Men, Women, and
Issues in
American History
VOLUME I

Men, Women, and Issues in American History

VOLUME I

edited by

HOWARD H. QUINT

and

MILTON CANTOR
University of Massachusetts

 1975

The Dorsey Press   Homewood, Illinois   60430

Irwin-Dorsey International   Arundel, Sussex   BN18 9AB
Irwin-Dorsey Limited   Georgetown, Ontario   L7G 4B3

Shown on the cover are Margaret Fuller,
Alexander Hamilton,
Abraham Lincoln, and Henry Thoreau.

First Printing, March 1975
Second Printing, February 1976

ISBN 0-256-01686-0
Library of Congress Catalog Card No. 74–24453
Printed in the United States of America

LEARNING SYSTEMS COMPANY—
a division of Richard D. Irwin, Inc.—has developed a
PROGRAMMED LEARNING AID
to accompany texts in this subject area.
Copies can be purchased through your bookstore
or by writing PLAIDS,
1818 Ridge Road, Homewood, Illinois   60430.

For our sons and daughters—
—scholars all—
May they have inherited our strengths,
not our shortcomings.

Janet and David Quint

David, Elisabeth, and Daniel Cantor

Introduction

College and university undergraduates are often as interested in the characters on the stage of history as in the historical process itself. For more than anything else it is the dramatis personae who bring history alive and make it not only the record of what men and women have thought and done but, in most instances, an exciting story in itself. Many are the students unfortunately who find history uninstructive and irrelevant, but rare are these same students who do not find themselves absorbed by historical biography, particularly when it presents people as they were and not what mythologizers have made them.

The essays in these volumes seek to place individual men and women within the context of their age, and, at the same time, to explore what contributions—political, economic, social, or intellectual—they have made to their society. In attempting to understand their values and goals, it is essential to understand those forces that shaped them; namely, family traditions and background, friendships which influenced them, religious and educational attachments which had an impact, economic commitments to which they may have been devoted, the social class to which they were seamlessly wedded, the changing historical circumstances that formed the backdrop against which they played out their lives. Knowing this congeries of attitudes and events, we know the men and women themselves; and, knowing them, we throw a spotlight on the society itself and the historical period that bounded their time on earth.

Contributors to these volumes include men and women of all academic ranks, from professors emeriti to assistant professors, as well as the distinguished former director of the Folger Library. They come from private and tax-supported colleges and universities and without exception are highly respected for their work in the fields of American history and American studies. They represent a wide spectrum of viewpoints, though on the whole we should have to say that their approach is essentially in the so-called Whig tradition of historical writing that has been the dominant one in this country. In the planning stage for *Men, Women, and Issues in American History,* the editors suggested a general format for the organization of the individual essays, but the reader will quickly realize that it has not been followed in all instances. We have accepted the departures because we endorse Carl Becker's dictum that every man must be his own historian and because we believe that every historian must organize the ideas presented in the manner most satisfactory to himself or herself.

The editors wish to acknowledge here, with appreciation, the assistance given them in various ways, large and small, by their colleagues in the Department of History at the University of Massachusetts/Amherst. Equally, they want to express publicly and thus for the record their gratitude for the secretarial help of Mary Reddington, Sandra Mailho, Susan West, Barbara Einfurer, and Jane Marino.

February 1975   HOWARD H. QUINT
                                                       MILTON CANTOR

Contents

1

English Civilization Transplanted in the New World

JOHN SMITH
JOHN WINTHROP
WILLIAM PENN

by Max Savelle
University of Washington

America was built by individual men and women. Many who first came to America were laborers, the workers who built its farms, docks, ships, and cities; others were architects, the master builders. The three greatest architects of this people—three of the most creative individual society-builders of 17th-century America—were John Smith, John Winthrop, and William Penn. Smith personified the pragmatic factor of English colonization, Winthrop the religious, and Penn the humanitarian.

*　　*　　*

Before them lay America, a continent to conquer and to occupy, a homeland yet to be created. Little did they imagine the magnitude of the task, or the historical significance of the enterprise upon which they were embarked. The three small ships, *Susan Constant, Discovery*, and *Godspeed*, sailed into the placid waters of Chesapeake Bay on April 21, 1607. In all, the colonists numbered a few more than one hundred souls, of whom 59 were "gentlemen" who were allergic to hard work.

One of the ships, probably the *Susan Constant*, carried a prisoner, a man who would one day become the leader and saviour of the colony—who would, indeed, emerge as one of the most significant leaders of that generation of English colonizers and imperialists—Captain John Smith.

1

John Smith was a member of the first generation that included Humphrey Gilbert, Walter Raleigh, Richard Hakluyt, Samuel Purchas, John Popham, Francis Drake, Thomas Smythe, Ferdinando Gorges, Edwin Sandys, Francis Bacon, and a host of others. In his philosophy of English imperialism, Smith was a disciple of Richard Hakluyt and a friend of Samuel Purchas. But as a man of action, fitting the end to the philosophy, he was his own man, a loner. Smith's impact upon Elizabethan expansion was crucial, although generally underestimated.

Smith was a man of action at the time that he mounted the stage of history in Virginia. He had narrowly escaped hanging for "insubordination" and "conspiracy" during a stopover of the fleet in the West Indies, and arrived at Jamestown still "detained" on board ship. But he came—it was discovered when the sealed instructions to the expedition from the London Company division of the Virginia Company were opened—as a member of the seven-man council that would govern the colony. The other council members were quarreling and intriguing among themselves—some of them against Smith—so the captain was not immediately admitted to full standing, despite the instructions. It was not long, however, before he came into his position and, in the second year (September 1608), he was elected president of that council, which meant, in effect, governor of the colony.

During the preceding year, Smith had already shown the pragmatic bent that made him the saviour of Virginia. He had managed to intimidate the Indians and had even succeeded in getting food from them. Now he purged the colony of its stagnation by making all the colonists, even the "gentlemen," work—with a stern order that "he who works not, eats not"—either in the production of food or in the preparation of commodities such as clapboard, cedar and cypress boards, sassafras, and other items that could be profitably shipped home to the Company. While the colonists were busy, Smith the explorer and anthropologist had also been at work. He mapped Chesapeake Bay and its tributaries as well as the distribution of the region's Indian tribes, an enterprise that resulted in the first of his famous maps, "The Map of Virgina."

John Smith returned to England, suffering from a gunpowder burn, in the fall of 1609. Thereafter, for several years, he lived in London in relative obscurity. But this was a period when he prepared his *Description of Virginia*, published (with his Map of Virginia) in 1612. These years, too, were filled with intense activity connected with the founding of the colonies in America; and we may be sure that he was moving about in the midst of it.

Smith next turned his attention to New England, and in March 1614 he commanded an expedition financed by Marmaduke Rawdon and his associates for "North Virginia." He was now instructed to search for mines of gold and copper as well as to hunt for whales—or, as a last resort, to obtain a cargo of fish or to trade with the Indians for furs. A purely speculative voyage, in the end it did not pay expenses.

Smith, meanwhile, was really thinking of more farsighted and scientific matters. While his crewmen hunted for gold they were not to find, pursued whales that would not be caught, and fished for cod that somehow failed to fill the ship's hold, Smith himself explored the coast of "North Virginia." Inspired by the French name for Canada, "New France," he now dubbed the region south of it "New England," a name that stuck. While exploring and trading for furs, he also formulated plans for a colony. This was his true love.

Once more, Smith the colonizer dominated Smith the commercial captain. His enthusiastic description of New England won the support of some members of the moribund "North Virginia Company," notably Sir Ferdinando Gorges and Sir John Popham, and he managed to scrape together enough capital for yet another expedition. Two ships, with the 17 men who actually were to found the colony, set out in the spring of 1615; the site of the colony would be chosen after the ships made landfall. Unhappily, while one ship sailed quickly to New England, the larger vessel—on which Smith was sailing—had to turn back because it was unseaworthy. Another ship was equipped and departed on June 24, 1615. But Smith's "bad hap by sea" still pursued him: he was caught by pirates, first English, who found his ship not worth capturing, then French, who also found little to take from him. While aboard the French vessel his own sailed off and returned to England.

It was while "marooned" on the French ship that Smith wrote *A Description of New England,* one of his most famous books. The French pirate—or privateer—the Sieur du Poiron, detained Smith for a number of weeks, during which time the Frenchman took several English, Portuguese, and other vessels. Smith was finally allowed to go to France on board a Portuguese caravel that Poiron had captured. Then, after a series of typically fantastic adventures, he eventually returned to England. Apparently he did not arrive penniless, because he seems to have received a share of the loot from the Portuguese caravel and financial assistance from a French lady of Rochelle (Smith, always a bachelor, was saved or dramatically assisted by high-born ladies—including Pocahontas—on an astonishing number of occasions).

John Smith still possessed a burning desire to push forward the expansion of the English empire in America. He would, however, never return to the colonies. He is properly thought of as a man of action and as a pragmatist, and his chief ambition was to build colonies but, paradoxically, his only experience with actual settlements was his relatively brief but significant career as the dominating spirit in the planting and the saving of Virginia. His really great contribution to the history of the founding of the British empire in America was intellectual. It was the contribution of a writer, a promoter, a thinker, a philosopher of imperialism.

John Smith began his career as a publicist for colonization with the publication of *A True Relation of such occurrences and accidents of noate as hath happened in Virginia* . . ., in 1608, while he was still in that colony. At least a half dozen books followed—on Indians, geography, settlements—all contributing to the literature of English colonial imperialism. His final book, *Advertisements for the unexperienced Planters of New England, or anywhere*, was published in 1631 and was a series of practical suggestions for colonizers and colonists. By this time the foundations of the English empire in America had been laid—in Virginia, in New England, and in the Caribbean area. It must have been a matter of great satisfaction to Smith, in the last year of his life, to contemplate this great event and his part in it.

For John Smith, colonizing was not to be entered upon lightly: "It is not a worke for every one to manage such an affaire, as make a discovery and plant a Colony, it requires all the best parts of art, judgment, courage, honesty, constancy, diligence, and industry, to do but neere well; some are more proper for one thing than another, and therein best to be imploied: and nothing breeds more confusion then misplacing and misimploying men in their undertakings." Yet it is a noble work; for "truly there is no pleasure comparable [to the creation of new societies] to a generous spirit; . . . to see daily new Countries, people, fashions, governments, strategems; [to] releeve the oppressed, comfort his friends, passe miseries, subdue enemies, adventure upon any feazable danger for God and his Country." But knowledge of the new land, and a realization of the problems to be faced could be acquired only by actual observation and experience. So many expeditions failed, he said, because of the imperfect knowledge and inadequate experience of the "home-bred adventurers" who started out ignorant of the nature of the land to which they were going and unprepared for the hardships and the problems they would meet.

Smith's pragmatic recommendations for the founding of colonies were based upon solid geographic descriptions, survey of the terrain and, most important of all, his two famous maps. He spent much time while in Virginia exploring and surveying Chesapeake Bay and its tributaries. Along with his *Map of Virginia* Smith published a description of the flora and the fauna of the country. He was especially interested, of course, in those products such as cedar, oak and walnut, woods for clapboards, sassafras and skins, that might profitably be exported to England, but he also displayed a sharp and curious eye for plants such as the chinquapin and animals such as the opossum that were peculiar to America.

Similarly, after exploring the coasts of New England, he published his equally famous *Map of New England*, the place-names on which, according to Smith, were designated by Prince Charles of England (later King Charles I). On this map, however, he omitted the names of the Indian tribes, since he never made any extended overland exploration of the region, and in his *Description of New England* he mentions them only briefly. As always, the geographer Smith was more interested in the merchantable products of the country—magnificent forests for masts, yards, lumber, and naval stores, furs to be had of the Indians, salt, whales, fruits, wild animals and, above all, many kinds of fish, the most important of which was cod. He hoped there were mines of copper, iron, gold and silver, but as a realist he could not promise them. "I need not despaire but that there are metals in the Country; but I am no alcumist, nor will promise more then I know...." He was nothing if not a realist. "Yet when the foundation is laid ..., and a common-wealth established, then such there may better be constrained to labour than here [in England]. But to rectifie a common-wealth with debaushed people is impossible, and no wise man would throw himselfe into such a society, that intends honestly, and knowes what he undertakes. For there is no country to pillage as the Romans found: all you expect from thence must be by labour."

Government in the New World should be in the hands of one strong man, a tough but benevolent dictator. Smith cited Cortez, Pizarro, and other great leaders; he was obviously thinking of himself, and the manner in which he had saved Virginia, as the successful colonial director and the perfect type of leader.

Smith was an integral part of the great economic expansion of England, and he knew and encouraged the economic motives of the merchants, the land speculators, and the common people who provided the brawn and sinew of the movement. But it seems clear that although he was certain, in his own mind, of the colonies' golden economic future, and although this conviction was the basis of his appeal to the merchant supporters of colonizing enterprises, his own interest in colonization was not primarily economic. Rather it was a vision of expanding the glory, might, and welfare of England and its people.

To be sure, the capitalists who funded the movement of people to the New World would, and should, Smith thought, receive a profit on their enterprises. Indeed, in one sense, colonies were commercial ventures; not only would the merchants profit but England itself would become richer and more powerful in the international balance of power. The ultimate basis of profit was commerce: for "there is nothing more inricheth a Common-wealth than much trade, nor no meanes better to increase than small [low] custome [duties] as *Holland, Genua, Ligorne,* and divers other places can well tell you; and doth most beggar those places where they take most [highest] custome [duties]...."

Once the process of peopling the empty spaces of the world was started, Smith believed, those who actually went overseas would find there a better life than they knew in England. "Who can desire more content that hath small meanes," he says, "or but onely his merit to advance his fortunes, than to tread and plant that ground he hath purchased by the hazard of his life; if he have but the taste of vertue and magnanimity, what to such a minde can bee more pleasant than planting and building a foundation for his posterity, got from the rude earth by Gods blessing and his owne industry without prejudice to any; . . . what so truly su[i]tes with honour and honesty, as the discovering things unknowne, creating Townes, peopling Countries, informing the ignorant, reforming things unjust, teaching vertue [,] and gaine to our native mother Country a Kingdome to attend her, find imploiment for those that are idle, because they know not what to doe. . . ." What could be more exciting, more exhilarating than participating in, even dominating, the great events taking place in the course of westward expansion? John Smith knew what was going on; if ever there was a man with a sense of the movement of history, he was that man.

And what of the inhabitants of the countries John Smith described—the Indians—the "salvages"? Here Smith the geographer became Smith the anthropologist. To be sure, his references to Indians were skimpy in his accounts of New England. By contrast, his Virginia studies were extensive, careful, and thoroughgoing. In them, he estimated the Indian population and described their tribal divisions, government, methods of making war, clothing—if any, personal ornamentations, lodgings, agriculture, family life, hunting and fishing methods, mores, and music (made with drums, rattles, pumpkin shells, in bass, tenor, counter-tenor, meane, and treble). "These mingled with their voices sometimes 20 or 30 togither, make such a terrible noise as would rather affright than delight any man." He describes their dancing, their medicine, and their religion, including child sacrifice. "But their chiefe God is the Divell. Him they call *Oke* and serve him more of feare than love."

The "salvages," he says, are strong and tough, inured to the most rigorous physical hardship, and possessing a knowledge of wood-lore that made for survival in the most desperate circumstances. But "they are inconstant in every thing, but what feare constraineth them to keepe. Craftie, timerous, quicke of apprehension, and very ingenuous. Some are of disposition fearefull, some bold, most cautelous [cautious], all Savage. Generally covetous of Copper, Beads, and such like trash. They are soon moved to anger, and so malicious, that they seldome forget an injury: they seldom steal from one another, least their conjurers [magicians] should reveale it, and so they be pursued and punished. That they are thus feared is certaine, but that any can reveale their offences by conjuration I am doubtfull."

As for Indian relations with whites, Smith was convinced that the vast culture-gap between the two peoples was unbridgeable; the Indians could never be won over by love. They were too inherently savage. They could be subjugated, however, and should be; eventually they would become a valuable labor force for the English.

Smith's descriptions constitute one of the most valuable early accounts of the Indians as they were when the white men came. But these descriptions are more: they also indicate a comprehension of the larger imperial problem of the relations of an expanding empire with native peoples.

In *The True Travels, Adventures, and Observations of Captaine John Smith* (published in 1630), he recognized that Englishmen had founded colonies in the West Indies. Thus the British empire now included three groups of colonies in America, all of which were by this time proving their value both to the motherland and to the settlers. The three, especially New England and Virginia, were interdependent, "and to those of *New England* may it not be a great comfort to have so neare a neighbour of their own Nation, that may furnish them with their spare cattell, swine, poultry, and other roots and fruits, much better than from *England*." There should never exist any envy between the two colonies, for it was always intended that they would complement each other. "Now when these shall have laid the foundations, and provided means beforehand; they may entertain all the poore artificers and laborers in *England*, and their families which are burthensome to their Parishes and Countries [counties] where they live upon almes and benevolence for want of worke. . . . For there is vast [waste] land enough for all the people in *England, Scotland,* and *Ireland:* and it seems God hath provided this Country [New England] for our Nation, destroying the natives by the plague. . . ."

Smith's knowledge of the West Indies was secondhand, and he always thought of Virginia and New England as his two "children." Nonetheless, he regarded the island colonies as indispensable to the English empire.

Underlying and permeating all of John Smith's thinking about colonization in America was a concept of manifest destiny inherent in the westward spread of peoples. "For God did make the would to be inhabited with mankind, and to have his name knowne to all Nations, and from generation to generation: as the people increased they dispersed themselves into such Countries as they found most convenient. And here in *Florida, Virginia, New-England,* and *Cannada,* is more land than all the people in Christendome can manure [cultivate], and yet more to spare than all the natives of those Countries can use and culturate. And shall we keep such a cayle [hassle] for land, and at such great rents and rates [in England] when there is so much of the world uninhabited, and as much more in other places, and as good or rather better than any wee possesse, were it manured and used accordingly."

Adam and Eve began it, and Noah continued it. Many peoples contributed to the spread of humanity—Hebrews, Greeks, Romans, and others. The "*Portugals* and *Spaniards*" led the way to America. Their achievements revealed, by contrast, the "idlenesse and ingratitude" of the English, "and neglect of our duty and religion we owe our God, our King, and Countrey, and want of charity to those poore Salvages, whose Countries we challenge, use, and possesse . . . , Where we doubt not but by Gods gracious assistance, and the adventurers willing minds and speedie furtherance to so honorable an action, in after times to see our Nation enjoy a Country, not onely exceeding pleasant for habitation, but also very profitable for commerce in generall; no doubt pleasing to almightie God, honourable to our gracious Soveraigne, and commodious generally to the whole Kingdome." England had both a right and duty to colonize America as a part of God's plan for peopling the Earth.

This was written of Virginia in 1608. But it was typical of John Smith throughout his career; he might as well have been describing the young three-part empire in 1631, the last year of his life. The founding of this empire was a national enterprise: it redounded, under God, to the benefit of the Nation, the King, and the whole people. "For my part," said Smith, "I cannot chuse but grieve, that the actions of an Englishman should be inferior to any, and that the command of England should not be as great as any Monarchy that ever was since the world began, I mean not as a Tyrant to torment all Christendome, but to suppress her disturbers, and conquer her enemies."

John Smith was one of the greatest voices of Elizabethan-Jacobean imperialism. He was a pragmatist, a colony builder, a propagandist, a promoter. But he was also a statesman, with a vision of a wider, more powerful empire and of a new English people in America. His ideas were not exactly original, but he seems to have been more a nationalist than most, more a conscious imperialist, more a man of action. He seems to have caught a clearer vision than many of his contemporaries of the potential splendor promised by the new English nation in the western world. As one of the Jacobean poets wrote, of the three little ships,

> Let England knowe our willingnesse,
>   for that our work is good,
> We hope to plant a Nation,
>   where none before hath stood.

*   *   *

Somewhere on the Atlantic, on board the good ship *Arbella*, Master John Winthrop addressed his fellow-passengers thus: "Wee are a Company professing our selves fellow members of Christ, wee ought to account our selves knitt by this bond of love, and live in the experience of it ... for the worke wee have in hand, it is by a mutuall consent through a speciall overruleing providence, ... to seeke out a place of Cohabitation and Consorteshipp under a due forme of Government both civill and ecclesiasticall ... for wee must Consider that wee shall be as a Citty upon a Hill, the eies of all people are uppon us. ...." A true expression of the spirit of the settlement of Massachusetts, this remark set the tone of the history of New England for a century or more. It was quite unlike the pragmatism of Captain John Smith and introduced a new and different factor—that of religion—into the formation of the American nation.

John Winthrop was a leading stockholder in the Massachusetts Bay Company, a corporation formed by a group of merchants and landed "gentry" with Puritan convictions. The Company received its charter in March 1629. A week later Charles I dissolved Parliament, not calling it again for nearly twelve years. Political, ideological, and religious persecution was abroad in England. The Puritans were frightened—and not on the score of repression alone. Young people, including John Winthrop's own two sons, were falling into worldly, even dissolute ways. For the Puritans, English society appeared to be falling into a slough of sin. Surely it was high time to consider snatching the Puritans' families out of this miasma of moral and social degeneration into the cleaner, purer "wilderness" of America.

John Winthrop certainly considered it. As he wrote his wife Margaret in May 1629, "I am very persuaded, God will bringe some heavye Affliction upon this lande [of England], and that speedylye: but be of good Comfort. ... If the Lord seeth it wilbe good for us, he will provide a shelter & a hidinge place for us & others. ..." Whatever happened, he would place himself entirely under the guidance of God.

But that was not all. As the possibility grew in his mind, he systematically and carefully weighed the pros and cons. "This lande growes wearye of her Inhabitantes"; life is vile and base, children and friends are only burdens, not blessings. Living is so expensive and luxurious that it is impossible for a man to exist on honest wages or "keepe sayle with his equalls" (that is, in modern terms, "keep up with the Joneses"). By contrast, the world in America is wide open for occupation, neither crowded nor corrupted. Why should a man fight to own and wrest a living from one acre of land in England when he can have hundreds of acres there just for the taking? Finally, would it not be wise and worthy in God's eyes to lead an infant church of Puritans into the wilderness to grow and flourish there? Surely it was preferable to facing the harsh oppression and destruction of this church by the juggernaut of state and church in England. He would go: he would sell his home; he would answer God's calling; he would lead his people to America.

Now here he was, with a thousand people following him, and he had set the tone for their subsequent history, a tone of high commitment to an intensely religious, intensely idealistic migration. The colonizers paused at Salem and, after looking around for the best place to settle, went on to Shawmut Peninsula where they founded Boston. Here they began their religion-infused society, one step toward the redemption of the world.

From Boston as a hub the colonists spread out upon the land. The communities they built were modeled largely upon those in England. Each town was also a church congregation, received a patent from the General Court, and in turn parceled out land to its members. Winthrop, the Governor, remained in Boston, but the settlers carried with them into their new communities his high dedication to the purpose of founding societies based upon covenants: the bonding force of the covenants was Christian love.

The merchants of Boston and Salem built ships and began a trade that radiated outward like the spokes of a wheel. They furnished manufactured goods to the inland towns; they sent schooners out on the fishing banks and brought back fish for themselves as well as for export to Virginia and the West Indies; and they soon were exporting fish to England itself and to Spain and Portugal as well. Already, in 1630, within a year of his arrival, Winthrop had had built the 30-ton bark, *The Blessing of the Bay,* which he dispatched to trade with the Indians and to carry furs to England.

After a while Margaret and her sons joined John Winthrop in Boston, and there they made a home they came to love. Margaret died in 1647 and John married again. His new wife, Martha Caytmore, presented him with another son, but he himself died on March 26, 1649, at the age of 60. Through 20 years he had led his people in the building of the "City upon a Hill," and he had been the most important single figure in this work.

If John Smith was a man of action and ideas, John Winthrop was a man of ideas and actions. With Winthrop, ideas came first. Above all, he was a theological-political philosopher, the first and surely the most important to appear on American shores before William Penn.

As he said in his "City upon a Hill" speech, the society—the body politic—was founded upon a social compact, a "covenant" among its members that bound them in Christian love. But this society had also a covenant or compact with God who would "expect a strickt performance of the Articles contained in it [our compact with Him]." Therefore, they must build the institutions of their "City" in such a way as to make sure that the covenant with God would be faithfully carried out.

But how? The Massachusetts Bay Company was a business corporation; its voting members or "freemen" were simply stockholders in the

Company. As the colony took shape, it was discovered that only about 15 stockholders were present, eight of whom were members of the governing council. By reason of sheer necessity this small group ran the colony for the first year or two; in 1631 it called a meeting of "all the freemen of the commons" (probably all or most of the male settlers) to take an oath of allegiance to the government, to ratify the work the council had thus far done, and to authorize the council to elect the governor. All of these were done.

But these people (each was now called "freeman," in the sense of "citizen") were not all stockholders of the Company. Nor, apparently, were they all committed to the ideal of the godly commonwealth envisaged by Winthrop and his fellow Puritans. If the "mission" were to continue to conduct itself according to the "Articles" of the covenant with God, it must be kept in the hands of the godly. For this reason, therefore, when the council undertook to expand the number of freemen with full voting rights in the company—now a commonwealth—it enacted that "noe man shalbe admitted to the freedome [citizenship] of this body polliticke, but such as are members of some of the churches within the lymitts of the same." Religion and government were thus brought together in a single body of religious men. Their agreement to do so was a sort of "covenant" or social compact. By this act the Massachusetts Bay Company disappeared and the Commonwealth of Massachusetts was created. Also, the religious idea and the political institution were fused into one.

Step by step the General Court of the colony became a representative body; it separated the council from the assembly, thereby transforming the original one-house general court into a two-house legislature. It also adopted the "Massachusetts Body of Liberties" to govern the entire colony. These derived in part from English common law, in part from the Bible, and in part from the measures already passed by the General Court. By the mid-1640s the political structure had taken shape. John Winthrop took part at every step in its evolution, in the formulation of the ideology that rationalized its structure, and its ongoing relationship with the ideal of the city on a hill.

In the first place, as Winthrop had said in his *Arbella* discourse, God, in his wisdom, had "soe disposed The Condicion of Mankinde, as in all times some must be rich some poore, some highe and eminent in power and dignitie; others meane and in subjeccion." It was God's will that authority be vested in men who were "highe and eminent in power and dignitie." Once given authority, the magistrates were to be trusted to rule benevolently and wisely.

Massachusetts Bay, then, was a government by the Magistrates who were elected by the representatives of the church-member freemen of the commonwealth. The people elected these officials but, once chosen, their authority was unchallengeable. In 1645 Winthrop, then deputy-governor, was accused of exceeding his authority as a magistrate and was tried by the General Court. On his acquittal, he asked permission to make a "little speech" to the people explaining the relationship, as he saw it, between the people and their governors. This "little speech" is the classic explanation of the Puritan theory of government:

> The great questions that have troubled the country are about the authority of the magistrates and the liberty of the people. It is yourselves [the people] who have called us to this office [of magistrate], and being called by you, we have our authority of God, in way of an ordinance, such as hath the image of God eminently stamped upon it. . . . The covenant between you and us is the oath you have taken of us [made us take], which is to this purpose, that we shall govern you and judge your causes by the rules of God's laws and our own, according to our best skill. . . . For the other point concerning liberty, I observe a great mistake in the country about that. There is a twofold liberty, natural (I mean as our nature is now corrupt) and civil or federal. The first is common to man with beasts and other creatures . . . it is a liberty to evil as well as to good. [The exercise of this liberty leads to evil and to the degeneration of men into wild beasts.] The other kind of liberty I call civil or federal, it may also be termed moral, in reference to the covenant between God and man, in the moral law, and the politic covenants and constitutions, amongst men themselves. . . . This liberty is maintained and exercised in a way of subjection to authority; it is of the same kind of liberty wherewith Christ hath made us free. The woman's own choice makes such a man her husband; yet being so chosen, he is her lord, and she is to be subject to him; yet in a way of liberty, not of bondage; and a true wife accounts her subjection her honor and freedom, and would not think her condition safe and free, but in her subjection to her husband's authority. . . . [Complaint, resistance to government, rebellion, are all exercises of "Natural liberty" and, therefore, evil], but if you will be satisfied to enjoy such civil and lawful liberties, such as Christ allows you, then will you quietly and cheerfully submit unto that authority which is set over you, in all the administrations of it, for your good.

Winthrop's philosophy is clear: government is the product of a compact between the people and their rulers, who administer for the people. Magistrates are elected by the people, but once in office they are responsible to God: the people must trust them and obey them. Criticism, demands for reform, the very idea of governmental accountability, are contrary to the will of God in whose name government acts. Such actions are manifestations of the rankest, rowdiest, most reprehensible democracy. Winthrop was a benevolent, godly authoritarian; he was no democrat.

Such was the benevolently authoritarian godly state of the Puritans according to their foremost New World political philosopher. But the city-on-a-hill was not happy, despite its high political idealism. Within the first five years of its founding and for at least two decades afterward, the colony was torn by religious and political dissension. As an escape-hatch for dissenters from Anglicanism in England, Massachusetts had attracted a horde of strong-minded men and women, Puritans all, who disagreed, sometimes bitterly, among themselves and with Winthrop over the question of how the city-on-a-hill was to be built and administered. These radical dissenters caused trouble. Roger Williams, for example, criticized the colony for occupying land that rightfully belonged to the Indians, for its religious requirement for citizenship, for its intolerance, and for its continuing pretense that its religion was not and should not be "separated" from Anglicanism. Mistress Ann Hutchinson and her brother-in-law Reverend John Wheelwright and their followers struck at the very marrow of Puritan divinity by preaching the heretical doctrine that the Holy Ghost dwells in every man after his salvation, and that "good works" were not necessarily a sign of salvation. Samuel Gorton questioned the doctrine of the Trinity, denounced a "hireling ministry," and even denied the existence of heaven and hell. Finally, Dr. Robert Child petitioned for a presbyterian form of government and more religious toleration. All of these dissenters, and many others, in the 1630s and 1640s, tore at the seamless fabric of the model society that John Winthrop was giving his life to establish.

Winthrop and the Puritan establishment fought back; one after another all of these troublemakers were banished from the city-on-a-hill. Winthrop and his "orthodox" Puritan colleagues were explicitly and convincedly "intolerationists," determined to maintain the purity of their Puritan society against all the malignant disciples of the Devil who had the temerity to challenge it. In other words, anything that interfered with the work of God, and threatened to overthrow it, could never be tolerated. Intolerance of dissent was completely logical if one were convinced that the dissent was a threat to God's work. The ideal of service to which Winthrop subscribed could never be permitted to be destroyed by a Roger Williams, an Anne Hutchinson, a Samuel Gorton, or a Robert Child. This had ever been the justification of intolerance; it remained the basis for intolerance in Massachusetts and in America long after Winthrop's death. It was written into the rationalization of the Puritan state, just as later it was written into the life-style of the United States. Love existed within the city, to be sure; but not the slightest toleration for such dangerous divisions and putatively destructive doctrines.

Winthrop and his dominant group of Puritans did not come to America to establish religious freedom. Far from it: they came to establish a society based upon the truth as they saw it. Anyone who challenged that truth must stay away—or enter Massachusetts Bay at his peril.

Within the colony, then, the Puritan ideal of the exclusive, tribal city upon a hill had succeeded in establishing itself, though not without trial and trouble. Winthrop might very well have congratulated himself and his co-workers upon their success. But the Puritan state was a member commonwealth in the nascent English empire of which Captain John Smith was the prophet. What were, or should be, according to the political philosophy of the Puritans, the relationships of the new state with the parent state of England? The matter had to be confronted, for in 1634 the king created the "Commission for Foreign Plantations" to supervise colonial affairs. Moreover, this commission, headed by the Puritans' old arch-enemy, Archbishop William Laud, decided to call in all colonial patents and charters.

How should they meet this challenge? The colony decided to resist the order, and by force, if necessary. Under their charter they were empowered to govern themselves as a "body politicke"; they would have to defend their possessions; otherwise, as Winthrop says, it must be their policy "to avoid or protract." Avoid and protract they did, for the next three-quarters of a century, and the policy was successful. The question arose again in 1638, and Winthrop was commissioned to write to the commission. His letter—or petition—was evasive, to be sure, in that he took no step to return the charter; but it also contained something of Winthrop's view of the nature of the empire. We humbly profess, he says, "that we are ready to yield all due obedience to our Sovereign Lord the King's Majesty, and to your Lordships under him. . . . We came under the authority of the great seal of England; we transferred our families, our estates there, and we have enlarged His Majesty's dominions. If we were to lose our patent," he continued, "we should suffer much distress; and people here will think His Majesty has cast them off, and that hereby they are freed from their allegiance and subjection, and thereupon will be ready to confederate themselves under a new government, for their necessary safety and subsistence, which will be of dangerous example unto other plantations. . . ."

The most dramatic part of the remonstrance is Winthrop's bold suggestion that if the charter were recalled, the people of Massachusetts Bay would consider themselves absolved of their allegiance to Charles I and would be compelled to seek the protection of some other government, perhaps (by implication) that of France. What, in short, he was demanding was nothing less than internal sovereignty for Massachusetts. His conception of empire, albeit dimly perceived, was a federal empire composed of internally sovereign states under the king of England. Indeed, he anticipated the thinking of most American Whigs in the imperial crisis that preceded the American Revolution.

John Winthrop had little or no such anthropological interest in the Indians as characterized the writings of John Smith and William Penn.

Like other Puritans, he thought of the Indians as being of another nation, perhaps descendants of the ten lost tribes of Israel, with customs and institutions other than those of the English. But they were "benighted" heathens, largely dominated by the Devil and, therefore, fit subjects for conversion to the Puritan form of Christianity.

Winthrop's own concern with the Indians was chiefly political and economic and revolved around such issues as occupation and ownership of the land. Some of the colonists themselves—notably Roger Williams—questioned the right of the English to take land already occupied by the Indians. This problem had arisen even before the Puritans left England and it continued, with increasing intensity, to plague the relations with the Indians in the early years of settlement. Winthrop, with his legalistic mind, was led to try to find some rationalization—some legal justification—for the Puritan occupation. His search concluded with a quasi-legal concept that served as precedent for later Euro-American empires and for their relations with native peoples: that is, the doctrine of effective occupation, or, as he called it, the doctrine of *vacuum domicilium*. As Winthrop stated: "That [land] which lies common, and hath never been replenished or subdued is free to any that possesse and improve it." Indians have a natural right to occupy and use the land, but since they have not enclosed it (fenced it in, that is) or improved it, or cultivated it in any extensive way, they cannot be said effectually to occupy it. They have not established a "civil right" (a right under international law) to it. Such being the case, the English may occupy the land to which the Indians have not established a legal title. Finally, to cap the argument that the English are doing right in occupying the unoccupied land, it is evident that God intended them to do so, since "God hath consumed the Natives with a great Plauge [plague] in those partes, soe as there be few inhabitantes left."

The Indians were an ever-present factor—an external factor, to be sure—in the life and growth of the city-on-a-hill. They were a fearsome element, and some Puritans were more conscious than Winthrop of the reality of the vast culture-gap between the two peoples. But the Puritans were most careful to do the Indians justice as they (the Puritans) understood it. Winthrop, himself convinced of the applicability of the doctrine of *vacuum domicilium*, scrupulously adhered to it. There, by and large, his interest in the Indians ended.

John Winthrop, then, is to be seen as a political philosopher, but his political philosophy was a system of thought in the service of religion. People make government on the basis of a social compact, but once the government is established, it draws its inspiration from and is responsible to God, not the people. The people must obey. The government is absolute, in a sort of benevolent absolutism. Similarly, in Winthrop's gestating philosophy of the federal English empire, God's intent for the new society comes first; practical relationships follow.

Winthrop was educated at Cambridge and was a member of the Inner Temple. The formulations of his political convictions, however, arose out of specific, *de facto* situations, and were the religiously suffused and dictated responses to them. One might call his thinking "theological politics"; i.e., political ideas cast in a religious mould. It is for this, the religious coloration of political theory, that he is most significant in our early history.

*   *   *

When on October 28, 1682, William Penn stepped ashore from the ship *Welcome* at Newcastle on the Delaware, near his new city of Philadelphia, just then a-building, he came with the intention of creating a new society. Its chief characteristics, as he envisioned it, would be Christian love, religious freedom, and the rule of justice. He planned to spend the rest of his life there.

William Penn was a Quaker. Of the Quakers and of their doctrine of the "inner light" or "inner voice" he wrote that "We believe this gift of light and grace, through Jesus Christ, to be universal; and that there is not a man or woman upon earth that hath not a sufficient measure of this light, and to whom this grace hath not appeared, to reprove their ungodly works of darkness, and to lead them that obey it to eternal salvation." Here also was a universalism which, in contrast to the exclusive tribalism of the Puritans, embraced all men everywhere. His new society would be built upon this universal principle.

But Penn was much more than a Quaker. After all, the Quakers were a tiny minority sect in England and on the continent of Europe. Penn was deeply motivated by religion in everything that he did; but to exaggerate the place of religion in his career would be to distort his life and diminish his achievement. Penn trod the boards of a much broader stage. He was a world statesman, a political thinker, and a humanitarian whose purview included the whole human race. He would expand the burgeoning British empire; but he would also extend the benefits of his new society to all who emigrated, especially from the continent of Europe but, eventually, from all over the world as well. He expected to be a leader of many peoples and, incidentally, to make a lot of money.

Penn brought with him three now-famous documents that remain important to our understanding of the history of Pennsylvania, of the continuing growth of the Empire, of the later United States, and of Penn himself. These were his charter to the vast dominion given him by his friend Charles II in payment of a debt that the sovereign owed Penn's father, the Frame of Government (constitution) he had drafted for the province, and a body of laws he had drawn up for the colony while in England.

Penn's charter was an essentially feudal document illustrative of the feudal—or personal—relationship between king and subject. It made Penn and his heirs "the true and absolute Proprietaries." But there were also several modern touches. For example, the charter required that Penn make his laws "by and with the advice, assent and approbacon of the freeman [citizens] of the said countrey, . . . or of their Delegates." Here was a recognition of the modern constitutional principle of representative government. He had to promise to enforce the English navigation laws, to maintain a permanent agent or attorney in England, and to allow appeals from his courts to the king. Taxation must be by the consent of the people; the king, for his part, promised never to tax the colony except by act of Parliament! Pennsylvanians would one day appeal to this document as the fundamental and inviolable charter of their right to govern themselves. This charter to Penn, binding Pennsylvania to England as it did, is one of the clearest links in a chain of institutional relationships then being forged confirming the federal compact view of the empire.

The "Frame of Government," the constitution for Penn's new state, was a clumsy affair, almost wholly unsuitable for efficient operation in a struggling frontier society. It was built on theory, sprung from the minds of Penn, Algernon Sidney, and probably John Locke as well as James Harrington. Because of its unwieldiness, it had to be revised again and again until Penn and his people finally devised the Charter of Privileges of 1701, which remained the constitution for the colony until the American Revolution.

But the philosophy of government that William Penn wrote into it was of dramatic and eternal significance. This philosophy voiced his humanism and his faith in the capacity of men to manage their political affairs. Thus we find Penn saying, in the preface to the Frame, "When the great and wise God had made the world, of all his creatures it pleased him to choose man his deputy to rule it; and to fit him for such a charge and trust, he did not only qualify him with skill and power, but with integrity to use them justly. . . ." When men turned away from the voice of the divine law within them, an external law, or government, became necessary. As the apostle Paul stated, Penn continues, "The powers that be are ordained of God. Whosoever therefore resisteth the power, resisteth the ordinance of God. . . . This settles the divine right of government beyond exception, and that for two ends; first, to terrify evil-doers; secondly, to cherish those that do well."

But government is of no fixed and inflexible nature. Thus, Penn declared, again in the preface, "I do not find a model in the world, that time, place, and some singular emergences have not necessarily altered; nor is it easy to frame a civil government, that shall serve all places alike. . . . Government, like clocks, go from the motion men give them, and as governments are made and moved by men, so by them they are ruined too. Wherefore governments rather depend upon men, than men upon governments. Let men be good, and the government cannot be bad; if it be ill, they will cure it. But if men be bad, let the government be never so good, they will endeavour to warp and spoil it to their turn." Penn meant what he said. Governments were made by men and for men; and they could change or improve it whenever and however they might wish. "He who thinks it to be an end, aims at a profit—to make a trade of it—but he who thinks it to be a means, understands the true end of Government."

How different was Penn's relativistic, flexible, humanistic concept of the state from the absolute, inflexible, authoritarian commonwealth of the Puritan John Winthrop!

Nowhere, probably, is Penn's humanitarianism more clearly manifest than in the laws he drew up for Pennsylvania while in England and which were then adopted (with additions) by the assembly itself. The very first chapter of the laws provided for complete religious freedom for all but atheists. Beyond that, in a day in which England had some 200 laws carrying the death penalty, Penn's laws reduced the number to two —treason and murder. In a day, too, when prisons were noisome dens of misery, filth, and vice, Penn's laws provided a radical measure of reform that anticipated the incipient prison reform of the Enlightenment. His laws also provided for divorce, and there were many measures dealing with morality (incest, sodomy, rape, bigamy, etc.) with the severe (to the modern mind) penalty of life imprisonment for second offenses. The selling of rum to the Indians was prohibited, and provision was made for public care of the indigent poor. The practice of "due process" was required in all cases, as was jury trial; but witnesses were required only to make a solemn promise to tell the truth, thus abolishing the oath, since Quakers could take no oaths.

The code of laws of Penn's new colony was surely the most humane code in effect in the entire western world at that time. After Penn's death, it became somewhat more severe, but he had introduced into American jurisprudence a body of law that was both humane and just, based upon the principle that the severity of punishment should be proportionate to the seriousness of the offense—an ideal that American jurisprudence has been working toward, if somewhat irregularly, ever since.

Seen against the background of Restoration England, William Penn was a radical worker for human freedom; his government and laws for Pennsylvania amply demonstrate the fact. But the most precious of all freedoms, for him, was the freedom to worship God as one thought best— that is, following the dictates of the Voice within.

Penn had come to this conviction through two routes: his own persecution as a youth because of his Quakerism, and by his observation of the cruelties and absurdities of religious persecution both in England and on the Continent. He had composed one of his most famous works, *The Great Case of Liberty of Conscience* . . . , while a prisoner in Newgate jail. In the first place, he insisted, persecution for one's beliefs is futile and absurd. Moreover, it is a disruption of the good order of an otherwise peaceful state. Persecution was also anti-Christian; it was a violation of the fundamental rights of Englishmen; it was a usurpation of the authority and the prerogative of God. "Force never yet made either a good Christian, or a good subject."

So far, Penn's argument for freedom of conscience is negative, permissive, defensive. But freedom of religious belief, or of thought itself, is also positive. Freedom of worship, like freedom of thought, means freedom of expression. A Quaker, moved by the Inner Light, speaks not merely of himself, but of God. But he does not merely "suffer" God to speak: he listens to what He says, and learns thereby. Thus freedom of worship, freedom of thought, freedom of assembly, and freedom of expression are the means toward a positive forward movement of human life. Freedom thus becomes a creative force in human affairs. Men learn from one another, and any man may have the answer to a present problem. Representative government, says Penn, is based upon reason and the exercise of reason. Reason must be free to solve the problems of the state as well as of religion. Penn was no democrat. He deplored and opposed revolutionary violence. He did not go beyond the positive aspects of freedom of religion. But he was also a lifelong advocate of the doctrine of freedom of the mind, which, when carried over into secular thought, is, needless to say, the *sine qua non* of democracy.

Given Penn's unchanging conviction of the social and political necessity of freedom of religion, it was no accident that both the first chapter of his "Great Law," and the first article of the Charter of Privileges of 1701, should provide for complete freedom of worship for all persons who believe in one God. By implication, at least, this would include Buddhists, Moslems, Catholics, Indians, Africans, and even the benighted Anglicans of Penn's own native England! Office holding, however, was limited to those who accepted the divinity of Christ. To the 20th-century mind, this might appear a serious reduction of Penn's professed principles. Yet the Charter of Liberties of Pennsylvania was probably the most liberal constitution, so far as religion was concerned, in the western world. It also set a model for the later constitutions of the states that would emerge during the Revolution.

The people who came to Pennsylvania with William Penn were all Englishmen. But already scattered along the Delaware were settlements of Dutchmen, Swedes, and Finns. Within the next year or two many Germans began to come. By 1685 Penn could report that the population of his colony numbered over 8,000 people, who "are a Collection of divers Nations in Europe: As French, Dutch, Germans, Swedes, Danes, Finns, Scotch, Irish and English; and of the last equal to all the rest: . . . they live like People of One Country, which Civil Union has had a considerable influence towards the prosperity of that place."

Within another generation more non-English groups had accepted his invitation to enter into the experiment—among them Jews, Scots, Negroes, French Hugenots, and others, not to mention the native Indians. Pennsylvania was clearly the most polyglot colony in America. And out of this reality—out of Penn's own intent, indeed—was born the New World image of the "melting pot."

One of William Penn's major concerns, both humanitarian and pragmatic, were the Indians. He did not question the right of the king to give him a huge tract of land, but he also recognized that it was owned by the Indians and that, for him legally and justly to possess it, he must buy it from them. Besides this pragmatic consideration, however, he was genuinely interested in the Indians and their ways, and he was determined to avoid the abuses and misunderstandings that had led to savage warfare, mutual distrust, and bitter hatred between white and redman in colonies founded earlier. He was determined that his people and the Indians, as children of God, should live alongside each other as good neighbors, bound together by mutual respect, justice, and Christian love. When Penn sent his representatives ahead of him to lay the foundations of his colony, he strictly instructed them to respect the Indians' feelings: "Be tender of offending the Indians . . . we have their good in our eye, equal with our own interest . . . make a friendship and league with them. . . . Be grave; they love not to be smiled on."

Legend has it that soon after his arrival William Penn held a "treaty" with the Indians of the region under a great elm tree at Shackamaxon, at which the two groups pledged mutual friendship and the Indians sold Penn a tract of land along the Delaware River. The legend is almost certainly based on fact. In any case, Penn reported in 1685 that he had made seven such purchases of land. And he rejoiced in the cordial relations that existed between his people and their Indian neighbors: "so far are we from ill terms with the Natives, that we have liv'd in great friendship. . . . if any of them break our laws, they submit to be punisht by them: and to this they have tyed themselves by an obligation under their hands. We leave not the least indignity to them unrebukt, nor wrong unsatisfied. Justice gains and aws them."

William Penn, like Captain John Smith before him, had a genuine anthropological interest in the Indians. After living two years near them he wrote a clear and sympathetic description of their mores. Their language, he stated, "is lofty, yet narrow; but like the Hebrew, in signification full [Penn inclined to the belief that the Indians were descended from the lost ten tribes of Israel]; it is relatively unstructured. He described the Indians' customs with their children, as well as their marriages, houses, diet, hunting, hospitality, burials, and use of wampum. "They are great concealers of their own resentments ... but in liberality they excel: nothing is too good for their friend ... the most merry creatures that live, feast and dance perpetually; they never have much, nor want much ... a little contents them. ... Since the Europeans came into these parts they are grown great lovers of strong liquors, rum especially." Of their religion, Penn observed, "These poor people are under a dark night in things relating to religion. ..." Yet they believe in one God and in immortality, he reported; they make sacrifices to their great god, usually the first fruits, and they express their worship in songs and dances.

Penn describes the Indians' government in great detail, and procedures at their councils: "they speak little, but fervently, and with elegance: I have never seen more natural sagacity ... he will deserve the name of wise that outwits them in any treaty about a thing they understand." He also notes their arrangements for the maintenance of the peace and good relations between the two societies. We have agreed, he declares, that all differences shall be decided by six men on each side. The decision of this group was final. "Do not abuse them," he enjoined, "but let them have justice; and you win them: the worst is, that they are the worse for the Christians; who have propagated their vices, and yielded them tradition for ill, and not for good things. ..."

How different was William Penn's attitude toward and understanding of the Indians from that of Captain John Smith!

William Penn was in England during the Glorious Revolution of 1688–89 and the accession of William and Mary to the English throne, and he viewed with dismay the outbreak of the War of the Palatinate that took place almost immediately afterward. These were sad years for him in any case. The colonists back in Pennsylvania were squabbling, which led him to rebuke them and to speak of himself as a "man of sorrow." Meanwhile, owing to his known friendship with the exiled James II, his enemies at court attacked his charter and succeeded in having it suspended in 1692. (He was exonerated, however, and his charter restored in 1696.)

It was during this period of unhappy retirement that Penn turned his mind to the problem of war and peace and wrote his famous *Essay Toward the Present and Future Peace of Europe.* As many political thinkers have done since then, he asked the predictable questions: Why do nations fight with each other, and how can war, an atrocity in itself, be avoided?

There are three causes of war, he reasoned: the first is the necessity of defense against an aggressor; the second is the need to recover territory seized by an enemy; the third is the imperialistic drive of one nation to take the possessions of another. War is undertaken, in the first two cases, in the name of justice; if justice can be achieved without fighting, war becomes unnecessary. In the case of an imperialistic aggression, if the combined power of the community of nations is brought to bear upon the aggressor, he can be forced to desist; justice will thus be achieved by collective action. Let there be an international diet, or parliament, therefore, to decide the justice of international causes, with a sovereignty that transcends the sovereignties of the component states and that has the power to enforce its decisions. Penn then listed the many benefits to be derived from such an international institution for the preservation of peace.

Speaking here was Penn the idealist, Penn the humanitarian, Penn the rational internationalist, but not Penn the realist. He failed to recognize, in this problem as in many others, that it was not in the nature of other men, especially statesmen, to be as humanitarian and idealistic as he was.

It was because of the international situation, apparently, that William Penn turned his thoughts to the desirability of organizing a union of the English colonies along the American seaboard. On February 8, 1697, Penn presented to the English Board of Trade a plan for a union of the North American colonies. He proposed creation of an intercolonial assembly composed of deputies from all the colonies (two from each colony); the president of this assembly would be a "commissioner" (or governor-general) appointed by the king; this assembly would meet in the most nearly central colony, presumably New York, as often as need be in time of war, and every two years in time of peace. Even though a pacifist, Penn recognized war as a fact of political life that had to be acknowledged. The business of the assembly would be "to hear and adjust all matters of complaint or difference between Province and Province" or disputes between private citizens of two different colonies, or the return of fugitives from justice. The assembly would also consider matters concerning intercolonial commerce. But it would be especially charged "to consider of ways and means to support the union and safety of these Provinces against the publick enemies" such as the French or the Spaniards. In such cases it would contrive united armed forces and decide the quotas of men and supplies to be furnished by each colony for the common defense.

The idea of an ongoing, permanent colonial assembly for peacetime purposes was apparently unprecedented. Like his plan for international peace, Penn's scheme fell on deaf or disinterested ears. But here, again, he articulated an idea that was to grow dramatically among Americans of the 18th century, one that would be re-formulated by Benjamin Franklin in 1754 and actually implemented in the Articles of Confederation and in the Constitution of the United States of 1787.

William Penn finally returned to his colony in 1699. Once more he sought a peaceful solution to the factional struggles and succeeded in formulating the Charter of Privileges of 1701, which, as has been noted, remained the colony's constitution until the Revolution. Departing for England shortly thereafter, he never returned to Pennsylvania. He knew, however, that his new society, based on his own humanitarianism, was a success.

*   *   *

Captain John Smith, Master John Winthrop, and Friend William Penn, so different from one another, nonetheless had certain basic characteristics in common: each was an outstanding empire-builder driven by the forces of his time to found new societies and to expand the bounds of the British empire in America. Each was a man of ideas who had the stature and the power to carry these ideas into action. Each had an impact upon the course of history that was powerful and undeniable; each illustrates the possible significance of the individual in history. At the same time, each applied the ideas of his time to the course of history, thereby demonstrating the reality of the role of ideas in human history. Finally, their three colonies, while vastly different from one another, were the chief germinal beginnings of a new society. Each man was conscious that he was building a new "nation," but never dreamed of the form and the spirit it would take; each one brought to this work distinct values and these were indelibly written into the character of the new nation that they founded: pragmatism, religion, and humanitarianism.

2

Gentlemen and Men of Property

WILLIAM BYRD
SAMUEL SEWALL
WILLIAM JOHNSON

by Louis B. Wright
National Geographic Society

Many reasons prompted emigration to the New World in the early periods of our history, but few motives were more powerful than the lure of easily procurable land. Land not only insured a livelihood but it held out the promise of status. In 17th-century England, however, land was hard to come by. Inherited property descended to the eldest son; little land came on the market, and when it did the price was beyond the means of most would-be purchasers.

But in the English colonies across the Atlantic, land in almost limitless quantities was available on terms not beyond the means of even a yeoman farmer. In Virginia and in some of the other colonies, any immigrant able to pay ocean passage for himself and his household was given 50 acres as a "headright" for each member of his family as well as for each servant. Anyone with a little capital could also purchase land at such modest prices that younger sons who had no hope of an inheritance at home could establish themselves overseas as landed proprietors.

From time immemorial, the possession of land in England had conferred a status. A yeoman with a farm in fee simple had a respected place in society. Larger holdings might insure that the owner would be classed among the gentry, hold county offices, and perhaps even sit in Parliament. Great acreages with many tenants usually meant that the possessor be-

24

longed to the upper aristocracy, frequently with a title of nobility. Thus land was a stepping stone in the individual's rise in the social scale.

Besides the acquisition of land, other opportunities in the colonies induced emigrants to try their luck overseas. Most came for the betterment of their economic lot, whatever it had been, and a few prospered in trade beyond their expectations. Traffic with the Indians for furs as well as fishing were the earliest sources of substantial revenue, but soon other avenues opened. In New England particularly, shipbuilding and shipping laid the foundations of many a family fortune. In South Carolina, trade for deerskins with the Indians of the highlands and the marketing of forest products (turpentine, rosin, and ship timbers) were combined with the production of rice and indigo to bring fortunes to Charleston gentlemen who feared no "taint of trade." In a new country, colonists experimented with any suggestion that seemed to promise a profit. At the same time they retained memories of the hierarchy and status that prevailed in the old country and frequently sought purposefully to reproduce the best of the social conditions they remembered.

The ideal of the English country gentleman had a persistent appeal, especially in the agrarian colonies. Much ink has been wasted by contemporary genealogists in trying to prove the aristocratic origins in England of American families; but this effort, frequently unconvincing, is far less important than a study of what they became once established on these shores and of how they achieved their status. For many colonial families, in a generation or two, were living in a state that gave them the right to be considered members of a rising aristocracy.

The word "gentleman" in the 17th and 18th centuries was a technical term connoting something more than a well-behaved individual, the usual definition at the present time. In England, at that time, a gentleman was normally a landed proprietor, with sufficient property to enable him to live without manual labor himself, though he might carefully supervise the workers on his estate. William Harrison, a writer in Shakespeare's day, made the point, however, that others besides landowners might expect to be designated gentlemen and have the right to be called "Master" (our word Mister). "Whosoever studieth the laws of the realm, whoso abideth in the University giving his mind to his book, or professeth physic [medicine] and the liberal sciences," or serves as a captain in the wars or benefits the commonwealth by his counsel, "can live without manual labor and thereto is able and will bear the port, charge, and countenance of a gentleman, he shall be called 'master,' which is the title that men give to esquires and gentlemen, and be reputed a gentleman ever after." A proverb of the day declared that "gentility is nothing but ancient riches," and some commentator observed that riches need not be very ancient. In colonial America riches could be very recent, indeed, to enable a man to write "Mr." in front of his name or "Esquire" after it.

During the 17th century a number of Virginia families emerged who were to play a prominent part in the country's later history. Such were the Lees, the Fitzhughs, the Carters, the Byrds, and a score of others. Few were more conspicuous than the Carters, who were both rich and prolific. The second of the name in Virginia, Robert Carter of Corotoman, known for his pride and wealth as "King" Carter, eventually acquired some 300,000 acres in that portion of the colony designated the Northern Neck. Serving as justice of the peace, colonel of the militia, member of the Council of State, rector of the College of William and Mary, and holder of other offices, Carter illustrates the devotion to duty that characterized the gentry of this period. Few emoluments went with these offices, which the holder occupied as a civic duty, and for the privileged this tradition carried with it a sense of responsibility. Carter managed to accumulate his land, not because he held public office, but because he served as agent for the Fairfaxes who held a royal patent for the proprietorship of all the Northern Neck.

*   *   *

Perhaps the best remembered member of Virginia's ruling class is William Byrd II of Westover, for he kept a well-publicized diary, wrote one of the most urbane narratives of the period (*The History of the Dividing Line*), occupied many high offices, and fathered a dynasty that has wielded political power to the present time.

Byrd's father, William Byrd I, who emigrated to Virginia sometime before 1670, was the son of a London goldsmith. His maternal grandfather, Thomas Stegg, was a ship captain in the Virginia trade who had already acquired land on the James River. After this grandfather was lost at sea, young Byrd went to live with his Virginia uncle, also named Thomas Stegg, and eventually inherited his property. Thus the first William Byrd came into possession of a substantial acreage and a trading business with the Indians, which he subsequently increased.

William Byrd I married Mary Horsmanden, the daughter of an emigré Cavalier. They sent their son, William Byrd II, to England to be educated at Felsted Grammar School in Essex; and, later, the father sent him to Holland. Here the son would learn about business from one of his commercial correspondents, and then serve for a term in the business house of Perry & Lane of London.

Eventually Byrd II entered the Middle Temple and was called to the English bar. Thus he received basic classical training in grammar school (essential, it was believed, for a gentleman), gained practical business experience, and came back to Virginia with the prestige of an English legal education. Furthermore, on the death of his father in 1704, he inherited a comfortable fortune, a thriving trade with the Indians of the interior, a family seat in Henrico County on the James, and the help of influential friends who saw that he soon received appointment to high offices in the colony. William Byrd II was already on his way to becoming one of Virginia's ornamental as well as important members of the ruling hierarchy.

In the course of his life Byrd made five journeys across the Atlantic to serve as the official emissary of the colony in dealing with governmental authorities in London. He employed the skills of a diplomat and a lobbyist in arguing for advantages favorable to Virginia. His stays were usually for long periods, in one instance for over five years, which gave him an opportunity to cultivate the friendship of important officials and friends among the British aristocracy. He was conscious of being a member of the gentry himself and was readily accepted by his English counterparts. When he returned to his plantation home at Westover he brought back portraits of these friends, ranging from scientific colleagues in the Royal Society (which he was invited to join) to the Duke of Argyle. A few of Byrd's Virginia neighbors smiled at his vanity in displaying his friendship with so many prominent Englishmen.

Byrd deserves an honored place as a man of letters, though he published little in his own lifetime. *The History of the Dividing Line,* on which his reputation earlier rested, was first published by Edmund Ruffin at Petersburg, Virginia, in 1841. A modern version of his *Prose Works* (edited by Louis B. Wright) was brought out in 1966.

Byrd is one of the best documented of colonial Americans. In addition to his literary pieces like *The History of the Dividing Line Betwixt Virginia and North Carolina Run in . . . 1728, A Progress to the Mines in the Year 1732,* and *A Journey to the Land of Eden, Anno 1733,* Byrd through much of his adult life kept a diary in shorthand in which he entered highly intimate details of these years. Three portions of this diary are now in print, and other portions, yet undiscovered, may appear someday. He also wrote numerous letters that throw light on himself and his times. His prose works are lightened with humor and have an urbanity and grace rarely found in other colonial writings.

But Byrd was more than a skillful author. He was the counterpart of the European virtuoso of the 18th century, the period of the Enlightenment. He was interested in science, in learning, in classical languages and literature, and in the world about him. He also cultivated the social graces that characterized the gentleman: hospitality, good manners, good conversation, music, and dancing. Much of the Renaissance tradition of the well-rounded man persisted in Byrd—and would find a culmination in Thomas Jefferson. With all his faults, which were numerous, William Byrd II personified the ideal of cultivation that distinguished Virginia's ruling class, an aristocracy that provided a leadership of extraordinary talent in a later generation when Americans were trying to hammer out the framework of a new nation.

Fortunately for our understanding of Byrd, the first of his known diaries begins as early as 1709. It was published in 1941 as *The Secret Diary of William Byrd of Westover 1709–1712* (edited by Louis B. Wright and Marion Tinling). A few excerpts illustrate his many-sided interests. Passages may be picked almost at random. This, for example, is the entry for October 31, 1709:

> I rose at 6 o'clock and read two chapters in Hebrew and some Greek in Lucian. I said my prayers and ate milk for breakfast. About 10 o'clock we went to court. The committee met to receive proposals for the building [of] the College [William and Mary] and Mr. Tullitt undertook it for £ 2,000 provided he might [take] wood off the College land and all assistants from England to come at the College's risk. We sat in court till about 4 o'clock and then I rode to Green Springs to meet my wife. I found her there and had the pleasure to learn that all was well at home, thanks be to God. There was likewise Mrs. Chiswell. I ate boiled beef for supper. Then we danced and were merry till about 10 o'clock. I neglected to say my prayers but had good health, good thoughts, and good humor, thanks be to God Almighty.

The opening sentence of the above is no surprise. A cultivated gentleman in the early 18th century was expected to know the classical tongues. Familiarity with Latin and Greek literature was taken for granted. But Byrd had more than a bowing acquaintance with these literatures. Owning a fine collection, he made constant use of his books. Since the press of work and the visits of neighbors made consistent reading problematical, he adopted the system of beginning his day with Greek and Hebrew. Occasionally he read some Latin author or something in Italian or French, but Hebrew and Greek were his normal pre-breakfast fare. This daily stint of Greek and Hebrew he maintained throughout his life.

Other items in this passage deserve comment. Already a member of the Council of State, which sat as the highest court in the colony, Byrd had gone to Williamsburg to attend a routine meeting of the Council. He belonged to a Council committee that let a contract for the erection of a building at the College of William and Mary. Further entries in the diary show his continuing interest in the College and in education. Like other members of his group, he was trying to provide for the perpetuation of higher learning, which our ancestors believed essential for an enlightened leadership.

Byrd's regret over forgetting to say his prayers is not mere rhetoric. An 18th-century gentleman of Byrd's class had a profound belief in the value of religion. A society without religion was, in his opinion, a contradiction in terms. Decency, decorum, and good order required men to show respect for religion, and a member of the ruling class had to set an example by going to church and observing at least the outward forms of worship.

Although Byrd's private life demonstrated many weaknesses of the flesh, he was sincerely religious. Classifying his beliefs is difficult. The rationalism that characterized many 18th-century intellectuals touched Byrd but did not envelop him, for his diaries not only record his daily prayers and those times when he neglected them, they also tell us of an insatiable appetite for sermon reading.

The randomly selected passage cited above indicates a few other things about Byrd. It shows his interest in people, his love of gaiety, his concern for his home, and certain peculiarities of diet. These things might be passed over as trivial if they were not indicative of wider interests that throw further light on the man.

An 18th-century aristocrat had to exhibit the social graces expected of a member of his class. But Byrd was no gilded butterfly. Colonial planters by and large were industrious and thrifty folk instead of the silken Cavaliers of popular fiction. Nevertheless, Byrd, like other members of his group, delighted in dancing and in the social gatherings that were part of life in Tidewater Virginia. To the end of his days he was never too tired to turn out for a ball at Williamsburg.

The excerpt above that records the presence of Mrs. Chiswell has more meaning than is at first apparent. Byrd clearly was interested in this pert and pretty woman. Three days later, on November 2, he again began his routine at 6:00 A.M., read some Hebrew and Greek, said his prayers, had milk for breakfast before settling some accounts. But in the evening, he continued,

> I went to Dr. [Barret's] where my wife came this afternoon. Here I found Mrs. Chiswell, my sister Custis, and other ladies. We sat and talked till about 11 o'clock and then retired to our chambers. I played at [r-m] with Mrs. Chiswell and kissed her on the bed till she was angry and my wife also was uneasy about it, and cried as soon as the company was gone. I neglected to say my prayers, which I should not have done, because I ought to beg pardon for the lust I had for another man's wife. However I had good health, good thoughts, and good humor, thanks be to God Almighty.

A wistful note later crept into Byrd's *A Progress to the Mines* when he reported a visit with Mr. and Mrs. Chiswell and found that Mrs. Chiswell, whom he had not seen in more than twenty years, had aged sadly.

Through a long life (he died in 1744) Byrd struggled to improve his plantation at Westover, to make a profit from the Indian trade that his father had developed, to increase his landed holdings, and patriotically to serve the colony of Virginia. Despite the multiplicity of his duties as a member of the Council, as a colonel of militia, and as a consultant in every important matter concerning the colony's welfare, he never neglected the improvement of his mind. He remained a student of the classics and a man of letters. In his library, one of the best in North America at the time, he found both delight and instruction. Other members of the ruling class shared many of Byrd's interests, his ideals—and some of his shortcomings. He was, then, typical of a small group who managed to dominate colonial society in Virginia.

*   *   *

In Massachusetts, the second region to be settled by the English, Samuel Sewall, another diarist, even more diligent in recording events than William Byrd, rose to prominence as a merchant and a jurist in the late 17th and early 18th centuries. Sewall's parents had emigrated from England in 1634 but returned to the homeland where Samuel was born at Bishopstoke in 1652. Nine years later, after Samuel had attended grammar school for a few years, the family returned to Boston. Samuel completed his secondary education and attended Harvard College, from which he graduated in 1671.

Massachusetts Bay in its early years had been dominated by the Puritan clergy. Its charter said that only "freemen" should vote. But to be admitted to the ranks of freemen, one had to be a church member in good standing; and in effect the clergy had succeeded in restricting the right to vote to church members. Joining a Puritan church was not easy. A candidate for admission had to stand up in open congregation and testify that he or she had experienced conversion. While young Sewall was a schoolboy in Boston, the churches found themselves hard pressed because members of the younger generation, who were unwilling to testify that they had experienced conversion, were clamoring to be admitted as freemen so they could vote. Consequently, in 1662, the churches adopted what was called the Half-Way Covenant. That is, unconverted children of church members were admitted to church membership and thus became freemen. Although these unregenerate members could vote, they were not permitted to take the sacrament of the Lord's Supper. This weakening of theocratic control of the colony influenced Sewall in the choice of a career.

After completing his education at Harvard, Sewall had to decide between becoming a minister or entering business. Had he graduated a generation earlier he undoubtedly would have chosen the ministry, a vocation then leading to power; but Sewall, though deeply pious, was also ambitious, and so he decided upon a career of business and politics. First, however, he served briefly as a Harvard tutor and "keeper of the college library."

Sewall's rise in the world was accelerated by a fortunate marriage in

1676 to an heiress, Hannah Hull, daughter of John Hull, the colony's master of the mint and a wealthy merchant. Hannah bore him 14 children, but her inheritance from her father, who died in 1683, helped to keep this numerous progeny from becoming a financial burden.

The term merchant in this time did not mean a tradesman who sold goods in a shop. A merchant was an importer and exporter of general merchandise which he then sold wholesale from his ships or warehouses. Although Sewall began keeping his famous diary in 1674, he tells very little about his business affairs. He displays far greater interest in social conditions in the community, the sermons he heard, and particularly the funerals he attended. Indeed, the diary often reads like a necrology as Sewall comments on the dead, lists the pall bearers, and reports on the funeral sermons.

In 1676 Sewall and his wife moved into his father-in-law's house on Washington Street, Boston, where he was to live for the rest of his life. Under the tutelage of John Hull, from this time onward, he "followed merchandise" (to use his own phrase) and prospered. He also quickly began to take on civic responsibilities and honors. During the outbreak of Indian hostilities known as King Philip's War, he served as a major commanding a detachment of Massachusetts troops. Three years later he became a member of the Ancient and Honorable Artillery Company, an organization known more for its social prestige than its military prowess. Many years later he was elected its captain. In the meantime, however, he served in 1683 as captain of John Hull's Company and in 1685 as captain of the South Company of Boston. He resigned his commission in the latter company in the following year because of an order to put the cross of St. George in the company's colors. To Sewall the cross with "popish" and idolatrous, such were his Puritan prejudices.

By 1684 Sewall was already a member of the Court of Assistants and presided as a magistrate, an office that started him on a long career as a jurist. In this period one did not have to be a trained lawyer to become a judge. Sewall, like many other colonial jurists, had never studied law but he had a fund of common sense and a deep concern for justice. In the same year that he became a magistrate, he was also appointed to the Board of Overseers of Harvard College. He was now firmly established in the political and social hierarchy of Boston where he would remain for the rest of his life with ever increasing honors and responsibilities.

Sewall went to England in November 1688 and therefore witnessed the "Glorious Revolution" of that year which deposed James II and crowned William of Orange and his wife Mary (daughter of King James). The purpose of Sewall's journey was to further his mercantile affairs, but he also attempted to assist the Reverend Increase Mather, who had gone to London to argue for a renewal of the colony's charter, which had been cancelled. Mather showed scant appreciation of Sewall's offers of help, which he thought officious. The King decided to grant a new charter but reserved the right to appoint the governor. Mather persuaded the King to choose Sir William Phips, who had married the widow of John Hull, Sewall's father-in-law.

Phips, a typical self-made man, was never accepted by the Boston social aristocracy; he had been knighted by James II for his exploit in discovering and raising in the Caribbean a Spanish wreck loaded with treasure. Although Phips had married a socially prominent wife, he never forgot his upbringing as a ship's carpenter and sea captain; he preferred the company of seamen, retained the manners and behavior of the quarter-deck, and showed a tenderness toward pirates who frequented colonial harbors. Perhaps Phips's most commendable act was his stopping the Salem witchcraft trials in which Sewall served as one of the judges.

Sewall's journal notes of his visit to London, which lasted from January 13 to October 10, 1689, reveal a side of the author not made explicit elsewhere in the diary. He recorded fewer funerals, since he knew fewer of the deceased in England and felt no duty to mention so many deaths. Although no less observant of the Sabbath, Sewall's travels from place to place left him less opportunity to listen to sermons. Nevertheless, he managed to find many non-Conformist preachers he knew by reputation, and he expressed his pleasure in hearing them.

What is otherwise recorded of his English visit throws light on Sewall's business activities. He visited an amazing number of relatives, some of whom owed him money, and carefully noted his collection of debts. Sometimes, in lieu of cash, he accepted gloves, silk stockings, and other light manufactured articles in payment. He had inherited land and rental property that he inspected, renewed leases, and attended to other business matters. All in all, he had a profitable and pleasant time.

Like any tourist, Sewall visited as many places of interest as time permitted and contrived to see a large part of England, from Plymouth to East Anglia, the Midlands, and of course London. On his way from Dover, his port of entry, he stopped at Canterbury; his Puritan prejudices, however, allowed him to say only of the Cathedral that it was "a very lofty and magnificent building but of little use."

Upon reaching London, Sewall at once sought out Increase Mather, official lobbyist for Massachusetts, and offered his unwanted help. When Sewall could spare time from business matters and from seeking out famous Puritan preachers, he saw the sights: the Guild Hall, Westminster Abbey, St. Paul's Cathedral and other churches, the Tower of London (and the zoo then kept at the Tower), and countless other spots that still attract visitors. Sewall displayed a particular curiosity about architectural specifications. He carried a folding yardstick and was forever measuring floor spaces. The Guild Hall, for example, he noted was 50

yards long and 16 yards broad. At Eton and Hampton Court, which he
visited on May 8, 1689, he seems to have been chiefly interested in dimensions, for he noted in his journal: "Eton College Library, 69 foot
long, the shelves four." At Hampton Court he took the trouble to measure
some of the rooms open to visitors: "Queen's bedchamber, 24 foot square;
King's public dining room, 32 foot and near square."

A gregarious man, Sewall contrived to find cousins or cousins of friends
nearly everywhere, and he enjoyed the hospitality shown him. Puritan
though he was, he was no ascetic and relished good food and drink, never
refusing cider, ale, or wine. Near Southampton he dined at Cousin Jane
Holt's and had "very good bacon, veal, parsnips, very good shoulder of
mutton and a fowl roasted, good currant suet pudding, and the fairest
dish of apples that I have ever eat in England." So it was on numerous
occasions. Like William Byrd, he carefully enumerated the items of food
and drink that were served.

In an age when the only means of travel was by coach or horseback,
Sewall contrived to get around to many of the most interesting spots in
England. At Winchester he looked up the librarian of Winchester College and gave him a copy of John Eliot's Indian Bible, which can still be
seen there. Few sights escaped him as he rode across the land: Stone-
henge, Salisbury—where he was more impressed by the original site of
Old Sarum than by the cathedral—and numerous towns and villages on
the road back to London. In late March he set out from London for a two
week trip to Abingdon, Oxford, Warwick, Coventry, and other points of
interest. If he thought of visiting Shakespeare's Stratford, he does not
mention it. After all, Shakespeare was merely the author of profane plays.
To relatives and friends along the way, Sewall gave gifts of sermons
written by Increase Mather's learned son, Cotton, of Boston. Sewall must
have brought over a bale of these pamphlet sermons, which he distributed
widely. On April 3 he was shown the Bodleian Library in shape of an H,
he reported, "a very magnificent thing. The galleries very magnificent,
about 44 of my canes length and nearly 8 in breadth. . . . Mr. Gilbert gives
us a pint of wine. Lodge at the Bear Inn."

Sewall was not one to go overboard in admiration of any sight. Visiting
Cambridge in late June, he went first to Emmanuel College, from which
many of New England's preachers had come. King's College Chapel, one
of the architectural wonders of England, he dismissed as "very stately."
He found St. John's College more interesting, especially its "library and
many rarities, among which was a petrified cheese."

Finally on October 10, 1689, after much travel, many visits to relatives
and friends, and important business transacted, Sewall sailed from Plymouth on a vessel aptly named *America*. He reached Boston on December
2, and immediately resumed his political, military, religious, and com-

mercial activities. Soon after his return, Sewall was appointed a member
of the provincial Council to which he was reelected every year until 1725
when he retired.

The Indians on the frontier, on instigation of the French, were giving
trouble, and one of the first pieces of bad news Sewall heard after his
arrival was an account of depredations in the interior. On February 8,
1690, he noted in his diary the massacre by Indians of 60 men, women,
and children at Schenectady. Massachusetts mobilized its militia, and
Sewall, formerly captain of the South Company, turned out for drill.
On March 24 he recorded in his diary that "I go into the field, pray with
the South Company, exercise them in a few distances, facings, doublings
. . . told them the place I was in required more time and strength than
I had, so took leave of them."

Two years later Sewall played a significant role in one of the most
tragic episodes in colonial history, the Salem witchcraft delusion, in
which scores of citizens were accused on the testimony of a group of
hysterical or sensation-seeking teen-age girls. When Governor Phips
reached Massachusetts in May 1692, more than a hundred persons were
in jail or under indictment for the crime of witchcraft. He immediately
appointed a panel of nine members of a commission of Oyer and Ter-
miner, a special court, to bring those accused of witchcraft to justice.
Sewall was one of the nine. His brother Stephen was clerk of the court.
At the first sitting of the court on June 2, Bridget Bishop was convicted
and sentenced to hang. Her execution followed on June 10. By the end
of the summer, after many sensational trials characterized by flimsy
"spectral" evidence that no modern judge would admit, 19 persons had
suffered death. Even Increase and Cotton Mather, who had originally
demanded that the court root out the heinous sin of witchcraft, realized
that things had gone too far. With pressure from some of the more
rational citizens of the region, Governor Phips in September stopped the
trials.

Sewall says little about the witch trials in his diary. Clearly he was
not proud of his role and felt uneasy in his conscience. Of the nine
members of the court he was the only one to confess publicly his regret
over participating in the miscarriage of justice. Five years later, on January 14, 1697, he stood up in Old South Church and had the minister
read a statement he had drafted in which he said he desired "to take
the blame and shame of it [the witchcraft trials], asking pardon of men
and especially desiring prayers that God . . . would pardon that sin."
Many must have admired Sewall's courage in taking the blame upon
himself, something none of the others involved showed a willingness to do.

On December 6, 1692, Sewall had been chosen one of the justices of
the Superior Court of Judicature, a post to which he was constantly re-
appointed until 1728 when he retired for age. On April 16, 1718, he was

made chief justice. Sewall's judicial duties took much of his time, but he was never too busy to attend to other obligations expected of a civic leader of his station. He served as an overseer of Harvard College, judge of probate of Suffolk County, commissioner, secretary, and treasurer of the Company for the Propagation of the Gospel in New England and Parts Adjacent. Furthermore, he prized his commission as captain of the Ancient and Honorable Artillery Company. Again, he was conscientious about attending the funeral of nearly every prominent citizen of the region, male and female. His journal also records his attendance at church on nearly every Sunday and Lecture Day (Thursday), with a statement of the preacher's sermon text. A reader is left wondering how Sewall found time for his business affairs, but his journal gives few clues.

Sewall was oppressively pious, but this was characteristic of many of the old school of Puritans in Massachusetts. Times were changing, and Sewall frequently expressed regret at the increasing wickedness of the age. He was scandalized at "mixed dancing"; he was shocked at Cotton Mather's defense of wearing periwigs, especially his mention of so worldly a matter in the pulpit; he disapproved of boys playing tricks on April Fool's Day and on Shrove Tuesday; and he voiced approval when Boston's citizens failed to observe Christmas, a "Popish" festival.

The diary is full of moralizing. On January 13, 1677, for example, he observed: "Giving my chickens meat [food], it came to my mind that I gave them nothing save Indian corn and water, and yet they eat it and thrived very well... which much affected me and convinced [sic] what need I stood in of spiritual food...." Almost every event provided an opportunity for Sewall to draw a moral. Another typical instance appears on October 1, 1697. At dinner someone knocked over and broke a bottle of spirits that "stood upon a joint stool." "I said 'twas a lively emblem of our fragility and mortality."

Sewall was one of the first New Englanders to protest against slavery and in 1700 published *The Selling of Joseph*, a tract expressing his views on the subject. In this he was a pioneer, for even ministers like Cotton Mather kept black slaves as household servants, and many merchants were engaged in the slave trade. To Sewall's credit, his mercantile activities did not embrace trade with Africa in which New England shippers bartered their rum with African chiefs for captives taken in tribal wars.

In addition to *The Selling of Joseph*, Sewall published other tracts on pious subjects. He also wrote verses that he circulated in manuscript among his friends. Books were among the imports brought over from England for sale, but Sewall rarely mentions them by title.

Sewall's own literary taste ran to the reading of sermons, which he distributed freely. A sermon in his opinion was an appropriate gift with which to court a lady when he was a widower seeking a wife. One of the most interesting episodes in the diary recounts his effort in 1720 to persuade Katherine Winthrop, widow of Wait Winthrop, to marry him. Sewall's second wife had died in May of that year. In the autumn he was vigorously pursuing his courtship, calling on "Madam" Winthrop as often as possible and taking her sermons as well as sweetmeats, almonds, gingerbread, and other small gifts. He provides a full account in his diary for September, October, and November. Madam Winthrop strung him along for several weeks, first encouraging him and then being distant. On October 12 he called and was discouraged to find that "Madam Winthrop's countenance was much changed from what 'twas on Monday, looked dark and lowering. . . . I got my chair in place, had some converse but very cold and indifferent to what 'twas before. Asked her to acquit me of rudeness if I drew off her glove. Enquiring the reason, I told her 'twas great odds between handling a dead goat and a living lady. Got it off." Ardent as was his pursuit, it came to naught. Madam Winthrop insisted upon Sewall's keeping a coach and he refused such an extravagance. The courtship cooled, and Sewall with some regret sought elsewhere for a wife. On March 29, 1722, he married another widow, Mrs. Mary Gibbs.

Sewall represented the best type of New England Puritan of the late 17th and early 18th centuries. He exemplified the bourgeois virtues embraced in what is now called the "work ethic." He believed that God would reward him with material blessings if he lived righteously according to the rigid Puritan concept of behavior. He insisted upon a life of diligence, thrift, sobriety, and abstinence from extravagant waste. To have a coach, which Madam Winthrop demanded, would have violated his principle of avoiding useless ostentation. The accumulation of wealth in Sewall's eyes was evidence of God's approval. So Sewall practiced piety, attended to his business but did not let it envelop him, and died on January 1, 1730, prosperous and in the odor of sanctity.

*   *   *

Few greater contrasts in character could be found than that between Judge Samuel Sewall of Massachusetts Bay and Sir William Johnson of New York. Sewall, a prosperous merchant and judge, gave little evidence of an interest in worldly affairs in his long diary. Recording vast numbers of sermons and funerals, moralizing about the hope of the hereafter, he gives the impression of being more concerned about the next world. Sir William Johnson, on the contrary, revealed little interest in the future life. In his utterances "God" was usually followed by the word "damn." It is true that he had some concern about religion, but his interest was in the practical aspects of missionary activities with the Indians. He had a profound interest in the fur trade, and his greed for land was exceeded by that of few other colonials. Before he died he had accumulated a princely estate of more than 1,000,000 acres in the Mohawk Valley and adjacent territory.

Sewall's interest in women was strictly within the bounds of matrimony. He occasionally mentions in his diary an observation that a young lass was "comely," but if his thoughts ever strayed beyond that, he never revealed it. It is true that after the death of his wife Sewall was soon pursuing a widow with offers of marriage—subject to her acceptance of his somewhat penny-pinching domestic arrangements. Johnson, on the other hand, was attracted by all sorts and kinds of women and felt no compulsion to resist female temptation. His interest in the opposite sex was apparently well known and unflagging. Even in his old age, on a peace-making mission to Detroit, his host, eager to please, assembled 30 of the most beautiful women in the area at a banquet in Sir William's honor. Included was Angelique Cuillerier (*dit* Beaubien), regarded as the most alluring temptress on the frontier. Johnson had been attracted by her before, and on this occasion he succumbed to a torrid love affair— but shrewdly sidestepped the lady's efforts to trap him into matrimony.

Johnson and William Byrd might well have understood one another, but there was a vast difference between them. Byrd, too, had an interest in the Indian trade inherited from his father; he had the same land hunger displayed by Johnson and other prosperous colonials; and he also had a weakness for women often revealed in his diaries—particularly when he was a widower in London. But Byrd had an acute sense of decorum and guilt lacking in Johnson. When lured by feminine wiles, as happened on frequent evenings in London, Byrd spent some of the next morning on his knees in the church of St. Clement Danes asking God's forgiveness for his transgressions. Johnson, as far as the record indicates, never showed remorse for any affair of the heart.

Johnson, born in 1715 in County Meath, Ireland, was a nephew of Vice Admiral Sir Peter Warren, already the owner of a considerable landed estate in New York's Mohawk River valley. His uncle sent William to America, probably late in 1737, to look after his property. The young man of 22 immediately saw the possibility of expanding the fur trade. He opened a trading post and began to make friends with the Indians. Soon he acquired land of his own and continued for the rest of his life to expand his holdings.

The secret of Johnson's success lay in his ability to get along with people, especially the Indians. He began by treating them fairly. They soon learned that Johnson would not cheat them—an unusual phenomenon in the traffic with aborigines north of Albany. Many rascally Dutch and English traders infested this and other frontiers. Johnson's honesty proved a highly profitable asset.

By the 1740s Johnson had already created quite an establishment of his own north of the Mohawk River on the site of Amsterdam, New

York, to which he gave the name Mount Johnson. A large stone house served as both residence and fortress. Because of this dual use it was frequently referred to as Fort Johnson. Not far away, in 1762–63, he built a vast manor house near the present city of Johnstown, New York. This commodious building and its outlying units provided space for the entertainment of all classes of visitors, from half-naked Indians to European dignitaries. Here, in Johnson Hall, the proprietor lived out his days in grandeur that might have excited the envy of many a titled Englishman.

Johnson's domestic affairs in the early years were informal and somewhat obscure. He took as housekeeper and companion an indentured German girl who bore him a son and two daughters. At some point he legalized the union to legitimize his children.

After his wife's death he brought into Johnson Hall a Mohawk squaw whose uncle, Hendrick, was a powerful chief. This informal union proved extremely useful to Johnson because it cemented his relations with the Mohawks. He had three more children by her. After her death, his next companion was her niece, Molly, the sister of an even more powerful chief named Joseph Brant. A woman of great strength of character, Molly Brant proved a highly useful helpmate and bore him eight children. The union, once again, helped to further Johnson's friendship with the Mohawks, and he was taken into the tribe as an adopted brother.

Johnson's greatest contribution to the development of colonial America was the enduring friendship he established with the powerful Iroquois confederation known as the Six Nations, of which the Mohawks were an especially influential unit. The original Five Nations were the Mohawks, Oneidas, Onondagas, Cayugas, and Senecas. Early in the 18th century an Iroquoian tribe known as the Tuscaroras was driven out of North Carolina after a disastrous war and joined the Iroquois confederation to make the sixth nation.

Johnson's relations with the Indians were sometimes tempestuous and not always satisfactory to him or to the tribesmen. But over a long period, until his death in 1774, he contrived to keep the Six Nations usually on the side of the English. To be sure, he suffered defeat. For instance, the Senecas, proving most difficult, came under French influence and defected. But Johnson at times was able to lure them back into the fold and prevent any enduring schism.

Johnson's skill in dealing with the Indians resulted from his knowledge of their language, which he learned to speak fluently, his intimate acquaintance with Indian psychology, and his own eloquence in addressing the Indians in the figurative and flowery rhetoric that characterized their own speeches. Johnson became one of the country's most skillful forest diplomats. When patience was required, he could sit around the council fires smoking and listening for hours at a time. When the situation dictated force instead of words, he could make an instant decision and act accordingly. The Indians respected him, and many showed him deep affection.

In the numerous conflicts of the 18th century between the English and the French, as they battled for dominance in disputed territories in the north and west, Johnson was always ready to take the initiative in any military action. Early in the Seven Years' War, which saw Braddock's defeat in the 1775 campaign for Fort Duquesne, Johnson led some 2,500 provincial troops with 300 or 400 Indian allies in an effort to block the French and their Indians from pushing down from Lake Champlain. His immediate objective was Crown Point, which he never reached. But he did succeed in defeating the enemy in a battle at Lake George, the only English victory in 1755. So pleased was the Colonial Office in London with this unusual good news that King George II created Johnson a baronet, a hereditary title that he was able to pass on to his son.

The Lake George battle, characteristic of many frontier conflicts in this period, throws a vivid light on Johnson and the qualities of his leadership. To whip up enthusiasm among his Mohawk allies, who came to the rendezvous near Albany, he painted his face like a warrior, danced the war dance, and then gave them a feast of roast ox from which he cut the first slice with his sword. He had need to stir his Indian allies, even his brother Mohawks, for they were at this time reluctant warriors. Despite the feast and a discreet ration of rum, the Mohawks sent along only some 300 warriors. Although in the subsequent battle a few fought bravely, most did little; one commented that they had come to see their English brothers fight. With levies of provincial troops numbering about 2,200, Johnson marched toward Lake George. The militia, farmers who had never been in action before, regarded their local officers with more respect than Johnson, the over-all commander. Discipline was difficult. Yet Johnson showed great tact in dealing with these raw recruits and their untrained leaders. He invited the officers to his headquarters, gave them strong lemon punch and good wine, and held joint councils of war.

The French commander, a German named Baron Dieskau, had almost as much trouble as Johnson with his own troops, more than 3,500 regulars, Canadians, and Indians. The Canadians were unruly and the French Indians gave Dieskau so much difficulty that he wrote his superior that "one needs the patience of an angel to get on with these devils." This problem, common to both sides during the wilderness wars, makes Johnson's role more significant, for he managed to exercise more control over the Indians than any other colonial leader.

Early in the battle Johnson received a bullet in his thigh and had to take to his tent. This wound would plague him the rest of his life. Dieskau, also severely wounded, was taken captive and brought to the British commander's tent. Dieskau later declared that Johnson ordered the surgeon to treat the Baron's wounds before having his own dressed. Johnson also saved Dieskau from the vengeance of the Mohawks, who tried to seize and murder him because of the death of Hendrick, their chief. Such was Johnson's gallantry toward a brave enemy. Francis Parkman, the historian, wrote rather disparagingly of Johnson's failure to pursue and destroy the fleeing French troops, but Johnson understood the limitations of his forces. Always a pragmatic warrior, he knew better than regular British army officers what could be accomplished in the forests with unreliable Indian allies and ill-trained militia.

In later campaigns Johnson was profoundly irritated by the superciliousness of British commanders-in-chief, particularly with Sir Jeffrey Amherst whom he blamed for the slaughter and disaster on the frontier during Pontiac's conspiracy in the 1760s.

The year following Johnson's creation as a baronet, King George II also named him "colonel of the Six Nations" and sole superintendent of Indian affairs north of the Ohio. In the south he had a counterpart in John Stuart. Johnson was allowed to name as assistant George Croghan, a loyal and ingenious fellow Irishman who helped to implement his Indian policies.

Johnson hoped to restrain white invaders of the Indian hunting grounds. In 1768, to be sure, he held a great council at Fort Stanwix where, outdoing himself in oratory, he persuaded the Indians to sign a treaty ceding large tracts on the frontiers from Virginia to New York for settlement by whites. But lands beyond a boundary established at Fort Stanwix would be reserved to the Indians for their hunting grounds for "as long as the rivers run." Johnson himself acquired desirable tracts, for which he was later criticized. But if he enriched himself, he showed no more land-greed than hundreds of other colonials, including George Washington. He merely had greater opportunities.

In his later years Johnson took increasing pleasure in the baronial life. His wealth had enabled him to provide Johnson Hall with all the amenities that an 18th-century gentleman could desire. Not one to stint himself of any luxury, he loaded his pantries and cellars with the best food, wine, and liquors that money could buy. Johnson Hall teemed with swarms of white retainers, black slaves, and Indians of uncertain status. Always present were numerous Indian girls, some handsome, some fat and squat. Johnson was not always terribly fastidious. It was reported by contemporaries that he had fathered in his time some three hundred children. Few of these, of course, inhabited Johnson Hall. When George Croghan's own wife was pregnant, he sent her off to what he referred to as "fruitful Johnson Hall." Croghan himself, though constantly in debt, sought to imitate his leader by a similar display of luxury. He named his own log quarters on Lake Otsego "Croghan Hall."

Sir William Johnson was one of the most colorful figures in colonial

America. In his youth handsome, jovial, and friendly, he remained into his later years a strong and stalwart figure capable of winning friends among New York's aristocratic grandees and the warriors of the Six Nations. Though hated by many unscrupulous traders, and disliked by the pacific Quakers of Pennsylvania, he was extravagantly admired by frontiersmen everywhere. They believed Johnson capable of performing miracles with the Indians. European visitors to the estate enjoyed their host's hospitality and also remarked on his skillful diplomacy.

Like William Byrd of Virginia, Johnson took pleasure in his library at Johnson Hall, where he accumulated more than 2,000 volumes, chiefly on scientific, historical, and political subjects. As early as 1749 he had ordered the works of Sir Isaac Newton and numerous scientific treatises. Later he left a standing order with his London bookseller for "all new books on history, philosophy [science], and the lives of men worth reading about." He was especially interested in works on agriculture, which he, as a large landowner, was eager to promote.

Although having had little formal education, Johnson was a literate man, read a great deal in his later years, and wrote with vigor and clarity. His reports on Indian affairs (preserved among the Johnson Papers in the New York Historical Society and elsewhere) show a keen intellect and remarkable powers of observation and discrimination. He contributed to the American Philosophical Society, and his communications concerning the customs and languages of the Indians of the Six Nations were printed in the Society's *Proceedings*. Until the end of his life Johnson continued his anthropological interests and investigated variations in Indian dialects. Late in life he also became a trustee of the New Jersey school that ultimately became Rutgers University.

Although Johnson showed little concern for religion in his own personal life, like other leaders of his generation, he recognized its civilizing influence. In the town that he established near Johnson Hall (now Johnstown, New York), he built an Anglican church at his own expense and provided a canopied pew for himself—in case he should need it. He also encouraged the clergyman of this church to adapt the prayer book for the use of the Mohawks. His religious support was not exclusively confined to the Anglicans, for he helped build chapels for the Dutch Reformed Church in the Mohawk valley.

Among his contemporaries, Johnson demonstrated a remarkable combination of traits. He combined the qualities of an 18th-century landed grandee and the typical frontiersman of a later day, now popularized in both history and legend. He displayed some of the characteristics of the cultivated gentleman and virtuoso of his period; he felt at home with the great gentry of New York like the Schuylers and De Lanceys; and he could entertain English noblemen and their ladies at Johnson Hall with grace and ease. He also could display on occasion the manners and behavior of the typical "squaw man" known on all the frontiers. This unusually versatile colonial leader died on July 11, 1774, shortly after a speech to the Mohawks characterized by his usual persuasive tact in which he urged the chiefs to control their men. Some said his death was caused by syphilis; others diagnosed his fatal collapse as apoplexy.

Although controversies between the colonies and the mother country had become acute at the time of his death, Johnson never swerved in his loyalty to Great Britain. Had he lived, he would have been a Tory loyalist, and his influence with the Six Nations might have made their adherence to the British cause even more dangerous to the outcome of the War of Independence on the frontier.

3

Changing 18th-Century Religious Attitudes

JONATHAN EDWARDS
BENJAMIN FRANKLIN
THOMAS PAINE

by Paul F. Boller, Jr.
University of Massachusetts, Boston

During the 18th century the secularization of American life and thought proceeded rapidly and for more and more Americans the church was becoming less important with each passing day. "This *Worldly Spirit*," complained a Boston minister in 1733, "has in a great measure thrust out Religion, and given it a Wound which will prove *Deadly* unless infinite Mercy prevent. . . ." Religion was not dying; it was being transformed. The stern Jehovah of high Calvinism was gradually being replaced by the genial God of rationalistic Deism for many people and the doctrine of human depravity was giving way to a belief in the potentialities of human nature for good. The key words for increasing numbers of Americans were no longer grace, election, and redemption; they were freedom, independence, and natural rights. Jonathan Edwards, struck by the "extraordinary dullness in religion" around him, worked hard to stem the tide of secularism overwhelming the land, but while he was solemnly calling sinners to repentance Benjamin Franklin was busily spreading the gospel of reason and tolerance in his almanacs, newspapers, pamphlets, and journals. And toward the end of the century Edwards' worst fears were realized: in an outspoken freethinking (and enormously popular) book called *Age of Reason,* Thomas Paine abandoned Franklin's kindly tolerance for all kinds of religion and issued a bold declaration of war on organized religion in general and a militant call for universal Deism. Surely no three men could have been more unalike than Edwards, Franklin, and Paine when it came to religion. But their lives, too, were utterly at variance.

Compared with Benjamin Franklin and Thomas Paine, Jonathan Edwards lived a singularly uneventful life. Born in East Windsor, Connecticut, in 1708, the son of a Congregational clergyman, he entered Yale at 13, studied theology after graduation, had a church for a while in New York City, became assistant and then senior minister of the Congregational Church in Northampton, Massachusetts, led a great revival there in 1734–35, quarreled with his parishioners in 1748 over qualifications for church membership, left to take a post in the frontier town of Stockbridge, and then agreed a few years later to become President of the College of New Jersey only to succumb to smallpox shortly after reaching Princeton in December 1758. He never went abroad, saw military action, participated in politics, held public office, or became involved in burning social issues, and he never really learned much about America outside of his beloved New England. Franklin, by contrast, was printer, journalist, editor, civic leader, scientist, inventor, diplomat, and statesman; and Paine was also a journalist, politician, and humanitarian leader as well as something of an inventor and very much a revolutionary.

Edwards in a real sense never really left home. Franklin and Paine walked among the great both here and abroad and they both participated in momentous events on both continents. But Edwards traveled widely only in the City of God and the crises he encountered were largely spiritual. Though like Franklin and Paine he familiarized himself with the secular psychology of John Locke and the new physics of Sir Isaac Newton, he utilized his knowledge mainly to justify the ways of a Calvinistic God to man. In an Age of Enlightenment, he dwelt on mystery, miracle, and prophecy; in an Age of Reason he emphasized religious affections and saving faith. He remained quite other-worldly in an increasingly secular age and implacably opposed to the resolute this-worldliness of men like Franklin and Paine. He dedicated his life to restoring the faith of his Puritan fathers that Franklin and Paine were steadily undermining. But when he died, the drift of American thought was unmistakably away from Edwardseanism, especially among educated people in urban centers, toward the genial optimism of Franklin and even, in some cases, toward the militant freethinking of Paine.

Edwards, unlike Franklin and Paine, was a God-intoxicated man. His aim in life was "to lie low before God, as in the dust; that I might be nothing, and that God might be All. . . ." In sermons, essays, and treatises on Christian fundamentals, he depicted in loving detail the beauty, power, wisdom, and goodness of God and called on his parishioners (and people everywhere) to prostrate themselves before Him. God, he declared, had created the world and sustained it by his infinite power; He worked through secondary causes and natural law but intervened in His creation whenever He saw fit; He gave all men and women common grace with which to improve their natural abilities, but He also freely bestowed His supernatural grace on a chosen few so that they might possess the kind of faith in Christ that guaranteed them salvation. Edwards' God was both omniscient and omnipotent; He had foreknowledge of all that was to come because He had foreordained it through all eternity. He had created the world for His own glory and it was the duty of His creatures to reflect this glory back upon their Creator by continual acts of praise and worship. Edwards insisted that "the whole is *of* God, and *in* God, and *to* God, and God is the beginning, middle, and end in this affair."

In Edwards' predestined scheme, there was no room for human autonomy. Men and women could not choose their destinies for themselves; their fate lay in the hands of the Almighty. Edwards never doubted the absolute sovereignty of God after his conversion at college and he was convinced that the profoundest insights into the human condition were embodied in the Calvinist theology he learned as a boy in a Puritan parsonage. Above all, he insisted on the doctrine of original sin: the belief that because of Adam's sin in disobeying God all human beings were born weak and selfish, behaved wickedly, and fully deserved the eternal punishment He reserved for unrepentant sinners. Edwards thought that empirical evidence for human depravity appeared in all ages and countries and that the history of every community was a chronicle of almost unrelieved greed, cruelty, dishonesty, and oppression. But he was also convinced of the validity of four other Calvinistic doctrines that dealt with release from the consequences of sin: unconditional election (God arbitrarily selects a few people for salvation regardless of their merits); limited atonement (Christ died to save some, but not all, people); irresistible grace (people play no part in achieving salvation but passively receive God's saving grace); and the final perseverance of the saints (people who receive God's free grace never lapse from their regenerate state). There was no place for free will in any of this. The Calvinistic Five Points that Edwards expounded rested squarely on a belief in predestination.

Edwards thought that the doctrine of predestination, like that of total depravity, was intellectually compelling. Did not the great Newton declare that "every event has a cause"? And did not the causal necessity asserted by scientists rule out free will (that is, uncaused volitions) as emphatically as predestination did? In his celebrated treatise on *Freedom of the Will* (1754), Edwards argued that human choices always have motives, that people always act according to what seems best to them at the moment, and that what seems good in turn depends on a variety of hereditary and environmental causes. But though people's choices are motivated, not free, people themselves are nonetheless free so long as there are no obstacles to doing what they choose to do and if they are not forced to do things they don't choose to do. The volitions of both slave and freeman are causally necessitated, but the latter is nevertheless free to do things the former can never do. Freedom, in short, lies in overt action, not in internal volition, and with this kind of freedom comes responsibility for what one does. Given human depravity, the tendency of people will be to put themselves above God and their neighbors, choose and act selfishly, and commit the sins that merit God's punishment. And only God can interrupt the necessary sequence of causes and effects set in motion by the creation of the world and, by shedding His free grace on certain men and women, rescue them from the awful consequences of their evil-doing.

During the Great Awakening, the great colonial religious revival of which the Northampton revival was one phase, Edwards preached powerful sermons on the terrible fate awaiting sinners upon the day of judgment and called on his congregations to realize the enormity of their depravity and throw themselves utterly on the mercy of God. He even gave the impression at times that if people strove hard enough to resist their sinful temptations and dedicate themselves to God they might be rewarded by an act of grace. Strictly speaking, however, he did not make and could not have made any such promise. Human beings surely could not, according to his theocentric religion, coax the Almighty into altering His predestined plans. Salvation was in God's hands, not man's; to think otherwise was to depreciate His majestic sovereignty. It might be, indeed, that the profound sense of worthlessness, feeling of utter dependence on God, and loving faith in Christ that accompanied the conversion experience, as well as the greater ability to resist temptation following from conversion, were outward signs of invisible grace. It was important therefore to strive hard, by constant reflection on one's infinite sinfulness, for the experience of grace. But if it came, it was God's, not the sinner's, doing. Edwards' determinism was uncompromising, but he did not regard it as inconsistent with hortatory sermonizing. He preached predestination and called for repentance the way modern sociologists teach environmental determinism and call for social reconstruction. Above all, he preached a religion of the heart, insisted that doctrinal knowledge without emotional commitment was worthless, and made a psychological analysis of the conversion experience after the Northampton revival that, like his later treatise on free will, still commands respect. He was anxious for the church to be filled, not with formal or birthright members, but with people who had experienced the awesome crisis of conversion. One of the reasons his Northampton congregation decided to dissolve its connection with him was that he demanded too much religiously from them.

In his later years, Edwards devoted his energies to combatting what was loosely called Arminianism. The Arminians made a larger place for human enterprise in their scheme of salvation than the Calvinists did and their views became increasingly popular in Protestant religious circles during the 18th century. They rejected the Five Points because there was no place for human initiative in them, insisted that human nature was a mixture of good and evil tendencies and not predetermined to evil, and asserted that a conscientious person might, by his own efforts, as well as with the help of God, achieve salvation. By playing down God's arbitrary grace and stressing man's potentiality for good, Arminianism had the effect of raising man's status at the expense of God's. Edwards observed the spread of Arminianism (in the Church of England and among educated people in New England, particularly in eastern Massachusetts) with alarm. He was convinced that rejecting the doctrine of God's free grace was the first step toward deism, atheism, and the destruction of Christianity. In 1754 he published his massive treatise on free will with the hope of demolishing the Arminian heresy once for all.

*   *   *

Edwards' *Freedom of the Will* was a magnificent failure. Though difficult to refute, it did little to stem the tide of Arminianism in Edwards' day. The movement in America as well as in England was steadily away from Calvinism to Arminianism and then to deism and beyond. The evolution of Benjamin Franklin's thinking about religion was a perfect example of the kind of 18th-century religious trends that Edwards was combatting. Franklin, like Edwards, was born into an orthodox home in Boston, filled with books on "polemical divinity," baptized in the Presbyterian church, and instructed in the Calvinist "Quinquarticulars" as a child. But where Edwards spent his boyhood building prayer-booths, yearning for conversion, and striving mightily to accept divine sovereignty, young Franklin was learning to swim, make candles in his father's shop, perfect his writing style, and set type in his brother's printing shop. It would never have occurred to Edwards, as it did to Franklin, to urge his father to say grace over a barrel of fish once for all so he wouldn't have to do it each time the family ate fish at mealtimes. Or to suggest to a Presbyterian chaplain, as Franklin did later on, to dole out the soldier's ration of rum right after divine service in order to improve church attendance. Unlike Edwards, Franklin discarded Calvinism with relief as a young man. He read some books attempting to refute deism and was promptly converted to the deist outlook. He was a "staunch doubter" at 16; at that age Edwards was immersed in theology. From Edwards' point of view, Franklin's thinking went steadily downhill after he became a deist.

When he was about 19, Franklin amused himself by writing a *Dissertation on Liberty and Necessity* (1725) which proved that predestinarian assumptions like Edwards' shut virtue as well as freedom out of the world. If God is all-wise, all-good, and all-powerful, and determines whatever happens, he argued, it follows that there can be no evil, no free will, and no morality in the world. No evil, because nothing happens without God's consent and what He consents to must be good because He is good. (Edwards had argued that God "permits" sin, though He hates it, for His own mysterious purposes.) No free will, because if man can do only what God predetermines him to do, he cannot choose on his own. No morality, because if men do not choose for themselves, "there can be neither Merit nor Demerit in Creatures" and "therefore every Creature must be equally esteem'd by the Creator." It would have been foolish, Franklin added, for God to have peopled the world with free agents, because if people had to make their own decisions they would never know what was best to do and they would have only one chance in 10,000 of actually hitting on the right action. A predestined world, though lacking in freedom and virtue, was a smoothly operating and harmonious one. Man should be grateful therefore that he is "Part of this great Machine, the Universe," that "his regular Acting is requisite to the regular moving of the whole," and that his choices and actions were governed by an all-wise Providence. Sowing a few wild oats in London, as Franklin was doing when he composed his "little metaphysical piece," as he called it, was presumably part of God's great plan.

Franklin eventually decided that his "Dissertation" had "an ill-tendency" because it was so cavalier about virtue, destroyed most copies of it, and wrote an essay on "the Providence of God in the Government of the World" (1732) in which he argued the case for freedom. In this essay Franklin took the line that predestination and prayer were incompatible. God would be malicious, he said, if He allowed people to pray in a world in which everything was foreordained. But God was good, not malicious, and people do pray, and the upshot must be that things are not utterly foreordained. (Edwards of course thought that both the rain and the prayers for rain were foreordained.) Franklin did not think that God left *everything* in the world to free agency, for that would make Him indifferent to His creation. So having rejected universal determinism and absolute freedom, he reached a compromise: God permits the laws of nature and the free agency of men to shape what happens in the world, but on occasion, not to leave the rewarding of virtue and the punishing of evil entirely to chance, He "interferes by his particular Providence, and sets aside the Events which would otherwise have been produced in the Course of Nature, or by the Free Agency of Men. . . ." Franklin was convinced that God had imparted some of His freedom, along with some of His wisdom, power, and goodness, to men. But he did not so much argue the case for free agency as to show the incompatibility of predestination with human effort. Thereafter he took freedom for granted and abandoned metaphysical reasonings about it as exercises in frustration. Like most of his associates in colonial America he lost interest in Calvinistic issues and never again engaged in serious discussion of the predestination-free will question.

But if Franklin lost interest in theology, his interest in religion continued undiminished. He was unorthodox but not irreligious. In 1728, he drew up a little liturgy for his own private use entitled *Articles of Belief and Acts of Religion*. In it, he professed belief in "one Supreme most perfect Being" who was too infinite and incomprehensible for humans to be able to worship and who, as far as human praise was concerned, was "INFINITELY ABOVE IT." But the Infinite, according to Franklin, had created "many Beings or Gods, vastly superior to Man" who did comprehend and worship Him and who were wise, good, and powerful enough themselves to create suns and planets of their own to govern. Franklin wasn't sure whether these secondary gods were immortal; they might endure forever or they might die out and be replaced by other gods after many ages—but they deserved and welcomed acts of worship. Franklin reserved his devotion for the "wise and good God, who is the Author and Owner of our System" and he pictured Him as having some of the same passions as human beings and consequently pleased by praise and worship and hurt by neglect. Franklin was convinced that the God of our solar system was a "good Being" who created many things for the "Delight of Man" and who was pleased "when He sees His Children solace themselves in any manner of pleasant Exercises and innocent Delights." But without virtue, Franklin added, people could have no happiness in the world and so "I firmly believe he delights to see me Virtuous, because he is pleas'd when he sees me Happy." Having stated his "First Principles," Franklin went on to present an elaborate liturgy of adoration, petition, and thanks to the God of our planetary system. It is clear that the polytheism of Franklin's liturgy enabled him to accept the aloof and impersonal deist God (who created the great world-machine and then left it to operate on its own by the laws of nature) without entirely abandoning the personal God of traditional religion which, he thought, satisfied the "natural principle" all people possess "which inclines . . . to DEVOTION or the Worship of some unseen Power." But polytheism was no rigid belief for Franklin. Though he toyed all his life with the notion of a plurality of lesser gods under the direction of a Supreme Power (much as Newton did), he also frequently expressed monotheistic views. In his autobiography he declared that "there is one God, who made all things" and this was by no means unusual for him.

Franklin's *Articles* show that he was fond of ceremony and ritual. He was continually tinkering with traditional Christian forms, rites, and creeds and trying to make them more acceptable to freethinkers like himself. In 1773, he collaborated with Lord Le DeSpencer in revising the Anglican Book of Common Prayer, on which his *Articles of Religion* had been modelled, to make it more attractive to church-goers. Lord Le DeSpencer edited the liturgy and Franklin redid the catechism as well as the Psalms and together they succeeded in cutting the Anglican service in half. For his part, Franklin omitted the imprecatory Psalms which, he said, "appeared not to suit well the Christian doctrine of forgiveness of injuries," abbreviated the prayers for the visitation of the sick, and shortened the "Order for the Burial of the Dead" in order "to preserve the health and lives of the living." Franklin hoped the shortened service would bring more people into church but he later admitted that the "Abridgement of the Book of Common Prayer" attracted little interest. Nevertheless, he joined David Williams, an English political philosopher, in preparing another system of worship which was even more deistical than the "Abridgement." He also went to work on the Lord's Prayer, which he thought badly needed modernizing, and turned it in effect into a Deist's petition; proposed a new version of the Bible in modern English and rewrote some verses from Job as an example of what he had in mind; and composed new chapters for the Old Testament containing parables about brotherly love and religious toleration. His "Parable Against Persecution," presented as the 51st chapter of Genesis, recounts how Abraham turned a stranger away from his house because he worshipped a different God and then relented after being severely rebuked for his intolerance by Jehovah.

Franklin thought religious intolerance was the curse of humanity and he did everything he could as editor and civic leader in Philadelphia to combat it. In 1735, he vigorously championed Samuel Hemphill, a Presbyterian minister under fire for heresy in the Synod of Philadelphia; in 1740, helped secure a building in which evangelist George Whitefield (who had been barred from the city's pulpits) might hold forth; and in 1747, while organizing a voluntary military "Association" for the defense of Pennsylvania, warned his supporters against animosity toward the pacifist Quakers who "from their religious *Scruples*, cannot allow themselves to join us." In his autobiography, he expressed admiration for the Dunkers who, though much misunderstood, refrained from publishing their Confession of Faith lest it bind and restrict them and make them "unwilling to receive Farther Improvement." During the Hemphill controversy, Franklin evinced considerable anticlerical feeling, referring to the ministers who put Hemphill on trial as "Rev. Asses," but on the whole his relations with clergymen of all denominations were amicable. He was on excellent terms with Whitefield, though the Anglican revivalist's Calvinist views were much closer to Edwards' than to his own, and he told his brother: "He is a good Man and I love him." But when he invited Whitefield to stay at his home and the latter thanked him for making the offer "for Christ's sake," Franklin exclaimed: "Don't let me be mistaken; it was not for Christ's sake, but for your sake." Whitefield despaired of ever converting his journalist friend.

Franklin respected organized religion for its emotional as well as moral value and though not a regular church-goer himself (after all, he had his own private liturgy), he gave financial support, first to the Presbyterian and then to the Episcopal church in Philadelphia (where he had a pew from 1760 to 1790), observed Lent, probably took communion on occasion, urged members of his family to participate regularly in liturgical devotions, proposed fast days for colonial Pennsylvania, and suggested daily prayers in the Constitutional Convention of 1787. He also gave money for Whitefield's projects, helped establish the first Unitarian chapel in England, and contributed to a fund to keep the Jewish synagogue in Philadelphia from being auctioned for debt. After the Revolution, Franklin helped the American Protestant Episcopal Church establish its independence from the Church of England; he also advised the Holy See on the organization of the Catholic Church in the new nation and played some part in the decision of the Spanish Cortes to end the Inquisition. "The Catholics thought him almost a Catholic," observed John Adams. "The Church of England claimed him as one of them. The Presbyterians thought him half a Presbyterian, and the Friends believed him a wet Quaker." Franklin was of course none of these; he was a Deist who believed in God and immortality but did not accept either the divinity of Christ or the superiority of Christianity to other world religions. But he did believe in a superintending Providence and he thought churches performed a useful function in society and, as we have seen, felt a personal need for some kind of religious devotions himself.

Still, Franklin's religion was largely practical. He regarded the inculcation of practical morality as a religion's chief function. The "best service toward God," he told a friend, "is doing good toward men. . . ." He thought "works of kindness, charity, mercy, and public Spirit" were far more important than "holiday-keeping, sermon reading or hearing, performing church ceremonies, or making long prayers" and he was sure that Jesus also preferred the "*doers* of the Word, to the mere *hearers.*" When his sister Jane expressed misgivings about his religion, Franklin referred her to a passage in Edwards' *Thoughts on Revivals* (1742) which placed such fruits of faith as "Self-denial, Righteousness, Meekness, and Christian Love, in our Behavior among Men" above such outward acts of worship as attending church, taking the sacrament, bowing, kneeling, and praying. From the beginning, Franklin enjoyed devising moral exercises as well as liturgies of devotion for himself. Two years before composing his *Acts of Religion,* he drew up a plan for regulating his "future Conduct of Life" in which he resolved to be extremely frugal, speak the truth in every instance, apply himself industriously to every task he undertook, and to speak ill of no man. A few years later he conceived an even more ambitious project for arriving at moral perfection consisting of 13 virtues—temperance, silence, order, resolution, frugality, industry, sincerity, justice, moderation, cleanliness, tranquillity, chastity, and humility—on which he was to rate himself day by day. He planned to concentrate on one virtue each week, thus making the rounds in 13 weeks and repeating the "course," as he called it, four times a year. He kept a record of his performance in a little notebook which he always carried with him, composed a little prayer to be used daily beseeching God's assistance in executing his resolutions, and followed out his plan of self-examination for a surprising number of years. He was dismayed to find himself "so much fuller of faults" than he had imagined and he admitted that the virtue, Order, gave him the greatest trouble, though he carefully drew up a schedule to follow for the 24 hours of each day. He also revealed in his autobiography that his list of virtues at first contained only 12, but a Quaker friend, informing him he was generally regarded as proud, advised him to add Humility to his list, which he agreed to do. Franklin thought there was "no one of our natural passions so hard to subdue as *pride*" and he confessed: "I cannot boast of much success in acquiring the *reality* of this virtue, but I had a good deal with regard to the *appearance* of it."

Franklin's emphasis on industry and frugality in his schemes of virtue led Max Weber in *The Protestant Ethic and the Spirit of Capitalism* (1905) to single him out as a perfect example of the bourgeois Economic Man of early modern times who identified godliness with hard work and by practicing the economic virtues—thrift, temperance, sobriety, frugality, and diligence—forged ahead rapidly in an expanding capitalistic economy. There was much in Franklin's writing illustrative of the Protestant or Puritan work ethic. For years, his *Poor Richard's Almanac* poured out preachy little admonitions like the following: "Early to bed, early to rise, makes a man healthy, wealthy, and wise"; "God helps them that help themselves"; "God gives all things to industry"; "Little strokes fell great oaks"; "Keep thy shop and thy shop will keep thee"; "No gains without pains"; "Idleness is the greatest Prodigality"; "Lost Time is never found again"; "Dost thou love life? then do not squander Time, for that's the Stuff Life is made of." Franklin also wrote essays on "Necessary Hints to Those That Would Be Rich" and "The Way to Make Money Plenty in Every Man's Pocket," and in his *Advice to a Young Tradesman* (1740) declared that the way to wealth "depends chiefly on two Words, INDUSTRY AND FRUGALITY." After the Revolution, he wanted the new nation to use coins inscribed with maxims from *Poor Richard's Almanac* as well as with Biblical injunctions. Franklin was no stuffy bourgeois devoid of *joie de vivre*. He included hedonistic as well as prudential maxims in his almanacs, wrote drinking songs ("For there can't be good Living where there is not good Drinking") as well as satirical, slightly cynical and sometimes ribald pieces, and enjoyed living lavishly in Paris where he developed gout. "Frugality is an enriching virtue," he once sighed; "a virtue I never could acquire in myself." In *The Way to Wealth* (1758), a compilation of *Poor Richard* maxims, Franklin has Father Abraham preach the gospel of thrift and industry to a crowd of people but he ends the book by reporting that the people "approved the Doctrine and immediately practiced the contrary, just as if it had been a common Sermon." Franklin regarded "the Pursuit of Wealth to no end" as foolish and while he thought that discipline and diligence were essential to the achievement of anything worthwhile, he also realized it was absurd to make them ends in themselves. He worked hard himself (though, as with all supremely talented people, there was something effortless about everything he did), but not all the time. He liked to swim, take air baths in the nude, participate in drinking sessions, and dally with the ladies. ("Somebody, it seems, gave it out that I loved ladies," he told his stepniece, tongue in cheek, in 1779.) If he was a "workaholic," his contemporaries were not aware of it. John Adams in fact thought him something of a rake and, when working with him on diplomatic missions in France after the Revolution, he was disgusted with the older man's late hours and generally frivolous behavior.

The Puritan ethic was unquestionably important to Franklin, but it represented only one side of his thinking. At 42 he was a rich man and he arranged to turn the management of his printing and bookselling house over to his partners so he could devote himself to science and public service. Yet he had always been concerned with non-pecuniary enterprises. While still building up his printing business, he found time to form the Junto club, a kind of adult-education society for young men; create the Philadelphia Library Company, the first subscription library in America; organize the Union Fire Company, the first in Philadelphia, and help establish the American Philosophical Society for scientific research and discussion. He also invented the Franklin open stove (which he refused to patent since he intended it for the benefit of mankind) and began his studies in electricity. After he retired, the pace of his scientific and civic activities increased. He founded the academy out of which the University of Pennsylvania developed, helped establish the Pennsylvania hospital, published *Experiments and Observations on Electricity* (1751), a path-breaking study which brought him fame in Europe rivaling that of Newton's, invented the lightning rod, studied the Gulf Stream, made numerous meteorological investigations, constructed a glass harmonica or organ which became popular in Europe (and for which Beethoven and Mozart composed music) and, after holding several local offices, began his long career as a public official outside of Pennsylvania: deputy postmaster general of North America, agent in London for several colonies, member of the Continental Congress that declared independence, commissioner in France negotiating the French alliance, member of the peace commission in Britain after Yorktown, and delegate to the Constitutional Convention. During an unusually long and busy life he also championed free speech, thought, press, and religion in his publications and in his last years lent his prestigious name to the burgeoning antislavery movement.

Franklin always remained something of a Puritan. He could not help thinking, particularly in his younger days, that poverty was an individual, not a social, responsibility, and that people were poor because of idleness and sloth, not because of fortuitous circumstances. He also occasionally expressed a gloomy view of human nature which Edwards would have heartily endorsed. In one of his rare speeches in the Constitutional Convention of 1787, he proposed a salaryless Chief Magistrate for the new republic. His reasoning: the two strongest human impulses are love of power and love of money and to unite both power and money in the presidency would attract people who were both greedy and power-mad and turn it into a monarchy. Yet Franklin was as much Deist as Puritan and he succeeded in shucking off much of the "sardonic optimism" (as George Santayana called it) of his Puritan heritage. He came to believe that people had innate benevolent impulses that could be nourished, as well as self-regarding instincts, and that with the help of a benevolent Providence they might learn to live together with generosity and goodwill in this world. He even came, perhaps because of his later association with French liberals, to take a social view of property. Private property, he declared, was "the Creature of public Convention"; natural right gave each men title to all the property necessary for the "Conservation of the Individual and the Propagation of the Species," but the remainder was "the Property of the Public, who, by their Laws, have created it, and who may therefore by other Laws dispose of it, whenever the Welfare of the Public shall demand such disposition." It was a point of view Thomas Paine, powerfully drawn, like Franklin, to laissez faire, was also to come around to in his later years.

When Franklin was an old man, Paine visited him in Philadelphia and was surprised to find him busily arranging books in his library. But Franklin told him it was his policy "to live on as if I was to live always." Franklin faced death, as he did life, with equanimity; he knew God was frugal and wouldn't waste anything He had created and he was confident that he would always exist in some form. Paine shared Franklin's belief in a benevolent God and a future state of existence, but he was far less patient with things as they were than Franklin and much more anxious to get on with the business of demolishing ancient superstitions and over-turning reactionary social institutions. Once he showed Franklin a strongly worded attack on organized religion he had just composed and Franklin strongly advised him to tone it down or destroy it. But the older Paine got the harder he found it to tone things down. Freeing the mind from bondage to the reactionary past, he had concluded, took extraordinary efforts. Paine was closer to Edwards than to Franklin in his unwillingness to compromise with what he regarded as evil.

"Where liberty is, there is my country," Franklin once remarked. "Where liberty is not, there is my country," Paine, an enemy of oppression wherever he happened to be, is said to have responded. Paine was more militant as a Deist than Franklin was and he had far less tolerance for organized religion (and for the pecadilloes of human nature) than his friend Franklin did. He was a religious as well as a political revolutionary and he wanted to overturn ecclesiastical as well as political establishments. His aim was to replace conventional religion with a "religion of humanity" and hereditary monarchies and aristocracies with republican institutions based on the freely given consent of the governed. He thought Deism and republicanism went naturally together. Unlike Franklin, he didn't take even a passing interest in theological questions; he had the typical 18th-century rationalist's contempt for such matters. He did write a piece on "the absurd and impious doctrine of predestination" toward the end of his life but he could scarcely conceal his exasperation over having to bother with the subject at all. In Paine's opinion, human beings were—or should be—"free agents," that is, autonomous individuals who could express their opinions openly, carry out actions of their own choosing, and participate in social decisions involving their happiness and well-being. Paine did not try to argue the case philosophically; he thought it was obvious to reasonable people. His major concern was with social and political arrangements guaranteeing and expanding man's free agency. In 1792, he made a proud inventory of the causes that motivated his life: representative government, universal education, public support for the poor and aged, world peace, free trade, and the eradication of superstition. He summed it all up in *The Rights of Man*: "... my country is the world, and my religion is to do good."

*   *   *

It is customary to explain Paine's love of freedom and his hatred of war, slavery, and oppression by his Quaker background. His father was a poor Quaker corset-maker in Thetford, England, and though Paine never formally joined the Society of Friends, he always spoke with affection of his Quaker rearing. He praised the Friends for "their care of the poor of their Society" and for "the education of their children" and, while critical of them for not supporting the American Revolution, said he shared their detestation of war. In *Age of Reason*, that powerful blast against all organized religion, he praised the Society of Friends as the only sect that had not engaged in persecution and said he reverenced their philanthropy. And though he added that he couldn't help smiling at thinking what the world would be like if the Quakers, with their plain ways, had been consulted at creation, he singled them out as being closer to "true Deism in the moral and benign part thereof" than any other religion. Coming from Paine this was high praise indeed. In plain fact, though, Paine's militant rationalism was about as far from the Quaker's mystical Inner Light as it was from the Calvinism of Jonathan Edwards and George Whitefield he so detested.

The natural bent of his mind, Paine once said, was toward science. When he was a young man, he recalled, he purchased a pair of globes, began attending science lectures in London, and became friendly with an astronomer who belonged to the Royal Society. He also studied mathematics on his own, made scientific and mechanical experiments, and followed Franklin's electrical researches with interest. Shortly after coming to America in November 1774, he became part of the little scientific community centered around Franklin, Jefferson, and other members of the American Philosophical Society. Like Franklin, he was fascinated by inventions. While editing the *Pennsylvania Magazine*, he published reports on various new English inventions and he also invented things himself: a planing machine, a new crane, smokeless candles (with Franklin's help), and, above all, an iron bridge (in which Franklin was also interested). The universe for Paine was an immense machine and God a great mechanic. God was also an "Almighty Lecturer" who displayed the principles of science in the structure of the universe. Paine saw unerring order and universal harmony in every part of God's works and believed the laws governing the physical world were eternal. But moral truths for Paine were just as self-evident and immutable as scientific truths. He dismissed with scorn the notion that abstract ideas and general principles were human contrivances devised to facilitate human understanding; he thought of them as truths of divine origin which were accessible to reason (the highest authority) if it were given a free rein. His epistemology was both optimistic and authoritarian.

Paine thought the social, religious, and political institutions of the Western world were horrendously unscientific. Cumbersome, unwieldy, devious, and oppressive, they prevented people from apprehending things as they truly were and living naturally by them. He took upon himself the gigantic task of setting people right on basic principles and he had no Quaker humility about the validity of his opinions. "What I write is pure nature," he averred, "and my pen and my soul have ever gone together." Though his philosophy was based on ideas familiar to all educated and informed people in the West in the late 18th century (especially those of Locke and Newton), Paine thought it came from acts of pure reason on his own part and he sincerely believed he was a man of nature thinking about certain issues for the first time. Actually, only in the rigorous consistency and boldness with which he carried certain principles to their logical conclusion can he be considered original. But the lucidity, precision, and assurance with which he expounded his ideas gave them wide currency and his popular influence far outran his originality. "I am a *farmer of thoughts,*" he once said, "and all the crops I raise I give away."

Paine had not intended to become a farmer of thoughts when he left his excise post in London and came to America in 1774 armed with letters of introduction from Franklin whom he had met a few months earlier. He came looking for a career in science or teaching. But he soon secured a position on the *Pennsylvania Packet* and quickly discovered that his natural talents lay in journalism. With the outbreak of the American Revolution, he thought he saw "a vast scene" opening in America with momentous consequences for the freedom of mankind and he joined the rebels. In addition to contributing *Common Sense* (which Franklin said had "prodigious effects" on the movement for independence from Britain) and *The Crisis* to the American cause, he served in the Continental Army and also worked for the Continental Congress. After the Revolution he looked back with pride on the part he had played in helping found "a New Empire raised on the principles of liberty and liberality." In 1787 he left his adopted country, mainly to promote his plan for a single-arch iron bridge in Europe, and he intended to return the following year. But he was soon caught up in the swirl of events in France and he ended by remaining in Europe, shuttling, for a time, between Paris and London, until 1802. The outbreak of the French Revolution, Paine thought, opened up an opportunity to extend "the principles of liberty and fraternity through the greater part of Europe" and he felt duty-bound to remain on hand to contribute his services to the revolutionary cause. In Paine's opinion, the French cause, like the earlier American cause, was the cause of all mankind and involved the freedom and rights of all men. During the French Revolution he did what he could to help: consulted with French leaders, served in the French National Assembly, and participated in constitution-making. Above all, he defended the principles of the Revolution in his forthright essays and pamphlets and tried to promote a republican revolution in England. When Edmund Burke published *Reflections on the Revolution in France* late in 1790, defending hereditary monarchies and established churches against the attacks of revolutionaries, Paine converted an essay he was working on into a massive assault on monarchical institutions and a defense of republican government which was published as *The Rights of Man* in 1791 and 1792. Paine's book touched off a storm of criticism among exponents of privilege and prescription and Paine was charged with everything ranging from ignorance, mendacity, and vulgarity on the one hand to recklessness, demagoguery, and downright anarchism on the other. The British government declared Paine's book seditious and proclaimed Paine an outlaw in December 1792.

But Paine remained imperturbable throughout. To him it all seemed as plain as day. To support the French Revolution—and the earlier American Revolution—was, he thought, the most natural thing in the world for a rational person to do. The fight for free institutions was grounded in the very nature of things. God, Paine insisted, had created the world and endowed every human being in it with a natural right to self-determination. He had given man, moreover, the precious gift of reason by which he was to apprehend the magnificent laws of nature He had set in motion for regulating creation and govern his life accordingly. Somehow, though, human beings in the course of long history had become almost utterly estranged from nature and nature's God. (Paine was no better than Edwards or Franklin at reconciling the existence of evil in the world with a benevolent Creator.) A small clique of self-interested men (priests and politicians) had succeeded by force and fraud in erecting formidable barriers, in the form of artificial and corrupt institutions, between man and nature. Not only did they concentrate power and wealth in their own hands and develop stupendous privileges for themselves that they transmitted to their heirs and favorites by means of hereditary institutions; they also deprived the majority of people of their natural God-given rights of free agency, equal opportunity, and political participation and kept them in a state of bondage and misery. Privileged elites and hereditary governments of all kinds violated the natural rights of man, according to Paine, and were absolutely contrary to nature; only republican governments, whose officials were chosen freely by the people and dedicated to protecting the rights of all citizens, had the sanction of nature and nature's God.

In America, Paine had not been much concerned with religion and his attitude toward the churches, even the Calvinistic ones, was generally benign, for most of them supported the Revolution. There was no "adulterous connection" between church and state in the United States, as there was in Europe, he observed, and religious diversity produced a great deal of tolerance (though Paine disliked the condescension implied in the word) and freedom in religious matters. In France, however, as elsewhere in Europe, things were different. Paine was appalled by the close bonds between Christianity and the old regime in France and he became convinced that organized religion had for centuries been one of the main enemies of the free mind. In 1794, he published the first part of *Age of Reason* (the second part came out the following year) to set people straight on religion as he had earlier set them straight on politics. He dedicated it to "my Fellow Citizens of the United States" and subtitled it "An Investigation of True and Fabulous Theology." By the latter he of course meant the kind of theology that people like Edwards cherished.

Paine's *Age of Reason* was a frankly anti-Christian book, greatly admired by freethinkers in Paine's day and ever since, but he wrote it to counteract atheism as well as orthodoxy. (This did not prevent Theodore Roosevelt from calling Paine a "filthy little atheist" many years later.) He was worried, he confessed in the preface to the book, lest, in the general overturn of established religious institutions and practices in France during the Revolution, people might "lose sight of morality, of humanity, and of the theology that is true." Paine made his own confession of faith at the outset. "I believe in one God, and no more," he announced; "and I hope for happiness beyond this life." He also believed in the equality of man, he added, and thought that religious duties consisted of "doing justice, loving mercy, and endeavoring to make our fellow creatures happy." He then announced that he most emphatically did not believe in the creeds professed by the Jewish, Roman, Greek, Turkish, Protestant or any other church and he exclaimed: "My own mind is my own church." All national institutions of churches, whether Jewish, Christian, or Turkish, he went on to say, were "no other than human inventions, set up to terrify and enslave mankind, and monopolize power and profit." The rest of *Age of Reason* was a sustained attack on the Bible and on Christian theology.

Paine had little but scorn and contempt for the Bible. He rejected it as the word of God, questioned the historical authenticity of the events recorded in it, and subjected its doctrines to scathing criticism. He went through the Old and New Testaments, book by book, reducing most of them to absurdity. Except for the Psalms and the book of Job, in which he admitted there was a great deal of sentiment reverentially expressed about the power and benignity of the Almighty, Paine had nothing good to say about the Old Testament. He dismissed it as a mélange of "obscene stories, voluptuous debaucheries, cruel and tortuous executions, and unrelenting vindictiveness" and declared that it had corrupted and brutalized mankind. He was no easier on the New Testament. He ridiculed the immaculate conception, the resurrection, the Trinity, and the admonition to love one's enemies (though he rejected the idea of revenge for injury) and dismissed the New Testament miracles as "degrading the Almighty into the character of a showman, playing tricks to amuse and make the people stare and wonder." Paine did, to be sure, speak respectfully of Jesus: "He was a virtuous and an amiable man" and "the morality that he preached and practised was of the most benevolent kind ...." But he

denied the divinity of Christ, saying he was no more the son of God
than any other human being, and he pointed out that systems of morality
similar to Jesus' had been preached by Confucius and some of the Greek
philosophers many years before. He also declared that the Christian
church had set up a system of religion utterly contradictory to the character of the person whose name it bore: "It has set up a religion of pomp
and of revenue, in pretended imitation of a person whose life was humility
and poverty."

Was there, then, to be no word of God? Was there to be no divine
revelation for humanity? There was, indeed, Paine hastened to say. "The
WORD OF GOD IS THE CREATION WE BEHOLD," he exclaimed,
"and it is in this *word,* which no human invention can counterfeit or alter,
that God speaketh universally to man." God's power, said Paine, was
found in the immensity of the universe; his wisdom in the "unchangeable
order by which the incomprehensible whole" was governed; his munifi-
cence in the abundance with which he filled the Earth; and his mercy
in not withholding that abundance even from the unthankful. "In fine,"
said Paine, "do we want to know what God is? Search not the book
called the Scripture, which any human mind might make, but the Scripture called creation." Paine did not accept the idea of "particular Provi-
dences" (interpositions by God from time to time in the affairs of men),
as Franklin did, though he never doubted God's benevolent supervision
("general Providence") of the universe as a whole through the laws of
nature. Nor did he trouble himself, as Franklin did, with composing
prayers and liturgies of devotion; and he certainly did not think, as
Edwards did, that religion was mainly a matter of the heart. Religion
for Paine was purely a matter of reason, like science, with which it was
so closely identified in his mind, and he thought human beings were
worshipping God best when they were studying His creation and
discovering how it was constructed. Science and religion were virtually
interchangeable for Paine.

Paine's *Age of Reason* delighted freethinkers and appalled Christian
believers everywhere. In some ways the book created a greater storm
than *Rights of Man* had created and it alienated many of his former
admirers in America. Devout people called it "The Devil's Prayer Book"
and excoriated the author as an atheist, infidel, sot, adulterer, reptile,
monster, and "lily-livered rogue." In 1801, when President Jefferson invited Paine to return to the United States from France on a government
vessel, there was considerable indignation among the orthodox. "What!"
exclaimed a Boston newspaper, "invite to the United States that lying,
drunken, brutal infidel, who rejoiced in the opportunity of basking and
wallowing in the confusion, devastation, bloodshed, rapine, and murder,
in which his soul delights!" When Paine finally returned to America in
1802, to live out his remaining years, he was treated like a pariah. One

coachman refused to accept so notorious an infidel as a passenger and the town of New Rochelle, where he went to live on some land the State of New York had given him as a reward for his Revolutionary services, denied him the right to vote even though Congress had made him a citizen during the Revolution. Even the Quakers held him at arm's length; when he died in Greenwich Village in poverty and obscurity in 1809, they refused to let his body be placed in their burial grounds. But Deism, it turned out, was not as seductive to Americans as Edwards had feared it would be. In the 1790s, it is true, there was a decline in church-going and a drift away from orthodoxy, and pious people feared that a wave of Deism was engulfing the nation, especially the colleges, and blamed Paine for it. But a Second Great Awakening was beginning to develop, even during Paine's last years, and it was soon to sweep hundreds of Americans back into orthodoxy and make good church-goers out of them.

* * *

Edwards would have rejoiced to see the Second Great Awakening overwhelm the tide of Deism in America. He might even have looked on the Second Awakening, as he did the first, as a sign that perhaps the millennium might begin in America after all. Franklin's hopes for America were quite different: his emphasis was on material progress, though he admitted that progress in morality, though less likely, was more important. Paine was the most hopeful of all. Despite the personal rebuffs he received at the end of his life and despite the setbacks to the cause of republicanism and to the "religion of humanity" he witnessed in both Europe and America, he never doubted that they would triumph some day in America and that the United States, by her example, would inspire other nations to develop free and rational institutions. Many Americans came to share Paine's hopes. In American religious circles, the 19th century marked a steady trend away from Edwardsean pessimism about humanity toward the kind of hopeful optimism concerning human nature that Paine espoused. In the 20th century, many of the things that Paine said about religion would seem commonplace in the increasingly liberal churches of the nation.

Still, after World War I, there was an unmistakable movement in American religious circles back to Edwardsean pessimism or at least back to Franklin's mixed views about humanity. Reinhold Niebuhr, America's best-known theologian after the 1930s, insisted, like Edwards, that the ancient doctrine of original sin contained important empirical insights into human nature. While not denying that there were rational and moral resources available to human beings (as Paine thought there were) that enabled them to develop self-governing institutions that safeguarded the freedom and happiness of citizens, Niebuhr also insisted there was an ineradicable impulse toward self-aggrandizement in all people (including the most idealistic) that had to be carefully hedged about with democratic checks and balances. "Man's capacity for justice makes democracy possible," declared Niebuhr; but "man's inclination to injustice makes democracy necessary." Edwards and Paine would have been puzzled by Niebuhr's statement. Franklin would have understood perfectly.

4

The Rights of Man and the American Revolution

SAMUEL ADAMS
THOMAS HUTCHINSON
JOHN DICKINSON

by James Kirby Martin
Rutgers University

Even with 200 years of historical perspective, the American Revolution stands as an elusive series of events; no consensus has emerged about what factors caused the Revolution. Likewise, the consequences of the momentous decision of 13 colonies to unite as one and break away from the sovereign British empire are still heatedly debated. To suggest that these issues could be settled here would be somewhat presumptuous. They cannot. But the personal histories of Samuel Adams, Thomas Hutchinson, and John Dickinson allow us to consider the role that conflicting personalities and perceptions of political reality played in hastening the disruption of the British empire. Personalities in conflict had a great deal to do with the pattern of revolutionary causation. In turn the furor those personalities generated gave birth to a basic alteration in political relationships which is still affecting the American experience.

The 13 Anglo-American provinces that chose to turn against their parent state in the mid-1770s were very much a part of the political culture shaping the 18th-century British empire. For its time it was an enlightened culture, even though the assumptions were clearly different from those that contemporary Americans hold as self-evident truths. Above all else two terms—*balance* and *hierarchy*—characterized the values of that culture. Balance and hierarchy lent stability to political relationships and guaranteed all citizens, both in England and in America, their rights and liberties as freeborn Englishmen. However, the sense that established relationships were out of order led the pugnacious Samuel Adams of Boston to push with all his energies against the weight of imperial policy in the dawning years of revolution. A similar sense, but from a different interpretive point of view, trapped the urbane and scholarly Thomas Hutchinson into resisting the brute force of Samuel Adams and his "insurgent" cohorts. Adams pushed and shoved as the protagonist; Hutchinson resisted as the despised antagonist. Caught in the middle and nearly crushed for want of direction were citizens like John Dickinson, the moderate "Pennsylvania Farmer" who did so much to construct the intellectual grounds for American resistance but could not bring himself to sign the Declaration of Independence as a Pennsylvania delegate to the second Continental Congress.

The political culture of 18th-century Britons and Americans encased the perceptual differences that brought Adams, Hutchinson, Dickinson, and 2,500,000 other provincial citizens into open conflict with one another and with the home government of King and Parliament. Different personalities jostled against each other because of the multiplicity of interpretations that arose from a common body of political theory and explained what was going wrong with the system and what needed to be done. The placement of individuals in the imperial system affected their perception of political affairs. Adams concluded that revolution was necessary; Hutchinson chose the path of loyalism; Dickinson equivocated until it was almost too late. Behind this complex set of responses were varying perceptions of reality based on those assumptions about balance and hierarchy that gave form and meaning to the British political culture.

"Democracy" was a derisive term for the politically sophisticated in the pre-revolutionary British empire. The word did not refer so much to a system or a style of politics; rather it specifically denoted the masses of common citizens who inhabited society. More broadly, the 18th-century definition of "democracy," carrying over from the writings of Aristotle, reflected upon one of three socio-economic orders (or classes of citizens) in functioning societies. The *demos* or "general masses" needed to have their interests represented in at least one branch of government to give balance to overall policy formulation and decision-making; furthermore, the democracy needed representation to act as a counterweight against potential excesses by either or both of the two higher socio-economic orders—the monarchy and the aristocracy.

According to the most enlightened—though somewhat archaic and medieval—political science of those times, the English constitution embodied the quintessence of balanced government, mixing and blending the three socio-economic orders of monarchy, aristocracy, and democracy in the three working branches of government, as represented in the King, the House of Lords, and the House of Commons respectively. More than anything else, students of 18th-century political culture feared an imbalance in the distribution of authority and responsibility among the orders. They believed history demonstrated that too much monarchical domination in decision-making, without appropriate aristocratic and democratic checks through the other two branches of government, had the dangerous potential to destroy known *liberties* and to produce political *tyranny*. Capricious if not arbitrary royal rule would in time subvert the basic political rights and liberties of the aristocracy as well as the democracy. On the other hand, too much power in the hands of the democracy, the ordinary citizens, had the equally deleterious effect of forcing the body politic in *anarchical* directions. Imbalance in authority favoring the democracy would result in licentious behavior, threatening known liberties, as commoners vied with one another to grab scarce socioeconomic rewards, such as private or public property, higher social position, greater community prestige, or even raw power itself.

Too much democracy predictably would produce a reaction, a swing of the political pendulum back toward aristocratic and/or monarchical domination so as to end popular licentiousness and once again to restore peace and order in governance. In precise, rhythmic fashion, so characteristic of the thinking of the Age of Reason in Europe and America, the most stable polities carefully balanced the socio-economic orders of democracy, aristocracy, and monarchy in the branches of government so that no one order would gain ascendancy. It was the only way to avoid the extremes of tyranny or anarchy; the delicate balance guaranteed that the known rights and liberties of all citizens would then be secure from veiled threats and outright attacks.

These assumptions may be summarized in the phrase *hierarchical conception of balanced government*. It was not the familiar notion of checks and balances among executive, legislative, and judicial powers that we accept today as axiomatic for even-handed government. Rather there was the tacit awareness of an indivisible relationship among leadership in state and society. Every subject in the realm had his or her place; to violate that place was to threaten the very foundations upon which known liberties through the ages had been constructed.

Well read and politically sophisticated colonial Americans by the beginning of the 18th century were drawing analogies between the working parts of their provincial governments and the English model. Using somewhat faulty if not porous logic, prominent American leaders were claiming that governors represented and substituted for the monarchy; councilors forming the upper houses in Assemblies and serving as advisers to governors represented and substituted for the aristocracy; delegates to the lower house represented the general citizenry—the democracy.

The analogy was far from perfect. There was no resident titled nobility in the provinces; yet individual and family wealth did serve as the basis for distinction between the "lower sort" and the higher orders in the provincial social hierarchy. Prospering colonial families were forming themselves into community and colony-wide leadership elites. Committed to the proposition that success in the socio-economic sphere conveyed the right to legislate and to execute that legislation for the general citizenry, the provincial upper classes believed that only those of demonstrated capacity should rule, especially in those upper-hierarchy offices representing the monarchy and the aristocracy of wealth and social prominence in America.

Colonial leaders, though, did not restrict their claims to higher provincial offices. In common with the "better sort" in England, they believed in comprehensive political stewardship. *Deferential* attitudes assumed that common citizens would submit in matters of state to men who by wealth, occupation, birth, and/or social position had the breadth of vision to act in the best interests of the body politic, thereby preserving and enhancing liberties. Wealthy and prominent men were less likely to be corrupted by power and to turn the public trust to private advantage. Socio-economic betters had demonstrated that their intelligence was keener, their wisdom perhaps more fully developed. One colonial Virginian pungently summarized deferential assumptions when he wrote: "It is right that men of *birth* and *fortune,* in every government that is free, should be invested with power, and enjoy higher honors than the people. If it were otherwise, their privileges would be less, and they would not enjoy an equal degree of liberty with the people."

Deferential assumptions in an age when the educated placed such a high value upon balance and hierarchy for the sake of political stability guaranteed provincial men of wealth and standing a major voice in their governments. Consequently, the lower houses of America's 18th-century Assemblies were largely controlled by the "better sort" of provincials, from which positions they perceived themselves as legislating most ably and wisely for the commonalty of citizens. Even though legislative seats were elective and voting rights widespread, the candidates usually were acknowledged "betters" in the pre-revolutionary socio-economic milieu. From their seats in lower houses and from appointive positions in upper houses they formulated local laws and statutes. Normally these same leaders set the colony-wide tone in accepting or challenging broader imperial policies enunciated by King and Parliament and given visible presence through royal governors and other Crown officials in America.

Such in brief were the integrating assumptions and structural components of imperial political culture. Men on both sides of the Atlantic contended over the prerogatives of authority. They sensed that political stability depended upon balance among socio-economic orders in society and state. Most politically-active gentlemen envisioned themselves as guarding the entire community against those few insidious individuals who would corrupt the accepted hierarchical relationships in governments as well as destroy liberties for private and petty interests. The life of the system, or the known liberties of all citizens, depended upon avoiding tyranny from above or anarchy from below. Even before midcentury some Americans were becoming fearful that English policymakers were distorting the balance and threatening liberties. A major shift in the direction of imperial policy during the early 1760s confirmed the worst suspicions of such men; among them was Samuel Adams.

*   *   *

Nothing in the early life of Samuel Adams would have led his parents to suspect that their energetic young son would be remembered as the chief revolutionary agitator of the next and more rebellious generation. Born during 1722 in the bustling seaport of Boston, young Samuel could take pride in his father and mother, Deacon Samuel, Sr., and Mary Fifield Adams. The Deacon was a prospering maker of malt, enough so that he earned the honor of serving as a local justice of the peace. He had money enough to send his son to Harvard College, then representing a level of educational opportunity that very few 18th-century Americans enjoyed. Most friends assumed that young Samuel would become a minister, since he himself had a penchant for systematic theology with a strong Calvinist flavor. But it would be otherwise. Little is known about Adams the student, except that he had an undistinguished academic record and that the school authorities once disciplined him for "drinking prohibited Liquors." He graduated just before his 18th birthday, during a crisis that would destroy the family fortune and turn him into a bitter foe of many prominently-placed leaders and supporters of imperial policies in Massachusetts.

The family crisis centered on the Land Bank scheme that Deacon Samuel and other local leaders were sponsoring in an effort to keep the Massachusetts economy fluid. There was never enough hard money (gold and silver) in the provinces to sustain the expansive tendencies of local economic activity. As a result, ingenious colonists (when not bartering) supplemented the sparse money supply with varieties of fiat currency. The Land Bank represented one such plan. Subscribers like the Deacon pooled funds—and their capital provided a modest backing for a large issue of paper money bills, loaned out by Land Bank directors at six percent interest and secured with mortgages against the landholdings of borrowers. Such precautions were taken so that the money would maintain as much of its face value as possible when circulating through the marketplace before retirement from circulation.

These currencies, when issued in modest amounts, tended to hold their values well, but merchants generally eschewed fiat money for fear that currencies with inadequate backing might plummet in value at any time. They did not want to be caught short. Leading merchants in Boston, among them the wealthy Thomas Hutchinson, had little use for fiat currencies of any kind. They were demanding before 1740 that the Land Bank plan of Deacon Adams and his cohorts be completely eradicated.

If the younger Samuel Adams had a respectable family background, Thomas Hutchinson had an even more prominent heritage. The family traced itself back five generations in Massachusetts history to Mistress Anne Hutchinson, famous for her radical Antinomian views among the first generation of Puritan settlers. Hutchinson's father ranked among the wealthier merchants in the province; he even had the distinction of sitting with the Massachusetts Council for several years. Colonel Thomas and his wife Sarah Foster Hutchinson had 12 children, among them Thomas, Jr., who was born in September 1711. The boy grew up in the stately family mansion in Boston until the age of 12 when his parents enrolled him in Harvard where he was an eager student and especially interested in history. Emerging with a degree before his 17th birthday and designated class valedictorian, this young man of immense family distinction, intelligence, energy, and personal rectitude was about to face a most tumultuous and controversial career.

To complete his education the younger Thomas joined his father's mercantile house as an apprentice and soon distinguished himself by his own business acumen. Everything about this glamorous young man marked him for leadership. Before his 26th birthday, he was named a Boston selectman; a few months later he found himself elected to the lower house of the General Court, Massachusetts' Assembly. In this lower chamber Hutchinson made known his opposition to paper money schemes. Speaking out as he did and associating himself with wealthy gentlemen of the Boston mercantile community, Hutchinson lost his seat in the 1739 General Court elections. But it was only a temporary reversal in a burgeoning political career.

The Adams faction wanted paper currency, but the merchants frustrated their best laid plans through the intervention of Governor Jonathan Belcher, royal appointee and hard money man. The Governor issued a proclamation stating that any person holding an office under royal authority who acknowledged Land Bank notes in any transaction would be removed from office. Deacon Adams then resigned his commission as justice of the peace and attacked the royal powers; he charged the Belcher faction with insensitivity to local economic needs. The quarrel spread, and the battle lines hardened. Governor Belcher removed other commissioned militia officers and justices of the peace from office. But the Land Bankers responded with enough popular support to carry the 1741

General Court elections and recommended Deacon Adams and a few other loyal fiat money men to the Governor's Council. (In Massachusetts an unusual arrangement in the royal charter permitted those elected by the populace to the lower house in turn to elect the members of the upper house or Council.) Belcher peremptorily vetoed the General Court's choices. Thus the elder Adams was unable to gain entrance to the inner circle where he and his associates could more effectively defend the collapsing Land Bank.

The uncertainty of heated political turmoil completely undercut the value of Land Bank notes. Even original subscribers, including Deacon Adams, became fearful of accepting the notes in exchange for goods. Belcher, Hutchinson, and others had ruined the Land Bank in the name of secure and stable hard currency. In the process they undercut the personal estate of Adams, who not only lost his part of the original subscription but also remained liable for debts against the Land Bank. Deacon Adams died in 1748 knowing that his son would have to make his way in the world with creditors hounding at his heels. Despising men like Hutchinson who seemed to be in league with royal officials and opposed to legitimate local interests, young Samuel would in time find other ways to refurbish the tattered family reputation.

After graduating from Harvard Samuel Adams had demonstrated no aptitude for or interest in business matters. Apprenticed to a merchant, he failed to respond to direction or instruction. Sent home, his father gave him money to go into business for himself, but Samuel soon lost it by loaning the currency to a friend. In 1748 he was working for his father. Preferring to keep himself solvent by remunerations from local political offices and by earning just enough to keep food on the table, Samuel let the business drift after the Deacon's death. More than business pursuits, he enjoyed local politics—and he would become a craftsman in the politics of vilification.

Through his father's contacts Samuel Adams ingratiated himself with the Boston political leaders who opposed imperial officials and with their supporters in Massachusetts. In 1746 he won election to the local post of clerk of the market; in 1753 he became the town scavenger; shortly thereafter he took the job as collector of the local liquor excise tax, to be followed a few years later by the more important office of Boston tax collector. These local offices were important for many reasons. They gave him the opportunity to be in constant contact with the common people of Boston. For instance, he built friendships by being a most generous tax collector—in that he was reluctant to perform the duties of his office, especially when citizens were in dire financial straits. By 1765 when he left the tax collecting post, he was some £8,000 in arrears. No doubt some of the funds had gone to keep his family in clothes; but the deficit accumulated largely because Adams did not always collect. As a result, he had a host of friends who listened with gratitude when he talked politics.

Very few men in the 18th century could make their way as petty politicians, living each hour by currying favor with the people. It might have been different had the modest Adams family fortune not been decimated by the Land Bank fiasco. But that is conjecture. Both out of necessity and temperament Adams reached out and touched the "poorer sort." He lived meagerly and closely to the people. Described by one contemporary as a "plain, simple, decent citizen, of middling stature, dress and manners," Samuel Adams was cultivating a constituency despite the accepted canons about hierarchy, balance, and political stewardship.

*   *   *

While Samuel Adams thrived on petty offices, the "tall, slender, fair-complexioned, fair-spoken" Thomas Hutchinson moved in the larger imperial officeholding orbit. During the 1740s he won election after election to the lower house of the General Court, eventually becoming speaker. In 1749 the lower house elevated him to the Council for the first time. By 1760 Hutchinson had emerged as a major plural officeholder. He held a commission as a commander of the fort on Castle Island in Boston and had also served since 1752 as a probate judge as well as a justice of the Suffolk County court of common pleas. He relinquished the latter post in 1758, perhaps because he became the province's lieutenant governor by royal commission the same year. Seemingly Hutchinson had an insatiable appetite for prominent offices. This hunger soon was to coalesce his Boston enemies and fix Hutchinson as a prime agent in what some believed was a plot to destroy American liberties, regardless of the amount of enlightenment this leader from the "better sort" demonstrated.

Hutchinson's officeholding appetite bloated his judgment. In 1760 Massachusetts welcomed a new royal governor, Francis Bernard, who in one of his official acts had to appoint a chief justice of the Superior Court, the highest in the province. Several candidates presented themselves, but none more ostentatiously than James Otis, Sr., then speaker of the house. Otis had been promised the office by a former royal governor, long since passed from the scene. While Otis, Sr., presented his claim, his more famous son, James, Jr., emerging as a powerful attorney and provincial leader in his own right, broadcasted it about that if his father was not appointed to replace the deceased incumbent, he would personally "kindle such a fire in the province as shall singe the governor, though I myself perish in the flames." Governor Bernard mused over the matter carefully and then chose Thomas Hutchinson. As one contemporary chronicler stated it, the younger Otis retaliated by joining "himself to the party which was jealous that the views of [the Bernard] administration were unfavorable to the rights of the colony . . . and soon became its chief leader."

James Otis, Jr., and Samuel Adams became closer friends after this contest over the chief justiceship. That friendship had some roots in mutual dislike for, if not personal revulsion with, the favored Hutchinson. Their ties became more resolute once ministerial leaders in England made it clear that the era of "salutary neglect" was coming to an end. The Bernard and Hutchinson royal faction would be charged with implementing the reinvigorated imperial program of the 1760s. The Otis and Adams combination would lead Bostonians in their resistance to the impending tyranny of the new policies being articulated by Parliament. First it was Otis, Jr., who more visibly waved the banner of liberty and then, as the decade progressed, Samuel Adams emerged as the hallowed figure—as Otis began to develop serious psychological problems as well as to flail about on issues. Personal animosities, though, hardened factional lines long before Otis gave indication of losing his mental stability.

The abrupt change in imperial policy crystalized in 1765 with Parliament's promulgation of the Stamp Act, though a host of less well-known statutes signaled the new departure. Great Britain had for decades fought wars throughout the world to maintain and extend her empire. She emerged triumphant among the imperial nations of Europe in 1763 with the signing of the Peace of Paris, ending the Seven Years' War (known in its American phase as the French and Indian War). This conflict resulted in the elimination of France's claims from the New World. The French menace no longer lingered in Canada and to the west. Home officials thought that Anglo-Americans should be forever grateful, sufficiently so at least to share more directly in the costs of imperial administration. British leaders knew that the English national debt had risen from £75 million to nearly £130 million during the Seven Years' War. They realized that part of that enlarged debt went to the advantage of all Americans who would be more secure without French competitors in North America. Funds, too, were lacking to back up the decision to maintain a 10,000 man regular British army on the American frontier for the ostensible purpose of keeping peace between aggresive settlers and warlike Indians. The course of action seemed obvious: Parliament must tax the sometimes troublesome and less than appreciative colonists.

The decision to tax directly represented a bold departure from established policy. Heretofore Americans had paid a variety of duties on trade into imperial coffers. But direct taxes had been the prerogative of local American assemblies. Now Parliament was asserting full legislative sovereignty over all subjects of the realm. Fiscal stability at home and the presumed need for greater consolidation in imperial administration expressed itself perhaps too plainly in the 1765 Stamp Act.

The Stamp Act proposed to draw money out of provincial pockets by placing stamps on some fifty items, including newspapers, pamphlets, playing cards and dice, wills, deeds and other land sale documents, marriage licenses, college diplomas, bills of lading, and ship clearance papers. The price of stamps varied according to the nature of each item, but none of the listed commodities could be bought, sold, or used after November 1, 1765, without stamps. To make matters worse, Americans would have to purchase stamps with hard money, always scarce. Violators could be tried in vice-admiralty courts (where there was no trial by jury) as well as in regular civil courts. Comprehensive enough to affect all Americans, the Stamp Act seemed to violate a host of basic political liberties, including the right to trial by jury and to taxation only by representatives elected by the voting citizenry.

First reports of Parliament's approval of the Stamp Act arrived in the provinces during April 1765. There was ample time to organize resistance against both the taxation plan and those royal officials in the provinces, such as Francis Bernard and Thomas Hutchinson who would be charged with administering the tax in Massachusetts. Samuel Adams proved a most effective organizer. Attacking the Stamp Act was one way to get back directly at his old enemy, now ensconced as Lieutenant Governor and Chief Justice of the Superior Court. How much of the assault was in defense of liberties and how much represented an opportunity to crush old foes may never be determined. Both factors surely were operative for Adams.

During the summer of 1765 Samuel Adams called upon old friendships (some no doubt formed during his tax collecting days) and assisted in organizing Boston's Sons of Liberty. He brought together two warring groups of Boston ruffians, the North End and South End gangs, and molded them into a powerful tool of local resistance under the street leadership of a cobbler, Ebenezer Mackintosh. With an organized mob—one could be more polite and say "crowd"—of liberty-loving citizens ready to perform violent acts in defense of community interests, the scenario was set for the memorable August riots. The script was quickly completed when Bostonians learned that Andrew Oliver, the province's secretary as well as closely-tied brother-in-law and political ally of Thomas Hutchinson, was to be the Massachusetts stamp distributor.

Trouble began on the morning of August 14 when the local populace awoke to find hanging from the "Liberty Tree" effigies of Oliver and Lord Bute, previously ministerial head in England. A shocked Governor Bernard demanded that the effigies be torn down; but no one dared to touch them. In the early evening the Sons of Liberty took both the effigies to a warehouse recently constructed by Oliver. In short order they tore the building apart, perhaps because it was rumored that the warehouse would be the distribution center for the stamps. Next they carried wood from the building's site to a nearby hill and ignited the effigies amidst a thunder of cheers. With Oliver's gracious home nearby, the mob turned on it, ripping apart the first floor and drinking unsparingly from the wine supply in the cellar. The merriment lasted until midnight. Early the next morning, according to Hutchinson, Andrew Oliver, "despairing of protection, and finding his family in terror and great distress . . . came to the sudden resolution to resign his office before another night." Indeed, no one in Massachusetts dared to think about distributing stamps after Boston's August 14 riot.

If the local Sons of Liberty had only wished to check the administration of the Stamp Act, they would then have stopped rioting, having proven their point with force. But a false rumor began twisting its way through Boston's byways and alleys to the effect that Hutchinson through his royal offices had argued in favor of the tax. Worse yet, local gossips were stating categorically that Hutchinson had clandestinely helped write the legislation. Unconcerned with hard evidence, the Sons of Liberty appeared in moblike fashion twice again and on the evening of August 26 wrecked Hutchinson's lavish Boston residence, one of the finest in the province. Hutchinson described the scene as follows: "They continued their possession until daylight; destroyed, carried away, or cast into the street, everything that was in the house; demolished every part of it, except the walls, as far as lay in their power." No one knows who started the rumors, but Samuel Adams and his cohorts were not out in the streets suppressing the gossips.

During the fall, violence spread to other communities in the 13 provinces where mobs intimidated other stamp distributors into resigning their commissions. Adamant colonists began to plan a boycott of English goods if Parliament did not back down. Provincial assemblies and an intercolonial Stamp Act Congress sent petitions to England. These remonstrances reiterated the theme that taxation without representation threatened the very foundation of political liberties and was a violation of constitutional rights. As the Stamp Act Congress summarized it, since it was unfeasible for Anglo-Americans "from their local circumstances" to be adequately represented in Parliament, the one way to sustain "all the inherent rights and liberties" of Englishmen in America was for the sovereign Parliament to concede that only elective assemblies in the provinces could tax citizens. Given the rioting, the intimidation, the boycott, and the petitions, Parliament accepted the obvious. The Stamp Act could not be executed without forcing even more heated confrontations. In March 1766 Parliament repealed the tax, but not before declaring that it alone had "full power and authority to make laws and statutes of sufficient force and validity to bind the colonies and people of America, subjects of the Crown of Great Britain, *in all cases whatsoever.*"

These words provided little consolation to Thomas Hutchinson, back in Boston and looking for financial reimbursement for his home. For him the devastated residence served as a symbol of the common people's licentious behavior. When there were no appropriate aristocratic- and monarchical-like checks upon the branches of government, the uncontrolled populace would tear all institutions of society apart in a frenzy of anarchy. Hutchinson remained committed to balance among the social orders. Above all else, stability had to be maintained in the realm. In 1767 Hutchinson wrote despairingly that "the town of Boston is an absolute democracy," which seemingly could not be constrained by royal officials representing the higher socio-political orders. By 1769 his concern with maintaining the hierarchical conception of balanced government for the preservation of society led him to express the conviction that "there must be an abridgement of what are called English liberties. . . . I wish the good of the colony when I wish to see some further restraint of liberty, rather than the connection with the parent state should be broken; for I am sure such a breach must prove the ruin of the colony." These indiscreet words would later haunt him. After 1765 Hutchinson dedicated himself to keeping in check those whom he believed were seriously threatening the very stability and good order of Massachusetts. Separation from Great Britain, he was sure, would mean total anarchy.

Samuel Adams drew upon the same political heritage and assumptions, but he interpreted events very differently. In line with other insurgent activists, he was conjuring up a conspiracy aimed against American political liberties by unbridled ministerial tyranny. Ministers in England and their sycophantic agents in America were being corrupted by power. If anarchy resulted from too much power in the peoples' hands, tyranny resulted from too much power in the hands of the monarch and his ministers. In 1768 Adams wrote in the *Boston Gazette* that "when the People are oppressed, when their Rights are infringed, when their property is invaded, when taskmasters are set over them, . . . when placemen and their underlings swarm about them, and Pensioners begin to make an insolent appearance . . . In such Circumstances, while they have the spirit of freedom, they will boldly assert their freedom; and they are to be justified in so doing." Adams was not worried by popular licentiousness and anarchy; rather he feared tyranny. On more than one public occasion he alluded to Thomas Hutchinson as the man who would shackle Massachusetts in political slavery.

Thus the destruction of liberties from above convulsed Adams, while Hutchinson despaired of political ruin from below. To Adams the reinvigorated imperial program and the continued elevation of men like Hutchinson to high provincial offices, meant that there could be no accommodation with the Crown; in peril were such rights as taxation only by consent. Adams and Hutchinson were at the opposite poles of the same set of ideas. Their diverging interpretations of reality reflected their relative placement in the political and social milieu of pre-Revolutionary Massachusetts. In fact it was this very placement as well as their previous personal experiences that shaped the development of their perceptions and gave them meaning.

In 1765 Adams won election to the General Court for the first time; in 1769 Francis Bernard left the province to be replaced in the royal governorship by none other than Thomas Hutchinson. Unconsciously the first was becoming a revolutionary, the second a loyalist.

*　*　*

Like Adams and Hutchinson, John Dickinson grew up with many advantages. His father owned extensive property in eastern Maryland, Delaware, and Pennsylvania. On the family estate at Croisiadore, Maryland, Mary Cardwell Dickinson gave birth to John on November 13, 1732. Little is known about his childhood, except that the family moved to sparsely populated Kent County, Delaware, when he was eight. There this son of a prospering planter grew to manhood. He was "tall and spare" and "simple and unostentatious in his habits." The family placed a great value upon education and provided their son with a private tutor. By his 18th birthday John Dickinson had decided to begin legal training in Philadelphia. After a three-year apprenticeship in William Penn's provincial capital, he completed his legal education at the Inns of Court in London. Studying in England represented the sort of exposure that few Americans enjoyed; yet wealthier families like the Dickinsons knew that such educational advantages almost assured economic success for children who did not squander such opportunities. For four years John Dickinson went about his legal studies in London with unusual diligence and rigor. He was to become one of the finest legal minds in 18th-century America.

By his mid-twenties Dickinson's world had been made. He knew that the family estates would eventually belong to him. Moreover, he had passed the bar examination in Philadelphia, the most populous and thriving provincial city of the time. While Philadelphia would be the base for his legal practice, Dickinson often traveled to Delaware to watch over business activities on the family estate. His was the life of a wealthy gentleman planter and a talented legal adviser.

Like so many other well-educated 18th-century provincial gentlemen, John Dickinson considered it his duty to take an active part in politics and lead the citizenry in enlightened directions. Elected to the Pennsylvania Assembly in 1762, Dickinson appeared at first to blend in with the "Quaker Party" of Benjamin Franklin and others who pitted themselves against the "Proprietary Party" supporters of the Penn family. There was nothing of real distinction in Dickinson's early Assembly career, except that he split with Franklin in the latter's consuming desire to see Pennsylvania taken away from the Penns and turned into a royal province. Given the beginnings of the new imperial program in the early 1760s, he saw no particular advantage to having Pennsylvania fall directly under the aegis of the Crown. Persisting in his convictions, Dickinson refused to be intimidated by powerful Quaker interests.

Although John Dickinson's early years in the Pennsylvania political arena were lackluster, he was developing a reputation for independence of thought and action; and he deserved it. At no time in his life did John Dickinson depart from his values and ideals under the heat of transient issues and events. He believed that any person who wished to live well had to be reasonable and moderate, not only in dress and manners but also in the formulation and articulation of his opinions. Moderation in all things became the trademark of this wealthy lawyer-planter who at times could be independent to the point of indecisiveness.

John Dickinson earned an intercolonial reputation as a spokesman for the American cause during the fight over the so-called Townshend Duties, which were hatched in the mind of a ministerial leader, Charles Townshend. In June 1767 Parliament approved his scheme to draw tax monies out of colonists in the guise of trade duties. The British ministry believed that Americans in resisting the Stamp Act were objecting only to "internal" or direct taxes, not to "external" or indirect taxes which in this case were duties on trade goods for imperial revenue. Americans long had paid duties on varieties of imperial goods, but Townshend made it clear that the duties to be collected in provincial ports on British-manu-factured glass, red and white lead, paper, painters' colors, and tea would be used to defray the costs of imperial administration in the New World. With heavy-handed subtleness, Townshend and Parliament seemed determined to prove that colonists could and would be taxed.

Unified colonial resistance was slow in developing, largely because the Townshend Duties, unlike the Stamp tax, burdened only a few. Except for tea, the duties were on essentially luxury items, rarely needed by the vast majority of Americans. It would take untold energy and nearly two years to mount an effective intercolonial boycott of all British trade goods as one form of pressure on Parliament. In the meantime, John Dickinson forcefully and persuasively articulated the full ramifications of the American position on taxation. Literary conceit probably led Dickinson, the wealthy lawyer-planter from Delaware, to entitle the several newspaper editorials making up his closely-reasoned statements, *Letters from a Pennsylvania Farmer.* The editorials were read widely as other provincial newspapers reprinted what he first published in the *Pennsylvania Chronicle* during late 1767 and early 1768. Pamphlet copies were later circulated among the colonists. All along the Atlantic seaboard literate provincials toasted their "Farmer," who made Townshend's rationale for taxation by trade duties seem absurd to them.

Dickinson wrote to defend fundamental political liberties. He stressed that "the single question is, whether the Parliament can legally impose duties . . . for the sole purpose of raising a revenue, on commodities which she obliges us to take from her alone, or in other words, whether the Parliament can legally take money out of our pockets, without our consent." Duties to regulate the flow of imperial commerce with revenue being an incidental consideration were one matter and were perfectly acceptable by precedent. But duties that so obviously were for the purpose of taxation could not be accepted in any guise. "If they can," surmised Dickinson, "our boasted liberty is but 'a sound and nothing else.'" Payment of such duties signaled the end of liberty by ministerial tyrants and the beginning of political slavery.

All enlightened men, Dickinson continued, had to align and resist that desperate condition. He called for unity of colonial action while speaking out against those—like Samuel Adams—who instantly would resort to violence and destruction of property to carry their position. First and foremost, citizens had to petition through their governments for a redress of grievances. If constitutional methods did not work, then Americans should adopt measures that were slightly coercive but non-violent, such as trade boycotts and nonimportation agreements. The weapon of force through violence should be unsheathed only when all else failed. Dickinson, moreover, warned that violence would result in retaliation by King and Parliament. Ultimately the colonists would be the losers and "bleed at every vein," since the "Farmer" did not believe that the American provinces could stand alone among the nations of the world. The acceptable course of action was to petition for a revocation of duties first, that is after enunciating the basis of the grievance, and hope that the home ministers would yield to pleas for the preservation of liberties.

What Dickinson failed to perceive was that his tightly-drawn arguments about taxation would not be accepted by ministerial leaders. More than any other writer, he established that Anglo-Americans would not accede to taxation by Parliament, no matter how packaged. But he and indeed most other colonists in the late 1760s did accept the general principle that Parliament as the sovereign body of the realm could legislate in general terms for Americans. British ministers never appreciated the distinction because it implied divisible sovereignty. What they did understand in the heat of the moment was that the nonimportation agreements that colonists began to support in reaction to the Townshend Duties were seriously impeding the flow of goods from English to American ports. It was the threat of economic prostration in Great Britain that led Parliament in 1770 to rescind the Townshend program, that is except for the duty on tea. Indeed, the repeal turned out to be a pyrrhic victory for Dickinson; Parliament had recanted again, but not because ministers understood, appreciated, or accepted the reasoning behind his position. The violence and destruction that Dickinson worried about was not far off.

The remaining duty on tea precipitated the final crisis that both Dickinson and Thomas Hutchinson feared might ensue. Because of the tea duty, colonists found it convenient to purchase smuggled Dutch tea from local merchants. Injured by the serious decline in sales as a prime supplier of English tea, the powerful British East India Company sought from Parliament a drop in the price of its tea below that of Dutch brands, even with the tea duty added to the base price. The ministerial head, Lord Frederick North, saw many advantages to the plan. Not only would the Company lose some of its authority over political affairs in India in exchange for such trading concessions, but colonists would find it to their economic advantage to buy less expensive Company tea. Furthermore, when Americans bought the tea, they would have to pay the three pence a pound duty; they thereby would be accepting the proposition that Parliament had the right to tax them. In June 1773 Parliament approved Lord North's East India Company legislation.

Lord North's calculations proved incorrect. He reopened an old wound by violating a perception of reality which men like Samuel Adams held dear. The East India legislation seemed but one more element in the ministerial conspiracy to subvert and destroy American liberties. When two sons of Thomas Hutchinson were named among the tea agents for Massachusetts, it only confirmed the hardening belief that ministers and royal agents seemed bent upon a plot to put the colonists in chains. No economic advantage in pricing, however real, could outweigh what appeared to be a tyrannical act. East India Company tea had to be returned to England or its sale suppressed. The tea shipments en route would be seen as visible proof of a conspiracy by a corrupted ministry to aggrandize power at the expense of colonial liberties.

Even though tea agents had been named for many American ports and tea consignments went to several colonies, it was in Boston where once again a confrontation with far-reaching implications took place. Samuel Adams and his old enemy, Thomas Hutchinson, were in the vortex of the storm. This time local gossips were noising it about that Hutchinson was lining his sons' pockets with proposed profits from tea sales. Citizens were wondering whether anything could stop their governor in his quest for riches and power. Such thoughts must have been in the mind of the mob that formed in early November 1773 and tried to force the tea agents into resigning. But the Hutchinson sons and other agents refused; they had not as yet received commissions and were unwilling to renounce positions not formally authorized. Then the first tea ship, the *Dartmouth*, entered Boston harbor on November 28. The Boston committee of correspondence placed guards on the *Dartmouth* and the other two tea ships as they docked. Samuel Adams and other local leaders insisted that the vessels return to England without unloading; but a legal technicality and an obdurate Governor Hutchinson thwarted the demand.

Victimized for years by the vilification of Samuel Adams and his cronies, Hutchinson was determined to take a stand and face issues squarely. The Boston "democracy" had painted him as a foolish sycophant too many times. For the sake of stability and the preservation of imperial ties vital to the survival of America, Hutchinson would force the tea on his fellow Bostonians. A customs law stated that once a ship entered the Boston harbor, it had twenty days to unload its cargo and pay necessary trade duties. But if any vessel did not unload, then the customs commissioners were empowered to seize its goods and store them in warehouses on land until all duties were paid. As governor, Hutchinson could authorize vessels to leave port before the twenty-day period elapsed. But he refused to issue the necessary papers; and instead he called on the Royal Navy to block off the harbor. The tea ships could not escape. The period of grace was over on December 16; then by law the tea had to be landed. For once Hutchinson sensed a victory for imperial interests over the disorderly Adams crowd.

But Samuel Adams never took a political challenge lightly, especially when it came from Hutchinson. On the afternoon of December 16 a mass meeting turbulently tried to determine a course of action. No one seemed to know what tactics to pursue. Finally, Adams stood up and reportedly yelled: "This meeting can do no more to save the country." It was time for mob action. Several citizens disguised themselves as Indians, went to the wharves, and dumped into the harbor some 342 chests of tea worth nearly £10,000 sterling. This dramatic act of open defiance set the pattern of confrontation that accelerated rapidly.

Reports of the Boston Tea Party shocked the English ministry. As John Dickinson had warned, confrontation led to retaliation in the form of the "Coercive" Acts, passed by Parliament in the spring of 1774. One act closed the port of Boston to all commercial activity until the city's citizens paid for the tea; another vastly increased the authority of Massachusetts royal officials in constraining local legislative bodies; and a third afforded greater protection to royal officials by guaranteeing them trials outside Massachusetts if they harmed anyone in executing their duties. Even though tea ships had not been allowed to unload in other ports, British officials concentrated their wrath against Massachusetts, largely because of the destruction of tea and the recalcitrant record of insurgents like Samuel Adams.

This parliamentary reaction to the Boston Tea Party seemed like a massive assault on liberty, even to colonists outside Massachusetts. No longer was the conspiracy hidden. First Massachusetts would be put in chains; then the other colonies would become victims of political tyranny from England. American resistance in the fall of 1774 focused on Philadelphia and the first Continental Congress, where Samuel Adams was among the leaders pushing for a complete economic boycott in the form of the "Continental Association." Once the Congress met, chances for reconciling differences rapidly diminished as British ministers ignored its petitions and almost disappeared when, in April 1775, British regulars and "embattled farmers" clashed in open and bloody combat at Lexington and Concord.

The second Continental Congress met in Philadelphia under the shadow of conflict. Samuel Adams was there; so was John Dickinson. Relations with England had deteriorated to the point that the only real question facing the delegates was whether independence should be declared. Adams and many New England delegates were ready to face the issue, but John Dickinson with a larger following still insisted that every avenue to a possible reconciliation of differences be explored. Dickinson and his adherents were able to control the Congress for nearly a year. They believed, as had Thomas Hutchinson, that the provinces could not survive as a viable nation. And they feared that the licentiousness of unlettered common citizens would result in internal economic, social, and political chaos in all the colonies. Consequently, the reconciliationists demanded that petition after petition be sent to King and Parliament. When Congress organized the Continental army in the summer of 1775, Dickinson insisted that a document be directed to the King explaining such apparent belligerence. The "Declaration of the Causes and Necessity for Taking up Arms," written by Dickinson and Thomas Jefferson, stated that the purpose of the army was not "to dissolve that union which has so long and so happily subsisted between us." Rather the Continentals would defend American lives, property, and liberty until "hostilities shall cease on the part of the aggressors, and all danger of their being renewed shall be removed, and not before."

And so it went during the next several months. The Dickinson group, clearly committed to upholding American liberties, would not allow open insurgency to become overt revolution. The Adams men, though, barely tolerated what they perceived as faint-heartedness. John Adams, another Massachusetts delegate in league with his cousin Samuel, no doubt stated his kinsman's misgivings when he wrote of Dickinson that "a certain great fortune and piddling genius, whose fame has been trumpeted so loudly, has given a silly cast to our whole doings. We are between hawk and buzzard."

The weight of events, especially spreading military confrontations, finally undermined the Dickinson group. In the debates over the Declaration of Independence Dickinson again reiterated his concern for political stability. He feared what other nations would do with "this stranger in the states of the world." He projected images of civil convulsions in the colonies unless "first we . . . establish our governments and take the regular form of a state. These preventive measures will show deliberation, wisdom, caution, and unanimity." Dickinson pleaded, but the other delegates found his arguments wanting. For them reconciliation had become a delusive impossibility. The moment had come for the birth of a new nation. Convinced to the end that formal revolution must be avoided at all costs, Dickinson abstained in the vote of July 2, 1776, approving the Declaration of Independence. His name does not appear among the signers.

* * *

Dickinson's failure to back the American cause in 1776 was less serious than Thomas Hutchinson's miscalculation of late 1773 in challenging the Boston insurgents to a showdown. Hutchinson believed that the integrity of the empire was at stake; at some juncture the Adams group had to be defeated if the vital, indeed life-sustaining cord, was to be maintained with Britain. But Hutchinson chose the wrong moment to assert his will against the Boston "democracy." The Tea Party was a challenge that English ministers could not ignore—and save face. Like Hutchinson, John Dickinson could not imagine that the colonies could long survive as an independent nation. If not torn apart by enemies from without, then civil turmoil and political insurgency by the licentious democracy would undermine any attempt at nation-building from within. The imperial connection meant stability, security, balance, and order; neither man wanted to face the next day without those elements. Perhaps for both it was a failure of vision.

Cast as tyrant when he saw himself as a defender of the British constitution against the turbulent masses, Hutchinson received in late 1773 a special leave from the governorship to go to England. He was tired of the political battles. Sailing in June, he hoped to return soon to his beloved native land. But the opportunity never came. As the imperial crisis intensified and insurgency turned to revolution, Hutchinson became *persona non grata* in Massachusetts as the primary symbol of the ministerial plot. First Boston's revolutionaries seized his property; then they declared him an enemy to the state and marked him as one who could never return to his home upon penalty of death. Thus Hutchinson lived on in London, first a knowledgeable celebrity among the ministry and then as a friend of other loyalist refugees who had not fared so well as he in escaping. In his last days Hutchinson's consuming passion was once again to be with his friends and neighbors in New England. He died at his London home on June 3, 1780, at the age of 68, despised to the end as a purveyor of offices, a power-hungry fiend, and a destroyer of liberties. The soothing effect of time has been a more reasonable judge.

Despite his seeming apostasy, John Dickinson did better. He finally cast his lot with the American cause, devoting himself to finding the constitutional means of building a stable, orderly American republic.

There were those who taunted him because of his refusal to sign the Declaration of Independence, but none could attack him as an enemy of American liberties. Yet they had to admit that Dickinson remained consistent during the revolutionary crisis in his position that liberties could only be preserved when there was a restraining hand on the potentially turbulent and anarchical citizenry. Thus Dickinson worked first to create a strong national government through the Articles of Confederation. Failing in that but remaining active in Delaware and Pennsylvania politics, he joined the distinguished group of nationalists who drafted the Constitution of 1787 and carried it to the citizenry as a document that truly would draw the 13 struggling states more closely together into one nation.

Since national unity was one key to stability, Dickinson seemed satisfied that the more-powerful national government resulting from the Constitution of 1787 could control popular anarchy. By remaining with the American cause despite his qualms and anxieties, Dickinson ultimately was able to assist in formulating the kind of constitutional settlement that he so wanted before a formal declaration of independence. For the rest of his life the "Farmer" generally eschewed politics, preferring to live on his estates. He was satisfied that the Constitution gave the republic every hope for survival, regardless of internal or external political pressures. John Dickinson died in 1808 at the age of 76 knowing that the experiment in nation-building was working.

If Dickinson in 1776 seemed for a moment to lose his way by recoiling at the thought of a complete severance of ties with Great Britain, Samuel Adams appeared to lose his political compass permanently after 1776 once the prelude to revolution was over. Adams was in many ways a driven man in his hatred of Thomas Hutchinson. For years he had resorted to every imaginable tactic in attacking his visible and well-placed adversary. One energizing source of that rage was the Land Bank controversy, which seriously undercut the Adams' family financial base. The Hutchinson clique even then seemed to be destroyers of liberty and political tyrants operating with the backing of imperial officials. Having personalized the area of disagreement, every significant issue after that time, so Adams thought, seemed to cast Hutchinson more and more in the role of ministerial sycophant and tyrant. Hutchinson's presence in so many high Massachusetts offices during the 1760s and early 1770s heightened tensions and abetted political disequilibrium. He was always there, representing the conspiracy from above. Adams again and again sought his humiliation and political destruction, characterizing him as a power-hungry enemy of the "democracy" of common citizens. When Hutchinson's downfall came in 1774, it was too late to regain political equilibrium. Too many leaders on both sides of the Atlantic had become involved in the larger ramifications of that struggle.

Rejoicing in Hutchinson's departure, Samuel Adams seemed thereafter to grope for political focus. He worked diligently for independence; but once it had been declared, Adams drifted in opinionated fashion from one personality and issue to the next, making few significant contributions either as a representative in the Continental Congress during the later 1770s, as a state senator in Massachusetts during the 1780s, or as the governor of his state for a brief period during the 1790s. There was no longer any person or group to rail against with sustained credibility. An old friend stated in the 1780s that Adams had "become the most arbitrary and despotic Man" in Massachusetts, a rather ironic comment given the latter's many venomous attacks on Hutchinson. When Adams died in October 1803 at the age of 81, Bostonians came out for a grand funeral procession. Obituaries spoke of a man who had fought diligently for liberty but who later in life had become an anachronism in the political arena. Adams the agitator, then, earned no real distinctions in postrevolutionary Massachusetts.

But the efforts of Samuel Adams as the protagonist in the revolutionary crisis should not be clouded by his failure to distinguish himself after 1776. Because Adams and others pushed, shoved, and challenged the British empire and its rulers, colonists gained the opportunity to rethink traditional assumptions about hierarchy and balance in state and society. The socio-political orders of monarchy and aristocracy rapidly lost their importance without the imperial connection. Some men started to speculate about an open political arena where the people themselves rather than stewards from higher orders would control decision-making in all branches of government, would enunciate and defend liberties, and by extension would shape the nation's destiny. Popular sovereignty was in the air. The question in 1776 seemed to be how far constitution-makers could go in allowing the people to govern themselves. Among other factors the fear of popular rule, reflected in the thoughts of men like John Dickinson, moderated the majority of the first state constitution-makers. They preferred constitutional checks on the common citizens. But a seed was being planted, a seed that transcended the rather petty and vituperative defense of liberties as conducted before 1776 by Adams and his associates. It was the seed of self-government by the citizenry itself through popular sovereignty. That was an emerging concept of political possibilities that became a very real part of the American Revolution. It would take time for the seed to sprout and grow. It would mean a fundamental change in the definition of democracy. But that too in time would flower.

5

Philosophers of the New Republic

THOMAS JEFFERSON
JOHN ADAMS
ALEXANDER HAMILTON

by Henry Steele Commager
Amherst College

No other people are as fortunate in their founding fathers as are the American. What a galaxy of statesmen presided over the birth of the American nation, and presided, too, over its formative years! Benjamin Franklin and George Washington, Thomas Jefferson and James Madison, Alexander Hamilton and John Adams, James Wilson and Thomas Paine —why, we have not been able to match them in 200 years! And, what is no less astonishing, the generation that won independence and created the nation, lived on for another half century. Continuity thus was woven into the very fabric of that nation that had been born out of revolution.

It was Washington who contributed most to the creation of the nation, for he was not only the Father of his country, but its symbol as well. Jefferson and Hamilton were "the movers and shakers," the men who put their stamp on ideals and on institutions, who set the pattern for the America of the future. John Adams, overshadowed a bit by both of them, was both a collaborator and a foil.

It is Adams, Jefferson, and Hamilton who command our attention. They fought together in the Revolution, they served together in the Washington administration, they helped to lay the foundations of our national institutions—not least of which are the political parties. Yet they were not a triumvirate; each was distinctive and independent, each made his own contribution—or perhaps, at times—counter-contribution. It is the differences that interest us, differences that, in the limited American theater, seem dramatic and even fundamental. But it is easy to exaggerate these differences, to assume that because they seem fundamental in an American context they were indeed fundamental and irreconcilable. What is historically most important is that these statesmen were on the same side in the great events of the 70s and the 80s: on the side of revolution, independence, commonwealth-making, and nation-making. To put it somewhat simply, they were on Washington's side. No one of them was tempted to be a Loyalist, none opposed independence or the philosophy that justified it, none challenged the new federal constitution, none withheld his support from the new government that guided the nation through the treacherous waters of the 90s. We attach the term "Republican" to Jefferson and "Federalist" to Hamilton and Adams, but it was Jefferson who said, in his Inaugural Address, that "we are all Republicans, we are all Federalists"; it was Hamilton who assured the peaceable election of Jefferson over Burr in the crisis of 1800; it was Adams who eventually associated himself with the Republican Party. We take much of this for granted, as we take consensus for granted in our history, but you do not find anything like this in the Europe of the Age of Revolution. Edmund Burke was not a champion of revolution, nor William Pitt, and the British revolutionaries for their part were either silenced or—as with Paine and Joseph Priestley—driven out. Nor was the situation different on the Continent. Adams, Jefferson, and Hamilton wore out their hearts and their lives in the same cause: and both of Adams' associates could have subscribed to what he said in that moving letter to his beloved wife Abigail, written on the day after he had voted for independence:

> I am well aware of the toil, the blood and treasure, that it will cost us to maintain this declaration and support and defend these States. Yet through all the gloom I can see the rays of ravishing light and glory. I can see that the end is more than worth all the means, and that posterity will triumph in that day's transaction.

We must then be constantly on guard—especially in an enterprise of this nature—against the professional vice of the historian; that of being more impressed with what men say than with what men do, and of looking for motives rather than looking at conduct. Both Adams and Hamilton sounded a good deal more High Tory than they actually were in their political character. Both tended to look on the people as a mob, and to identify American commoners with the mobs of the Old World; both feared democracy and were inclined to approve a class society. Hamilton thought the British system the most nearly perfect in the world; he thirsted for monarchy and was ready to argue that corruption was an essential part of the beauty of that government. If Adams did not go quite that far, he nonetheless confessed that "chance was better than choice" and a hereditary prince better than an elective. Hamilton rejoiced in the military, yearned to don a uniform and to lead an assault on the ramparts of the enemy; Adams did not. But both detested the French Revolution, rejected the possibility of genuine equality, and thought talk of progress mostly cant. Jefferson, too, was given to hyperbole. Did he really mean that the tree of liberty must be watered with the blood of martyrs? Was he really ready to scrap all constitutions every 20½ years because each generation should make its own constitution? Was he really persuaded that there was a plot to establish a monarchy in the United States? We must remember, rather, that whatever Hamilton said in that famous speech at the Constitutional Convention on June 18, 1787, it was he who led the fight for ratification in New York State and who bore the major burden of writing the *Federalist Papers;* that however much he endorsed the British Monarchy and admired the British Empire, he fought to destroy them both and to set up a system without King or Colonies. So with Adams: he detested the French Revolution and Napoleon but risked his presidency to prevent a war with France; he did not oppose the liberalization of the Massachusetts Constitution he had originally written; and he ended up—thanks in part to the Hamiltonians—in the Jeffersonian party. As for Jefferson, he proclaimed the doctrine of state sovereignty in the 1798 Kentucky Resolutions and hinted at secession, but proved in the end the most ardent nationalist of all; he adored France and Italy but was ready to pray for an ocean of fire between the Old World and the New; he was a communicant of the Anglican Church, but helped topple it from its established position in Virginia.

They had more in common than a revolution, a constitution, a nation. They were also dreamers of dreams, Hamilton less than the others. The climate of opinion moulded their thought; circumstances and necessity dictated their conduct. Two of them, Jefferson and Adams, fulfilled the Platonic ideal of philosophers as Kings, and what a tribute to the new American people that they should be the first in history to elect philosophers to their throne. Hamilton was not really a philosopher—perhaps not even a *philosophe* (the distinction is subtle and elusive)—nor did he ever become king, though he wanted to be and in a sense deserved to be. They were at the same time activists; they created institutions that were logical products of their philosophy; they could be abstract, but for the most part were not; they were practical and consequential. With them there was no dichotomy between thought and action, between ideal and reality; they were not only the most philosophical of American statesmen, they were the most effective and creative.

It is their creativity that impresses us most, perhaps because we are so shamefully unable to emulate it. Together with their associates in Revolution, they created every important political and constitutional institution in our history: six generations have added nothing of importance in this realm, and we are still living on the capital they piled up in that remarkable quarter century between the Declaration of Independence and the inauguration of Thomas Jefferson. Adams, Jefferson, Hamilton, and their associates did far more than win independence; they *"realized the theories of the wisest writers."* They confronted the problem of how men make government—of how government "derives its powers from the consent of the governed." And they responded to it with the constitutional convention, the basic institution of democracy. They also confronted the problem of how men can limit government, and responded with written constitutions, separation of powers, Bills of Rights, and judicial review. Organizing 13 independent States into a single nation, they invented the first successful federal system in history. They faced the challenge of the organization and administration of what was in effect a colonial empire west of the Alleghenies, and solved the intractable problem of imperial-colonial relations by the simple device of doing away with colonies altogether and recognizing western territories as equal commonwealths in the federal system. They banished the spectre of religious wars by providing not only for complete toleration but also for separation of church and state. They made impossible—so they thought—the danger of a Cromwell or a Napoleon by subordinating the military to the civilian authority. They did not do away with slavery, but that was not the fault of the American *philosophes*, and certainly not of Jefferson and Adams who regarded the institution with loathing.

Intellectually, Revolutionary America was very much part of the Enlightenment, and Jefferson, Adams, Hamilton, each responded to and reflected the Enlightenment in his own special fashion. All three accepted the Newtonian world, governed by laws of Nature and (if you wished to make rhetorical gestures, as did the signers of the Declaration) of Nature's God. They accepted (Adams with some misgivings for others though never for himself) the principle of the sovereignty of Reason and the axiom that Reason could penetrate to and master the laws of Nature and persuade men to conform to them. Looking back over half a century Jefferson selected this as the animating principle of his age:

> We believed that man was a rational animal. . . . We believed that men, habituated to thinking for themselves, and to follow their reason as guide, would be more easily and safely governed than with minds nourished in error and vitiated and debased by ignorance.

From Newtonian premises, too, there followed a passion for order that permeated alike the great affairs of nature, the great affairs of government, the affairs of society, and of economy and of learning; that ordered even the architecture of buildings, forms and balances in music, the landscaping of gardens. Adams committed himself to this chiefly in the arena of government; Hamilton in government and the economy; Jefferson in almost all of his multivarious interests and activities.

A third common denominator—far more prominent in the New World than in the Old—was a commitment to freedom of the mind, freedom from the tyranny of the church or of the state, freedom to follow the teachings of science wherever they led, freedom from ignorance, from authority, from the past. No one put this better than Jefferson, or more eloquently: "I have sworn upon the altar of God eternal hostility against every form of tyranny over the mind of man." Adams shared this passion for freedom, though rather for himself than for others; Hamilton took it for granted, but contributed little to it.

Their objective was, of course, to liberate the minds and the energies of men; to enable them to achieve what God or Nature had so clearly intended that they should achieve; to persuade them to conform so perfectly to the laws of Nature that the errors and corruptions which had for so long afflicted mankind would fall away, and man would enter a golden age. In Europe that was impossible, and there only the most infatuated *philosophes* talked in this fashion. Adams thought it was impossible in America, too, for he had little faith in Progress and none in Utopia. Hamilton would have put the matter in more secular terms: an enlightened government—defined as one that is managed by men like himself—could indeed solve most of the problems that afflicted most societies, could create an orderly system of political economy. Beyond that he was reluctant to go. With Jefferson this objective was of paramount importance and its realization a consuming passion for 50 years.

Already the differences are beginning to emerge, differences that in the Old World would have assigned each of them to warring camps, for there Hamilton would inevitably have been like his fellow American, Count Rumford, advisor to one of the Enlightened Despots; Adams, for all his misgivings about England, would have gravitated to Dr. Samuel Johnson and his circle; Jefferson—alone of the three—would have been, and indeed was, at home with the *philosophes*.

*   *   *

Thomas Jefferson was born in 1743 in the county of Goochland (now Albemarle) on what was then the Virginia frontier. His father, Peter Jefferson, was a surveyor who had helped run the boundary line between Virginia and North Carolina. A man of substance and position in his own right, he had married into the powerful and distinguished Randolph family. From childhood, then, Thomas belonged both to the frontier and to the tidewater. Through his father he was familiar with that great West for which he later became the pre-eminent spokesman; through his mother he had entrée to the best society of colonial Virginia—which had some claim to be the best society in America. As a young man Jefferson studied Latin and Greek with the Rev. James Maury, who first initiated him into the pleasures of learning—an initiation he never thereafter betrayed. At the age of 17 he enrolled in the little provincial college of William and Mary; there he had the good fortune to study under the distinguished mathematician and philosopher, Dr. William Small, who introduced him to the pleasures of natural science and to the attention and favors of Gov. Fauquier and George Wythe—most distinguished of Virginia lawyers who later became the first professor of law in America and Chief Justice of the Commonwealth of Virginia. It was heady company for a lad from the frontier, but Jefferson proved himself ready for it. At the age of 24 Jefferson was called to the bar; in seven years of practice he rose to be one of the leaders of the bar and—more importantly—found time to collect the ancient laws and the judicial cases of the Virginia courts, thus early displaying that talent for the practical and the scholarly that characterized him for the next half century. In 1772 he married Martha Skelton who brought substantial estates and gave him four children. Already he had begun to build what was to be the most beautiful house in America—Monticello, for his talent for architecture and gardening emerged as early as did his talent for law, politics, agriculture, science, and learning. In 1769 his neighbors had sent him to the House of Burgesses; that began a public life that stretched over a span of 56 years. Like John Adams, he was early caught up in the controversy with the mother country and like him, too, contributed to that controversy a pamphlet of lasting value in our literature: the *Summary View of the Rights of British America*. In 1774 the Burgesses chose him as a delegate to the Continental Congress; he returned there in 1776 to achieve immortality.

Clearly there is no more cosmopolitan figure in the whole of our history than Jefferson—this man who could sit "gazing for hours at the Maison Quarrée, like a lover at his mistress," and then reproduce it in the State Capitol at Richmond; who was not only America's most ardent disciple of Palladio, but reproduced two of that great Italian architect's masterpieces—the Villa Rotunda and the Villa Malcontenta—in his own exquisite Monticello and then adapted the master's style to that great architectural achievement—the University of Virginia; who delighted in gardens as in temples, villas and stately homes, and studied these in France, Italy, and England; who laid out the gardens at his own University, and kept a fascinating garden book throughout his life; who imported exotic plants from every quarter of the globe; and who confessed that "no occupation on earth is so delightful to me as the culture of the Earth, and no culture comparable to that of the garden." At another time it was music that was "the dearest passion of my heart," and Jefferson delighted in the opera and the chamber music of Paris, compiled a large collection of music—

alas, lost—and himself played the fiddle. He had other passions, too—how did he find time for them all?—a passion for "natural philosophy," which we call science, and he added to it both on the practical and the theoretical side; for book collecting, and he amassed the largest and best selected library in America, and refounded the Library of Congress after its destruction by the British in 1814; for classical literature. He translated what he needed of Sophocles and Euripides, and to the close of his life sprinkled his correspondence with quotations from the Greek and the Latin. No other American of his generation contributed so richly to the arts as did Jefferson. Hamilton could design a state but imagine him designing its capitol building as well: there is no evidence, indeed, that for all his passion for high society Hamilton had any interest in the arts. John Adams was a farmer, but imagine him visiting the vineyards of the Loire or the Moselle, or laying out the gardens of a university. Though he did write into the Constitution of Massachusetts an admonition to the Legislature "to cherish the interests of literature and the sciences," he resolutely put aside all temptations to indulge in the arts: as he wrote his Abigail in 1780

> I must study politics and war that my sons may have the liberty to study mathematics and philosophy. My sons ought to study mathematics and philosophy . . . commerce and agriculture, to give their children the right to study painting, poetry, music, architecture, statuary, tapestry and porcelain.

But 30 years later he was prepared to dismiss even such study as flummery. "Statues, paintings, panygerics, in short all the fine arts, even music and dancing," he wrote, "promote virtue while virtue is in fashion. After that they promote luxury, effeminancy, corruption, prostitution, and every species of abandoned profligacy."

Yes, Jefferson was cosmopolitan, affluent, patrician, happier in Paris than anywhere else in the world except Monticello. It is a critical exception. For Jefferson mixed romanticism with classicism and provinciality with cosmopolitanism. He really belonged in Virginia. His romanticism, was not *contrived*, as it were, but spontaneous; it had strong personal connotations, obvious enough in his passion for Monticello and Poplar Forest, for the Palladian villa perched on a mountain top on the very edge of a romantic wilderness, and for the boundless West Monticello looked out upon.

Jefferson's romantic view of America had decisive political connotations as well. It was Jefferson, after all, not Hamilton or Adams, who rejected Europe—the European past, and the European present. His admiration for the Old World rested on nothing so corrosive as envy of, or longing for, those institutions that perpetuated the rule of his class; his antipathy on nothing so vulgar as a sense of discomfort, resentment of snubs, the difficulty with the language, exasperation at being considered a provincial. It was precisely the glitter, the charm, the social seductions that put Jefferson off. His isolation rested, after all, on moral grounds. Writing from Paris in 1785 he warned against sending an American boy abroad to study:

> He acquires a fondness for European luxury and dissipation, and a contempt for the simplicity of his own country; he is fascinated with the privileges of European aristocrats and sees, with abhorrence, the lovely equality which the poor enjoy with the rich in his own country . . . he is led, by the strongest of all the human passions, into a spirit for female intrigue, destructive of his own and others' happiness . . . and learns to consider fidelity to the marriage bed and an ungentlemanly practice. . . .

Nor did he ever depart from these views. It was Jefferson who, for all his affection for France, supported the Neutrality Proclamation; Jefferson who warned against "entangling alliances" with the countries of Europe; Jefferson who first used the Embargo as an instrument for peace; Jefferson who called for a "wall of fire" between the Old World and the New; Jefferson who urged on President James Monroe that doctrine that came to bear his name. Listen to him after 50 years in public life:

> Our first and fundamental maxim should be never to entangle ourselves in the broils of Europe. Our second never to suffer Europe to intermeddle with cis-Atlantic affairs. America has a set of interests distinct from those of Europe, and peculiarly her own. She should therefore have a system of her own, separate and apart from that of Europe. While the last is laboring to become the domicile of despotism, our endeavors should surely be, to make our hemisphere that of freedom.

Hamilton—who never visited Europe—admired not so much the Old World as the British segment of it, and there his admiration was boundless. He admired its government, monarchy and all, its far-flung empire, its class system, its affluence and elegance: he even had something good to say about its corruption as the lubricant of the Parliamentary system. Adams, on the other hand, detested Europe—after all, had not the French treated him shabbily, had not the English snubbed him? Like Jefferson, he was put off by its class system, by its painful contrasts of wealth and poverty; like Jefferson, he was affronted by its palpable immorality. Homespun, provincial, irremediably Yankee in his interests and attachments, he was radically suspicious of all that smacked of the effete, the polished, the mannered, the luxurious, the extravagant and the sinful. And yet in his thinking—not in his conduct—he was, in a sense, a prisoner of the Old World, unable to emancipate himself from its past and what he thought were its lessons. He could not say, with Paine, that the American was "as a new Adam in a new Paradise." He could not write, with

Jefferson, that "this whole chapter in the history of man is new," for he could not delude himself that there was anything really new about human nature or about history. No! With Adams it was the Past, it was History that was in command: we shall return to this, for it had consequences far beyond the realm of historical philosophy.

Certainly no other American was so thoroughly suffused with Enlightenment philosophy or contributed so much to it as Jefferson, and no other so symbolized the American Enlightenment. His commitment and his conduct was all of a piece. What he said at the beginning of his career in Philadelphia where he wrote the Declaration of Independence, in Virginia where he drew up the Revisal of the Laws, he also said at high noon as Secretary of State and Vice President and President, and in retirement at Monticello as the evening shadows fell. The very last letter he wrote breathes the same commitment to freedom, the same faith in progress that he had professed in his youth. It was on the occasion of the 50th anniversary of the Declaration and—as it turned out—the beginning of his own immortality:

> May it be to the world what I believe it will be, the signal of arousing men to burst the chains under which monkish ignorance and superstition had persuaded them to bind themselves, and to assume the blessings and security of self government. That form which we have substituted restores the free right to the unbounded exercise of reason and freedom of opinion. All eyes are opened, or opening, to the rights of man. The general spread of the light of science has already laid open to every view the palpable truth that the mass of mankind has not been born with saddles on their backs, nor a favored few, booted and spurred, ready to ride them legitimately. These are grounds of hope for others. For ourselves let the annual return of this day forever refresh our recollections of these rights and an undiminished devotion to them.

From time to time Adams would allow himself this kind of sentiment, but mostly he looked with deep misgivings on the rhetoric of revolution, and as for Hamilton, he was far less interested in the rights of man than in the power of government. The differences were more than rhetorical; they were, or became, philosophical. Let us explore these differences.

*   *   *

And let us begin with one of those great controversies that erupted again and again in the 18th century and did so much to illuminate the mind of the age: the Ancients versus the Moderns, Nature versus Civilization, Mercantilism versus Physiocracy, the causes of the Rise and Decline of Empires and—of primary interest to us—Was America a Mistake?

It was an old question, this; one that had its origins in the discovery of the New World and that had raged, in various forms, over the following three centuries. By the time of the Enlightenment, Europe had in a sense come to terms with America, and no one now debated whether man had violated the will of God in lifting the veil on the new continent, or whether the Indians were indeed human beings, or whether there had been a single or multiple creations. But even the most enlightened of the *philosophes* had not wholly rid themselves of the notion that America was somehow inferior to Europe, its climate miserable, its flora and fauna degenerated, its people enervated, stunted, and doomed to permanent inferiority. Why was America so backward? Why had it never produced a civilization? Why was its effect so malign even on those Europeans who migrated there? These questions came not only from crackpots but from distinguished historians like Abbé Raynal, whose *Philosophical History of . . . the Europeans in the East and West Indies* was one of the most influential books of its day.

It was in 1780 that a young Secretary to the French Minister in Philadelphia, Francois Barbé de Marbois, forwarded to all the American governors a list of inquiries designed to provide his government with useful information about the new United States. The questions covered pretty much everything except politics—geography, natural resources, native races, the economy, commerce, and even history. Only one Governor bothered to answer this formidable set of queries, and that was the busiest of them all, Thomas Jefferson. Even he might not have troubled to do so, had it not been for a lucky accident. Riding around one of his farms, Poplar Forest, Jefferson fell off his horse and was for some weeks incapacitated. It is to that horse—and Jefferson's inveterate habit of making use of every moment—that we owe his reply to Marbois, the *Notes on Virginia.*

"This country," he wrote, "affords to philosophic view an extensive, rich and unexplored view." It is the philosophic view that make *Notes on Virginia* one of the great books of our literature, one of the important books of the whole Enlightenment. For Jefferson answered not only the formal queries, but thought up others of a more philosophical character —and answered them. The *Notes*—how desultory that sounds!—covered not only obvious things like geography and geology and commerce and finance, but also population (one of the crucial indices to civilization and population in the Enlightenment age), religion, education, slavery, and law; they included dissertations on the native races, the Negro, the past and the future of the State and, by implication, of America. In the end the *Notes* added up to a repudiation of the European animadversions against the New World, a celebration of religious liberty, an attack on slavery, a ringing declaration of scientific and intellectual independence, and a theory of History that subtly shifted the center of gravity from the past to the future. It probed the American character, and presented, more fully than any other treatise of the time the agenda of the American Enlightenment.

Observe first—and it was a feature far more characteristic of Jefferson than of Adams or Hamilton—the reliance on the inductive method, which was the method of science. After all, Jefferson was himself a scientist (the term then was Natural Philosopher), President, for many years, of the American Philosophical Society, American substitute for the great Royal Society of London. He did not disdain rhetoric, but he relied on facts. And here are the facts, comprehensive and conclusive. Are American animals enfeebled? Let us measure them. Here is the European and the American bear, the first a mere 153 pounds, the second 410. In Europe the beaver grows to 18 pounds, in America to over 40. Or contemplate the American bison of almost 2,000 pounds, or the bullock of over 2,500, or the hog—Jefferson himself had seen one that weighed 1,000 pounds.

What then of the native races? What of Europeans in the American climate? Here the story was the same. After all, Americans knew the Indians as European scientists did not, and of all Americans none knew them better than Jefferson, who has some claim to be the father of American ethnology. No one of his generation, unless it was his friend and disciple Albert Gallatin, contributed more to our knowledge of the Indian than did Jefferson—certainly not Adams, certainly not Hamilton, who had no interest in them, either scientific or practical. The Indian, Jefferson made clear, was a product of climate—as men were everywhere —climate as environment and climate as social and economic organization. An almost perfect product of that climate, he was perfectly adapted to it. The Indian was ardent and brave, strong and agile, resourceful and sagacious. Physically he was a splendid specimen: he had ardor and virility, the ability to withstand a hostile environment, and to provide for all his necessities; he had even—and here Jefferson yielded to that romanticism never far from the surface of his mind—eloquence and nobility of character.

But the nub of the matter was, of course, what happened to Europeans when transplanted to the New World. Were they indeed enfeebled by the new climate, distracted by the importunate necessities of the struggle for existence, hopelessly isolated from the centers of civilization? So said Corneille De Pauw, who claimed that "through the whole length of America, from Cape Horn to the Hudson Bay, there never appeared a philosopher, an artist, a man of learning whose name has found a place in the history of science." Even the friendly Abbé Raynal repeated the canard: "How astonishing that America has not yet produced a single good poet, an able mathematician, or a man of genius in any one of the arts or the sciences." Nonsense, said Jefferson. We have produced in one generation a Washington, a Franklin, a Rittenhouse—he might have added a Jefferson but let others do that: can France, with six times the American population, show six comparable men? But what is more to the point, we have produced a wholesome society, one where there are few extremes of wealth and of poverty, where there are few who are without schooling, where none live in fear of tyranny, where happiness is generally suffused. Look aside from the achievements of empires and armies and navies; Americans "have given hopeful proofs of genius of the nobler kinds which arouse the best feelings of man, which call him into action, which substantiate his freedom, and conduct him to happiness." Here is the Jeffersonian test of civilization—something that eluded not only the monarchs and the *philosophes* of the Old World, but Adams and Hamilton, too, —the test not of power but of freedom and happiness.

There was not only happiness, there was progress too, progress such as no Old World people could display. For what was the ultimate test of a successful and progressive society in the 18th-century? It was not wealth, it was not power, it was not even, in the long run, aristocratic culture and the social graces. It was population. After all, Oliver Goldsmith had put it simply enough: *ill* fares the land, to hastening ills a prey/where wealth accumulates and men decay." No other country in the western world, perhaps no other country in history, could show an increase in population such as that which America enjoyed—and showed promise of continuing to enjoy into the indefinite future. Why it took a century for population to double in Old World countries—and some of them—the Italian states, for example, boasted little increase from generation to generation. But in America population doubled every 25 years: even John Adams could look forward to one hundred million Americans a century hence, and the infatuated Reverend Edward Wigglesworth confidently predicted a population of 1,280,000,000 by the year 2000! And not only did population double every quarter century, but the whole of America seemed to be a kind of fountain of youth where men and women lived well beyond the Biblical life span of three score and ten. All this was a product of environment to be sure, but of more than environment —more than an abundance of land, richness of soil, fecundity of animal life. It was a product of a social system where mothers and children need not toil in the fields or in shops or domestic service; of a religious system where the church did not monopolize the land or wrest tithes from an impoverished peasantry; of a political system that encouraged freedom—at least for the whites; of industry, simplicity, and purity of morals. It was, in short, something that set the new United States off from all other nations, something that vindicated—you can take your choice of these explanations—either the special favor of Providence, or the special good fortune of climate, or the special virtue of the American people. Jefferson, Adams, Hamilton all might give lip service to the first explanation without putting much stock in it; all, too, might endorse the second, though Hamilton had little faith in climate and much in government; only Jefferson would accept the third.

*   *   *

John Adams was born in Braintree, Massachusetts, in 1735, of a family respectable but not yet distinguished. His Yankee forebears had been farmers, and their days were spent in the routine of planting and harvesting, schoolroom, town meeting and church; Adams himself, notwithstanding more than half a century of public life, never departed very far from this routine, for he kept the ancestral homestead in Braintree and did not think it beneath his dignity to pitch hay in his meadows. John's father had been clever enough to marry a Boylston of Boston, just as John himself was clever enough to marry a Quincy of Boston; the marriages were happy but the relationship between Braintree and Boston was always an uneasy one: as John's great-grandson, the famous historian Henry Adams, was to write, there was a "hereditary warfare between State Street and Braintree." For all their worldliness, the Adamses were unregenerate provincials with their roots deep in their own soil. At 16— not uncommonly young for those days—Adams went off to Harvard College, graduating, without any special distinction, in 1755. A brief experience with school teaching persuaded him that he preferred the public to the private life, and within a year he managed to get himself admitted to the colonial bar, under the auspices of the powerful Jeremiah Gridley of Boston. Though Adams was eventually to be appointed Chief Justice of Massachusetts, his interest in the law was never professional: the law opened to him, as to so many others, a path to public life that was always his meat and drink. As early as 1765 Adams plunged into the controversy with the Mother Country with a *Dissertation on the Feudal and Canon Law,* which attracted widespread attention, and in no time at all he was hobnobbing with men like Gridley, James Otis, Sam Adams, and others who were leaders in the anti-Hutchinson faction of colony politics. He was elected to the General Assembly, he rejoiced in the Boston Tea Party, he was chosen a delegate to the First Continental Congress; by 1775 he was so prominent in revolutionary activities he was one of the few radicals specifically exempted from the blanket pardon George III was ready to extend to the American rebels if only they would promise to behave themselves. Already it was clear that John Adams was the kind of man who would never be counted on to behave himself.

Unlike Thomas Jefferson, however, Adams had no faith in the virtue of man, not even of man in America, and he did not believe that even the most favorable climate could overcome man's innate perverseness and corruption. "There is no special Providence for Americans," he wrote, "and their nature is the same as that of others." As he surveyed the history of mankind, he found men and governments everywhere the same—men the same in their passions, greed, ambition, venality; governments the same in their propensity to tyranny. No other colonial political philosopher was so completely the prisoner, almost the victim, of History. It is all set forth in those three tumultuous volumes of the *Defense of the Constitution of the United States* and a fourth volume called *Discourses on Davila*. Almost every page plagarized from older histories. No matter, it came out as Adams anyway. Adams saw in History "eternal, unchangeable proof" of the corruption and depravity of man. What a contrast to Jefferson who was quite as much at home in history as was Adams, who had read the same books, but who rejected almost contemptuously the "Gothic idea that we are to look backwards rather than forwards, for the improvement of the human mind, and to recur to the annals of our ancestors for what is most perfect in government." The Earth belongs to the living, not the dead, Jefferson insisted and so, too, mechanisms controlling government and prosperity. This was something Adams could never understand, for his instincts were not only conservative but almost antiquarian.

History, Adams knew, was philosophy teaching by examples. What lessons did it teach, what that Americans should take to heart?

That men are irremediably corrupt, the creatures of passions and of interests;

That neither education nor religion could control the appetites of men; nothing but "force and power and strength" in the State;

That though all men are the same in their moral depravity, they are not equal, but incurably unequal—in their physical, intellectual, social, and economic character—and that this inequality is the point of departure for any sound political philosophy;

That these basic inequalities divide every society between the few and the many: that the few were the rich and the well-born, the many were the masses of society whose lot would never be greatly improved;

That these divisions in society were distinguished chiefly by ownership of property, which in turn compels those who control it to exercise the tyranny of property—Adams preferred the term "dominion";

That the tyranny of property was matched, however, by the tyranny of the majority who were without property;

That the only way to protect both society and liberty from these twin tyrannies was by contriving a system of checks and balances so elaborate that they would inevitably frustrate corruption;

That "nothing but three different orders of men, bound by their interests to watch over each other, and stand the guardians of the law" could achieve the balance essential to the preservation of liberty, and that this threefold balance was that of an independent executive and two legislative bodies, each with a veto upon the other two;

That such a balance was far more than a mere political contrivance; it was rooted in natural law, for these three branches "have an unalterable foundation in Nature";

And finally, annotating it all—an annotation Adams shared with Hamilton—that the British Constitution was "the most perfect combination of human powers in society which infinite wisdom has yet contrived and reduced to practice for the preservation of liberty and the production of happiness."

Now it is hard to know whether to be more impressed by the narrowness of this entire argument or by its palpable irrelevance to the American experience. It was directed almost entirely to a single problem and with a single solution and that one of utmost simplicity. The problem was, basically, the innate depravity of man; the solution that of counteracting depravity by mechanical contrivances. Never, apparently, did Adams ask himself the most elementary of questions: how could merely mechanical obstacles really frustrate the ambitions and aggressions of men who were irremediably selfish and corrupt? But perhaps even more astonishing was the almost total inapplicability of the Adams argument to the American scene. Had Washington, had Franklin, or Jefferson, or Madison, or John Jay, or George Wythe, or Charles Carroll, or Benjamin Rush—had John Adams himself—most of them rich (by the simple standards of America) and all of them, surely, "well-born," succumbed to the temptations of power? Had they sought to enrich themselves at the public expense, to prolong their tenure of office, to subvert the Constitution of the laws? Could fatuity go any farther? Indeed it could, for here is Adams writing to Dr. Rush at the very time Washington was ascending to the Presidency: "Have not our Parties behaved like all Republican Parties? Is not the history of Hancock and Bowdoin, the history of the Medici and Albizi?"

What is startling is not only Adams' failure to understand the irrelevance of his major argument to the American scene, but his concentration on that one argument and that one solution as the beginning and the end of political wisdom. That the purpose of government was to preserve liberty was nowhere challenged, but was it the only purpose and, for that matter, was it the only method? Adams, to be sure, did make one contribution not so much to political theory (for the theory welled up from the New England town meetings) as to political practice: he was perhaps the first to "realize" the principle of popular sovereignty in the processes of constitution-making through the device of a popularly elected constitutional convention and subsequent popular ratification. Other than this, what is most impressive is perhaps the paucity of Adams' contributions to the solution of those great questions that confronted the American people in the early years of the Republic. To the solution of the problem of federalism—in many ways the toughest of them all—he made no contribution; indeed it is not clear that he even understood it. Nor did he have anything to contribute to the vexatious problem of the organization of the West and the necessity of transforming potential colonies into co-ordinate states: indeed throughout his long life he remained curiously indifferent to the trans-Appalachian West and even to the native inhabitants—in contrast to Jefferson's almost obsessive preoccupation with the Indians. He was a lawyer and, technically, Chief Justice of Massachusetts, but gave so little thought to the judicial power that he did not even include the judiciary in his philosophy of the separation and balance of powers. And though Adams had himself drafted the Massachusetts Declaration of Rights, he showed no interest in a federal Bill of Rights and, as President, signed and enforced those Alien and Sedition Acts that palpably violated the guarantees of the First and the Fifth Amendments.

"Author of the Declaration of Independence, the Virginia Statute of Religious Liberty, and Founder of the University of Virginia." This was the epitaph Jefferson wrote for himself. His passion for freedom in all its manifestations suffuses the *Notes on Virginia,* especially those chapters devoted to slavery, to education, and to religious freedom. Listen to his answer to the innocuous Query XVII: "The Different Religions received into that State?"

> The rights of conscience we never submitted, nor could we submit [to the coercion of laws]. We are answerable for them to our God. The legitimate powers of government extend to such acts only as are injurious to others. But it does me no injury for my neighbour to say there are twenty Gods, or no God. . . . Reason and free enquiry are the only effectual agents against error. . . . they will support the true religion, by bringing every false one to their tribunal. . . . It is error alone which needs the support of government. Truth can stand by itself. Subject opinion to coercion, whom will you make your inquisitors?

The great Statute of Religious Liberty bore out the promise of these observations, but with an additional touch of eloquence and of passion:

> Truth is great, and will prevail if left to herself, she is the proper and sufficient antagonist to error, and has nothing to fear from the conflict unless by human interposition disarmed of her natural weapons, free argument and debate, errors ceasing to be dangerous when it is permitted freely to contradict them.

Nothing that Adams wrote or said can match this; nothing, needless to say, that we have from the pen of Hamilton is its equal. They were, each in his way, devoted to freedom, but it was freedom from Britain, from awkward political regulations, from the tyranny of the majority. It was not freedom as Jefferson cherished it. Adams feared the tyranny of George III and of the military, but he feared even more the tyranny of majorities, and he has some claim to have introduced that pernicious concept into American political thought. He was not responsible for the illiberal attitude of the Massachusetts government toward dissenting sects, nor for its retention of many of the prerogatives of the Congregational establishment, but he was wholly unable to understand why the Quakers or the Baptists should object to those arrangements. Indeed, he tried to fob off on the distinguished Quaker, Israel Pemberton, the argument that "the laws of Massachusetts were the most mild and equitable establishment of religion that was known to the world"; and he dismissed the powerful Isaac Backus and his Baptist followers as troublemakers. With the passing of years John Adams' illiberalism grew upon him, and the climax was his endorsement of the narrow and vindictive Alien and Sedition laws of 1798. In their disregard for the guarantees of the Bill of Rights and their acceptance of arbitrary executive authority, these laws went well beyond anything that the British had tried to impose on the American colonials. Hamilton was critical of the measures, but on grounds of political expedience only; Adams did not even doubt their expedience.

On that one great issue of the paradox of freedom and slavery that glared ceaselessly upon the American people, Adams and Jefferson were in substantial agreement on philosophy but not on policy. Both detested slavery on moral grounds and deplored it on practical grounds. But Adams, so far as the present record reveals, was content to refrain from public (though not from private) judgment, to avoid overt attack on the institution, and to let history take its course. That was doubtless natural enough in one who had so little faith in the improvability of human nature and who was persuaded that all men were the creatures of passions and interests. Adams was a member of the committee to draft the Declaration of Independence, but made no effort to retain Jefferson's fiery denunciation of George III for perpetuating slavery and the slave trade. As Vice President, in 1796, he reprobated a petition from the Quakers denouncing slavery, because he felt that it could have "no other effect than to stir up sectional animosities." The Missouri crisis of 1819–20, which Jefferson called "a firebell in the night" that "filled him with terror," persuaded Adams that humanity dictated the adoption of "every measure of prudence for the extirpation of slavery from the United States," but that "the same humanity requires that we should not by any rash act or violent measures expose the lives and property of those who are so unfortunate as to be surrounded with these fellow creatures . . . without their own fault." While Adams' abhorrence of slavery was genuine and deep, it did not lead to action.

Jefferson saw the fatal consequences of slavery at firsthand, and it is not perhaps astonishing that his response should be bolder and more effective. In his *Notes on Virginia,* "The whole commerce between master and slave," he wrote, is

> ... the most unremitting despotism on the one part, and degrading submissions on the other. Our children see this and learn to imitate it. . . . The man must be a prodigy who can retain his manners and morals undepraved by such circumstances. And with what execration should the statesman be loaded who, permitting one half the citizens to trample on the rights of the other, transforms those into despots, and these into enemies, destroys the morals of the one part and the *amor partriae,* of the other. . . . I tremble for my country when I reflect that God is just; that his justice cannot sleep forever, that considering numbers, nature, and natural means only, a revolution of the wheel of fortune . . . is among possible events; that it may become probable by supernatural interference. The Almighty has no attribute which can take side with us in such a contest.

At the time he published his *Notes on Virginia,* no one had contributed more to the struggle against slavery in his own State, and perhaps in the nation, than Jefferson who was himself a slaveholder, and whose private relationship to slavery was marked by ambiguities almost inescapable in a southerner. As early as 1770, in an obscure local case that involved the freedom of a third-generation mulatto, Jefferson had pled that "we are all born free" and that slavery was contrary to nature; the court dismissed the argument out of hand. Time did not reconcile Jefferson to the paradox of a society proclaiming freedom and perpetuating slavery. Six years later he vainly tried to identify the political rights of Americans with the personal rights of Negro slaves, but the Continental Congress was not ready for such sentiments, and the passage, which meant so much to Jefferson, was omitted from the Declaration. That fall Jefferson returned to the Virginia Assembly. His proposed Revisal of the Laws of Virginia contained the bold proposal of the emancipation of all slaves born after 1800 with the added provision that those born slaves should be "brought up at public expense to tillage, arts or sciences." Two years later he introduced a bill putting an end to the importation of slaves—"which passed without opposition, and stopped the increase of the evil by importation, leaving to future efforts its final eradication." In 1784, he had proposed the total abolition of slavery in all the vast territory west of the Alleghenies—a proposal that lost by only one vote, but that was subsequently incorporated, for the territory north of the Ohio, into the Northwest Ordinance of 1787. Nor should we forget that it was President Jefferson who signed the bill which, at the earliest moment permitted under the Constitution, permanently outlawed the importation of slaves to the United States.

Yet Jefferson and Adams for all their differences of politics, philosophy, and temperament had much in common. Both were in a sense provincials, with their roots deep in the soil. Both were schooled in classical literature and history and drew their intellectual juices from that schooling. They had agitated and labored for independence and won it; together they had served their newly found country at home and abroad; each of them helped create a commonwealth; and each had served the new republic and General Washington. By the 1790s they had drifted apart—the Alien and Sedition Acts and the Kentucky and Virginia Resolutions dramatized how far apart—and there was a long hiatus in their association, a long suspension of their friendship. But "I have always loved Thomas Jefferson," Adams wrote in old age, and Jefferson responded with one of his most felicitous letters:

> A letter from you calls up recollections very dear to my heart. It carries me back to the times when, beset by difficulties and dangers, we were fellow laborers in the same cause. . . . Laboring always at the same oar, with some wave ever ahead threatening to overwhelm us, and yet passing harmless under our bark, we knew not how we rode through the storm with heart and hand, and made a happy port. . . .

And the ancient friendship was renewed, and with it the most fascinating correspondence in the history of American politics.

*   *   *

We know almost everything we need to know about the family, childhood and education of John Adams and Thomas Jefferson, but our knowledge of the youthful Hamilton is meager. He was born on the island of Nevis, in the British Leeward Islands, in 1755, perhaps in 1753. His mother, Rachel Faucette, the daughter of a French Huguenot physician on the island, had left her husband after five years of unhappy marriage, and attached herself to an indigent Scots merchant, James Hamilton: there is no record of marriage, but the family lived together until Rachel's death in 1768 when it appears that Hamilton abandoned his son who was thereafter dependent on the uncertain aid of relatives, and on his own resources. We know little about his boyhood, except that he worked for a merchant on the island of St. Croix, picked up a desultory education with a local Presbyterian dominie, and was early fired with an ambition that never deserted him—or left him in peace. In 1772 he found his way to America and the next year wound up in New York as a student in King's College where he quickly distinguished himself by his energy and address. A handsome, brilliant and ebullient young man, with a lively sense of his own worth, Hamilton quickly attracted the attention of men of power and influence. For all his admiration for the British constitution—an admiration that persisted to the end—Hamilton quickly joined his fortunes with the patriot cause, and as early as 1774 emerged as one of the leaders of that cause in the colony of New York. A series of pamphlets early displayed his talent for literature and for logic; his zeal for military action commended him to those who were preparing for possible war, and early in 1776 he received a commission as commander of an artillery company authorized by the Provincial Convention.

"Mine is an odd destiny," he wrote to one of his few intimates, Gouverneur Morris, in 1802:

> Perhaps no man in the United States has sacrificed more or done more for the present Constitution than myself; and contrary to all my anticipations of its fate, as you know from the very beginning, I am still laboring to prop the frail and worthless fabric. Yet I have the murmurs of its friends as well as the curses of its foes for my reward. What can I do better than withdraw from the scene? Every day proves to me more and more that this American world was not made for me.

He was, alas, right: his contribution to creating the American world was prodigious—who except Washington and Jefferson contributed more? —but the American world was not for him. He owed much to King's College and he was the most trusted of Washington's lieutenants; he fought before the redoubts at Yorktown; he married into the aristocratic Schuyler clan of New York, and glittered with the glamor of that family socially as he glittered with his own well-earned glamor professionally. He was the most effective of all those who labored to create a strong union out of what was a rope and sand, and he was successful. With Madison he provided, in the *Federalist Papers*, the best commentary on the art and science of politics in 18th-century literature. He was the guiding intelligence of Washington's administration, carrying through, almost singlehanded, a program of economic nationalism unmatched elsewhere in that century for boldness and effectiveness. He was the organizing genius —and the avenging genius, too—of the Federalist Party. He helped shape the American nation and government in his own image, but he lacked faith in that nation or in its government ("a frail and worthless fabric").

No, Hamilton did not really belong in America. He belonged in Britain —which he admired above all other nations: there he might have been another Camden, another Fox, another Pitt. He belonged in Europe— which had expelled his mother's people, and which would never have given an opportunity to a young man whom John Adams called "the bastard son of a Scots pedlar." What he really admired was not just the British Constitution but Enlightened Absolutism. He did not like Washington, but confessed that "he was an aegis very necessary to me"; might he not have been happier with a Frederick the Great, a Louis XV, a Gustavus III, a Joseph of Austria? His purpose was not to sweep away ancient injustices or archaic institutions, nor to promote the happiness of men; it was to strengthen the power and augment the wealth of the state.

Nationalism meant to Hamilton the dignity, the authority, the power, the wealth, of the state. To this end he was ready to sacrifice all other considerations. He was ready to wipe out state lines and consolidate the union; he was ready to enlarge the authority of the executive, for "energy" was the prime requisite of good government; he was ready to sacrifice the supposed interests of the people to the very real interests of the state. He had a genius for bringing order out of administrative chaos; he admired the military and believed in war as an instrument of national policy; he was prepared, like Karl Fredrick of tiny Baden, "to make his subjects into free, opulent, and law-abiding citizens whether they liked it or not." Born in the West Indies, Hamilton never understood that deep attachment Americans had first for their colony and then for their state. Trained in a counting-house and in the law, he had little feeling for the land or for farming, and no sympathy for that peculiarly Jeffersonian form of physiocracy, agrarian democracy. A parvenu who had pulled himself up by his bootstraps, and then married into the Hudson River aristocracy, Hamilton had no interest in the people and no patience with the romantic pretentions of democracy. He was prepared to reprobate the "spirit of persecution" against Loyalists, but at the same time to call for laws restraining "seditious and incendiary publications . . . if levelled against any officer of the United States," since it was more important to preserve "confidence in the officers of the general government" than in the principles of the Bill of Rights. He helped draft the American Constitution, but had no faith in its permanence; he helped create the Federalist Party, but never understood the unique character of American politics, and instead of following the Jeffersonian policy of merging all ingredients into a single political organization, he embraced the British practice of fomenting factionalism within his own party.

He was, in short, a man who had faith only in his own star and his own genius, and in the end it was his lack of faith in the American people that destroyed him. He did not believe in duelling and had no desire to fight Aaron Burr but accepted the challenge of Weehawken for the highest of motives—just such motives as might exalt a sovereign. He was sure that the American union was falling apart; he believed that he and he alone could save the American people from ruin; he was persuaded that if he were to command their support and allegiance, he must prove himself a man of courage and of honor. For this gross misjudgment of the American situation and the American character he paid with his life.

It is in the light of these traits of character that Hamilton's relations with Adams and Jefferson take on firmer contours. In his deep distrust of human nature, his detestation of democracy and his readiness to embrace a class society, his admiration for the British Constitution and his horror of the French Revolution, his advocacy of a strong executive, his keen sense of the economic basis of politics, he was closer to Adams than to the master of Monticello. Yet he neither liked nor trusted John Adams: nothing in his own experience disposed him to appreciate the homespun, the provincial, the garrulous, the pugnacious honesty, or the intractable Puritanism of the man who threatened to take *his* party away from him, and it was not merely differences on foreign policy—deep as they were—that persuaded Hamilton to risk destroying the Federalist to deny Adams the presidency in 1800.

To the end of his life, Hamilton's attitude toward Jefferson was ambivalent: he thought his great rival weak, devious, cunning—and dangerous; at the same time he displayed a grudging admiration for him. Certainly Hamilton found it easier to understand, even to work with, Jefferson than Adams. When he read the Kentucky and Virginia Resolutions, he burst out that this was the spirit which, unless crushed, would destroy the union; but when the crunch came, just two years later, it was to Jefferson that Hamilton threw his support, not to Aaron Burr. As he wrote James Bayard, "I admit that his [Jefferson's] politics are tinged with fanaticism; that he is too much in earnest with his democracy; that he has been a mischievous enemy to the principal measures of our past administration; that he is crafty and persevering in his objects; that he is not scrupulous about the means of success, nor very mindful of truth; that he is a contemptible hypocrite, but"—and this counterbalanced the whole damning indictment—"he is as likely as any man I know to temporize, and the probable result of such a temper is the preservation of systems which, being once established, could not be overturned without danger to the person who did it. To my mind a true estimate of Mr. Jefferson's character warrants the expectation of a temporizing, rather than a violent system." And then a postscript that spoke volumes: "Add to this that there is no reason to suppose him capable of being corrupted."

Yet this acceptance of Jefferson—an acceptance colored, we cannot help thinking, by the fact that socially Jefferson represented what Hamilton wanted to be—was nevertheless misleading. For Hamilton's philosophical differences with Jefferson were both more extensive and deeper than his differences with Adams. It is not fortuitous that there is no Jefferson-Hamilton correspondence to compare with that of Jefferson and Adams, or that Jefferson should name Bacon, Newton, and Locke, while Hamilton would nominate Julius Caesar, as "the greatest men the world had ever produced."

It is perhaps sufficient to list the philosophical and pragmatic differences that divided these two great founders of the American republic.

There was, first, an ineradicable difference of temperament that permeated both the characters and the philosophies of the two men. Jefferson was, by nature, sanguine, buoyant, hopeful, and indefatigable. "I am among those who think well of human nature," he wrote. "I believe, with Condorcet, that man's mind is perfectible to a degree of which we cannot as yet form any conception." Hamilton's view of human nature was, by contrast, dour, sceptical and misanthropic. He thought the idea of perfectibility one of the vagaries of a romantic imagination. He assumed the worst of men, and appealed—in this he was not unlike Adams—not to their better natures, but to their passions and interests: to him practical statesmanship was the successful manipulation of these interests.

But with Jefferson the concept of perfectibility was not a romantic fancy but rested on logical and scientific foundations. Here we have a second difference between the two men, and one that permeated their thinking and their conduct. Jefferson's conclusions were dictated by the teachings of science and Hamilton's by practical calculations: here Jefferson was one with the *philosophes* who provided the ideas of the Enlightenment, while Hamilton may be identified with the administrators who sometimes, but not often, put those ideas into effect. It was Professor William Small who made the greatest impression upon the youthful Jefferson; it was with the members of the American Philosophical Society —of which he was a long-time President—like David Rittenhouse, and Drs. Franklin and Rush that Jefferson was most at home; it was Old World scientists like Dr. Priestley, Helvetius, and Lavoisier he cultivated abroad. Nor did he himself fail to make important contributions to science, especially to the science of agriculture. When he tried to lure Priestley over to America "to drink the cup of knowledge with us" at the new university he was already planning, he listed as "first among the objects to be taught botany, chemistry, zoology, anatomy, surgery, medicine, natural philosophy, agriculture, mathematics, astronomy, geography." And at the close of his life he could still write with enthusiasm about "the most extraordinary of all books"—one that explained Dr. Flourand's experiments on the function of the nervous system.

But there was more to science than sheer intellectual delight. For if you accepted the almost universally endorsed Newtonian principle of natural philosophy—that those cosmic laws that governed the movement of the stars in the heavens and the tides in the oceans, the circulation of blood in the body, and the functioning of the eye—also governed the operations of politics, law, administration, the economy, and morality, then you could look forward with confidence to the achievement of ultimate perfection. Man had but to use reason to conform to these laws and thus solve all the problems that confronted him. In a more immediate way, science was of particular importance to Americans, since it taught them how to adapt to a new world—how to drain the swamps, clear the forests, accommodate the plow to its soil, the axe to its trees, the canoe to its streams; how to transfer old plants to new soil, and how to domesticate plants that grew wild; how to cope with the diseases of a strange environment; how to guard against the excessive cold of the North and the excessive heat of the South—all the things that helped create a society healthier, more long-lived, and more progressive than any heretofore known to history. These were the things that made for civilization, and that provided a scientific basis for Jeffersonian idealism and optimism. Thus science was an essential ingredient in that Jeffersonian philosophy that affirmed that the New World was an improvement on the Old, that America was opening a new page in history, and that in the abundance and the richness of land, the potentialities of science, and the rewards of general education there was a far more solid basis for faith in progress than a Turgot or a Condorcet had imagined.

All this was part, too, of an even deeper difference, one that went to the very heart of social philosophy. Hamilton was not interested in science, or the philosophy of progress or in such notions as happiness or popular education, because with him the center of gravity was the state. What did interest him was the power and wealth of the nation, the energy of government, the efficiency of administration. He did not go quite so far as to assert that men were made for government, but he was incapable of understanding the Jeffersonian principle that government is made for men—or that the Earth belongs to the living, not the dead and that each generation may therefore start afresh. In the crisis of 1799 he could call for the extension of federal jurisdiction to "libels, if levelled against any officer whatsoever of the United States," but Jefferson said—with some exaggeration—that given a choice between "a government without newspapers, or newspapers without government, I should not hesitate a moment to prefer the latter." Jefferson, in fact, did not care much for a *strong* government; what he cared deeply for was a *just* one.

> Still one thing more, fellow citizens—a wise and frugal Government which shall restrain men from injuring one another, shall leave them otherwise free to regulate their own pursuits of industry and improvement, and shall not take from the mouth of labor the bread it has earned.

These different philosophies of government were dramatized by the very different attitudes toward two governmental instrumentalities, one very old, one new: the military and judicial review. Though Jefferson had helped precipitate one war, he was a man of peace. He was all but ready to liquidate both the Army and Navy upon becoming President; later he persuaded Congress to impose an embargo on both imports and exports as a substitute for war—a plan that turned out calamitously in part, at least, because he thought too highly of human nature. Notwithstanding all the high offices he held during his long life, it is relevant to observe he was always *Mr.* Jefferson, but that Hamilton preferred to be *Colonel* Hamilton. Hamilton confessed early that he loved to hear the whistle of bullets; one sometimes thinks that he all but concocted the "Whiskey Rebellion" just so he could display the power of the new government and lead the militia against the rebels; when, at a later time, he imagined open resistance to the Alien and Sedition Acts from Virginia, he warned the Secretary of War that "whenever the government appears in arms, it ought to appear like a *Hercules,* and inspire respect by the display of strength."

As for that uniquely American instrument of strong government, judicial review, it was Hamilton who first perceived its potentialities and who first and most powerfully formulated its logic. Not even Chief Justice John Marshall would improve on the argument of No. 78 of the *Federalist Papers,* one of the great contributions to jurisprudence of our literature. Jefferson approved of an independent judiciary, but the notion that independence somehow implied superiority was alien to his political philosophy. Yet his opposition to judicial review—especially when exercised by the federal judiciary—was tardy, and flawed by personal considerations, for it was not really until Marshall made *Marbury v. Madison* a vehicle for a personal attack on President Jefferson and his Secretary of State, James Madison, that Jefferson awoke to its dangers. To this day it is not quite clear whether Jefferson rejected judicial review more because of its undemocratic or its partisan nature; more, that is, because it substituted the judgment of the one non-democratic branch of the government for those of the two democratic branches, or because Justices Marshall and Joseph Story used it so palpably as a weapon to preserve Federalist policies after they had been repudiated at the polls.

The most ostentatious contrast between Jefferson and Hamilton was in their attitude towards the economy. Neither was primarily an economist; both were statesmen who proposed to use the economy to achieve larger ends—with Jefferson social, with Hamilton political. Both sublimated the economic activities with which they were most familiar into moral principles. Jefferson was not converted to physiocracy by French thinkers: it was because he was himself a farmer who had lived all his life in the agreeable society of farmers and planters, that he found so much to commend in physiocracy. Hamilton was not attracted to mercantilism by studying the classics of these economic doctrines; rather he gravitated to mercantilism because it best fitted his political preconceptions.

The difference went deep and its consequences were far-reaching. Jefferson wanted to make sure that the new United States would remain an agrarian democracy into the most distant future. "Those who labor in the earth," he wrote in the *Notes on Virginia*

> are the chosen people of God, if ever He had a chosen people, whose breasts he has made His peculiar deposit for substantial and genuine virtue. . . . Generally speaking the proportion which the aggregate of the other classes of citizens bears in any State to that of its husbandmen,

is the proportion of its unsound to its healthy parts.... While we have land to labor, then, let us never wish to see our citizens occupied at a workbench, or twirling a distaff.... For our general operations of manufacture, let our workshops remain in Europe.

This commitment to agriculture led Jefferson to look ever westward for the future of the Republic; persuaded him to forego his constitutional scruples and acquire Louisiana; strengthened his determination to acquire New Orleans and West Florida as essential for the control of the Mississippi and the prosperity of the West; and justified a policy of geographical isolation. For Jefferson shared with most physiocrats the conviction that the growth of commerce and trade would inevitably lead to the acquisition of colonies and of an empire, to a great military organism which would devour the substance of the people or subvert their government. In short what Jefferson feared was the Europeanization of America through mercantilism.

Unlike the French physiocrats, however, Jefferson was able to do something about it. Almost alone of the great agrarians of that age, he stood not in the shadow of power but at its center. As a member of the Virginia Assembly, he took the lead in abolishing those remnants of feudalism—primogeniture and entail, and his program of disestablishment of the church carried with it the ultimate forfeiture of its glebe lands. His proposal to grant 50 acres to every adult male who was landless was rejected, but while it failed in Virginia, it succeeded on a larger theater, for the acquisition of Louisiana doubled the agricultural domain of the nation and—together with those enlightened ordinances for the Northwest that Jefferson helped write—guaranteed a flourishing agrarian republic in the West. He tried to prohibit slavery throughout that entire West; he succeeded only in forbidding it in the territory north of the Ohio River—a great boon, that, to the ideal of agrarian democracy.

Hamilton envisioned an economy not unlike that of most Old World nations, one in which agriculture, manufactures, commerce, banking worked together to assure self-sufficiency, encourage immigration, stimulate the growth of cities, assure financial solvency, enhance the national wealth, and strengthen the national government by making it increasingly the arbiter of the economy and the guardian of major economic interests. Thus the United States would be able to hold her own with other nations, strong enough to bargain on terms of equality with the great powers of the Old World. Thus she could protect her interests against those threats history taught were inevitable. To achieve all this, Hamilton recommended creation of a national bank; assumption of state debts in order to attract the support of security holders to the central government; and encouragement of manufactures by tariffs, bounties and monopolies. To the Jeffersonians this program conjured up the spectre of re-creating at home conditions long familiar abroad—the growth of great cities with all their poverty and misery and vice; the emergence of a capitalist class that would eventuate into a class society; the struggle for markets that would encourage the growth of the military; the penetration of the central authority into every nook and cranny of the economy. There were social implications, too, in Hamilton's argument that in his system "the farmer might experience a new source of profit and support from the increased industry of his wife and daughters," and that it would make certain that "in general women and children are rendered more useful, and the latter more early useful, by manufacturing establishments, than they would otherwise be." It is of course misleading to read back into the 18th century modern attitudes toward child labor, but it is not misleading to recognize that the successful, implementation of the Hamiltonian program entailed a shift in the center of gravity from countryside to city, and from local to central political controls.

Jeffersonian agrarianism and Hamiltonian mercantilism involved different concepts of life and of society. Jefferson's was romantic—by implication anyway—individualistic, simple, equalitarian, close to nature and to all that nature intended for a virtuous and enlightened people. Hamilton conjured up a shift from farming to industry, from rural to urban, from isolation to involvement, from a classless to a class society, from a mild and passive government to one that would inevitably aggrandize power over society and economy alike. Clearly Jefferson was most in touch with reality in the early years of the Republic. But it turned out that it was Hamilton who anticipated the future, and by anticipating it hastened its approach. Clearly Jefferson presided over the birth of the Republic; Hamilton presides over its maturity. But do not feel sorry for John Adams. He presides over the most famous family in American history, and to a member of a generation that thought its obligation to posterity the most solemn of all obligations, that is sufficient glory.

6

The Collapse of the
One-Hoss Shay

TIMOTHY DWIGHT
CHARLES G. FINNEY
WILLIAM E. CHANNING

by Milton Cantor
University of Massachusetts, Amherst

Between the Revolutionary years and the industrial take off of the mid-19th century, great and fundamental changes occurred in American society. Outwardly, the old colonial institutions of family, church, political faction, social class seemed stable enough, but in reality all of them were gradually coming apart at the seams. Their unravelling, more-over, paralleled that of the rural community itself; and, in combination, had the effect of freeing men from the constraints of traditional social values. Small wonder that many of the religious orthodox found the Revolution fatal to the old morality.

Meanwhile, to turn to politics, the Federalists dominated the nation's political life in the 1790s. They distrusted the ordinary man and affirmed the wisdom of a ruling elite—unlike Jefferson's rising Republicans, with their confidence in public opinion and popular rule. These Federalists had recoiled from the execution of the French King, the subsequent Terror, and the seeming destruction of religion, even if it were a Catholic faith. Jacobinism came to seem not merely anti-Catholic, but anti-clerical and even anti-Christian as well. Voltaire and the *philosophes*, so it seemed, had let loose doctrines that any breeze might sweep across the seas and infect America's increasingly fragile religious and political communities. To a mounting number of both Federalists and Congregationalists it seemed

111

that the respectable people, those of property and standing, might ultimately suffer the fate of France's aristocracy. Anti-Jacobinism, then, became a highly attractive ideology for many Americans. More than ever before, in the generally prosperous 1790s, the possibility of mob uprising and social revolution lurked as the spectre at the feast.

Believing in the rule of moral man, as they of course defined him, the Federalists evoked a basic and deeply embedded Protestant piety and inevitably lured New England's Congregational clergy into their camp. Many of this clergy had been prominent in resisting English tyranny from mid-century onward, and the American revolution had simply enhanced their good name. They had been, for instance, the immediate beneficiaries when New England Anglicans, owing to their Toryism, were cast in the villain role during the War of Independence. But Congregationalism, the first religion of New England, began to show signs of slippage. Its growth was the slowest of any denomination in Massachusetts during the 1780s and 1790s. Nor did ethnic and population changes help it—as Irish Catholic migrants began to settle in the growing seaport towns. A swarming and largely foreign working class, mostly Irish and "papist," new working class organizations, and riotous urban conditions called for immediate restraints—by the "strong arm of the law," declared Lyman Beecher, the prominent Congregational minister.

A host of votaries shared such ministerial apprehensions about the growth of new denominations; the more permissive ways of the world; the seeming erosion of the old community and the concomitant rise of commercial centers that encouraged seemingly un-Christian life styles; the decline of morals—the drunkenness, vice, Sabbath-breaking; the influx of new Irish immigrants who quickly identified with the "licentious" Republican Party.

The old "Congregational way" was also plagued by mounting doctrinal problems, with New England's urban ministry beginning to rework the traditional Calvinism. Influenced by Enlightenment currents, this ministry was increasingly drawn toward belief in a benevolent Providence. By 1825, to jump ahead momentarily, schism would come to what had been *the* established church of the northeast—in the form of Unitarianism. Itself a product of growing urbanity, enlightenment and self-confidence, Unitarianism gained adherents among the wealthy and educated of New England's seaport cities—and won over most of the faculty and students at Harvard College. Defectors from orthodoxy were drawn to the newest of denominations by its Arminianism, which emphasized human agency and human will rather than divine will and guidance; by its Arianism, the ancient heresy that questioned the doctrine of the Trinity; or by its overtone of 18th-century Christian rationalism. Calvinist Congregationalism, then, would fragment after 1800, with followers of Reverend Samuel Hopkins, who were strongest in central and southern Massachusetts, joining orthodox Calvinists in the Berkshires against the rising menace of religious liberalism in the coastal counties.

* * *

Among the most alarmed of New England's Congregationalists was the Reverend Timothy Dwight, President of Yale College (1795–1815). Dwight was convinced that the United States was being subverted by an international conspiracy, the Bavarian Illuminati—"those enemies of Christ"—and by the infidelity and immorality of Revolutionary France. The latter was "a kind of suburb of perdition . . . ," he warned. "Her embrace is death." He asked a Fourth of July audience in 1798: "Shall we, my brethren, become partakers in these sins? Shall we introduce them into our government, our schools, our families? Shall our sons become disciples of Voltaire and the dragoons of Marat, or our daughters the concubines of the Illuminati?"

Timothy Dwight, then 40 years old and possibly Connecticut's most respected citizen, was born in 1752. For over a century before, the family fortunes had been interwoven with the history of Massachusetts. On his father's side, he came from five generations of farmers, yeomen, and public servants—men who tilled the soil, served the community, sturdily believed in the God of John Calvin. His maternal line also had impressive Congregational credentials. Dwight's brown-eyed, dark-haired mother was the third daughter of no less than Jonathan Edwards. It was in Edwards' Northampton, a town nestled in the Connecticut Valley, that Timothy grew up, the first of a brood of 13 children.

Young Timothy had a bookish cast of mind. He was early taught to love God, to walk strictly in the narrow way of the Ten Commandments, to be acutely aware of the differences between right and wrong, to know his own depravity. At the age of six, this proper grandson of the great Edwards had already learned that good conduct was unavailing, that he was predestined, that his fate was in the hands of a righteous, inscrutable, justly angry God. And yet, as his deeply reverent mother taught, he must model his conduct on that of Jesus.

Timothy's formal education also began at six—down the road at a local grammar school. Gradually he developed a thirst for knowledge that would never be satisfied. His world slowly expanded. He studied everything that came his way, especially Latin, and made astonishing progress. He ransacked his father's library, devoured histories of Greece and England, and wrestled with accounts of early New England settlements and the first Indian wars. Outgrowing Northampton's limited educational facilities, which had been augmented by his mother's tutoring, the 12-year old was shipped off to Middleton, Connecticut, where he would be prepared for college under the supervision of the town's minister. Yale accepted him in 1765, at age 13. While enjoying card playing and under-graduate pranks, Timothy continued to read voraciously. He graduated in 1769, remained at Yale for graduate studies, and supported himself by teaching grammar school, a common practice for young men fresh from college.

In 1771, Timothy Dwight became a tutor at his Alma Mater, remaining at this post for six years. With two other tutors, he championed the cause of belles lettres and provoked an intellectual ferment unprecedented in the life of the little provincial college. In addition to teaching Yale's rough country boys, he labored over a gigantic epic, "The Conquest of Canaan," which was typical of the mock-heroic poems of that day. Working long hours by candlelight, he subjected his eyes to strains from which they never fully recovered. Indeed, he was forced to rest them by taking a moratorium from books.

The roar of cannon would further lengthen his exile from the library. Called to fight in the Revolutionary conflict, Dwight's period of army service was a short one. It included a leave to deliver the 1776 "Valedic-tory Address" to Yale's graduates. A model of that stirring and optimistic nationalism then drenching American letters, the address prophesied that the empire of America would be the most glorious of all, the last and the brightest of time, the final kingdom, God's glorious plan fulfilled. By 1777, with the death of John Dwight, his soldiering came to an end. He received a license to preach, becoming army chaplain to General Samuel Parson's Connecticut brigade. He found time for another nation-alist paean, "Columbia, Columbia, to glory arise," which cheered the soldier audience who heard it. Finally putting the army forever behind him, he moved into the old Northampton homestead with his wife and small child.

Timothy Dwight had become the main support for a large family of younger brothers and sisters. He managed two large farms, but still had energy enough to teach school and continue his studies in literature and philosophy. Moreover, the young minister-schoolmaster-farmer was elected Northampton's representative in the State legislature in 1781. But it was a short tour of duty, for he received a call to the Congregational ministry at Greenfield Hill in Connecticut and put the dust of North-ampton behind him.

By the mid-1790s, Dwight had acquired a national reputation. Though minister of a small rural church, he was celebrated for his preaching, poetry, political satires, and liberal educational policies. His sermons, often composed while hoeing in the garden, usually were delivered ex-temporaneously, owing in part to his congenitally feeble eyesight. They were renowned for their broad and searching rhythms, their eloquence and power, and the rich, mellow voice of the preacher.

Loyalty to Yale as well as unquestioned ability made Dwight an obvious candidate for the school's presidency when Ezra Stiles died in May 1795. Heeding "an important call of Divine Providence," Dwight was inaugurated in September 1795, a date that marked a new era in Yale's history.

At Greenfield, and later at Yale, Timothy Dwight was convinced that his country was in danger. He had long recognized that "benevolence toward man" was a Christian virtue having the highest priority. And such charitable impulses, that sense of noblesse oblige axiomatic of Puritanism, were in the hands of the wise and good—to be directed toward the community itself, especially toward one's social inferiors. Dwight continually practiced moral and social stewardship, and believed that he was thereby doing God's great work. It follows that he would support foreign missions for Africans, tract societies—so popular in Jacksonian society—and all the products of the Christian tradition. He encouraged a number of charitable and missionary agencies—and they in turn absorbed some of the religious energies catalyzed by revivalism and by an ethic of benevolence. Dwight himself helped establish the Missionary Society of Connecticut; he was a founder of the American Home Missionary Society; and he was a committed member of the American Board of Commissioners of Foreign Missions. He assisted the campaigns for prison reform and poor relief; indeed, he helped any agency working toward the alleviation of human distress. So he also endorsed a school for young Negro girls, commending three socially prominent New Haven ladies who would teach them how to read; he even helped raise a "considerable fund" for the school.

Education and religion were Timothy Dwight's lifelong concerns. Both were essential, he believed, to the dissemination of knowledge and piety, qualities absolutely necessary to the community that wished to enjoy divine favor. "Without churches," he declared, "men will be vicious of course; without churches they will be ignorant." Such sentiments suggest the same fear of social change, the same dread of spiritual contamination, the same belief in orthodoxy so important to his Puritan ancestors. And it was important, too, to Connecticut's orthodox, the Standing Order as it was appropriately called, that mix of the Congregational elect and solid Federalists. They would stand athwart the terror of the French Revolution, now horridly stalking New England's shores. And they would combat the "unAmerican" party of Jefferson that was then threatening national security, and frustrate the democratic masses—tradesmen, mechanics, small farmers, mostly "infidels"—already clamoring for greater political power in Connecticut and the nation.

Dwight's views recalled those early Puritans who had steeled their hearts by the fires of faith, those who had sought order, social stability, the discipline of the senses, and the maintenance of the cohesive community. Much like the Puritan fathers, he assumed that government was ordained by God and must dispense the divine law. Everything he had been taught argued that religion alone could guarantee that high level of public morals essential to good government. Everything that he saw about him, in the four frenetic post-Revolutionary decades, suggested the breakdown of the old religious life. He would, it followed, lead the host of the righteous against Arminianism, Arianism, Catholicism, and French philosophy. He would champion the moral renovation of society through sumptuary legislation and a quiet revivalism. Recalling Yale's undergraduates to the original mission of Connecticut's settlers, he proclaimed: "This land was settled by Christians. God brought his little flock hither; and placed it in this wilderness, for the great purpose of establishing permanently the church of Christ in these vast regions of idolatry and sin, and commencing here the glorious work of salvation. This great continent is soon to be filled with the praise, the piety, of the Millennium."

Dwight would use revivalism as a practical weapon in the crusade to restore religious orthodoxy. Moreover, he subscribed to most of the tenets of the New Divinity men who had revised and liberalized Calvinism. He even rejected the Half-Way Covenant by which persons who could make no claim to a conscious regenerate experience were admitted into the church and their children were allowed to take the baptismal rite. But more adroit than the followers of Edwards, he was willing to compromise, and his moderation helped overcome objections to his appointment at Greenfield Hill and to the Yale presidency. Nevertheless, he worked successfully toward the gradual elimination of the Half-Way Covenant in Connecticut's Congregational churches.

In addition, Dwight held to nearly the entire battery of Biblical truths. He accepted the story of the Flood and believed in the existence of Adam and Eve. But he refused to endorse the orthodox claim that Adam's children carried his sin. They had Adam's propensity to sin, to be sure, but did not bear his depravity or his guilt.

Dwight was closer to his grandfather and to Calvinist orthodoxy on the question of future rewards and punishments. He drew a vivid picture of the horrors of Hell and the bliss of heaven. He knew, furthermore, that straight was the way and narrow the gate, and repentence and regeneration in earthly life was necessary before entry into the celestial city; the unregenerate on earth would not be rewarded with heaven. But unlike the implicitly man-centered theology of revivalism, Dwight was convinced, at least in his early ministerial years, that only God could transform the sinful nature of man by His benevolence.

At the outset, then, Dwight was much like his fellow Yale man, the Reverend Samuel Hopkins of Newport, Rhode Island. But Hopkins was more a theologian than Dwight, now the recognized leader of the

New Divinity clergy. Dwight was relatively unconcerned with speculative thought per se. His mind was more receptive than creative. He was practical and commonsensical, a man with a job to get done. Hopkins, much more unbending, and much like Jonathan Edwards, insisted upon God's absolute sovereignty and man's utter moral powerlessness when it came to faith and repentence. So at the outset did Dwight, but he increasingly moved away from this antinomian cult of helplessness. Quite understandably, he emphasized Bible reading, church attendance, and meditation, and connected them with man's ultimate hope for conversion. Man, Dwight insisted, must become aware and be convinced of his sinful state. He must pray to God and ask forgiveness, since only He could deliver man from sin and eternal punishment.

Dwight, therefore, preached the sovereignty of God but would enlarge man's moral and intellectual agency. Beyond what his grandfather might affirm, predestination was a diminished thing: man had the ability and the absolute obligation to "make great effort." Dwight's emphasis on the practical carried him toward a "system of duties"—the duties of a Christian life on Earth—which was enmeshed in a utilitarian notion of happiness far removed from Edwards' insistence upon depravity and exclusive dependence upon God.

It is ironic, then, that Dwight also fought a lifelong battle to revive his grandfather's faith, to halt the lamentable decline of morals, to save the Standing Order, to revitalize Congregationalism in New England. And the irony is embedded in the implications of revivalism, which assumed that human nature was not inherently depraved. Jonathan Edwards' theological system had not only claimed man was sinful by nature, but that any attempt by an unconverted heart to seek God's grace was a defiance of His will. It is, in fact, almost impossible to combine Edwardsean theology—which imputed inability to believers, which literally claimed that the unconverted could not even pray properly, which inspired a cult of passive obedience, which called for the sheer surrender of man to his Creator—with the contrary assumptions of revivalists that every person can help himself. Dwight nearly pulled off the impossible. In an age that had clearly lost much of its moral earnestness and inner convictions, he tried to finesse the issue in the interest of bringing people into a conversion experience—of reawakening the sense of sin, of turning men's hearts again toward God.

Again like his grandfather, Dwight was goaded by contemporary indifference to religious faith in New England, by the prevalence of irreligion and immorality. He had, after all, a fiercely proprietary interest in the region and it compelled him to use revivals as a means of restoring religious convictions and worship. So in 1806, he became president of the Connecticut Religious Tract Society, which had as its sole objective "the promotion of evangelical religion." And he would be the single most important early leader of Connecticut's Second Awakening. He knew, of course, that the First Awakening, which Jonathan Edwards had led in New England, was marked by egregious emotional excesses, an "enthusiasm," and hoped to avoid it. In any case, he initiated a quiet revival in 1801. It was, he believed, a mighty weapon in the ceaseless struggle against infidelity.

Previously, in 1795, infidelity at Yale had been Dwight's overriding concern. When he took over the reins, Yale was in his estimation a "ruined college." One contemporary found it in "a most ungodly state"; another observed a dreadful "state of disorder, impiety, & wickedness." Probably little had changed since Dwight studied there, beyond the deepening fears of Connecticut's Standing Order. Yale certainly seemed the same physically: four motley buildings set on the commons, along with a few shade trees, a nearby barbershop, some taverns, a jail, and a few boarding houses. But Dwight believed things had changed. For one thing, undergraduates seemed to be indulging excessively in pranks, profanity, petty thefts, intemperance and gambling, and one and all had to be combatted. However, "Pope" Dwight, as Connecticut's Republicans had begun to call him, gave higher priority to other transgressions; namely, denial of the Scripture, desecration of the Sabbath, propagation of heresy.

Dwight was determined to recapture this Congregational bastion. Yale did indeed begin to hum under his leadership and it would be transformed over the next two decades. Dwight served as both President and professor of divinity. He introduced new texts, new subjects, new methods, new professorships—most significantly in chemistry, a field then in its infancy. Owing to his skilled maneuvering, new lands were purchased for new buildings; the library holdings were doubled; the College's endowment increased; medical and divinity schools had their start; and good relations were established with the State legislature.

Equally important in Dwight's scheme of things was his successful campaign against dwindling chapel attendance, the appeal of the Enlightenment, the popularity of Tom Paine and Ethan Allen whose writings the farm boys devoured, especially when religion, priestcraft, and the Genesis version of creation were being arraigned. The new President struck hard and uncompromising blows at such heretical thoughts in lectures on "evidences of Divine Revelation." Furthermore, his campaign for moral purification eventually would have its rewards. The handsome and magisterial Dwight, with his broad-brimmed beaver hat and imposing presence, commanded respect. Some students, like Lyman Beecher, even loved him. And the President helped his own cause by building bridges to them. He eliminated fines for infractions of College rules, substituting private admonitions and personal suasion. Eventually, discipline was such that fines were unnecessary. Some students, possibly only a handful, admired his capacity to broaden their education and intellectual horizons even while restoring orthodoxy. And restore orthodoxy he did—by encouraging free and open discussion of religious doubts, inviting students into his house, especially those concerned with their salvation, and debating undergraduates on the truth of the Bible versus the agnosticism of Tom Paine and English rationalists.

Rare was the occasion when Dwight failed to proclaim the meaning and beauty of the Bible. In a four-year cycle of discourses on Christianity, he explored its nature and defended it against assaults from those who despise God and know "a priori that there is nothing beyond the grave." Dwight's sonorous and extemporaneous sermons avoided jargon as well as complex theological issues. Gradually, he brought Yale's rowdies and sceptics back to the "service of God." By 1797, in a period of rising revivalism in Connecticut, Dwight sponsored the Moral Society, which students willingly joined and which stimulated religious debate on campus. In 1801 Yale experienced another mild Awakening and in 1812, during still one more revival, Dwight converted nearly a hundred boys.

For Dwight, as we have seen, religious revivalism and political orthodoxy were inextricably enmeshed, with religious faith yoked to social stability, and Federalism, the politics of the Godly. He had long felt this way. The collapse of stable government during and directly after the American Revolution had greatly troubled him. So had the subsequent currency depreciation which contributed, he felt, to social instability. Understandably, he had turned to the cause of strong central government. His sermons frequently combined Federalist panic toward France and its Jeffersonian followers with an apocalyptic vision presented in millennarian rhetoric. Dwight's July 4, 1798, address, "The Duty of Americans at the Present Crisis," was delivered during the cold war with France. It called the roll of fallen republics and proclaimed the New World a unique refuge of pure religion. Three years later Dwight would become a prominent political satirist in the service of God and Federalism.

By now Dwight's belligerent message was familiar throughout New England and beyond it. Any preacher who predicted that Republican victory would mean the deflowering of Connecticut females by Jeffersonian democrats was bound to win the attention of pious Federalists. The latter had long been convinced that the Republicans were morally depraved and Jefferson's 1800 victory was a galvanic shock to those who had made Jacobinism, the Illuminati, and conspiracy theories household words. Now they looked to Dwight for further guidance and he was not timid about giving it. Indeed, he was happy to declaim against French and Jeffersonian infidelity and subversion from the rooftops of New

Haven. For over two decades he would battle in the cause of true religion, good morals, and sound government—seeking to save Yale College, the State of Connecticut, and the New England he loved.

*   *   *

Perhaps the most prominent evangelist of the Second Awakening was Charles Grandison Finney. Born a Connecticut Yankee in 1792, Finney was the son of a Revolutionary army veteran and an heir of 17th-century Puritanism. Following the westward trail of many earlier New Englanders, his parents took their two-year-old son to Kirkland in the central part of New York State—into what was then part of the Burned-Over District, so called because of the innumerable religious fires that had already scorched it. Young Charles Finney attended the common schools of the frontier that was Oneida County and then, in 1812, he returned to his birthplace in Warren, Connecticut, for a high school education. For the first time he encountered formal religious teaching, which he largely ignored. Rather than seeking to enroll at Yale, he chose to go instead to New Jersey where he taught school for two years. He contemplated establishing a private school in the South, but nothing came of it. With no other prospects in view, Finney, now a 25-year-old man, decided to study law. Returning to Adams, New York, he easily read through some dusty law books in a local attorney's office, joined the bar, and settled down to practice.

Six feet two, physically impressive, and in robust health, Charles Finney seemed content with life. He was rightly popular with his peers; he played the cello, loved Shakespeare, sang solos in the church choir, enjoyed horseback riding, and excelled as a marksman. George Gale, the energetic young Presbyterian minister of Adams did not believe the sinful Finney would ever be converted but worked on him nonetheless. And then, in October 1812, Charles Finney had a conversion experience; he was then nearly 29 years old. Sitting in his law office, he had a vision of confronting Christ and received, as he described it, "a mighty baptism of the Holy Ghost." So overwhelming were successive waves of feeling that he cried out: "Lord, I cannot bear any more; I shall die if these [feelings] continue." His violent conversion also included a vision of Christ on the main street of Adams as well as an encounter with the Lord in the nearby woods where, as he recounted it, "I could feel the impression, like a wave of electricity going through and through me."

Out of this sudden and spectacular mystical experience came Charles Finney's single-minded determination to enlist in Christ's army and to preach his gospel; his lucrative law practice was forgotten. During the course of his conversion, Finney realized that salvation was complete only when he consented to give up his sins and accept Christ. There was no need to wait for God's regenerative power to enter him; no need for probationary good works. It was his "decision" to make—and he did so. In lawyer's language, he stated, "I have a retainer from the Lord Jesus Christ to plead his cause, and," he told a client, "I cannot plead yours."

Finney next brought Adams' townsfolk together in a meeting house and gave them no rest until all but one were converted. After a week without food and sleep, his feelings were as inflamed as ever. In this giddy state of mind he met Reverend Gale at the church door, and an "ineffable" light flooded his soul and he found himself sobbing hysterically. But this personal state of elevation was a passing phase, and his real mission began to take shape: he would forge an evangelical Christianity, first locally, in Adams, Evans Mills, Antwerp, and Gouverneur, and then in the State's larger cities. And this handsome, sandy-haired preacher with burning convictions would have phenomenal success by appealing to the practical and common sense tastes of the area's shopkeepers and farmers.

Finney did not graduate from a major seminary or pass through a university theology course and thereafter few revivalists would go this route. He had been urged to enroll at Princeton, where Gale had been trained and the local Presbytery even offered to pay his expenses. But Finney refused: "I plainly told them that I would not put myself under such an influence as they had been under; that I was confident that they had been wrongly educated, and they were not ministers that met my ideal of what a minister of Christ should be." A superbly contemptuous statement, it was a straw in the wind. In 1823, with understandable reluctance, the Saint Lawrence Presbyterian licensing board examined and ordained him. The following year, the Female Missionary Society of the Western District of New York commissioned this imposing man with the hypnotic blue eyes to thunder the Word.

From the beginning, Finney relied upon the Bible and worked toward a religious faith based on scriptural literalism. For him, the most important religious agency was the revival and it had been perfectly designed, as he understood it, to convince the unconverted of their sinfulness, thereby beginning the process of repentence and conversion. A revival, he insisted, must dwell "on that class of truths, which hold up man's ability, and obligation, and responsibility. This was the only class of truths that would bring sinners to submission." And by "submission," he meant conversion, which had three stages: conviction, repentence, reformation. Finney rejected Reverend Gale's contention that salvation was for the elect. Not so, the novitiate declared, it was for all men. His gospel, then, was close to that of Dwight, who would liberalize the old Calvinist view of God's arbitrary will and emphasize His transcendant goodness.

Revivalism was to split Presbyterian ranks, with the absolutist Old

Light ministry eventually bringing charges against many New School revivalist preachers. Finney seemingly didn't care. He went ahead as if there were no stopping him. For his part, the theological critics could literally go to Hell; his successes in conversion, his results, were what counted and they validated his methods. This rebuttal was more than sublimely defiant; it said something about Finney's pragmatic criterion, indeed, his opportunism. He firmly believed that conditions demanded a new religious emphasis, even if at a cost of abandoning strict Calvinism and doctrinal distinctions.

As a rampaging frontier revivalist, Charles Finney broke all the rules. In a score of sermons, he emphasized human agency in the work of an individual's redemption; he maintained that God was benevolent and reasonable; he affirmed man's ability to know God. Open your souls to the Lord, he exhorted audiences: the Holy Ghost did not miraculously enter a man and alter his debased condition. Agreeing with the now deceased Yale President, Finney believed that man could not save himself, that God alone knew who He had willed to salvation. But salvation, Finney thundered in 1834, "is the work of man. It is something for man to do. . . . It is a man's duty. It is not a miracle, or dependent on a miracle in any sense." Man could save himself by an effort of will, Finney was fond of asserting: "The agency is the sinner himself. . . . The conversion of a sinner consists in his obeying the truth. It is therefore impossible it should take place without his agency. . . ." Man, by virtue of his conscience and of "all things that conduce to enlightening the mind, chooses God's way and at that very moment [conversion] God accepts him and he is born into the Kingdom [regeneration]."

Finney ranged across New York State at a time when the Erie Canal was bringing urbanization and a new wealth into the region. And in the process the upstate farmers and townsfolk saw their isolation end, their communities fragmenting, their verities being corrupted by new and alien ideas. Nostalgia for their lost world and fear of the new made the old inhabitants grist for every revivalist who came down the sawdust trail. Finney comforted them, fueling a religious enthusiasm that swept across the Burned-Over District like wildfire. He expressed perfectly ante-bellum moralizing theology and he made clear to his listeners the relation between man as a moral agent and God as his moral governor.

Finney's message, delivered in plain and powerful rhetoric, was uncomplicated. Vice was sin, not merely bad intention, he explained to penitent and unrepentent alike. And sinners would suffer the fires of hell. He portrayed its horrors with enormous energy and imaginative invective: the fiery lake filled with burning wretches moaning and screaming through eternity. Unquestionably he believed in this vivid picture and so did his hearers. There was indeed a personal devil as well as a personal God. Such a message was presented without erudite discourse or ornamentation or equivocation. Finney could not abide the timid and moderate preacher. He rejected the orthodox view that the sinner could not repent. Repudiating "cannot-ism," he deplored the jingle: "You can and you can't; you will and you won't; you're damned if you do and damned if you don't."

From the outset, the manipulative preaching of this back-country amateur created a sensation, the more so because of his innovations. He was willing to scrap traditional worship in order to get across his Arminianized Calvinism; he spoke at outdoor meetings, barns, and schoolhouses; he departed from the regularly scheduled times for religious services; he made extensive use of the "protracted meeting," which went day and night for a week or more; he introduced the "anxious bench," to which came the most promising potential converts, who were culled from the mass of parishioners, to subject themselves to special exhortation and prayer, he encouraged women to pray and to testify in meeting, though St. Paul had admonished their silence in the churches; and he openly encouraged the "fallings" and "weepings"—those well-known physical manifestations of revivalism—though avoiding incitement to bodily convulsions such as "jerking," "rolling," "jumping." Nonetheless, some of these "exercises" were present at his gatherings, especially in the early phases of his work. Small wonder, when he believed that "mankind will not wake until they are excited." And Finney would excite men. He was perhaps the most American of all contemporary preachers, and his practical, nonsectarian, implicitly anti-Calvinist message inevitably stirred things up. It struck an immediate responsive chord.

Wherever Finney went, men and women crowded around the pulpit, begged for mercy, pleaded with him to stop, reacted with hysteria. "If I had a sword in my hand," he contentedly exclaimed, "I could not have cut them down as fast as they fell." After successful revivals in Rome, Utica, and Auburn, New York, Finney seemed like the wave of the future. He was emerging from the back country as a power to be reckoned with. This tall, long-armed preacher could gesticulate; he could bully—and triumphantly announce that "he beheld the angels of God sealing their eternal doom"; he could thunder; he could literally frighten people into submission. But Finney could also persuade with a lawyer-like brief. Nonetheless, it was his whirling arms, his flailing of unbelievers, his passion that worried both conservatives and urban revivalist preachers. The Unitarian Henry Ware, for example, watched disgustedly Finney's "abject groanings, his writhing of his body." Actually, Finney's emotionalism became more muted as he neared New England, and he began to caution himself against loud praying and bench pounding. But conservatives were not persuaded. The man was a menace. They objected to his emphasis upon "free and full salvation," worried over the connection between revivalism and social reform, were affronted by handbills that proclaimed his coming "by command of the King of Kings," and of course they opposed his methods.

The Reverend Lyman Beecher, himself an acknowledged revivalist leader, was aghast. Finney, emerging from western obscurity, was now standing on the border of New England. "I know your plan," Beecher declared, "and you know I do. You mean to come into Connecticut, and carry a streak of fire to Boston. But if you attempt it, as the Lord liveth, I'll meet you at the State line, and call out all the artillery-men, and fight every inch of the way to Boston, and I'll fight you there." So frightened were Beecher and other conservative clergy that they held a meeting at New Lebanan, New York, on July 18–27, but Finney decisively bested them in debate. He was not to be curbed. Indeed he was remorseless, "made for action" as Beecher reported, and his only pausing was for marriage to Lydia Andrews in October 1824. Crossing over from New York State, he assaulted—and there is no other word for it—Wilmington; Lancaster, Philadelphia, where he spoke nightly for a year; Rochester, for three months of meetings attended, among others, by lawyers, bankers, judges; New York City; and, finally, Boston. Beecher couldn't fend him off—not when earlier meetings in the East failed to produce the legendary "outbursts." As a consequence, a number of deacons and ministers sought to have him speak. Beecher himself surrendered—even to the point of expressly inviting Finney into his own Hanover Church; and Finney drew large crowds and aroused great excitement. And then he advanced into Connecticut where, *mirabile dictu*, some of the settled clergy endorsed his presence.

In 1832, this phase of itinerant revivals came to an end when Finney accepted a pulpit at the Broadway Tabernacle Church in New York City. The church itself had been especially built for him by Lewis Tappan, the New York merchant prince and reformer. Three years later, he became Professor of Didactic, Polemic, and Pastoral Theology at Oberlin College in Ohio. Founded by a band of pious New Englanders and open to Negro students as well as to women, Oberlin primarily prepared ministers for frontier duties. Finney, however, continued to make occasional evangelical forays from there, including two trips to England. There was also a six-week campaign at Boston's Park Street Church in 1857, which more than any previous appearance signalled the approval of revivalism by New England's Congregationalists. And he continued to make religious news. He scored unparalleled triumphs whenever welcomed to New York City. After Reverends Albert Barnes and Lyman and Edward Beecher were tried on heresy charges, Finney became a Congregationalist, leaving Presbyterianism in disgust. Finally, in 1850, he was appointed President of Oberlin.

These Oberlin years were important ones. For some time, Finney's confidence in the conversion experience had been shaken by the large number of backsliders. To be sure, he unwaveringly believed that a divinely ordained assignment had been given him, but the ambiguous results of these revival conversions were confusing. These results indicated that conversion itself was not enough; it did not lead to that exalted Christian life demanded by evangelical Christianity. He was forced to the dismaying conclusion that sainthood might not be for everyone who experienced a "decision." Disillusioned, he began, first at the Broadway Tabernacle and then at Oberlin, to work out a theology of his own. It emphasized God's perfection as its ideal and selfless love as its central proposition. All the converted, he declared, "should aim at being holy and not rest satisfied till they are as perfect as God." Man could grow in Grace, Finney told his students, until they reached a state of virtual sinlessness. He called it "entire sanctification" and in effect it amounted to a second conversion or "higher blessing." Christian perfection fed that hunger for holiness that existed among Protestants. But it meant a willful abandonment of revivalism and Finney's fellow evangelists charged that this doctrine of divine government smacked of heresy. Finney, once again, therefore, proved an extremely divisive figure and contributed to the tensions within the ministry that led to recurring schisms.

Charles G. Finney and the revivalists helped undermine Calvinism in one way; Unitarianism did it in another. Coming from a different direction—eastern Massachusetts to be precise—and with its own distinct emphasis, Unitarianism would also call into question the Congregationalist positions on sin, depravity, free will, and the granting of grace. From modest beginnings in the 1790s, it would become a separate sect and eventually take over a considerable number of the oldest Calvinist churches in New England.

Harvard men and Boston merchants bulked large among the Unitarians. They were part of a distinctive social and intellectual class, an "elite of wealth and fashion," so Harriet Beecher Stowe reported. The church of this cohesive and patrician elite was destined to be only a small backwater in the tidal wave of religious awakening then sweeping across the country. Nor were Unitarians competitive with the evangelical sects. They did not wish to be. They distrusted religious emotionalism, since they believed its hysteria robbed men of their reason. They held that man needed only to follow his conscience, cultivate the higher faculties, educate himself, and model his life on Jesus. They believed, as the old jest had it, in the fatherhood of God, the brotherhood of man, and the community of Boston; and he who was born in Boston did not need to be reborn.

*   *   *

Unitarianism's greatest leader, William Ellery Channing, was born in April 1780—and not in Boston, but in Newport, Rhode Island, a community whose wealth had derived in large part from the notorious rum and slave trade. His father, the State's Attorney General, had a flourishing law practice as well as a family of ten children. Generally too busy to spare time for his sons and daughters, he nonetheless was a strict disciplinarian who believed children should be infrequently seen and never heard. Not surprisingly, the boy looked elsewhere for guidance and affection, and received both from his maternal grandfather, William Ellery. Young Channing was sent to school early because his mother was in poor health and, when old enough, was enrolled in the local boarding school of Master Robert Rogers, a disciplinarian who bequeathed a hatred of flogging to Channing and apparently little else.

The slight but muscular schoolboy was fond of solitary ways, usually content to play alone with his kite or to take a lonely walk on the beach. But he was also exposed to some of the leading personalities and best minds of the day. Ezra Stiles, the family minister before Yale called him to its presidency, was a greater influence upon young Channing than any other man, except possibly Grandfather Ellery. There was also the Reverend Samuel Hopkins, though his gloomy Calvinism repelled the sensitive boy. The Channing house, moreover, was a center for both social gatherings and Federalist political activity, and to it came, among others, John Jay and George Washington.

Young William Ellery Channing also had a close-up look at both slavery and the rum trade along Newport's wharves. Indeed, there were domestic bondsmen in his own house, some of them possibly brought home by his highly respected merchant grandfather who imported slaves. Lawyer Channing never openly opposed slavery and would manumit his own black domestics after the Revolution. Very conceivably, it was at this point in his life that young Channing began to develop that sensitivity for human beings which later made him an abolitionist.

As childhood passed into adolescence, William Ellery Channing prepared for college—in the household of his uncle, Reverend Henry Channing in nearby New London, Connecticut. The latter was a clerical maverick who ardently supported revivalism and adamantly denied the divinity of Christ. Under his tutelage, young Channing was further liberated from Calvinism. In 1794, at age 14, he enrolled at Harvard, where his classmates and friends included Joseph Story, a future Justice of the Supreme Court; William Emerson, father of Ralph Waldo Emerson; and Joseph Tuckerman, who would become his beloved colleague in the Unitarian ministry. Harvard was then not quite ready to go over to Unitarianism but the bracing winds of religious liberalism were clearly affecting faculty and students alike. Few if any of them were unacquainted with the readings of Bishop Berkeley, David Hume, the idealism of Richard Price, or the appealing men of the Edinburgh Enlightenment like Francis Hutcheson.

The same unsettling social and political conditions Timothy Dwight encountered when he took over the presidency at Yale were also present during Channing's years in Cambridge. "The old foundations of social order, loyalty, tradition, habit, reverence for antiquity," values that Channing held sacred, "were everywhere shaken, if not subverted." As at Yale, Harvard's Federalist teachers and overseers saw infidelity in every troubling development, including student pranks and Jacobinism. Channing's Federalist background placed him squarely in the camp of the opponents of the French Revolution. His grandfather also fed his Gallophobia. Jacobinism, for this gentle, slender schoolboy, was "synonymous with a dishonest, immoral, factious, and disorganized man."

Graduated in 1798, William Ellery Channing was restless and unsettled. While having learned much under Harvard's willows, he was still uncertain in religion. Sentiments had not yet hardened into convictions, nor had knowledge matured into philosophy. He was nothing formed or clear, merely a learned young man who had still to ask critical questions and to feel his way toward "spiritual things." He was even uncertain about a career to pursue when he met David Randolph of Virginia, then visiting Newport. At the latter's invitation, he went south to Richmond, to tutor the Randolph children. Richmond, far away from the confines of New England, was a window on a larger world. Channing commended Virginians for their manners and for loving "money less than we do." Without "their sensuality and their slaves," they'd be the "greatest people in the world." For once again he had encountered Negro wretchedness, even on the relatively humane Virginia plantations, and it hardened his sentiments that slavery was an affront to God. His rigid Federalist persuasion, on the other hand, began to soften—to the extent of opposing President John Adams' military preparedness against France as well as the Alien and Sedition Acts. Whatever hours were his own after completing the day's chore of educating 12 children he spent in reading—mostly Rousseau and Godwin—despite failing eyesight, by candlelight. Cultivating loneliness and privation, he adopted a spartan existence. He wore improper dress, slept on the bare floor, neglected to eat, and punished the flesh as a way of exorcising his "shameful" passions. The stress and strain of these "sore trials" produced hallucinatory moments and a deep and moving conversion experience; he would be "a servant of God."

But first Channing had to recover from his weakened physical state. In 1800 he decided to leave Virginia and return to Newport, a pale and emaciating young man badly in need of rest. Both at home and later at Cambridge, he devoted most of his hours to preparation for the ministry. His orthodoxy satisfied the Cambridge Association, and he was licensed in the autumn of 1802.

Short, slender, with stooped frame and worn appearance, Channing gave an impressive initial performance at Medford's First Church in October 1802. Listeners unanimously observed "that wonderful voice—so distinct and strong and sincere"; and the sermons themselves—so plain and undogmatic. Soon Channing was preaching in Boston, at the large and fashionable Brattle Street Church and before the Federal Street Church congregation. Both churches needed a minister and extended invitations to him. Channing accepted that offered by members of the old wooden Federal Street Church and was ordained on June 1, 1803. He would remain there almost 40 years and during that time would travel very far from the Calvinism and Federalism of his youth. In fact he would become the acknowledged leader of American Unitarianism.

Channing loved Boston and knew its patricians, those who had made this "hub of the universe" a center of charity, culture, wisdom, and stability. He invariably associated with the city's moderate, cultivated, cool-tempered ministers who had Arminianized Calvinism and were slowly making Boston their stronghold. Such ministers emphasized the ethical elements of love and good conduct in a Christian's life. And so did Channing. He had not yet broken with orthodoxy, however, and as late as 1807, he thought man's depravity "should be most deeply and painfully felt." But he was moving toward the camp of religious liberalism and had concluded by 1812 that Calvinism "chills the best affections," that it could have a "dreadful influence" on "susceptible minds." He would come to virtually deny the existence of Hell, and to believe in the perfectibility of man, and hold to a concept of God in man's image. Confident of man's destiny, he exclaimed, "I do and I must reverence human nature."

Most of these views were incorporated in Channing's famous and widely circulated 1819 Baltimore sermon, a 45,000 word statement that was perhaps the most comprehensive and most subtle expression of the Unitarian position. A stirring call to the colors of liberal Christianity, this manifesto opened with a clear assertion of God's beneficence, the significance of Jesus as a divinely appointed model for mankind, the love of God for man, and the dignity of man himself. An expression of the secular humanitarianism that had been developing in New England, the sermon rejected the doctrine of election, the Trinity, dogmatic scriptural authority, and all religious agencies that curbed man's freedom. Channing wished men would engage in a "deliberate, devout, fearless study of God's word."

Countless sermons followed. They all dwelt on aspects of the doctrinal synthesis of 1819. Human reason had centrality in most of them, but it was not unequivocally affirmed. There were, to be sure, beautiful tributes to reason, as would be expected of an advocate of rational religion and Christian humanism. "Christianity," he declared, "is reason in its most perfect form." That "ultimate reliance of a human being," Channing further stated, "is and must be on his own mind." Even revelation was based on reason, he stated in 1828. But such claims were hardly an absolute for a minister who declared that the spiritual message was not to be found in book or creed but in "the human heart"; nor for one who asserted elsewhere that man's "rational nature is from God" and that Christianity was miraculous in origin. Unlike the English Unitarians and the American Transcendentalists, Channing never considered Jesus as merely human; he always insisted on the special divinity of Christ as the first of the sons of God. But, like the Transcendentalists, he exclaimed: "In ourselves are the elements of divinity."

Reason, then, was obviously a very inclusive term for Channing, at once intellectual and spiritual. This maddening ambiguity was aggravated by his proximity to Transcendentalism. He came close to their treatment of reason as a faculty to be exercised in feeling; he shared their belief in a self-directed life; he agreed that his Unitarian colleagues had "a want of vitality and force." However, he was willing to go the entire route with these young men and women who, recalling Jonathan Edwards' "sense of the heart," would turn religion into an ecstasy, a saturnalia of faith. Channing was troubled by their tendency to substitute private inspiration for Christianity; he balked at their conviction of an actual union of Self and the Divine. Channing's own note is nonetheless clear in his claim of man's "likeness to God," of "impenetrable mystery in every action . . . in the universe," presumably impenetrable to the thrust of reason.

Unitarian rejection of Calvinism, and its cautious belief in man's capacity for perfectibility, strikes a chord familiar to Charles Finney and to evangelical Christianity. It was consonant as well with the spirit which animated many of the communities that mushroomed in these decades, the golden age of utopian experimentation. Channing would not accept social predeterminism any more than he had endorsed religious predestination. Men could manipulate their society and alter the character of their institutions. Indeed, man himself "was also equally improvable, for he was endowed with reason, will, and conscience, inwardly impelled by God's decree to seek betterment."

Social-economic change, it followed, could ultimately be effected only through perfection of the individual and only through voluntary action. Channing himself was not much of a joiner. "Let not the individual enslave his conscience to others," he exhorted. He affirmed the principle of Fourier's "association," and cautiously endorsed Brook Farm as well as Adin Ballou's Hopedale Community but, always the supreme individualist, he warned that any and all organizations, public or private, ecclesiastical or secular, had "a tendency to fetter men, to repress energy." He emphasized instead self reform and "self-determination" above all.

By 1830 Channing was the chief ornament of the Unitarian pulpit, but he was also the paradigm of the high-minded Protestant who had been reared in the spirit of charity and liberality. He had increasingly emphasized the social value of the Bible, the importance of inculcating morality, and the need to evangelize the entire nation. To this end, he published the *Christian Disciple,* a journal of liberal Christianity. In addition, he was a member of the Boston School Commission, a founder of the Harvard Divinity School, a member of the Harvard Corporation, a pioneer in adult education, and an advocate of publicly-supported schools. He always displayed great concern for the education of the children of the poor. He was a friend and confidante of Horace Mann and influenced Mann's elementary school reform proposals for Massachusetts. In large measure, Elizabeth Peabody owed her interest in kindergarten reform to the "personal exertions of Dr. Channing."

There was more. Channing did not limit his reform energies in any direction. Rather, despite recurrent ill health, he engaged in a strenuous array of activities. He grew bolder with the years. Encouraging Dorothea Dix, he allowed her to prepare the moving "Memorial on the Condition of the Insane" in his study. He championed penal reform and the abolition of capital punishment; and he informed his proper middle-class parishioners that the criminal caught the infection of vice from the respectable element in society. He drew up the petition in defense of Abner Kneeland who was jailed for atheism, for he "would call that mind free which calls no man master." And none was more vehement than Channing in condemning the sins of property.

Like so many practitioners of religious benevolence, Channing struck hard at war, urban poverty, intemperance, and slavery. He was, for instance, the heart and soul of the Massachusetts Peace Society whose 22 founders first met in his study. Although believing wars of self defense were justified, he held that war itself was "a tremendous evil" and that the "profession of a soldier . . . is immoral."

Channing's reaction to urban poverty was even more ambivalent. Most ministers, as of old, attributed it to idleness and immorality, and to deficiencies of character. His own analysis, which was a model religious response, blamed poverty on the poor themselves and showed little sympathy for the urban poor or for factory operatives. But he did on occasion concede that "a man half fed, half clothed . . . will be too crushed in spirit to do the proper work of a man," and he did believe workers "must share more largely in the fruits of their toil." Like his co-religionaries, Channing mostly urged "self-culture" upon workers; however, he also campaigned for more practical reforms—such as new approaches to juvenile delinquency; "manual labor schools," like the one Tuckerman proposed; abolition for imprisonment for debt. Channing also helped organize, in 1824, the Association of the Members of the Federal Street Society for Benevolent Virtues, an agency typical of that extraordinary array of voluntary societies from Boston to Baltimore which channelled the anti-pauperism energies of merchant elite and Christian liberals alike.

Always seeking to avoid controversy and notoriety, to live above the clamor of political and theological strife, Channing approached the slave controversy with the same desire to appear "mild and amiable" and "not mingle with the contentions of the world" that had guided him in all reform efforts. Hardly a militant, therefore, he shunned a meeting with William Lloyd Garrison, whose verbal fury scandalized proper Bostonians after 1830, and his early anti-slavery critiques were wooden and labored. The Abolitionists were admittedly "a noble set of men," but intemperate and excessive as well. Still slavery was "essentially evil"; and he would abolish it—in the North by statute and in the South by moral suasion and voluntary action, by appeals to reason and conscience. By 1835, however, Reverend Samuel May chided him on neglect of the great issue: "Why, Sir, have you not spoken before?" and evoked this admission: "I acknowledge the justice of your reproof: I have been silent too long." And he was not silent again. By 1836, he was attending a session of the New England Anti-Slavery Convention and attacking Cincinnati's anti-abolitionists who had destroyed James Birney's anti-slavery press. He spoke at Faneuil Hall in the following year, at a mass meeting protesting the murder of Elijah Lovejoy, the Illinois printer. He signed petitions for the elimination of slavery in the District of Columbia; in 1839 he defended the Abolitionists who called "the slaveholder hard names"; and two months before he died, in an 1842 Lenox, Massachusetts speech, he violently arraigned the "evil" and "outrage" of slavery.

Such sentiments distressed his Federal Street Church members who regarded them as an endorsement of Abolitionism. Channing struck hard at these gentlemen of standing and property who made "gain ... their God" and would sacrifice human rights to it. But the congregation prevailed and had virtually cast him out by the late 1830s. It was a bitter blow. He was forced to give up cherished personal associations and endure hostility from friends of a lifetime. Nonetheless, he had no regrets. It had been a privilege "to have lived in an age so stirring, so pregnant, so eventful." And he had moved with the age. His decade-long journey from moderation to militancy on the issue of slavery was matched by a similar emancipation from conservatism on other reform issues—much as he had evolved from a tentative and cautious young man who held to religious orthodoxy to a bold spokesman against it in his middle years. And in the course of this devolution to reform, to radicalism even. Channing, more than most, questioned the goals and values—such as materialism—held by his countrymen. He loved quiet and preferred to "work alone," but in the end none spoke braver or wiser words to his generation, none were superior in ability to galvanize belief in the certainty of human improvement.

*   *   *

Channing's commitment to reform was hardly unique. In varying degree, Dwight and Finney both shared it, as did most evangelical ministers; witness the near-universal clerical concern for temperance and educational reform. Moreover, all three ministers eventually concluded that emotion was superior to reason—though its victory was not clear-cut with Dwight or Channing; all would nonetheless assent to Dwight's judgment about the evanescent nature of metaphysical speculation; all would appeal to the "heart" and to plain common sense. Nor were their inconsistencies, we have seen, limited to the contrasting virtues of reason and faith. Each vacillated between the useful and the intuitive, science and miracles, self-reliance and divine guidance, social reform and rugged individualism, social obligations and otherworldly concerns, secular humanism and religious benevolence. None held unswervingly or consistently to a single lifelong position—not Channing, the moderate religious and social reformer; not Finney, the pietistic radical and the social conservative; not even Dwight, whose abiding conservatism drenched every aspect of his life and thought. Each in differing degree reflected that cultural and social mix characteristic of all those who lived in the first 50 years after the Revolution—between the afterglow of the Enlightenment and the dawn of American romanticism. From the former, they drew something of their faith in progress and in education; from the latter, their trust in humanitarian evangelism and in the possibilities of man.

7

Gentlemen Democrats
at Home and Abroad

ALEXIS DE TOCQUEVILLE
SAMUEL F. B. MORSE
JAMES FENIMORE COOPER

by R. Jackson Wilson
Smith College

Down the stretch of United States history running from George Washington's inauguration to Abraham Lincoln's assassination, no development was more obvious and exciting to Americans than the survival and triumph of their republican democracy. Lincoln was astonishingly skilled at finding words to sanctify facts, and he never exercised his skills more effectively than when he put together phrases like "dedicated to the proposition that all men are created equal," or "government of the people, by the people, and for the people." By the 1860s, Lincoln's phrases—for all their peculiar grace—captured only the commonplace understanding of most politically conscious men and women in America: theirs was a society whose essential meaning was to be sought in their experiment in the practice of human equality.

Lincoln's words have droned through the minds and mouths of so many school children for so long a time that they have an almost ritual character. It is not easy to be curious about what they really meant, and even more difficult to remember that an important misunderstanding was just below their surface. For the nation's "fathers" had not "conceived" the nation as a democratic enterprise. "Democracy" to them was a word to be seldom used and usually as a fright-word, another name for mob rule. The notion that all men are created equal was an abstraction for

133

Thomas Jefferson and for most of his contemporaries, an appeal to an almost metaphysical principle. Functioning democracy was a phenomenon of the 19th century, not of the period of the Revolutionary years, a fact of life younger than Lincoln himself.

By the time of the Civil War, of course, democracy had become an article of faith in the United States. And one requirement of the faith was that the idea of "government of the people" be rudely pushed back in time, enfolded into the 18th-century Revolution. This reverent picture of our national history had the odd effect of ignoring one of the great mental efforts of Americans born *after* the Revolution: their own awkward, halting, but monumental attempt to comprehend the seeming triumph of Democracy in their political and social lives.

This effort was especially trying for those who—by birth, talents, education and fortunes—were marked as gentlemen. There was, of course, no American "aristocracy"; the Constitution itself forbade titles of nobility. But there were thousands of Americans who were persons of "refinement" and "quality." There was, in other words, a self-conscious elite whose members thought of themselves as set apart from the enveloping democratic mass. The gentleman might be a planter in the South, or a merchant in New York or Philadelphia; he might be a landowner along the Hudson or the Connecticut, or he could be a lawyer or a minister in New England. But however they were situated, gentlemen in America in the decades after 1820 understood one thing very clearly: an 18th-century social order that had entitled men like them to the automatic deference of their social inferiors was dying. A new world was being born in which they had lost access to power and position, a world that jostled them rudely and embarrassed them by its roughness, its crudity, and its lack of controlled expectations.

One logical response to such deep and threatening changes would have been to repudiate democracy in both theory and practice, to ask simply for the return of a time when ministers could be confident of their congregations' regard, gentlemen on the street would not be insulted, manners would have their supposedly ancient social value, and styles of dress would still mark men and women in recognizable ranks. But, after about 1820, this response had become unworkable. To reject democracy in favor of "aristocratic" values would brand any gentleman (even in the South) as a mere crank. None of the political parties of the period—Democratic, Whig, or Republican—had room for anti-democratic ideas; and no tradition of religion, no scholarly career, no learned profession served as a barrier to the tide of equality. For any educated and articulate member of the elite—any person of "breeding"—accommodation to Democracy was an urgent necessity. A generation of American gentlemen (and European gentlemen, too) had to come to terms, to adjust to the ominous, powerful and encircling fact of equality.

One outcome of this encounter between an anxious elite and a triumphant social "principle" was the emergent gentleman democrat, a temporary but interesting social type. Before 1820, the type could not flourish; there was simply too little democracy to form it. After 1870 there simply were not enough self-conscious gentlemen. But from about 1825 until the Civil War, gentlemen democrats turned out a sizeable body of political essays, novels, speeches, histories—even poetry and paintings—dealing with an absorbing dilemma: how could they consent to the mounting democratic tide and still preserve the manners, graces, and social stability they thought had belonged to an older "aristocratic" world?

*   *   *

To those Americans grappling with this dilemma, the distinction between the stereotypes of "democracy" and "aristocracy" parallelled another contrast: between the United States and Europe. And so it seemed, too, to Europeans who believed they could read some of their own future in the American experience. Europeans, especially in England and France, were almost as preoccupied with democracy as Americans. Simple antidemocratic opposition was a more frequent option for Europeans; but an option that had its costs, and endorsed less often than Americans have supposed. Like their American counterparts, French and English aristocrats had to learn ways of accepting, rationalizing and even seeming to promote the new democratic ethic. And they were inevitably drawn to two momentous events: the great Revolution in France, with its Napoleonic sequel, and the Revolution of 1776 in the United States, with its own democratic sequel. The French Revolution made the democratic force seem as destructive as it was powerful. The American experiment appeared to offer more hope.

More than any other European of his day—and perhaps more than any European since 1776—Alexis de Tocqueville strained to read the European future in America. The outcome was *Democracy in America*, a massive and intricate analysis of American life that Tocqueville published in two parts in 1834 and 1840, and which Americans ever since have read more seriously than any other large analysis of their society.

Tocqueville was only 25 when he came to the United States, and only 30 when he published *Democracy in America;* but he wrote with a loftiness and majesty that earned him an enormous and quick reputation. His American readers, especially, found him far more balanced, detached and therefore "objective" than most foreigners who wrote about the United States—the easily offended English travelers, or the other Frenchmen who often romanticised America out of existence. But, in fact, *Democracy in America* was written not in loftiness and detachment, but with intense involvement. In many important ways, *Democracy in America* was a kind of projective autobiography. The book contained an implicit but important statement of what Tocqueville thought he was and might become socially and politically. His observations of particular facts, and his grand generalizations about the nature and meaning of American life all hinged on a perception of his own "delicate" (as he called it) position in French society: a gentleman, decidedly, but a gentleman trying to find ways to be a democrat.

In his introduction to the first volume, Tocqueville made a gloomy estimate of the state of affairs in France. He identified two important types of Frenchmen advocating two different social strategies. There were, first, men of "high and generous characters ... virtuous and peaceful individuals whose pure morality, quiet habits, affluence and talents fit them to be the leaders of the surrounding population." But these gentry had fallen into a simple-minded, futile opposition to the democratic "novelty." On the other hand, there were democrats in France, anti-aristocratic men who assumed the role of "champions of modern civilization." But these *arrivistes* were nasty, pragmatic and utterly without principle. They were attempting (as any aristocrat would complain) to place "themselves in a station which they usurp with insolence."

These linkings of aristocracy with conservatism, democracy with social "unworthiness," were a "misery" to Tocqueville, they made a world

> where nothing is linked together, where virtue is without genius, and genius without honor; where the love of order is confounded with a taste for oppression, and the holy rites of freedom with a contempt of law ... and where nothing seems to be any longer forbidden or allowed, honorable or shameful, false or true.

By birth, education and attitude, Tocqueville was an aristocrat. He was Alexis Charles Henri Clerel de Tocqueville, a member of the Norman nobility. His grandfather and his aunt had gone to the guillotine during the Revolution, and his own parents had been put in prison. His family had reentered public life only when Napoleon was overthrown and the Bourbon monarchy restored. After he became a lawyer, Tocqueville himself had accepted an appointment as a minor magistrate from the Bourbon monarchy. And when the Bourbons were again overthrown in 1830, Tocqueville felt compelled to leave either the government or the country —which prompted him to ask for a slightly fabricated assignment: visiting the United States to study its prison system. Tocqueville's identity, in other words, was clearly with the old regime—with order, stability, hierarchy, manners and taste and breeding. Indeed, he personalized these qualities—to the extent that even Gustave de Beaumont, his friend and colleague on the American tour, could twit Tocqueville on his excess of genteel reserve: "a manner a little cold, and too reserved in society;

too much indifference toward persons who don't please him, and an attitude silent and calm, too close to dignity."

It was no incidental thing, then, that the July Revolution of 1830, which replaced the Bourbons with a constitutional monarchy, made Tocqueville feel his position in France to be "delicate." Almost any democrat would have welcomed the revolution, especially since it was fostered and supported by one of the saintly figures of both French and American republicanism, the Marquis de Lafayette. But Toqueville's inheritance and his sensibilities were too deeply conservative. At the same time, however, he was too interested in politics and too concerned with finding a role for himself merely to withdraw. He needed most of all a strategy of reconciliation between his ancestry and what he had already come to see as the irresistible force of democracy. And if French society offered no ready clues toward such a strategy, then perhaps the United States might.

Tocqueville thought the problem out carefully before he and Beaumont left France. He brooded over the history of France, and he read carefully and widely about America. Even before arrival in the United States, he had already reached some fundamental intellectual conclusions. Tocqueville later began *Democracy in America* by referring to American equality as a "novel object" that "struck me forcibly during my stay in America." But this opening was disingenuous. He had decided, before embarking, that democracy was the most important force in world history, and that equality had made the most important and rapid inroads on the old "feudal" culture in the United States. And he had already decided, too, that if democracy had had beneficial social consequences anywhere, it was probably in America. So he went looking not for "novel objects" but for confirmations of a position that he had read about and reasoned toward in France—in response to French stimuli, not American.

Tocqueville's philosophical position was really quite simple, and not very original. From aristocratic beginnings, society in Europe was moving steadily and inevitably toward democratic ends. The old ways, perfected around the 12th century, had emphasized order, hierarchy, and subjection of plain people to a powerful and brilliant aristocracy. Men then had to pay a high price for social order: cruelty was a frequent feature of aristocracy, and suffering and ignorance the portion of the poor. But there had also been rewards: "the pursuit of luxury, the refinements of taste, the pleasures of wit, and the cultivation of the arts." Above all, men had felt bound together. The nobility could be benevolent and the people felt a deep attachment to their betters. Men understood who they were and what their obligations and rights were. "The social state thus organized might boast of its stability, its power, and, above all, its glory." Tocqueville almost never described the aristocratic state of society without obvious wistfulness and nostalgia; if he were now going to embrace democracy, the embrace would be gingerly and fastidious, the embrace an aristocrat might give a yeoman ally with whom his lot was cast by crisis.

Against the old order, which represented for Tocqueville a fixed point of beginning, the democratic tide had been breaking steadily for seven centuries. And, he reasoned, there was no way to turn it back. One of Tocqueville's subtle ways of accepting democracy without surrendering his refined bearing was to describe it as an impersonal force over which he and men like him had no real control. So Tocqueville objectified democracy, made it into an abstract power, a force to which he could succumb—a virgin submitting innocently to an irresistible seduction:

> The gradual development of the principle of equality is . . . a providential fact. It has all the chief characteristics of such a fact: it is universal, it is lasting, it constantly eludes all human interference, and all events as well as all men contribute to its progress . . . The whole book that is here offered to the public has been written under the influence of a kind of religious terror produced in the author's mind by the view of that irresistible revolution which has advanced for centuries in spite of every obstacle and which is still advancing in the midst of the ruins it has caused.

Here was the key to Tocqueville's objectivity, the reluctant objectivity of a man accepting what he could not avoid, counting its costs, stoically seeking some redeeming features in it. But the detachment was a function of passion, not indifference: the "ruins it has caused" were not merely historical facts to Tocqueville; they were personal. His ancestors' tragic sufferings at the hands of the Revolution were acted out again, almost as farce, in his own life. When he was forced to take the oath of allegiance in 1830 to the constitutional monarchy, he was self-consciously wracked:

> I have just taken the oath! [he wrote his wife] and I will count this day as one of the unhappiest of my life. For the first time since my birth, I have to avoid the presence of persons whom I esteem. Oh! Marie, the idea of it racks me! How my voice changed as I uttered those three words! I felt my heart beat as though it would burst from my breast.

This was the dramatic stance of a 25-year-old who had given in, sacrificing his "honor." From this point of shame, an almost logical chain led Tocqueville to and beyond *Democracy in America*. If he could believe that he had sacrificed family honor to an irresistible "force," then his heart need not "burst"; giving in to a vast tendency of history would provoke less guilt than surrendering to ordinary human beings. But the logic led forward. If the democratic force could be shown to have even one grand and good outcome—in the United States, if anywhere—then it just might be a force that a young man of aristocratic hauteur could accept and move with. And if he could perform such an intellectual somersault, then he could return to France and pursue a career in democratic politics without shame—not only without shame but with a positive mission, explaining the new world to the old, the future to the present, democracy to his fellow aristocrats.

The quasi-logical character of Tocqueville's dilemma helps explain one of the most striking peculiarities of *Democracy in America*. It had the form and manner of a geometry textbook: a schedule of theorems about democratic society. And, as in a geometry, the demonstrations were more important than the particular political planes and angles serving as examples. In both senses, American democracy was exemplary: it was the most favorable case of a general type; but it was also *only* an example, a case in point. This did not mean that Tocqueville's observations were not astute; in fact, he was a cunning observer precisely because he knew what he was looking for. He also knew where to look. He talked mostly to literate members of the American elite—who would also provide him with his American audience. *Democracy in America* was a book on the logic of democracy, written by an anxious young aristocrat, helped along by refined Americans. It was a class book, both in its origins and its reception, a genteel endeavor (which may help explain Tocqueville's great vogue after World War II among America's refined and anxious intellectuals.

Tocqueville found much to celebrate in American democracy. Though lacking elegance, the manners and morals of the people were sound. Property was respected and secure. The middle class, which he believed dominated society, was really conservative, since it (like Tocqueville) thought of democracy in America as a finished product, an inheritance from the 18th century, to be protected and secured. Because of their widespread political participation, Americans were much more sophisticated than most Europeans. Literacy was almost universal. Women and children were better off than in Europe—single women, in particular, though married women had some special problems. In general, Americans had developed an acute sense of political and social responsibility that could replace the vanished hierarchical stability of the aristocratic old regime. American constitutions, both state and federal, were cleverly designed to balance opposing forces and tendencies in democracy. The United States, in other words, satisfied Tocqueville's expectations.

But the logic of his situation required that democracy have faults; if it were both irrestistible and excellent, then what role could he and gentlemen like him play except that of spectator? And so Tocqueville set out to discover failings in democracy as well as successes. And his discoveries—even more than his positive observations—read like deductions from abstract principles. Democracy, he argued, made every man into a facsimile of every other, and this created the danger of gross mediocrity. Similarities between men also had the paradoxical effect of establishing distance between them; similar people suffered from feelings of alienation: they did not *need* society, and so they easily fell into isolated "individualism." But their isolation, in turn, made them constantly anxious about their social identity. And to try to control their anxiety they tried to control each other's lives. Americans, however, had given up all the old means that aristocratic society once used to enforce control, so they resorted to control by "public opinion." This, in turn, laid democratic societies open to the awful "tyranny" of public opinion.

Such masterly balancing of admiration and acceptance of democracy on one side and suspicion and resistance on the other was not merely a personality trait of Tocqueville's, or a simple triumph of reason over passion. For Tocqueville, as for any other member of what Mark Twain hilariously called "the quality," such balance between class instinct and political necessity was both difficult and precarious. Under pressure, Tocqueville (like gentlemen democrats in America) could revert quickly to aristocratic instinct. In an unpublished "confession" that he entitled "My instincts, my opinions," Tocqueville faced this truth about himself:

> Experience has proved to me that almost all men, but most certainly I, return more or less always to their fundamental instincts, and only do well those things that conform to these instincts. Let's try, sincerely then, to discover where my *fundamental instincts* and my *genuine principles* lie.
>
> My mind has a certain taste for democratic institutions, but I am aristocratic by instinct, that is to say I despise and fear the mob.
>
> I passionately love liberty, legality, respect for rights, but not democracy. There are the depths of my soul.

Hundreds of Americans, democrats by opinion and gentlemen by instinct, would have read his confession with quick transatlantic sympathy.

*   *   *

During the summer of 1830, when Alexis de Tocqueville was undergoing his humiliation in Paris, and making the decision to visit the United States, an American gentleman in Rome was beginning his own period of reflection about the meaning of being an American in a democratic age. Samuel Finley Breese Morse was, like Tocqueville, a man of refinement. Morse would later have a huge reputation as the inventor of the telegraph and of the code that still bears his name. But for the moment he was an artist, in Europe to study and copy, to try to revive an artistic career that had begun 15 years earlier with great promise. During 1830–31, Morse reversed Tocqueville's geographical movements: he went from Rome to Paris during Tocqueville's first summer in the United States, returning to America in 1832, the same year Tocqueville went back to Paris. The paths of the two men crossed intellectually, too. Morse was straining in a European setting to discover the significance of being an American democrat, just as Tocqueville was using the United States as a way of defining his European identity. For both men, the years were momentous and anxious; and for both American democracy was an opportunity as well as a peril.

Morse was, by American standards, as much an aristocrat as Tocqueville. He was the son of a well-placed minister and scholar, Jedediah Morse of Charlestown, Massachusetts. Jedediah Morse was the author of famous and influential books on American geography, a passionate and well-known defender of Congregationalist orthodoxy, and pastor to an important congregation. A graduate of Yale, friend of scholars and university presidents, he was learned and impeccably distinguished. Nor was he unique among the Morses in such honors. A great-grandfather had been president of Princeton, and one of his grandfathers was a judge. The Morse name had been in New England since the 1630s. The family was Federalist in politics long after Federalism had become hopelessly identified with New England reaction. Morse had, in other words, a "nest of associations"—in Henry Adams' nice phrase—that marked him from birth as a member of the elite.

A mild tension always existed between Morse's background and his own ambitions. Even at school, he found it difficult to submit to the dark discipline of the family's Calvinism. He liked to skate, to shoot, to pick blackberries and, above all, to draw. But there were always parental admonitions: keep death and the fate of the soul uppermost. When he was 14 and away at school, Morse received a letter from his mother about the death of a Boston girl:

> She ate her dinner perfectly well and was dead in five minutes after. Her name was Ann Hinkley. You see, the importance of always being prepared for *death*. We cannot be too soon or too well prepared for that all-important moment, as this is what we are sent into this world *for*. The main business of life is to prepare for death.

Within the Morse family, such ideas were not isolated religious sentiments. They expressed a world view. For Jedediah Morse, and for men like him, society was in crisis. Jeffersonianism in politics, Unitarianism in religion, the French Revolution, unruliness in Boston streets, the capture of Harvard College by men of "liberal" ideas—all these and half a dozen related tendencies spelled impending disaster. Change was everywhere, almost all of it bad. Foreign ideas, democratic nonsense, frivolity and irreligion were rife. And, it was clear to men like Jedediah Morse, members of the elite must use every opportunity to root out evil, rationalism, and loose morals. Charlestown, Massachusetts, was in fact a rather calm community during the first two decades of the 19th century, but the disturbed Morse household passed through days of gloom and fear quite like the anxious moments of Tocqueville's family of Bourbon loyalists. Jedediah Morse was a gentleman, but he was certainly no democrat. His son had to learn to try to be both; however, such learning was never free of the lurid, fearful social reflexes of the family.

How could it be otherwise, when one experience after another confirmed these reflexes? When Morse, while at Yale, was reprimanded for his frivolity and wastefulness after he went shooting a little too often? Or when his desire to become an artist was turned aside by his parents, and he was forced for a time to accept a dull apprenticeship to a bookseller? Or, when his parents finally consented to let him go to England to study art, his mother warned him that the theater, Madeira, and cigars were "ruinous to both soul and body," and that Americans studying in Europe were a lot of "dissipated infidels"? Morse was indelibly marked by all this experience; he could not even court his first wife without warning her to beware of her soul's state:

> I might flatter you, dear, I might tell you that your amiable disposition and your correct conduct would certainly recommend you to God, that you need only to go on, live correctly, be charitable, and you have nothing to fear. But think, my dear, what a part I should act: I could see one whom I loved so tenderly resting in false security, and I could live with her through life, and when death separated us, know for an awful truth, that if I was saved, we were separated *forever.* Could I love you, dear girl, if I could do this?

Such attitudes were an American equivalent of the Tocqueville family's Bourbonism. Within Morse's lifetime, religious ideas like his father's were transformed, and became primarily the property of revivalism—which appealed more and more to the lower middle-class and to the poor. But when Morse was growing up, Protestant "fundamentalism" still belonged primarily to respectable families, especially in New England. It was still the religion of a sector of the American elite.

Morse first definably parted with his father's world while studying art in London, during 1811–15. The United States and England were at war for most of these years, and Morse underwent the odd experience of being an enemy alien. He responded naturally enough by becoming archly patriotic, defending his country's war policies, and praying for American victories. But this natural response set him at odds politically with his own family. Like most New England Federalists, his father opposed the conflict and thought of it as a trick of the Jeffersonians, the party of infidelity. And his mother wrote him in 1812 to bewail the Republicans' war policy: "We rejoice that you are at so great a distance from our wretched, miserably distracted country, whose mad rulers are plunging us into an unnecessary war." And so when Morse, writing home, confessed that he favored the war, the implication was plain: "Some of you at home, I suppose, will call me a democrat."

Morse's political break had nothing to do with American domestic realities. Being a "democrat" meant nothing more to him in 1812 than being a patriot. He retained the values of the gentleman: Calvinism, fear of social change, distrust of "the people." He continued to identify with the Democratic Party, even in the years when the Party was being redefined by Andrew Jackson. But the identification was always casual, and did not involve him directly in politics. During the 1820s, for example, he busied himself with painting instead.

But even painting had ideological implications. Morse's career as an artist contained a double danger to his identity as a gentleman. In the first place, there was the growing notion that artists were "dissipated." And he was far from that. And, secondly, there was still a lingering identification of the artist as a craftsman, the practitioner of a trade that was beneath a gentleman's standards. Morse struggled against both dangers. And fortunately the solutions to each were identical. He painted only noble and "refined" subjects, designed to improve the morals of his audience—surely a fit occupation for any gentleman. And he painted portraits of the elite. First in New England, then in Charleston, South Carolina for several years, and finally in New York, Morse painted Americans who, in class terms, were indistinguishable from those with whom Tocqueville passed most of his time in America. Morse had a great deal of trouble making money as an artist. But he never dropped the dress, the style, the manners and the relentless dignity of the gentleman. After 1823, he settled in New York, where his friends were the cream of society. And painting subjects like President James Monroe and the fabled Marquis de Lafayette would hardly induce social unease.

In 1829, when Morse returned to Europe for more study—leaving behind, this time, his dead wife, father and mother—he was a man with a low level of explicit political concern, a nominal democrat, a practised gentleman and a successful (if poor) painter. He settled in Rome, and began an unanticipated process of political awakening. Almost everything roused Morse. Rome, to him, was an old, "artisocratic" world of Catholic superstition and ritual, of ignorance and poverty and, above all, arbitrary subjection. Much as it had been in England during the War of 1812, his consciousness of American identity was heightened. Morse was especially intrigued by the Church's architecture and art, its ritual, and its hold on the imagination of its people. But he was also repelled. Gradually, he became preoccupied with the ideology of his own citizenship. He become a heated republican and democrat, not out of any awareness of American conditions, but in response to his encounter with European and with Catholic "autocracy."

Morse's political conversion was completed during the revolutions of 1830 and 1831. Lafayette, the subject for two of Morse's portraits and the type of aristocratic republican to be revered, lent his name and influence to the July Revolution. But he also supported an attempt by Poland's republicans to free themselves from Russian control. At the same time, a revolutionary army in Italy tried to bring down the Church government of the Papal States. An excited Morse set out for Paris, the center of the revolutions. Lafayette received him warmly, and initiated him into an exclusive "Polish committee."

Morse's experiences in Italy and Paris prompted the straightforward and obvious conclusion: a great struggle was in progress between republican freedom and autocratic tyranny. The United States, he thought, was the purest example of republicanism; and, conversely, Roman Catholicism represented the purest form of autocracy. Europe was already torn between these contending forces, and American democracy might also soon fall prey to the sinister, always advancing, power of the Church. "American liberty," Lafayette warned, "can only be destroyed by the Popish clergy." And Morse took the warning to heart. Returning home much more poltically conscious than when he had left, he became a partisan of freedom and equality—of everything that smacked of republicanism. Now he was also required to combat the autocratic menace, to become a gentleman democrat in politics.

To Morse, back in New York, the enemy was not just an abstract and distant Popish danger. More alarming, he believed, was the growth of ignorance, poverty and plain boorishness at home. That New Yorkers would not buy paintings prompted genteel bitterness as well. "There is nothing new in New York," he wrote his friend James Fenimore Cooper, "except that they are not the same people that are driving after money, nor the same pigs at large in the street. Come prepared to find many, very many things in taste and manners different from your own good taste and manners."

Morse was caught between two worlds, geographically, ideologically, and socially. His own ideals of "refinement" and order clashed with what he considered to be American realities. But Europe was too full of popery and "aristocracy." Like Tocqueville, Morse often thought of Europe and the United States as abstractions. When the abstractions became too concrete, both men had an instinctive weakness for the old and the European. In Europe, Morse could be captivated by the picturesqueness of peasants; in the United States, pigs in the street were an offense. His nearest approach to ideological wholeness was in Paris, in the elegant company of Lafayette and other gentlemen, both European and American, giving wholehearted support to distant revolutions. The contradictions inherent in his position as a gentleman democrat were so deep that Morse could rail against the "tyranny" of the Church over Italian peasants, but at the same time see no evil in the practice of slavery in the United States.

During the disturbed political decade of the 1830s, these difficulties and contradictions focused on a single problem. European immigrants were flooding the United States, many of them Irish and Catholic. This immigration offended both Morse's gentility and his "democracy." The immigrants had none of the virtues he still believed were the core of "good taste and manners." But, Morse believed, the immigrants were also a threat to republican democracy, since they were easy prey for the Roman conspiracy. And so he entered politics as a distressed amateur. He ran for Mayor of New York City twice, in 1836 and 1841, under the colors of the new Native American Party. His platform was simple: a Jesuit conspiracy was at work, organizing immigrants into a political tool. Once this goal was accomplished, he claimed, "Anarchy ensues; and then the mass of people, who are always lovers of order and quiet, unite at once in support of the strong arm of force for protection; and despotism resumes its iron reign." Morse lost both elections badly—as he did again in 1854 when he ran for Congress.

Morse's alarmed nativism was not a repudiation of his theoretical democracy. He believed that democracy had to be protected *from* the people, whose abstract "sovereignty" was always being undercut by their weakness and poor "taste." And if defense of such an abstract democracy in effect required repudiation of "the people," then Morse would do it—confident that, in the long run, he was only fighting to preserve the good order and good manners necessary to the survival of republican democracy. Underneath—as with Tocqueville—there was always class instinct, ready to assert itself in any difficult moment. In an unpublished note very much like Tocqueville's private "confession," Morse laid out his rejection of Jean-Jacques Rousseau's principle that "Man is born free":

> I repudiate his fundamental postulate. There is not a living thing born into this world which is at its birth so utterly dependent, more perfectly enslaved, as man. [This] is the source of error of the Dec. of Indep., the equality paragraph.

*   *   *

James Fenimore Cooper, gentleman and writer, reached Paris for the first time in the summer of 1826, his 37th year. By October, with the generous help of Lafayette, Cooper had penetrated well into the upper reaches of French society. "I go to soirées," he wrote a friend, "where Princesses and Duchesses are as plenty as hogs in the streets of New

York." In truth, fastidious gentlemen like Cooper and Morse were probably much more numerous in New York streets than the pigs they fussed about. And Cooper probably exaggerated the estimated number of princesses of Paris, too. But his observation was more than a pair of miscounts, and more too than a joke to amuse a refined correspondent. He was beginning a seven-year stay in Europe, and it was a time of ideological tension for him as it had been for Morse and Tocqueville.

Like most other genteel Americans, Cooper was both fascinated and shocked by Europe. He gloried in his contacts with aristocracy, but made the almost routine American observation that Europe was a very mixed blessing. France, he said shortly after arrival, was a "strange country made up of dirt and gilding, good cheer and soupe maigre, bed bugs and laces." Europe set Cooper to thinking about America in a more systematic way than he had at home. He wrote his first work of non-fiction, *Notions of the Americans*, in Europe. And his attitudes toward American democracy became both more conscious and more troubled under the pressure of these seven years of European experiences. Like Morse and Tocqueville, then, Cooper became preoccupied with democracy in an international context; as with them, his perceptions of America were shaped at least as much by European as by American realities. Upon returning home in 1833, he was filled with doubt about republican democracy, and even more troubled over his status as a gentleman and his career as a novelist in democratic society.

The decor of James Fenimore Cooper's own life was gilding, good cheer and laces—not dirt, thin soup, and bed bugs. His ancestry was not so distinguished as Morse's; he was the son of the founder of Cooperstown, New York, a self-made man who accumulated a large fortune through land speculation. But William Cooper was a solid sort, who eventually became county judge, Congressman for two terms (as a Federalist, like Morse's father), and owner of an estate worth about $750,000, a huge fortune by the standards of the day. The family tried to educate young James suitably at Yale, but he studied little and pranked his way into dismissal in 1805. He was 16 and needed a career, so his father sent him to sea as a common sailor for a year in preparation for a naval officer's life. Cooper was commissioned a midshipman in 1808 and served until 1811.

Then, when James Fenimore Cooper was 22, his life reverted into a more gentlemanly channel. His father had died, leaving him $50,000 immediately and an interest in the entire estate. And he married Susan DeLancey, whose family was even richer and more aristocratic than Cooper's. He built a large home in Westchester on DeLancey land, and settled into the life of gentleman farmer with a few entreprenurial interests on the side.

This quiet pattern was broken in 1820, when Cooper began to write novels. The first was done on a dare, but once started he was obsessively efficient. Cooper published almost a book a year for the next six years, including *The Spy*, *The Pioneers*, and his greatest popular success, *The Last of the Mohicans*. He also moved into New York City, at about the same time Morse did, and for the same reason: the city was the most obvious place to pursue a literary or artistic career. Cooper was even more closely identified with the upper reaches of New York society than Morse. He began a dining club, called simply The Lunch, which served as a resort for New York's most talented and elegant men of letters, money, or power.

Like Morse (who also belonged to The Lunch), Cooper had broken with family tradition to become a Democrat. But being a Democrat in New York still meant associating with men from refined Hudson River families who ran the Party. The shift was not ideological, and Cooper was not greatly concerned with the social implications of politics. For him, Andrew Jackson was a southern gentleman and military hero, not a leader of democratic masses. And Cooper was much more interested in the reputation his books were gaining at home and abroad than in the development of democracy.

It was only when James Fenimore Cooper carried overseas his social credentials, his reputation and his concern for refinement that the problem of being both a gentleman and an American democrat began to agitate him. Just two years after he arrived in France, he published *Notions of the Americans*, two longish volumes devoted to explaining America to Europe—and to any of his countrymen who needed instruction, too. The book was begun for an odd reason. Lafayette, whom Cooper had met in New York when Lafayette made a triumphal tour of the United States in 1824, asked him to write an account of the tour. It would be difficult to make such a book interesting, but Cooper began anyway, out of courtesy and gratitude for Lafayette's social efforts on his behalf. *Notions of the Americans* took a peculiar shape, however, and one to which its original purpose was almost irrelevant. Cooper invented a travelling European nobleman, "The Count de - - - - -," who carried on an unrelenting correspondence with aristocratic friends in England and France about his travels in America. The "Count" was, in other words, a kind of fictive Tocqueville, three years before the fact.

The "Count's" perceptions were indeed very similar to some of Tocqueville's. He learned that "equality" had liberated Americans from foolish aristocratic notions and cruelties, that the democratic mass was serious, hardworking, inventive, generous, and decent. Equality had not erased the privileges of wealth and talent: gentlemen were still held in careful and gentle esteem by Americans. And gentlemen themselves had learned to live comfortably with democracy: their manners and dress were characterized by a republican simplicity reminiscent of their great national hero, Washington, the very model of the aristocratic republican. Cooper's explicit conclusions were commonplace, as were his contrasts between American democracy and European society. And his patriotic conclusion prefigured Tocqueville's awe at the inevitable triumph of democracy and of America which, in the last word of *Notions of the Americans,* was "irresistible."

On its surface, *Notions of the Americans* was not a problematic book. Its position on democracy was clear; its patriotism unambiguous; its picture of American government, manners and morals uniformly favorable—except for occasional dark spots, like slavery, which Cooper regarded as a "scourge." But as an event in its author's life, it was very perplexing. While at work on *Notions,* Cooper was very much involved in Parisian high society and worked hard to develop a courtly life style. His letters home were full of detailed descriptions of his social successes —like the grand ball at the house of Count Pozzo de Borgo, to which he escorted a real princess:

> As for the party, it was magnificence itself. Sixteen or seventeen rooms open, and many of them princely. The rooms were crowded, perhaps 1,500 people, including everybody most distinguished at Paris. The Princess and myself [!] came away at 1 o'clock, like sober people. My servant told me that 600 carriages had entered the court at 12 o'clock.

Cooper had made something of a habit of having his servant count the carriages. And he kept remarkably careful track of the aristocratic personages whom he met at Lafayette's weekly soirées. In such a setting, *Notions of the Americans* was quite eccentric: a defense of Cooper's own "democratic" society, yes, but prompted by the request of a Marquis, published anonymously in Europe, told in the form of letters of a fictive nobleman, directed obviously to an elite audience, and written by a man for whom European princesses appeared more frequent and congenial than New York hogs.

This striking disparity between the ideas of *Notions of the Americans* and the circumstances in which it was written should have made its readers cautious. The book aimed at one essential point: there was no real conflict between democracy and aristocracy in America, because both plain people and the elite have managed to preserve the best features of aristocratic society while shedding its abuses and oppressions. But the point was mildly dishonest. The novels Cooper had already written about America were dense with conflict between the values of gentlemen and of democrats. Even when Cooper wrote about "noble" men of poor birth and circumstances—like Natty Bumppo, the scout, hero of the Leatherstocking novels—the nobility was almost a miracle, a striking exception to class realities, not a typical trait of plain men. And the scout's very nobility constantly brought him into conflict with the demands for social order inherent in Cooper's idea of civilization. Cooper always had Leatherstocking come out the loser in these encounters, and Cooper's own values were normally represented by a gentleman, judge or squire who was "forced" to impose social discipline on the scout. Novels like *The Spy*, Cooper's second, published in 1821, had also been peopled by unruly, dangerous, disrespectful crowds of the poor and ignorant, obvious threats to the decent classes—the very kinds of people that *Notions of the Americans* chose carefully to ignore. The book was the gesture of a man deeply caught up in a Parisian world and anxious to picture his homeland as a place where "true" aristocracy could flourish within a wholly decent and restrained democracy.

Cooper traveled for two years after the publication of the *Notions*, but, with the July Revolution of 1830, hurried back to Paris. For the next two years, he was more politically active than he had ever been at home. He headed the Polish Committee, wrote essays defending American government and republican institutions in general, and watched with fascination as Lafayette and the republican liberals first seemed to have won, then gradually lost power to the new monarchy they had helped create. But James Fenimore Cooper the republican did this watching from an elegant two-story apartment in what his wife called "a very *distingué* part of the Town." Support for this life style came from his books, which he still churned out almost once a year. His royalties were very considerable: income from his British publisher was almost $20,000 for 1831 and 1832.

Finally, Cooper was ready to leave Europe. In 1833, with four Swiss servants, he set sail in "three state-rooms *en suite* built expressly for us, and near the centre of the ship, so that I hope the *maladie de mer* will not be killing." Cooper came home already troubled about the United States. His republican sentiments had earned him some very harsh reviews in the European press, and a number of America's Whig papers had reprinted the attacks. And so, before disembarking in New York, Cooper was prepared to notice great "changes" in his homeland, to "retire" as a novelist, to buy back his father's great house, "Otsego Hall" at Cooperstown, to take his family, servants, and expensive Persian rugs there—away from the instabilities and crudities of New York. The "change," of course, was at least as much in Cooper himself as in America. And what he chose to regard as a sudden "decline" in American manners was a decline not from the America he had actually known in the 1820s, but from the abstraction he had invented in *Notions of the Americans*.

Men looking for trouble seldom have any trouble finding it. Within months, Cooper was involved in newspaper feuds about himself, his work, the actions of Andrew Jackson's administration, and United States relations with France. In these feuds, Cooper, the Democrat, found himself cast by Whig papers as a Europeanized snob who, being spoiled by seven years abroad, was unable to tolerate the realities of American life. These charges had some truth to them. He was impatient with democracy, and he shared Morse's refined horror of New York's pigs and "nouveaux" entrepreneurs. It was a great consolation to buy his father's country seat and raise the ceilings three feet so he could put in Gothic windows to make the big house seem even more venerable.

Cooper's belief that American democracy had undergone a great corruption and decline got its strongest confirmation from a quarrel that he had deliberately provoked. The townsfolk had for years picnicked freely on a point of land owned by the Coopers and jutting into Lake Otsego. Cooper fretted about this incursion onto his family's "immemorial" rights. Finally, in 1837, he announced in the local Democratic newspaper that he intended to enforce the family's title to the Point. The first public reaction was an angry town meeting at which the local library was even asked to remove his novels from its shelves. The second was another newspaper war in which Whig papers in Cooperstown, Albany, and New York flayed his aristocratic pretensions. The third result was *The American Democrat* (1838), a book cataloguing the failures of American democracy.

In *Notions of the Americans,* Cooper had foreshadowed many of Tocqueville's optimistic assessments of the United States. In *The American Democrat,* he echoed many of Tocqueville's negative judgments. Cooper was still a theoretical democrat, to be sure. But now he was even more the gentleman, afraid of the tyranny of public opinion and of what he now saw as the dangerous conflict between rich and poor, gentry and people, order and anarchy. Most of all, he had decided, the public was to be feared: "The publick, then, is to be watched, in this country, as in other countries kings and aristocrats are to be watched." *The American Democrat* was an extremely abstract book, in which mere concepts like "classes," "men of cultivation," "the people," and the "the spirit of our institutions" collided on a blank geometrical plane. But its intentions were clear: to announce the collapse of the old, fictitious truce, stated in *Notions,* between democracy and aristocracy that had kept social peace.

The American Democrat was also a kind of schematic outline for two sets of novels: *Homeward Bound* and *Home as Found* in the 1830s, and a trilogy on a family of New York gentry, the Littlepages, in the 1840s. In these novels, aristocratic families recognizably like Cooper's found themselves in nasty encounters with democrats of all descriptions: ruthless entrepreneurs, demagogic politicians and journalists, Yankee farmers as crude and grasping as William Faulkner's family of Snopeses, and pretentious *nouveaux riches* whose manners merely betrayed an uncouth (and therefore democratic) obsession with the external badges of class. In all these encounters, Cooper's gentlemen could only be what they were: patient, moderate, and humane. They also turned out, as often as not, to be ineffectual, and to end in graceful retirement from scenes of action they could no longer control or even soften. In Cooper's world, there was no real alternative to democracy; he apparently shared an American consensus on that point. But the consensus was not always a willing one. Like many other gentlemen, Cooper felt himself born out of time, trapped in a world that had to be approved because it was the only one going, trapped too in the necessity to use the language and forms of democracy even when the purpose was to criticize or repudiate it.

Cooper never confessed, even privately, that he was no democrat. Nor did he ever formally reject the "equality paragraph" of the Declaration of Independence. But he did live a somewhat withdrawn life, interested himself more and more in religion as a check on the democratic "principle," and became visibly more bitter with the course that his country seemed to be taking. It was appropriate that he completed the Leatherstocking cycle of tales (which had begun with Natty Bumppo as a 70-year old man) with a pair of novels that retreated into the hero's youth. *The Pathfinder* and *The Deerslayer* pushed back into time and deeper into wilderness, to a period when there was less painful conflict between the hunter's "natural aristocracy" and the distressing "realities" that Cooper chose to see in American democracy. In the young Deerslayer, moving with efficient grace through his forests, Cooper could find imaginary relief from those selective "realities"; the novel ended with Cooper reflecting sadly that:

> We live in a world of transgressions and selfishness, and no pictures that represent us otherwise can be true; though, happily for human nature, gleamings of that pure spirit in whose likeness man has been fashioned, are to be seen, relieving its deformities, and mitigating, if not excusing its crimes.

For at least 50 years before Cooper wrote this ending to Leatherstocking's inverted career, it had been an axiom of American politics that the survival of republicanism depended on the "virtue" of the people. As the republicanism of the revolutionary generation was transformed into the democracy of the 1830s and 1840s, the people's "virtue" became an even more urgent need. But Cooper had concluded, finally, that there was very little virtue to be found in men in general. Leatherstocking, who was a magnificent accident of nature, represented, finally, no more than a consolation, a "gleaming" of light in a dark and distrusted world.

* * *

There was nothing in the actual history of the United States that *drove* Cooper (and Morse like him) to such a conclusion. The "people" were probably as virtuous on the whole in 1840 as they had been in 1800. It would have been just as easy, as a matter of experience, for Cooper to have decided that his Cooperstown neighbors were sturdy, decent yeomen, and to have thrown Three Mile Point open to their picnics, thereby fulfilling his own generous prophesies in *Notions of the Americans*. Morse, in a similar way, could have welcomed the Irish to New York as potential recruits to a new democratic culture. And Tocqueville could have seen any Paris crowd as the vanguard of a new awakening for France, instead of a fearsome mob. Men exercise a real choice in their perceptions, and their neighbors can become (within wide limits) symbols of almost any ideological fact or proof for almost any political theorem. Gentlemen's democracy, as it developed during the decades before the Civil War, was a paradoxical and unstable ideology. Men like Morse, Tocqueville and Cooper attributed a vague and elusive decency to "the people." But instead of building confidence, this hope could just as easily lead to fear—fear that the virtues so essential to the success of democracy might fade with alarming speed. In the end, it was fear, not hope, that governed the minds of most gentlemen democrats.

Soon, events would make the social perceptions of this trio of gentlemen democrats almost irrelevant. Immigration, geographical expansion, industrialization and urbanization—all punctuated by Civil War—transformed the face of the old republic much more radically than the short-term "declines" of the 1830s. The reflections and activities of gentlemen democrats were rudely treated by the processes of history, and the preoccupation of Tocqueville, Morse and Cooper with the international logic of democracy became half-relevant, almost antique.

8

Moral Man and Moral Society

LYMAN BEECHER
BRIGHAM YOUNG
HENRY D. THOREAU

by Charles A. Barker
The Johns Hopkins University

Lyman Beecher, Brigham Young, and Henry David Thoreau were three Americans who staked their lives on convictions they imagined would make society good. Two of them, Beecher and Young, won considerable support in their lifetime. Today Beecher is largely forgotten, Young continues to have followers, and Thoreau has emerged as a sort of patron saint for those who question the coercive power of the State.

The hope all three entertained, that their ideas would improve the behavior of human society, often fails to raise sympathy in 20th-century minds. A generation ago Reinhold Niebuhr, already beginning to be honored as the greatest American theologian in two centuries, expressed modern doubt about social regeneration, in *Moral Man and Immoral Society*. To be sure, Niebuhr restated Christianity's hope concerning individuals: by God's grace, His children on Earth can be, and often do actually become, just, altruistic, loving, and good. But society is different. Especially the national state is incapable of altruism, for by its nature it cannot transcend self-interest. And self-interest, and the sovereign power the state exercises with violence, are inseparable parts of a lump of immorality. There is no regeneration in it.

This judgment has hung on. Not at all the unique position of one theologian, but an attitude widely heard during the 1930s, it re-echoes

153

today. But it has never prevailed; and it seems less near doing so now than before World War II. Indeed recent social movements have sung a different tune. "We shall overcome." Today is too early to say whether our present crop of social injustice and violence will reinforce Niebuhrian pessimism or will relight the hope never extinguished that, once moral bottom has been hit, an upturn may be expected.

All this bears on the men who appear in the next three sections of this chapter. Were the immoral-society view to govern us, we should have to prejudge two of them—Lyman Beecher, churchman, reformer, and educator, and a man of the modes of his time, and Brigham Young, leader, organizer and policy-giver to the Mormons—to have been fools. For both of them literally expected that the law of God would imminently prevail. Still taking the Niebuhrian line, we should have to think well of our third principal, Henry David Thoreau, the member of the Transcendentalist circle who had the most to say about law and society. For, though he spoke in a time of superpatriotism, the decades of the 1840s and 1850s, he totally defied the state and denied any virtue in politics.

Still and again, if the immoral-society view perhaps expects too much virtue of a few individuals, and too little of most, and none of organized society as a whole, we may approach our three "movers and shakers" with expectations more nearly equal. Supposing that all persons are affected by circumstance, we may well notice at the outset that every one of our three began life in New England, the region most productive of moral ideas. The religious genius of New England—from Anne Hutchinson to Ralph Waldo Emerson, Jonathan Edwards to Mary Baker Eddy—has been proliferation and variety. We may reasonably look to each of our three, not alone to Thoreau, for something of what our time has learned to call "alienation." Lyman Beecher, Puritan held over from colonial Puritanism; Brigham Young, migrant and outpost builder; Henry Thoreau, devotee of solitude—the three raise just that question.

Thus today, in long-distance communication with them, we receive whispers that sound contemporary—whispers that must be especially audible to new-community men, to wilderness lovers, and to haters of regimentation.

*   *   *

Among the situations in history Lyman Beecher shares with Brigham Young and Henry Thoreau is that of having been the number-two man in the work with which he is identified. This condition is self-evident in the other cases as well: first Emerson, second Thoreau; first Joseph Smith, second Brigham Young. With Beecher the situation is less familiar, but the fact is that in Connecticut's moral-reformist history he was doubly a number two. He was second to President Timothy Dwight of Yale College, the man after whom he consciously modelled. In the 1790s Dwight had started the Connecticut work among students; 20 years later Beecher tried much the same reforms on the body of citizens. He also came second, in the sequence of thought rather than the sequence of time, after his friend and fellow Yale man, Nathaniel W. Taylor. From the pulpit of Center Church on New Haven's Green just in front of the college, and later from his chair of theology in the new Yale Divinity School, Taylor spoke brilliantly the lines of the "New Haven Theology." A variant of Edwardsean belief, it stressed man's free and sufficient "ability," under God, to live on Earth according to His law. Thus Taylor qualifies as the main theorist, and Beecher, accepting the theory, became its leading proponent.

*   *   *

Son and grandson of blacksmiths in lower Connecticut, Beecher began life on a social footing considerably lower than the famous Unitarians, who were born to such Harvard names as Channing and Emerson, and whose careers would run parallel to his own. But there was no lack of Puritan content in Beecher's background. A Beecher had crossed the Atlantic with John Davenport, the founder of New Haven; Lyman himself was born and brought up in nearby Guilford, fronting on Long Island Sound. He entered Yale College just before President Ezra Stiles finished. This means that he breathed of the twin currents of air that swept over post-revolutionary Yale: first, the warmth of new currents from the Enlightenment, to which Stiles had opened the windows, and second, the sharp wind of evangelism and of vigorous experimental science that entered with President Dwight. The combination made Yale popular; for some years it outstripped Harvard in student numbers and institutional growth. Long a home of nationalist feeling—for instance, of the Connecticut Wits—the college now made special contributions to social solidarity. Its science served the people of Connecticut, and its theology, the still-established Congregational Church.

Beecher's ministries took him away from New Haven. For the first decade of the new century, he served in a farming hamlet on upper Long Island, where he became restless, with too little money and too few chores. So when at age 35 he was called to Litchfield, a commercial town on the inland road from New York to Boston, he was delighted. It presented him with pleasant prospects: there were fine houses and gardens; Judge Tapping Reeve, who had more or less engineered Beecher's coming, had already established there his famous law school, the first in America. The new church was magnificent. Steeple and doors and windows, pulpit, and balcony supported by columns, all made the building a model. This was just what Lyman Beecher wanted his church as an institution to be.

At the time of Lyman Beecher's new beginning, the United States from southwest to northeast was experiencing the Second Great Awakening. If measured by the influence of revivalism on society, the second Awakening was more important than the first, of the 1730s and 1740s, the very well known one, of which Jonathan Edwards had been the great theologian. Generally speaking, where the 18th-century Great Awakening had strained near to breaking the century-old alliances between colonial churches and colonial governments, the 19th-century awakening sought almost the opposite: to impel the churches and the state and local governments into sympathetic efforts of reform. "Home missions" became everywhere important: training ministers; setting up churches, schools, and colleges in the West; supplying every encouragement to new settlements to nuture Christian youth who would be ready to meet their obligations, whether as churchmen and citizens or as creditors and debtors. From region to region the many churches acted differently, according to their organization. The four or five largest churches—the Congregationalists, Presbyterians, and Episcopalians, who had been numerous for more than a century; and the Methodists and Baptists, who had come to outnumber those three—accounted for a multitude of boards and commissions assigned to various undertakings of social action. Above all else the urgencies of population increase prevailed; if statistics are convincing, during the first half of the 19th century the United States was on the way, at last, to becoming surely and massively Christian.

Lyman Beecher's Connecticut had its small intense share of the excitements and hardships of growth. Farmers were moving west; debtors were numerous, and noisy about their grievances; clergymen were losing, and politicians were gaining in public esteem. The State's Congregational church, as in Massachusetts but nowhere else in the Union, still received tax money to support it; but embarrassingly that church was proportionately losing strength to the Methodists and the Baptists. Likewise the Federalist Party, the members of which characteristically were Congregationalists, was falling behind. Such adverse and challenging, but not yet critical, conditions were the reverse side of the coin that drew Lyman Beecher to Litchfield.

What he could do for his parish, and for Connecticut, occurred to him in terms of his training and recent experiences. On Long Island Beecher had tackled intemperance within his congregation. In and around Litchfield, it was a bit astonishing for him to hear, the same abuse existed in all classes, but conspicuously among the clergy! The farmers, mechanics, and manufacturers of the community all needed, in Beecher's words, "to diminish the quantity of ardent spirits consumed in their several employments." He thought that they should substitute "other palatable and nutritious drinks" and that "compensation" should be given, "if necessary, to laborers who will dispense entirely of the use of ardent spirits." But first of all, it was up to the ministers and magistrates to improve. "Let ministers, and churches, and parents, and magistrates, and all the friends of civil and religious order ... unite their counsels and their efforts, and make a faithful experiment."

These words by Beecher come from a committee report. Organized action followed. Whatever the substance of the abuse—whether the degradation that alcoholism now often accounts for, or something less—the writer does not know. We do know that, locally, other ministers joined Beecher, and public complaints diminished; that, nationally, excessive drinking challenged revivalist preachers in all regions; and that, historically, the churches tackling the problem preceded the first state legislative action in Maine by decades. We know also of Beecher that, while over and above parish routines he made temperance his first reform, he moved quickly on other causes. Before he arrived in the community, ministers had gone about raising money for the education of young women and for training men for the ministry. These efforts he promptly picked up. And in 1813 he took the principal lead in launching the Connecticut Society for Good Morals. Literally borrowing the name, the new society otherwise imitated one which Timothy Dwight had sponsored at Yale to Christianize student behavior. It spread a network across the state. Beecher served on the directing committee; the president was an ex-governor; the vice-president was Judge Reeve, Beecher's friend as well as parish associate. The program concerned manners as much as morals. It condemned blasphemy; it urged moderation of speech; it proposed strictness in keeping the Sabbath. In his 1827 farewell sermon to the people of Litchfield, Beecher uttered a kind of benediction on all that he and they had tried to do in their 15 years together: "Philosophers and patriots, statesmen and men of wealth, are beginning to feel that it is righteousness only which exalteth a nation." He quoted Revelations: "And He that sat upon the throne said Behold, I make all things good."

Finally, before summing up Lyman Beecher's efforts in Connecticut, an event of 1818, not something he did to the state but something the state did to him, requires a brief explanation. Much against his will, but according to the wishes of non-Congregationalists and more modern Congregationalists than himself, the convention that drew up a new constitution separated church from state. In his own retrospection: "I foresaw what was coming," he later reminisced. "I saw the enemy digging at the foundations of the standing order. ... I went with deliberate calculation to defend it." The decision by the convention hurt. "For several days I suffered what no tongues can tell." Yet somehow he recovered. On learning that Congregationalist colleagues felt relief not to be tied to the government, he decided that he did too. Soon and surprisingly he pronounced disestablishment to be *"the best thing that ever happened to the State of Connecticut."*

By present-day standards, Connecticut's agricultural, commercial and early industrial society seems almost incredibly simple; and so do its social problems and its leading social reformer. What could have been more shallow for a learned clergyman, who believed that through God's church His will could be done on Earth, than the program of the Connecticut Society for Good Morals? What change of mind (quite apart from the merit of the matter) could have been more facile than Beecher's, about the relations of church and state?

Still and again, such questions suggest more about the distance of a century and half between him and us than they do about the work of Lyman Beecher, or about Connecticut, or about the subject of this chapter—19th-century approaches to reform. Beecher did start statewide social reform in Connecticut. Soon after his departure, under such leaders as Henry Barnard and Horace Bushnell, systematic programs of education, some of them tax-supported and some of them church-sustained, succeeded well. They owed something to him: he had preached reform with enormous impact, and men had followed where he led. It was a tribute to Beecher when, in 1827 at age 52, he was called to Boston. The Hanover Street congregation, inviting him, asked of him just what he was prepared for—revivalist preaching of the New Haven doctrine. Rendered the more attractive by a good salary at a good address, the new situation compares at first glance with the Litchfield one in 1811, but in larger dimensions.

Yet there were also deep differences. Connecticut was known as America's "land of steady habits." Not Massachusetts and especially not Boston. In eastern Massachusetts religious ferment, strong enough to dissolve Christian orthodoxy with regard to the doctrine of the Trinity, was two generations old. Meanwhile social dislocations, owing in part to the rise of textile factories and exacerbated by Irish immigration, produced class conflicts worse than those in Connecticut. Both phenomena bore on Beecher's career. Naturally the religious one, now developed to the stage of open harassment between the Unitarians—who called themselves "liberal Christians"—and the conservative Congregationalists, was the first to draw his fire.

He arrived expecting and ready to battle the Unitarians. During the previous decade, in common with Taylor in New Haven, he had sensed that the liberals would extend their effort to capture control of Congregationalist parishes all the way into Connecticut. The two had taken protective measures: Taylor's anti-Unitarianism goes far to explain the founding early in the 1820s of the Yale Divinity School, a counter-offensive with Taylor himself in command. From his citadel on Hanover Street, Beecher likewise counter-attacked. His congregation was only one of several in Boston that supported the Andover Theological Seminary, the two-decades-old opposition school to the Harvard School of Divinity. But, because his own New Haven theology favored more social reformism than did Andover doctrine, Beecher thought himself better prepared than his allies to understand the liberals and to demolish their ideas forthwith.

He led off with the old vigor. His preaching brought recruits to his congregation, promoted the missionary movement, and launched in city and surrounding region a revivalistic campaign to compare in intensity with that of the 1740s. But any success he may have had against the Unitarians is dubious. Because Unitarian minds were closed to his ideas of regeneration, Unitarian ears did not hear his revivalist pleas. He failed to return many, if any, Unitarians to the fold of mother Congregationalism; he probably curtailed their growth. Rather than answering, they ignored him, a reaction that was hard to take.

The sector of Boston's social problems which most concerned Beecher was the startling increase of Roman Catholicism, largely but not altogether a product of immigration. No different from his ancestors, to whom the nearest Catholics in numbers were the French in Quebec, he conceived the Boston Papists to be enemies to be destroyed. As he envisaged them, Catholic ritual was archaic, the secrecy of confessional and convent was conspiratorial, and church authority was erosive of American freedom. In this mix of history and prejudice, Beecher abandoned the restraints that had moderated his assaults on evil in Connecticut; he became a rabble-rouser. One of his sermons, which alleged sexual misbehavior between priests and nuns, seems to have helped to incite, at very least to have shared the spirit of, the mob that broke into the Ursuline convent in Charlestown and burned it. This was the single most violent act in the anti-Catholic turbulence of the period, that guerilla warfare of the seaboard cities that historian Ray A. Billington has ironically called "the Protestant Crusade."

Partly because of this climax, rather anticlimax, of his pulpit career, Beecher's Boston period appears the most counterproductive part of a lifelong effort to make his people good. At this turning point of his life, while approaching 60, his mind once again seems not to have worked philosophically. In Boston the trouble was that, along with his total attachment to Congregationalism, he displayed no tolerance at all. Working for his denomination he gave no thought to the merits of Unitarians or Unitarianism, or to the merit of having them around. Still less did he comprehend, or even begin to consider, the value of welcoming Roman Catholics as neighbors.

Beecher moved to his last post of responsibility in 1832. While in Connecticut, he had feared the movement to the frontier as a process upsetting institutional and moral stabilities; but his decision now to go to Cincinnati awakened in him the feeling (common among those who went there) that the Old Northwest had become the last best hope for the Christian republic. In Cincinnati he was given charge of a leading Presbyterian congregation and the presidency of Lane Theological Seminary. The latter was a combined Congregational and Presbyterian training center for ministers, a recent institutional product of the Second Great Awakening and of the temporary union between the two churches. Possibly contemplating the origins and ideals of New Haven colony two centuries earlier, he managed to convince himself that Cincinnati would become America's London.

Soon after arrival Beecher ran into a second round of urban conflict. Some of his sermons disturbed the old-school Calvinists of his congregation. They brought him to trial for heresy, slander, and hypocrisy. Though the charges and the defense were very specific, procedures were relatively loose—as they were for all church trials at the time because ecclesiastical law was unsophisticated and trial officers rarely if ever were experienced. Heresy, consequently, had to be whatever the officers declared. Thus Beecher's ordeal stretched out: he was tried first before the local presbytery, second before the synod, and finally before the nationwide General Assembly. In the end he was found innocent and returned with honor to his appointments. But the trial was a hard beginning for Beecher in the West. After his own intolerance in Boston he may have had coming to him some anguish on behalf of his own belief. Certainly, he bore a great deal for his faith in the work of his 60s and 70s.

His more famous ordeal in Cincinnati, the best known episode of his life, occurred at the Lane seminary. During the early 1830s, when the antislavery movement was rising among the churches and the religious journals of the North and Northwest, his students insisted on meeting and discussing the subject. They were just across the river from Kentucky, and the South's peculiar institution had high and distressing visibility. But Lane's trustees, who were a mixed body of clergymen and businessmen, wanted quiet: "Education must be completed before the young are fitted to engage in the collisions of active life." Consequently it was wrong for the prospective ministers even to talk, and they forbade the meetings. During this discourse, President Beecher temporized. For most of his life he had been indifferent to slavery; but, before leaving New England, he had come to favor the Negro colonization movement, which aimed to settle American blacks in Liberia. (In point of fact, white Southerners saw colonization as a means of removing free Negroes from their midst.) Thus he was identified with a very slow method of emancipation and with a movement that acted out the common racist assumption that blacks were not to be assimilated as equal to whites in American society. Even so, Beecher did favor the students' demand, and when he finally insisted that the meetings be permitted, his trustees acquiesced.

Unfortunately Beecher's courage came late. The students at Lane walked out—the earliest and most memorable social protest of that kind in pre-Civil War history. They crossed the State northward to Oberlin College. There they were welcomed into an institution that not only had a few black students but also stood as the nation's principal academic citadel of antislavery. Oberlin was under the presidency of Charles G. Finney, who had been Beecher's rival in evangelism in the East. Moreover, the College immediately started its own theological seminary and its own "perfectionist" school of theology. In encouraging social reform, its ideas would carry considerably further than the New Haven theology. Thus in Ohio as in Connecticut, Beecher's cautious starts in reform and education were overtaken by men of larger commitment.

Unhappily for any sense of climax or culmination about Beecher's career, the long years before and after his retirement contained no memorable innovations and no successes that came near to matching his goals. After the tensions within church and seminary that upset his life during the early years in Ohio, the adversities of depression hit him in the late 1830s. In addition the strains of antislavery involvement mounted on him, as on all churchmen in the Old Northwest during the 1830s and 1840s. Instead of culmination, Lyman Beecher's later career brought him an increment of dignity, the reward—without either conspicuous success or conspicuous failure—of sustained effort made in a faith that was always sincere.

One special aspect of his life requires a kind of appendix because in a way it projects him ultimately into public affairs. President Abraham Lincoln, it may be recalled, once greeted Beecher's fourth daughter, Harriet (who was also the wife of his old close colleague at Lane, Calvin Stowe), as the woman who by her book had brought on the Civil War. She was one of his 13 children to whose upbringing he had contributed greatly, both during years of happy marriage and in years of widowhood. His oldest daughter, Catharine, as founder of a school and a missionary of women's education, is a larger figure now than her father in the history of education; probably she is a larger one than Harriet in the history of women's freedom and participation in society's work.

Beecher also fathered seven sons, every one of whom grew up to be a Christian minister, just as he wanted. Though today not one of them seems as important as their two famous sisters, one is well remembered, Henry Ward Beecher. For years the country's best known preacher, honored with the charge of the rich Plymouth congregation in the rich suburb of Brooklyn of the nation's richest city, he built on a talent which he would seem to have inherited from his father. As adapter of current thought, Darwinian evolution, to Christian doctrine and as preacher of moderate social reform, he echoed Lyman Beecher's effort to shape the New Haven theology to popular social improvement.

*　　*　　*

Brigham Young's number-two, but hardly secondary, position in Mormon history owes nothing to the date of his birth. He entered the world in 1801, four years ahead of "The Prophet," Joseph Smith. Both were Vermont farm-village boys and while young were part of the large migration from upper New England to western New York. They had no family connections. But where Smith began well before 20 to have uncommon religious experiences and by 25 had transmitted to the world the Book of Mormon and founded the Church of Jesus Christ of Latter-Day Saints, Young was 31 when converted to that church and 43 when he took charge. The two lives first came together in the fall of 1832 when Young visited the Prophet at the Mormon settlement in Kirtland, Ohio.

Thus the top two Mormon leaders were born in one state, taken to another state, and then worked together in a third state, where the folkways of New England religion persevered. Just how tenaciously they did so, Lyman Beecher's career illustrates well. But, the other side of the coin, religious innovation, occurred as well. The so-called "Burned-Over District" of upstate western New York, where Joseph Smith grew up and Brigham Young came into manhood, somehow became the special breeding place of radical faith. For instance, besides the Mormons there were the Oneida Perfectionists, who outdid all others in restructuring family organization and sex arrangements, and the Seventh-day Adventists, whose ideas about the calling of the saints were vivid and often upsetting. And in the same region the older churches competed with one another in revivalism, using Charles G. Finney's "anxious bench" and other new methods of conversion. "I am the way," became the repeated, essential message, not simply of radical leaders such as Joseph Smith, William Miller (another Vermonter), and John Humphrey Noyes, but of many another. It was a departure, but not a far departure, from evangelical norm. Although Lyman Beecher was never caught saying so, that was just about what he meant.

Among the special revelations of the period, Smith's Book of Mormon is by far the most imposing. It declares that tribes of Israel, unknown to Jewish history, were the forebears of the American aborigines. This was nothing new: many Americans, Lewis and Clark among them, had long since entertained such an idea of red Indian origins. But the Book of Mormon filled in the story in ways that gave it religious potency. In rough similarity to the historical books of the Old Testament, it chronicled complex wanderings and wars among the tribes. Jesus Christ was recorded as not only having come to Palestine with His message of salvation but also to America centuries ago. But no more this time than on His first coming, had His rule been accepted. Wars continued with bad Indians exterminating good until only one tribe of the good, the Nephites, survived. Finally that tribe too was annihilated, excepting a short remission for Mormon, its chief. God then punished the evil victors by darkening their skins. (Here was established Mormonism's special belief in the primacy of the white race; Joseph Smith and his successors would never recruit Negroes and Indians only to a limited extent for their new church. But, in truth, it was hardly more than a variation on the common 19th-century belief that God had made His creatures different, some high, some lower.) Thus the Book of Mormon concludes with a new picture of human destiny: American aborigines, like the ancient Jews from whom they were descended, had specially received the Savior; and like the Jews they had rejected Him. Among all the people of Earth, the readers of Mormon's book were now given a new New Testament. Like the early Christians receiving the Gospels and the church, they were called of God to lead all whites and Indians who would follow into righteousness during this life and beyond.

This remarkable book, and then over the years a flood of revelations, came to the Mormons in complex ways. (Smith had 133 revelations as compared with only one by Young.) According to Smith, he had early received directions for unearthing near his home the original Book of Mormon—the text Mormon himself had inscribed on plates of gold just before death. Next Smith was enabled by miracle to read the text and authorized to render it into English. Almost of equal importance to himself, to Brigham Young and to all their successors in Mormon leadership, Smith received continuing instructions from God, instructions which were to shape Mormon policies. One group of these instructions placed the government of the church on a totally authoritarian basis. Joseph Smith identified himself as the "first president" in a council of three presidents. Another set of revelations set Mormon rules about marriage. During the 1830s, God approved the plural marriages Joseph Smith had already made; in 1843 He sanctified plural marriage for any male approved by the church. (Strictly defined, Mormon "polygamy" should be called "polygyny," for extra partners were not allowed to females.) Thus Smith received and Young inherited two unique provisions of privilege: namely, one-man supremacy in the Mormon hierarchy and movement and as many women as they cared to marry. Over the years Young took 27 wives, 24 of them as a polygamist. He sired 54 children.

When his time came, Brigham Young proved no man to hold back. Within a year after becoming first president, he began his great act of moving his people far to the west, where they would be quite independent and he would be practically sovereign.

About six years were required to make the enormous transition. Before Joseph Smith was assassinated in 1844, the Mormons had been settled for several years in Nauvoo, Illinois, where they built a prospering community. Even so, as the violence of that year demonstrated, they had not achieved security; they had not outlived their previous condition as a rejected tribe. But Smith and Young had made one special provision of strength: a system for bringing converts from Europe. It quite reversed the usual way of American missionaries. Where the old churches, generally speaking, were based in the east and looked to the west for converts (in Oregon, in China) the Mormon movement looked east to the working classes in Europe—at first to the United Kingdom, then to the northern, later to the central and southern, parts of the continent. In today's language, the Mormons as an American counter-culture, sought recruits in Europe's subculture. With polygamy they appealed to women. To be sure, a missionary's plea must often have seemed startling to women; namely, that they join a new church with some likelihood of sharing a new husband in the bargain. The message bore comforts nevertheless. The church provided immediate aid for making the transatlantic and transcontinental journey; marriage, whether single or plural, was guaranteed and was sure to be sanctified. Above all, in the mind of the convert, the church signified life among saints on this Earth.

With female reinforcement coming in large numbers and male immigration not short, Brigham Young's situation invites comparison in the American history of immigration with that of Governor John Winthrop, two centuries earlier. Like Winthrop in the role of principal manager of settlement in New England, Young could not escape separatism; schismatic groups of Mormons broke away. Neither did he avoid Indian fighting and killing. But like the great migration of the Puritans during the 1630s, that of the Mormons in the 1840s belongs to the history of heroism. Its very size as well as its anguish and ultimate success separated the Mormons forever from the insecurities of Joseph Smith's years. The Mormons did not worry unduly about their isolation in what was Mexican territory until 1848.

At this point the designation, theocracy—which means government by God and implies a ruling high priest or other deputy for Him—is no longer to be avoided. Notwithstanding that the treaty of peace with Mexico in 1848 so redrew boundaries that Utah became a part of the United States, Brigham Young retained an ample supply of power. As if to confirm this fact, President Taylor appointed First-president Young to be the first governor of the territory that was created by act of Congress in 1850. If in theory such authority was incompatible with theocracy—there being no claim of divinity in the presidency of the United States—it neatly filled out on the secular side Brigham Young's consolidation of strengths. Certainly, in the most honored theocracy in American history, the Massachusetts Bay Colony, Governor Winthrop had had many advantages beside theory; but never had that church-and-state combination been as total and solid as this Mormon one.

On the church side, the church-state of Deseret (as the Mormons called it for years) developed as population growth demanded and as Brigham Young directed. As naturally as the now world-famous Temple and Tabernacle rose in stone and wood in the center of Salt Lake City and as small houses of worship were built in every farming settlement, so was the church hierarchy constructed, downward and outward from the first apostle to the people. From the presidency of three and the apostolate of 12 at center, church lines of command and invigoration reached the "wards," as the congregations under their "bishops" were known. Two religious brotherhoods, called Aaronic and Melchizedek, introduced some of the secrecy and comradeship that Masonry gave to eastern Protestants and reinforced the whole Mormon system.

On the governmental side of the theocracy, economic problems made early and urgent demands. The first need, posed by the unaccustomed climate, was water for very dry land. As to irrigation, Young and his colleagues can hardly have had any previous knowledge except from their Bibles. So his starting operation, which was laying out eight thousand acres of flatland in rectangular five- to ten-acre plots and directing the whole manpower of the community to dig intersecting canals, seems wonderfully imaginative and right. So also does his scheme of administration. He had plots distributed by lottery. Residential lots, with irrigation, were distributed in the city; and later on, as population growth required, the system was extended. Lotholders were sometimes required to plant fruit trees or shade trees or both. Today the regularity and beauty of Salt Lake City, a man-made oasis in a mountain-and-desert location, owes much to these beginnings.

The Mormons carried their ways of planning into their underlying institutions. All lands were assigned in usufruct, not in fee: that is, farmers and householders were given the role of steward rather than owner. Likewise the yield of grain was placed under a system of tithing. This meant that the product of a farmer's toil went 90 percent to him and ten percent to the community. By way of the church's tithing office, which was very close to President Young's own residence, the Mormons thus built up a durable food supply, insurance against lean years. Memory of the system would come to a second life during the 1930s in the New Deal's plan for an ever-normal granary.

Perhaps Brigham Young's three practices of theocratic management of the economy—landholding in usufruct, farming by irrigation, and tithing —did not strike him and his colleagues as being particularly connected in moral logic to polygamy. But the connection is evident in Utah's early history: for as a matter of course within the church "celestial marriage" was arranged early rather than late, often between teen-agers. And, as the female converts arrived, probably about 20 percent of the males took more than one wife. Few other Mormons matched President Young's total of 27, but others well up the hierarchical ladder counted wives in two digits. Concerning all this, it would be hard to certify that the harem-situation stories, which often appeared in American journals against the Mormons, contained no pebbles of truth. But the closer accounts indicate Mormon marriage to have been characterized by discipline, labor, and child-bearing, and harshness rather than ease. Quite as plots of land were distributed in a way to encourage high productivity, so also were women converts placed on arrival. Conceivably, other arrangements could have been tried, say, religious sisterhoods living in convents. But for durable marriages and the birth and raising of legitimate children in that time and place, the moral common sense of Mormon polygamy is hard to doubt.

Far distant as Brigham Young's Utah was removed from its New England origins, the Mormon theocracy proceeded, almost Puritan style, with education. Again as in the 1630s, a "university," secondary schools, and primary schools were provided early.

In Utah, as in states of colonial origin, compromises were made in time between the interest of the church and the interest of the state. Radical economic policies, and polygamy, were abandoned. Thus when normal American statehood finally arrived, half-a-century after the Mormon migration, tax supported, secular government followed as in the east. Church and state, separated by law but not fully divorced in practice, managed to mix, even to blend, their efforts.

In final hindsight, Brigham Young continues to look somewhat like the tribal leader, a kind of Moses of the 19th century. He and his people crossed the country, part of a huge and enveloping migration of peoples. But uniquely in America they stayed loyal to their inspiration and kept their community identity. To be sure, their women lost out in personal and economic freedom; but, just possibly they were more often fulfilled. Certainly the Mormons built a city of beauty, an unusual thing in that age. As to the common culture, they pulled themselves high by their bootstraps with their schools—and with music, dance, and theater, which departed old Puritan ways.

Measured beside the other principals of this chapter, Lyman Beecher and Henry Thoreau, Brigham Young succeeded far beyond their success as immediate changer of the moral order in which he and his people lived.

*   *   *

Where Lyman Beecher and Brigham Young spoke from pulpits, Henry David Thoreau (1817–1862) won an audience much more slowly through writings supremely well done. In his lifetime, outside his home circle at Concord he reached very few people. But today, over a century later, his ideas and his identity have carried around the world.

We know the proximity of Thoreau to Emerson as Transcendentalism's number two man in the 1840s. In the Concord circle, he was, in fact, the only native of that village. His studying at Harvard, his longest period ever away from home, gave him the very best preparation—under William Tyrrel Channing—for a literary life. Immediately after graduation in 1837, he taught school for a time; and he soon made the trip from which, ten years later, he drew his first book, *A Week on the Concord and Merrimack Rivers*. Having become close friends with Emerson, he lived in his home starting in 1841. Two years later, when he began his second longest residence away from Concord, he went as tutor to the household of Emerson's brother William on Staten Island in New York.

Though in college Thoreau ventured some teen-age defiance of discipline, he became no radical; nor did he mark up a high record as student. But he did become known as the most widely-read member of his class; likewise, a decade later, he was probably the best-read member of the Concord group if one does not count Theodore Parker. After Harvard, German and Greek (taught to him by the mystical poet Jones Very) were always available. And when one examines the Oriental interests of the Transcendentalists in the Neoplatonism of the Middle East or in the Bhagavad-Gita and other wisdom literature of India, there is Henry Thoreau with his quotations in order. About his mind opening wide to his great neighbor Emerson, the only questions are those of detail. It would be pleasant to know, for instance, whether Thoreau sat in the audience when Emerson, in his first Harvard address, "The American Scholar," admonished the students against bookishness and in favor of intellectual "action." Altogether certain is Thoreau's lifelong, admiring, and loving attitude toward the number one Transcendentalist. During the years that surrounded Thoreau's graduation from college, Emerson brought out Transcendentalism's philosophical charter, *Nature;* and, besides "The American Scholar," he gave the equally famous Harvard address wherein he advised divinity-school students and professors against the ministry as a career. That independence-declaring, nature-loving, now fully self-reliant Emerson gave Thoreau his model, philosopher, and friend.

Literary work began for Thoreau with contributions to the *Dial*, the journal edited first by Margaret Fuller and then by Emerson. In company with such older, distinguished people as Bronson Alcott and Theodore Parker, and with Emerson and Miss Fuller themselves, he contributed both poetry and prose.

His essay on "Friendship" was one piece. When Emerson assumed the editorship, Thoreau assisted at that work. Yet for all his elevated connections and opportunities during the first eight years out of Harvard and for all the comfort of his mother's home as well as Emerson's, this post-graduate period has for Thoreau the look of a young man at loose ends. Those months of tutoring in New York did uncommonly widen his vistas. There he became acquainted with reformers: with Horace Greeley, when the New York *Tribune* was two years old; with Lucretia Mott, five years before the women's rights convention at Seneca Falls; and with Henry James, Sr., then studying Swedenborg. But only after returning to Concord would Thoreau take the step that would carry him directly to self-realization.

On July 4, 1845, just a few days short of his 28th birthday, Thoreau withdrew from society. Physically he moved only a very short distance, from the center of Concord village to the edge of Walden Pond. But spiritually he reached solitude. He was ready to take whatever time might seem right under wilderness conditions—26 months later he decided.

Of course his principal work, *Walden*, published nine years from this time, was the appropriate product of the period of observing and thinking. But the direction of his ruminations appears also in earlier, lesser writings. One of those writings, which to millions has seemed not a lesser writing at all, *Civil Disobedience*, flowed directly from his reaction to the outbreak of war with Mexico. As Thoreau tells the story, on a beautiful summer-day walk through Concord on a berry-picking expedition, he ran into a friend, the town constable, Sam Staples. The officer interrupted him with a reminder that his poll tax was long overdue: "Henry, if you don't pay I'll have to lock you up pretty soon." To which Thoreau replied, "As well now as any time, Sam." Perhaps he was angry, as another report says; but, according to *Civil Disobedience*, he was philosophical while in jail, as surely he ought to have been. For by intention he had been withholding payment since 1843. In that year Bronson Alcott, his friend and the schoolmaster and philosopher of child-nature, had refused the tax and had been jailed. The Massachusetts measure had posed the issue of principle. But in 1846 the Mexican War had changed the frame of reference. It aroused Thoreau, as it did many others who had doubts about slavery or about war as an institution.

Already leaders of the antislavery movement were advocating tax refusal. Abolitionists feared that the coming acquisition of Mexico's northerly and westerly domains would lead to transplanting slavery there. Tax refusal seemed to them, as it has to 20th-century radicals, to offer a way of resistance. But how could refusing to pay a tax locally, one enacted by State lawmakers and executed by Concord authorities, restrain conquests by forces that were authorized, paid, and directed from Washington? Thoreau's own words give us his reasoning. "I quarrel not with far-off foes, but with those who, near at home, cooperate with, and do the bidding of, those far away, and without whom the latter would be harmless. . . . I do not hesitate to say, that those who call themselves Abolitionists should at once effectually withdraw their support, both in person and in property, from the government of Massachusetts. . . . Any man more right than his neighbors constitutes a majority of one already. . . . Under a government which imprisons any man unjustly, the true place for a just man is also a prison. The proper place today, the only place which Massachusetts has provided for her freer and less desponding spirits, is in her prisons. . . . I was not born to be forced. . . . I quietly declare war with the State."

These passages go far to justify the claim that has been made by modern anarchists, that Henry Thoreau qualifies philosophically as an anarchist. Yet *Civil Disobedience* contains a countervailing conviction as well, the almost universal confidence in the nation men of Harvard and men of Concord especially loved to assert. Again Thoreau's own words are not to be improved upon. As for the state and local government that surrounded him: "I have never declined paying the highway tax, because I am as desirous of being a good neighbor as of being a bad subject; and as for supporting schools, I am doing my best to educate my countrymen now." Directly to the point of the federal system, he acknowledged that the "Constitution, with all its faults, is very good; the law and the courts are very respectable; and even this State and this American government are, in many respects, very admirable, and rare things, to be thankful for." Thoreau's final word gives off an almost millennialist gleam: "I please myself with imagining a State at last which can afford to be just to all men, and to treat the individual with repsect as a neighbor. . . . A State which bore this kind of fruit, and suffered it to drop off as fast as it ripened, would prepare the way for a still more perfect and glorious State, which also I have imagined, but not yet anywhere seen." In this mode appears the Thoreau who wanted to be a reformer, or a "re-former" as Emerson himself proposed.

Thoreau had courted imprisonment. No doubt his expectation that his argument for civil disobedience would be reinforced by having an actual prison record was fulfilled; it was not much impaired anyway by his aunt's paying the tax. Released after only one night, he resumed the course which, according to Emerson, "He chose, no doubt for himself, to be a bachellor of Thought and Nature." Certainly it is easy to think of his two years at Walden as experimental work leading to a degree. It is yet easier to think of *Walden* as a thesis, to record his findings; the famous first chapter, "Economy," particularly qualifies as a summary of backgrounds and procedures. Thoreau had said when he was 20 that Mosaic law is wrong about the work-week. "The seventh should be man's day of toil, wherein to earn his living; the other six the Sabbath of the affections and the soul—in which to range this garden and think." Not only did the traditional work ethic offend him, but also, much more, the new industrial spirit. In a book review, before *Walden*, he levelled his charge. The book before us, he said, "aims to secure the greatest degree of comfort and pleasure merely. . . . There is far too much hurry and bustle, and too little patience and privacy, in all our methods." Not different in logic from white contemporaries in the South, who reasoned that slavery provided a better system of labor than hirelings working with machines, Thoreau offered an anti-industrial way of living.

He was very exact about it. In that opening chapter on "Economy," he published his personal records. On the debit side, for examples: $28.12½ for building materials for his cabin; $8.74 for store provisions to last eight months. On the credit side: $36.78, from the sale of vegetables he had raised but not consumed and from payment for doing neighbors' odd jobs. And so on. In the end he found himself $25.21¾ out of pocket, which he balanced against 26 months of leisure, comfort, and health. By contrast he had observed surrounding him his "townsmen, whose misfortune it is to have inherited farms, houses, barns, and plowing tools. . . . Who made them serfs of the soil? . . . The mass of men lead lives of quiet desperation. . . . There is no play in them, for that comes after work." Many later chapters tell us what "play" meant to Thoreau: they speak, for instance, of life in "The Bean Field," of our "Brute Neighbors," and of "Winter Animals." In *Walden* work and play, observation and meditation, and all else move rhythmically, according to nature's four seasons.

Not for everyone but for men who will venture, the literal meaning of *Walden* seems to be that life can be rich and good. Recently critics have told us how much more and other than an economic solution the book contains. One of them, Charles R. Anderson, insists persuasively that *Walden* is truly a poem, and that the ultimate concern of it is human regeneration. Here we see that passages are linked together in feeling, though logically they are as far apart as the opening ones about costs and earnings and the closing ones about sunrise and the life of insects. Thoreau managed beautifully the emotional distance between the everyday comity that man can establish with nature and nature's evidences of "resurrection and immortality." *Walden* marks him as America's best spokesman, so far, for living in love of nature.

*   *   *

"By Circumventing the State" could be applied with almost as much descriptive accuracy to Lyman Beecher and Brigham Young as to Thoreau in their respective approaches to social improvement. Beecher certainly did contemplate, and did win, mutuality between his church on one hand and the state and local governments of Connecticut and Ohio on the other. Equally, and more than equally while he held the office of territorial governor, Brigham Young played the sovereign game of power. Yet both men relied ultimately on church, not state. Beecher had little if any traffic with Washington; more characteristically Brigham Young held apart from the United States government longer than he conformed with it. All three of our principals lived their lives before most state governments had ventured into programs of social improvement and long before the federal government entered the field. In this respect the difference between Thoreau and the other two was that the latter were ready to take government or to leave it. They were pragmatic on that issue. Not in theory but for practical purposes, Thoreau's only option was to leave it.

Since the life span of the three, the United States has travelled a stop-and-go course of accepting the idea that the federal and state governments will replace the churches as the normal instruments of social improvement. Beecher would not have liked this. His anti-slavery children seem closer than he does to having achieved a prophetic view. Only in the temperance movement, and to the slight degree in which Henry Ward Beecher's Social Gospel reformism of the 1880s fulfilled his father's undertakings may Lyman Beecher be credited with affecting the long-run future of social reform.

Brigham Young's claim seems stronger. Admittedly since his time the United States has produced no new theocracy; and, as the Mormons continue to apply that word to themselves, to outsiders it sounds rather hollow. On the other hand, Brigham Young's forthright decisions about land and water use, about a special kind of family planning, and the Mormon achievement of social solidarity, do retain excitement and contemporary relevance. One at least wonders whether with God's help the Mormons might not extricate themselves from some of the lines of thought that separate them from potential allies, notably their ideas of white-race and male-sex superiority. Might they then not have a second turn in the work of large-community planning?

In the 1960s and 1970s, as American fondness for strong government has waned, and as among the young moral idealism has waxed and moved toward the left, Henry Thoreau has seemed more than ever special and the most prophetic of the three. Since the later 19th century he has been a household name to outdoorsmen, to conservationists in general, and especially so to wilderness lovers. With the passage of time he has become a hero to pacifists. To Martin Luther King and his followers, *Civil Disobedience* stated the best method of social protest. During the 1940s his moral outreach—by way of Mohandas K. Gandhi, into India's independence movement—carried the farthest ever, to a land very un-American and halfway around the world.

If one chooses to believe that moral ideals do in fact have long life in society, not apart from but in enhancement of their life in the hearts and minds of individuals, the ideas of Henry Thoreau offer a vital case in point.

9

The Role of Domesticity Transcended*

MARGARET FULLER
LYDIA MARIA CHILD
MARY B. CHESNUT

by Margaret R. McGavran
University of Massachusetts, Boston

To be born female in America during the first half of the 19th century almost automatically meant that one's future would be that of domesticity. Woman's lot was to rock the cradle, tend the house, and keep the peace within it. If she lived on a farm or plantation, she was usually expected to help out with the harvests and to oversee the hired hands or slaves. American women clung to the notion that they were inherently different from men. Indoctrination from childhood taught them that they were docile and submissive by nature. Only the "home," so they believed, could offer a refuge from man-made violence and an ever encroaching industrialism. Even outspoken women like Cotton Mather's grand-daughter, Hannah Mather Crocker, in her "Observations on the Real Rights of Women" (1818) conceded that "The surest foundation to secure the female's right, must be in family government, as without that, women can have no established right."

There were, of course, exceptions—even radical ones like those women who saw in the abolitionists' plea for black freedom direct parallels to their own unspoken wish for liberation from male domination. In the summer of 1848, many of the most assertive women from upstate New

* Unpublished material quoted from the Margaret Fuller manuscripts by permission of Harvard College Library and from the Williams-Chesnut-Manning Papers by permission of South Caroliniana Library. Excerpts from Mary Chesnut, Diary from Dixie (edited by Ben Ames Williams) (Boston: Houghton Mifflin Company, Sentry Edition, 1961), quoted by permission of the publisher.

172

York, along with an almost equal number of men, met in convention at Seneca Falls, where, in mimicry and perhaps somewhat in mockery of the *Declaration of Independence,* they wrote their own *Declaration of Sentiments* wherein they declared: "The history of mankind is a history of repeated injuries and usurpations on the part of man toward woman, having in direct object the establishment of an absolute tyranny over her. To prove this, let facts be submitted to a candid world."

But those who were willing to submit the "facts" were few. Women such as Lucy Stone, Lucretia Mott, Susan Anthony, and Elizabeth Cady Stanton (at whose home the Seneca Lake convention initially met) were among the notable exceptions. Their careers hardly give a clear indication of the temper of the time. And even they were embarrassed when they collectively acknowledged how few women before them in the 19th century could be singled out as proof of woman's ability to transcend her allotted "sphere." To work one's way free from indoctrination was a tricky business. Only in the most unusual circumstances could a girl grow up with the education and energy that would allow her to develop beyond narrowly circumscribed limits.

"It is a true, and therefore an old remark," wrote Lydia Maria Child in her book on domestic life, *The Frugal Housewife,* "that the situation and prospects of a country may be justly estimated by the character of its women." Among those who sought to transcend the limitations of domesticity assigned to American women in the first half of the century were Margaret Fuller, Mrs. Child herself, and to a lesser extent, Mary Boykin Chesnut. Certainly, Margaret Fuller and Maria Child defied those conventional definitions that categorized the female as a parlor ornament or as a pristine madonna, even as they themselves remained consistent in their belief in the significance of the harmonious union of self-realized men and women within a family context. Though not radical in the sense of being exclusively feminist, they nonetheless would define and redefine the role of woman with the goal of making her a more suitable companion of man.

*   *   *

As a dissenter within a straight-laced New England, Margaret Fuller championed the right of women to live in expressive interaction with men and thereby, she believed, in significant relationship to the community. Indeed she tested her radical theories to such an extent that the close-minded circle of intellectual elitists in Massachusetts turned from her. Lydia Maria Child, too, asserted her persistent vision that all people should be free whatever their race, religion, nationality, or sex. To her brother Convers Francis, she wrote in January 1841 her first self-consciously expressed thoughts on the matter: "I defy all the powers of earth and hell to make me scour floors and feed pigs if I choose meanwhile to be off conversing with the angels. . . ." For her work in behalf of abolition, she also won the scorn of many Boston Brahmins. In contrast to Margaret Fuller and Maria Child, both New Englanders, Mary Boykin Chesnut came out of the South Carolina gentility. She was the wife of James Chesnut, Jr., a prominent Palmetto State political figure in the immediate pre-war era and later a Confederate brigadier-general and a member of President Jefferson Davis' staff. An "iron-willed" secessionist like her husband, her fortitude was tried during the South's effort to secede from the United States and stand independent as a slave-holding nation. She kept her faith and her wits even as she watched the Confederacy crumble around her. Her fidelity to those she loved never faltered; and her belief grew ever stronger as the Civil War neared its end that the only causes worth fighting for were the right to life of the men, women, and boys whom she saw dying daily around her and the family's perpetuation and cohesion.

All three displayed varying degrees of valor in their lifetime effort to achieve their respective individual identities as women. Their courage was, in part, the product of an excess of energy—what in woman, Margaret Fuller called "electricity." And though differing in their views, they shared a belief in woman's subtle strength and power of endurance.

Some pertinent questions come to mind. How did these women go about contending with, and even transcending, the static definitions society assigned them? How did they overcome self-doubts and fear in the face of adverse criticism and/or the chaos of man-made war? More specifically, where lay the source of their strength and of their awareness that "true and perfect companionship," was that which gives both man and woman complete freedom *in* their places, without a restless desire to go out of them? While reading John Milton's *Paradise Lost* in the midst of war, Mrs. Chesnut saw "the speech of Adam to Eve in a new light. Woman will not stay at home; will go out to see and be seen, even if it be by the devil himself." Commenting at another point on the simultaneous creation of Adam and Eve, she noted succinctly, " 'Male and female, created he them,' says the Bible."

To appreciate fully these women, we must consider their childhoods and their relationship to parents who were sometimes difficult and demanding—particularly the father. It was through a "good father's early trust," Margaret Fuller noted in her radical feminist tract, *Woman in the Nineteenth Century* (1845), that a daughter learned to know "that what the soul is capable to ask it must attain." It is also helpful to look to their schooling to their intellectual ability to move beyond precast patterns and role models. If the three grew up in exceptional circumstances (as each did), then further questions come to mind. How did childhood training influence their adolescent relationship with men and their adult selection of a husband? How did it help determine career choices and/or the causes each defended? And how did it affect their actions during the trials of war when, in Mary Chesnut's words, "Grief and constant anxiety kill nearly as many women at home as men are killed on the battle-field." In short, what part did early personal interactions with their fathers have to do with their vitality as women and above all, with their public view of, and battle with, the male-defined society in which they lived?

To Sarah Margaret Fuller, born May 23, 1810, in Cambridgeport, Massachusetts, no person on earth meant more to her than her father, the high-strung, domineering, Harvard-educated lawyer and politician, Timothy Fuller. And little wonder: "Timo" Fuller had selected the first of his nine children to be the image of himself, a thorough-going rationalist with a demonstrable ability to antagonize people. Early he took his daughter from the care of his wife, Margarett Crane, who was a former school teacher; he talked to her and taught her as if she were a boy. Happily for the father, Margaret could adapt intellectually to his outrageous regimen. By age four she was reading English fluently; by six Latin; and by eight Horace, Virgil, and Ovid in the original. Her gift for learning was astounding; she memorized her lessons late into the night so that she might recite them to Mr. Fuller when he returned from his law office. In reality she sought to meet the all but impossible demands of his exacting intellect. In time, the training proved effective, even if the little girl had "no natural childhood." She wrote at age nine: "My father, When I get the card that has *Best* upon it at school, may I read it again?" And, then, at age ten, she confessed that "it is the first and dearest wish of my heart to conform *to your* wishes in everything."

Margaret, to be sure, had difficulty meeting demands she could never be certain of fulfilling. But she spent most of her time trying. When she could find no adequate means of expressing the confusion of feelings that he aroused, those emotions turned inward. Thus, not surprisingly, she become a sickly, high-strung, and lonely child to whom, by her own confession, "the life of dreams . . . has often seemed more real . . . than that of waking hours." In some dreams she could pacify her deeply ambivalent feelings toward her father. But other dreams were nightmares that thoroughly terrified her. Hiding in his book closet, she sometimes fancied herself a Don Quixote, a Caesar, or any male hero who might fulfill Timothy Fuller's high estimate of her future character. On occasion, she fantasized herself an abandoned European princess, a girl who was soft and feminine, but thoroughly worthy of her father's love. In reality, however, Margaret was ugly. She had coarse features, an elongated neck, and squinty eyes. She was also given to overweight and troubled by a poor complexion.

There is something sad, if not tragic, in Margaret's need to imagine herself worthy of parental affection. Moreover, she sorely missed her gentle mother's love. Her stubbornly obtuse father eventually took note of a child who hid for hours behind their Cherry Street house within her mother's garden and pretended to be as lovely as the flowers. Troubled by his daughter's eccentricity and what he thought was her "unnatural" and even passionate love for an older woman, who was visiting from England, he confessed "I am to blame." His solution was to send the 14-year-old Margaret off to the Misses Prescott's boarding school in Groton. But it was too late; the other school girls laughed at their strange, but brilliant, classmate and played cruel pranks on her.

Throughout her life Margaret suffered from the inadequacies of her early upbringing. Though intellectually a prodigy, she remained emotionally alone. Parental instruction and self-discipline had given her an education, as well as a "masculinity," comparable, if not superior, to the best of Harvard's youthful scholars. Despite her lack of physical attraction, she had become, through an act of sheer will, the perfect blend of intellect, wit, and charm. Many of Boston's educated men and women found themselves positively drawn to this brilliant ugly duckling who seemingly could converse on any subject under the sun. When she was 25 and critically ill on the family farm in Groton, her father sought to console her. "My dear," he said, "I have been thinking of you in the night, and I cannot remember that you have any *faults*. You have defects, of course, as all mortals have, but I do not know that you have a single fault." Proud of his daughter, Timothy Fuller had at last spoken aloud his high esteem, but again it was all too late; she had grown tired of his crankiness and refused to yield him any sign of respect or affection. Yet despite this slight show of independence, she could not escape her nurture. Even after his death, which came not long after her own near fatal illness, his unvoiced commands continued to exert their hold on her. She grieved by the bier of this man who in life had set such high standards for her and who, even in death, made a demand upon his daughter—to seal his eyes. Margaret would make a lifelong effort to comply with his commands. Of Timothy Fuller's forbidding presence his daughter long carried within her, she wrote in her Journal: "My father's image follows me constantly . . . May this sorrow give me a higher sense of duty in the relationships which remain." Fulfilling her "duty," Margaret Fuller henceforth would work to become what she believed ought to be the paradigm of the new 19th-century female—an aggressive and yet feminine woman. She would, moreover, make the theme of her book, *Woman in the Nineteenth Century*, the right of such a woman to live freely and creatively.

*   *   *

Lydia Maria Francis—she was called by her middle name—had an equally arduous youth; her father, David Convers Francis, was just about as difficult as "Timo" Fuller, though not so attentive to the intellectual growth of his youngest child. While both families could extol their colonial heritage (each had been among the earliest immigrants to the Massachusetts Bay Colony), Margaret unlike Maria could not boast of a grandfather who had fired a shot at Lexington, a matter of some importance to New Englanders. Moreover, David Convers Francis was a thoroughly self-made man. Without benefit of formal education, he had raised himself up from apprentice baker to foreman to successful bakery owner. His "Medford Crackers" were renowned throughout the Commonwealth of Massachusetts. "He was," wrote Convers of his father, "the most intensely industrious man, I think, that I ever knew. He was sturdy, and a great lover of right and freedom." He was, even more, a man of strong opinion and unbending will who "detested slavery and its apologists." However, Maria's mother, Susannah, like Margarett Crane Fuller, was a woman with a "simple loving heart, and a spirit busy in doing good"; similarly, she had an intense love of nature.

Maria's formal education was obtained at a "dame school" in Medford and at Miss Swan's Seminary. In 1814, when she was 12, her mother died of tuberculosis. The blow fell hard on this youngest of six children whose nearest sibling, Convers, was seven years her senior; the rest of the Francis children had long been grown-up and out of the house. Only Maria remained, and though she admired her father's industry, she missed her mother's presence. Heartbroken at his wife's death, Convers Francis sold his bakery, retired with the princely sum of $50,000, and sent Maria off to live with her newly married sister in Norridgewock, Maine, then a raw frontier town where marauding bears and howling wolves terrorized farmers. Understandably, Maria felt abandoned and alone. There is little remaining evidence that tells us much of these early years, but what does exist reveals a child who felt intensely her early separation from a home and the lack of a secure family, a place to which she could really belong.

And again like Margaret Fuller, this lonely girl turned to books as companions, particularly the romantic novels of Sir Walter Scott. Fortunately she saw in her brother Convers, then a student at Harvard, a positive intellectual model to emulate; her first letters about her reading and self-education were written to him. Picking up the familiar family theme of personal freedom at any cost, she related it to her readings in Gibbon, Shakespeare, Addison, and Samuel Johnson. Of Milton's writing she remarked at age 15: "Don't you think that Milton asserts the superiority of his own sex in rather too lordly a manner?" For, she continued, when Eve conversed with Adam, "she is made to say, 'God is thy law, thou mine: to know no more/ Is woman's happiest knowledge, and her praise.'" Maria preferred as her models not the downtrodden, meek women, but rather those of "wild dignity" and "pathos and grandeur." At age 19 she again wrote, "I hope, my dear brother, that you feel as happy as I do. Not that I have formed any high-flown expectations. All I expect is, that, if I am industrious and prudent I shall be *independent.*"

Maria Francis recognized the combined influence of her father and brother upon her life. All of her letters expressed gratitude to the latter, a long time Unitarian minister and later a Harvard professor; they attributed to his "early influence" the fact that her "busy energies took a literary direction at all." In 1820, she went to live with him and his wife in Watertown, Massachusetts. While brother and sister were mutually supportive, they had a lifelong disagreement about the origin of human strength. Although converted to Convers' Unitarianism, she could not believe that her faith could be the product of simple reason or of any formal "theological tenet." In her mid-30s she wrote him: "I know not how it is, but my natural temperament is such that when I wish to do anything I seem to have an instinctive faith that I can do it." And that included tending to the needs of her temperamental father toward whom she often felt intense anger, yet attended tenderly when the five other children remained uncaring.

Maria's relation to her father intrigues. He was ever present in her life, either to be contended with or to be cared for. He blustered; he was at times unbearable; he claimed with no basis in fact, to have sacrificed so much for his daughter that he had deprived himself of a home; he was enough, she said, to make a person turn to drink or suicide. Yet she loved him and watched over him. At the time of his death in December 1856, she wrote a good friend, "the occupation of my life seems gone." For, the "old man loved me; and you know how foolishly my nature craves love . . . Always when I came back from Boston there was a bright fire-light in his room for me, and his hand was eagerly stretched out, and the old face lighted up, as he said, 'You're welcome back, Maria.'" Maria cried herself "blind" at his death and thought she would "willingly be fettered to his bedside for years," if she "could only hear that voice again."

Many creative and successful women, it has often been noted, have had dynamic fathers toward whom they were almost magnetically drawn from an early age. Throughout their lives, they have had strongly ambivalent emotions of both dependence and resentment. Such women have characteristically released these internal tensions in aggressive though highly feminized ways. Certainly Margaret Fuller and Maria Child were aroused to anger, even rage—which was rarely articulated and hence internalized—through their interaction with difficult fathers. Intellectually each desired to be equal to that father and to share a position of power with him, while emotionally they remained dependent on him. They wished, as Mrs. Child put it, to remain "fettered" even as they asked to be free.

This desire for freedom, so often repressed in those who have been taught to be passive, childlike, and dependent, was brought to conscious recognition within them. Even as children they found in the unresponsive behavior of an emotionally remote father reason to believe that they deserved to share authority with him. Once mature, they realized their right to exist as independent personalities. If a "master" proved unjust, it was the moral responsibility of the fettered to seek an end to this bondage; or, as Maria Child angrily wrote before the Civil War about slavery in the South: "In this enlightened age, all despotisms *ought* to come to an end by the agency of moral and rational means. But if they resist such agencies, it is in the order of Providence that they *must* come to an end by violence." History, she added, "is full of such lessons."

*   *   *

If on the other hand, the father figure was just and good, the child, however enlightened, would not necessarily feel the need to question, upset, or destroy the structure that defined her in terms of passivity and dependency relationships with men. Such was true of Mary Boykin Chesnut who never doubted the legitimacy of Southern manners until the close of the Civil War. But, then, she had little reason to question her situation. Born near Camden, South Carolina in 1823, Mary Chesnut was the oldest of four children by the second wife of Stephen Decatur Miller, a self-made man who had risen from small-time farmer, to lawyer, to high public official; he was successively Congressman, Governor, and Senator from South Carolina. Mary literally worshipped her father, who was South Carolina's chief executive during the nullification crisis; she attributed to him her lifelong interest in public issues as well as her steady belief in the cause of states' rights. She implicitly accepted his authority, but she also early recognized her own right to self-assertion. Mary's reminiscences characterized her mother as open, honest, pleasure-loving and kind in the best manner of a Southern gentlelady. But she was also apparently a strong and practical woman.

The source of Mary Chesnut's stability as an adult was thus fairly evident. She had honest and emotionally open parents whose qualities she admired and whose love she never questioned. At age 12 she recalled her ill father travelling with the family south to Mississippi so he could take up cotton planting and hopefully improve his health. How happy and intimate, she commented, they all were on their journey. They read together till the books ran out; they sang together and slept together. In the words of Mrs. Miller, as her daughter recalled them, they were a "model family." Mother and children never allowed anything disagreeable to upset Mr. Miller. They consciously avoided annoying him and sought only "to make home happy." "I have never said a word to worry him in my life," wrote Mary of her father, "and I never will." Her mother added by way of explanation: "My husband looks upon his home as a heaven of rest and peace."

Mary was deeply instilled with the Southern belief that a woman's role, however prominent, was to serve her husband. And though she attended boarding school of Madame Talvande in Charleston where she exhibited some traces of intellectual detachment, she generally followed this Southern code. She frolicked with girls her age, was absorbed in schoolgirl daydreams of meeting a military hero and, by her own confession, concentrated, "the energy of (her) imagination" on this fantasy. At age 13, Mary Miller had the good fortune to meet James Chesnut, Jr., a member of the "elite of Southern youth" and by then Princeton graduate and student in the law office of James L. Petigru. She quickly made him the very real subject of her dreams. For his part, Chesnut found young Mary Miller not unattractive; but more important to one who had political ambitions, she was the daughter of Stephen Miller. Still, romance was the most important aspect of their covert courtship.

In fact, the father image of each of these three women influenced their perceptions of men. Margaret Fuller found in Ralph Waldo Emerson, high priest of the Transcendental movement, the same cold Anglo-Saxon qualities as she had seen in the intellectual and distant Timothy Fuller. Shortly after the father's death in 1836, and at the outset of Emerson's brilliant literary career, she sought his intellectual understanding and emotional help. For three weeks Margaret was a guest in Emerson's Concord home where she taught him German, talked to him of love, poetry, and religion, and wrote him impassioned notes and letters—delivered directly from room to room by his little son, Waldo. She desired in short to win from him and to give in return a daughter's love that was inhibited in her father's lifetime and left unexpressed at his death.

It was all very intense yet one-sided. For Ralph Waldo Emerson lived a settled domestic life with his wife, Lidian, while at the same time seeking intellectual and spiritual detachment. In his own words he desired to be "alone with the Alone." Emerson sought salvation for his own personal tragedies in his writing; those of Margaret were simply more than he could handle. In September 1840, Emerson read one note from Margaret, who was again his guest, inquiring, "Then indeed, when my soul, in its childish agony of prayer, stretched out its arms to you as a father, did you not see what was meant by this crying for the moon?" And as her would-be surrogate father, he heard her revealing appeal at the close of this letter: "I need to be recognized." From a distance he could see her despair and sometimes he could love her. But they could not meet emotionally. Rather they froze each other into silence.

Emerson could understand, but given her nature, he could not fully relate to such an aggressive woman. Margaret, for her part, adamantly refused to accept his union with Lidian as true or lasting, being convinced "that it will never be more perfect between them two." But for Emerson love was "only phenomenal." The soul knew "nothing of marriage, in the sense of a permanent union between two personal existences." The soul, he said, married only thoughts: "There is but one love, that for the Soul of all Souls, let it put on what cunning disguises it will, still at last you find yourself lonely,—*the Soul.*" Margaret conceded to none of his high-toned Transcendentalist talk. They conversed endlessly, but did not come to an understanding; they agreed only that her "god was love, his truth." Nevertheless, the encounter served Margaret Fuller well. It sharpened her understanding of her problematic father and helped her to come to terms with him.

Since her meeting with Emerson in 1836, Margaret had thrown herself tirelessly into a series of unsatisfying jobs both in and around Boston and in Providence, Rhode Island. As teacher, translator, conversationalist, lecturer, and editor of the Transcendentalist magazine, *The Dial,* she worked at an exhausting pace. So eager was she to excel that again and again she found herself the victim of piercing headaches and emotional strain. But she remained always alone. The chore of writing *Woman in the Nineteenth Century* had a dual function in Margaret Fuller's life. It served to resolve those emotional problems that she knew so well were the source of both her strength and her pain. It would also argue for the rights of a new kind of woman—one who was intellectually astute as well as aggressive and one whom man could deeply love. Like man, Margaret Fuller argued, woman must be allowed "as a nature to grow, as an intellect to discern, (and) as a soul to live freely and unimpeded . . ." In the United States there ought to be a way for a woman full in soul, mind, and body to interact with a man in harmonious reciprocity of respect and affection. "It is the very fault of marriage and of the present relation of the sexes that the woman *does* belong to the man instead of forming a whole with him," she concluded. Emerson was, of course, right in believing that marriage, as it stood, was not a meeting of self-realized souls: nor would it ever be until all of woman's attributes were fully recognized. When that day came, woman would be a fit mate for man.

Maria Francis shared Margaret Fuller's goal of feminine equality. Her early letters to her brother and her first novel, *Hobomok,* reflected the rage she felt toward her father and all of the other overtly cold and overly cerebral Puritan men. In writing *Hobomok* and *The Rebels,* or *Boston before the Revolution* (1825)—both stories of strong-willed and independent women—she announced her defiance; she would have nothing to do with emotionally inhibited intellects. Her formula for relationships between male and female, as well as for black and white, was simple: equality, open emotional expression, and mutuality.

Maria Francis was a young woman of seemingly inexhaustible energy. Not only did she conduct a school in Watertown, but she also began publication in 1826 of *Juvenile Miscellany*, the first children's magazine in the United States. She achieved wide popularity and entree into Boston's literary and intellectual circles where she met David Lee Child, a Harvard graduate of old Puritan stock, who resided in Watertown where he practiced law. Eight years her senior, Child had already served as secretary of the United States legation in Lisbon, had joined the Spanish in their fight against the French, and on his return to America was elected as a representative to the Massachusetts General Court. Like her father, he was a champion of human rights and freedom; he defended the Cherokee Indians when they were expelled from their Georgia lands and was among the founders of the Garrisonian New England Anti-Slavery Society. But David Child also had a restless spirit that fixed upon visionary schemes. Maria, lively and petite but not terribly attractive, fell deeply in love with this dreamer whom she married in 1828 against the advice of her family. Depending heavily on his wife's affection for stability, he thereafter devoted most of his life to fighting actively for abolition and to an unsuccessful attempt at cultivating beets for sugar to replace cane sugar produced by slave labor. Maria unwaveringly stood by him, for, though money problems were constantly recurrent, husband and wife were intellectually and emotionally compatible. Both believed that slavery must be eliminated. Both were certain that with its collapse in the South, the United States would at last become a land of and for "the people." Indeed, Maria Child was convinced that *only* with the collapse of the "peculiar institution" could women fully teach men the meaning of "gentleness and love."

Organized feminist groups did not appeal to Maria Child. Women should do what they could do well without making a fuss about it. She wanted women to keep their "charm" by consciously remaining unobtrusive and mild. Nonetheless, she insisted that they be strong personalities. In agreement with Margaret Fuller, she realized that dependency relationships between husband and wife began in the home. Though a woman must not cease loving her husband and children, she had to learn how to share in the business end of marriage. With her own situation in mind, she wrote in *The Frugal Housewife:* "Let women do their share toward reformation—let their fathers and husbands see them happy without finery; and if their husbands and fathers have (as is often the case) a foolish pride in seeing them decorated, let them gently and gradually check this feeling by showing that they have better and surer means of commanding respect."

Maria Child had to be content without finery and she also had to handle her husband's business affairs. For David Child seemed incapable of earning money or of managing family finances. She stood by him despite the loss of his legal career and lawsuits brought against him for his radical activities. "Few men in the world have done more good than you have done," she wrote him in his distress. "Few are more truly respected. God knows that I consider my union with you His richest blessing. It has made me a better and a happier woman than I ever was before."

To earn money she wrote a succession of books—mostly popular non-fiction—about the liberation that comes through a woman's commitment to domestic happiness. Unfortunately, as much as she and David loved children, they had none. Once during her marriage she wrote a friend "that to a childless wife, life is almost untenanted." Perhaps partly as compensation, as well as a means of defending her own independence, she stressed in her books the necessity of good educations for young girls so that they might be more than mere ornaments, wives, or mothers. In *Good Wives* (one of several volumes in her *Ladies Family Library*), she demonstrated through a series of brief biographies that women could indeed learn the art of good housekeeping without sacrificing their individuality. And, in later books like *Fact and Fiction,* she provided a fictional account of the abuse of women in a society governed by man-made laws.

Maria Child preached only what she herself practiced; she remained the devoted wife even as she exercised extraordinary independence. Following her husband's lead, she wrote the provocative *An Appeal in Favor of that Class of Americans Called Africans* (1836). The work was so bold a plea in behalf of immediate abolition and so sharp a criticism of both the subtle and unsubtle forms of discrimination practiced against free Negroes that sales of her other books dropped off precipitously. Indicative of the displeasure of conservative Bostonians was the fact that the Atheneum, which had generously given her a free subscription, suddenly closed its doors to her. Yet there were not a few Bostonians who, on the basis of Maria Child's book, began to see immediate abolitionism in a new light. Among them were Wendell Phillips, John Greenleaf Whittier, Thomas Wentworth Higginson, and William Ellery Channing.

Undaunted and certainly not intimidated, Maria Child continued to write abolitionist tracts. She also became executive secretary of the American Anti-Slavery Society. When in 1841 William Lloyd Garrison offered her the editorship of the *National Anti-Slavery Standard,* the Society's new journal, she accepted it, leaving David Child behind on their Northampton beet farm. However, she went to New York primarily to bring in money to help save the failing farm which had all but reduced them to poverty. Just weeks after her arrival there, she wrote of her editorship: "I hate it . . . I question the morality of letting one's soul thus be ground up, for a cursed reform!" Though detesting slavery, her first loyalty was to her husband. How she longed to be reunited with him "and have some quiet, domestic days again!" Later she wrote of her work in behalf of abolition, "I *am* a reformer, but please henceforth never to think of me thus. If anti-slavery made me take one particle less of interest in the sad music of the moon, the birth and death of the flowers, and above all, in the rosecolored dreams of youthful love, I would abjure it tomorrow, even at the risk of the Calvinist hell for my disobedience to my conscience!!" Nonetheless, Maria Child worked hard on the *Standard.* The literary quality of the journal was improved, and its editor defiantly insisted on directing it toward readers of the family circle rather than abolitionist zealots.

With reason, Garrison resented her moderation. But she remained stubbornly consistent and hung on as editor until 1843 when she finally resigned in favor of her husband who meanwhile had given up on his beet farm. But David Child lasted only a year as editor, and he too resigned over a policy dispute with Garrison. During the next few years Maria continued her writing while David went from one job to another. He was unsuccessful in all of them. In 1850, they returned to Massachusetts and two years later they moved into her father's house in Wayland.

Maria Child spent all of her life in the North where she believed that it was possible for men and women to form "free and kind" companionships. On the other hand she was certain that slavery had made Southern women mentally as well as physically indolent and consequently "far less capable, industrious, and well-informed" than their Northern counterparts who were "educated under a more healthy system."

To some extent Maria Child's observation applied to Mary Chesnut. The latter does not stand out in history necessarily as particularly intellectual, introspective, or self-conscious; but she does emerge as an attractive and perceptive woman, particularly in the war years when she candidly wrote down what she saw in *Diary from Dixie,* her only published book. That she could display such uncanny powers of observation while the Southern world she had known and loved crumbled daily around her was something little short of a miracle.

Mary Chesnut attended boarding schools designed primarily for the training of genteel Southern ladies. But her formal education was cut off abruptly when she was 15 with the death of her father. Almost immediately James Chesnut entered into her life. In a letter of May 1839, just 14 months after her father died, he wrote from Paris and proposed. He expressed himself with the proper decorum of a Southern gentleman: "To love you is not inconsistent with the love of heaven... *you* must become the link to bind me to that better world—through you I will learn to love it better."

They married in April 1840, and she quickly assumed the role of a dutiful wife to a Southern planter and fledgling politician. Toward the end of the war she wrote in words that echo those of her mother: "All the comfort of my life depends upon his being in good humor." Of course they sometimes disagreed and had marital squabbles. She argued that he was too self-controlled. He accused her of being a "miracle of sensibility." But in the end his word was law; or, as Mary Chesnut playfully put it: "He is the master of the house; to hear is to obey."

The worst result of slavery, Maria Child had pointed out in her abolitionist writings, was that it made the victims so accustomed to their condition that neither master nor slave would see any reason for a change in the system. Of his own servant, James Chesnut noted, "After all, what can he ever be, better than he is now—a gentleman's gentleman?" But Mary Chesnut looked at slavery from a different perspective. To maintain racial purity and white control, the social conventions of the antebellum South elevated the region's caucasian womanhood to an exalted status. Mary Chesnut knew better; she realized that it was all a sham. Slavery was a curse, a cancer in the body of Southern white society. "Men and women are punished when their masters and mistresses are brutes, not when they do wrong," she wrote to her diary. Even more bitterly, she continued:

> Under slavery, we live surrounded by prostitutes, yet an abandoned woman is sent out of any decent house. Who thinks any worse of a Negro or mulatto woman for being a thing we can't name? God forgive us, but ours is a monstrous system, a wrong and an iniquity! Like the patriarchs of old, our men live all in one house with their wives and concubines; and the mulattoes one sees in every family partly resemble the white children. Any lady is ready to tell you who is the father of all the mulatto children in everybody's household but her own. Those, she seems to think, drop from the clouds. My disgust sometimes is boiling over. Thank God for my country women, but alas for the men! They are probably no worse than men everywhere, but the lower their mistresses, the more degraded they must be.

In an equally biting passage, Mary Chesnut wrote:

> I hate slavery. You say there are no more fallen women on a plantation than in London, in proportion to numbers, but what do you say to this? A magnate who runs a hideous black harem with its consequences under the same roof with his lovely white wife, and his beautiful and accomplished daughters? He holds his head as high and poses as the model of all human virtues. To these poor women, whom God and the laws have given him. From the height of his awful majesty, he scolds and thunders at them, as if he never did wrong in his life. Fancy such a man finding his daughter reading "Don Juan." "You with that immoral book!" And he orders her out of his sight. You see, Mrs. Stowe did not hit the sorest spot. She makes Legree a bachelor. . . .

Such, then, were the fruits of the Southern system, if Mary Chesnut is taken at face value: manners were often more important than authentic expression of human emotion; blacks were casually bought and sold; women were trained to remain silent; and men and women customarily married for the continuation of the family line. Still, Mary Chesnut was not at all severe in her judgment. "In face of all difficulties," she wrote in her old age, "when a race continues from father to son, scrupulously correct in conduct, pleasant in manner, charming, high-bred . . . It is a thing to thank God for!"

Courage, needless to say, was also integral to that system, and faith endured beneath the ladies' bright facades. "The real ammunition of our war is faith in our-selves," she continued, noting that "Mrs. [Jefferson] Davis's ladies" were highly "wilful women . . ." She described the women of Richmond going in their carriages for the wounded in order to take them home and to nurse them. "One saw a man too weak to hold his musket. She took it from him, put it on her shoulder, and helped the poor fellow along." But in her heart, she knew that it would all be in vain. "We are as gay, as madly jolly, as sailors who break into the strong-room when the ship is going down." The sinking South could not be saved by its gentlemen, no matter how blue their blood or incarnate their chivalry.

That genteel Southern women like Mary Chesnut felt an unaccustomed exhilartion in these years was not surprising. For in a sense they thrived during wartime; they were needed as never before. Prior to the war, Mary Chesnut had been bored with her passive, silent role on the Chesnut's Mulberry plantation near Camden, one of several owned and lorded over by her elderly father-in-law. At Camden, her house was always crowded, she wrote in 1864. "It is the wind-up," she confirmed prophetically, "but the old life as it begins to die will die royally."

As an eye-witness account of the war years, Mary Chesnut's diary told of the death of this decorous system wherein slaves, and women, lived for their masters; even more, it related the suffering of Southern white women. Of one such woman who had lost a son, daughter, and husband in the war, her sister said, " 'How was she to face life without her husband and children? That was all she had ever lived for.' " And amid such tragedy, Mary Chesnut read *The Blithedale Romance*, Nathaniel Hawthorne's romanticized version of Brook Farm. "Blithedale," she remarked, "leaves such an unpleasant impression . . . now that we are so harrowed by real life. Tragedy is for our hours of ease."

Margaret Fuller could hardly have lived within Mary Chesnut's chivalric world. She was far too intellectual and assertive for that. Those who came—and paid—to hear her expound on literature, art, mythology, philosophy, women's rights, etc., in her famous Conversations, were aware that they were hearing one of the sophisticated minds of their day. But New England was not yet ready to accept fully a woman of her magnetism. Nor did she fare better in New York where she went to live and work in 1844. It was in New York that she had her first real love affair, one that unfortunately turned out badly. And so in 1846 Margaret Fuller left for Italy as correspondent for Horace Greeley's *Tribune* for which she had been working as a reporter (she was the first professional woman journalist in the United States). There she fell deeply in love with the young and impecunious Marchese Giovanni Angelo Ossoli and worked tirelessly in behalf of the Italian revolution. This uprising against papal tyranny, according to Margaret Fuller, was also against the priesthood in general. "I am deeply interested in this public drama," she wrote home from Rome, "and wish to see it *played out*. Methinks I have *my part* therein, either as actor or historian."

Perhaps woman's character could, after all, be best measured by her ability to rise above the chaos and destruction of war. Certainly Margaret Fuller played her part bravely in a struggle which, like her own, seemed destined to failure. In charge of the hospital of the Fate-Bene Fratelli, she tended the wounded and the dying who lay around her "in every form of pain & horror." Lewis Cass, Jr., the United States chargé d'affaires in Rome and an eye-witness to her heroism, wrote that she was like a European Queen whose "heart & soul were in the cause for which these men had fought, & all was done that woman could do, to comfort them in their sufferings." Cass watched "the eyes of the dying, as she moved among them, . . . meet in commendation of her unwearied kindness."

Margaret's activities and acquaintance with pain were highly visible, but she herself privately suffered from another source, an illegitimate pregnancy. The consequent guilt was almost unbearable. In her liaison with Ossoli, she had transgressed the moral code of New England Puritanism. During the bombardment of Rome in June 1849, she wrote some last words to Emerson: "Should I never return,—and sometimes I despair of doing so, it seems so far off, so difficult, . . . Meanwhile, love me all you can; let me feel, that, amid the fearful agitations of the world, there are pure hands, with healthful, even pulse, stretched out toward me, if I claim their grasp." Ultimately the rebellion of the people failed and with it, in Margaret's words, "Private hopes of mine are fallen with the hopes of Italy. I have played for a new stake and lost it. Life looks too difficult."

Ten months before the collapse of the revolution, Margaret Fuller gave birth to a child; in his existence she found reason to play for another kind of "stake" in life. Love for her son, Angelino, transcended both morals and war. The energy once given to the revolution was now diverted into merely writing about it; her child and to a lesser extent her husband were all that mattered. Of her son she wrote to one of her young admirers, Cary Sturgis Tappan: "You speak of my being happy; all the solid happiness I have known has been at times when he went to sleep in my arms." And she again prophetically wrote to this same friend: "This much I do hope, in life or death to be no more separated from Angelino." "The position of a mother separated from her only child is too frightfully unnatural."

Through her love for little Angelo, Margaret Fuller at last appreciated fully her own mother, "—so generous, so sweet, so holy! What on earth is so precious as a mother's love; and who has a mother like mine!" Beyond that there was the family to live for. To Margaret, the "earthly family" was "the scaffold whereby we build the spiritual one." Surely, she said, the family must be "of Divine Order."

Friends had urged Margaret Fuller to remain in Italy. Even Emerson counseled her not to return "home." But she had decided upon America. No longer employed as foreign correspondent for the *Tribune,* she had no source of income. Moreover, the Italian revolution had failed. There was, then, no cause, no reason, to keep her abroad. Finally, she knew that at home and within the circle of her family's love, she could find consolation and a refuge, insulation against a life-long suicidal anxiety. At the core of Margaret's new faith was a mother's love for her child; by it she could make her way in a hostile world and "take the worst bitterness out of life." Nothing else, she wrote, could "break the spell of loneliness." She would go home.

Margaret's ship, the "Elizabeth," set sail on May 17, 1850. Sometime in the morning of July 19, it struck a sand bar off Fire Island only minutes away from New York City. Often in her anxiety Margaret had dreamed of death by water; and now she watched, horrified, as the terrors of her night came alive. While others tried to swim ashore, Margaret, almost as if paralyzed, stood on the forecastle beside her praying husband. She made no effort to save herself, according to the ship's cook who survived the disaster. "I see nothing but death before me," she said. "I shall never reach the shore." She did not, nor did her husband and son. At Concord, Emerson wrote coldly of her death: "To the last her country proves inhospitable to her."

Not until the Civil War would America be forced to face head-on the issues raised by the existence of what Lydia Maria Child called "The Patriarchal Institution," the title of one of her antislavery tracts. From her home in Wayland, where she lived in retirement with David Child and her dying father, she wrote of the skirmishes in Kansas and of the forthcoming 1856 election: "There never has been such a crisis since we were a nation. If the slave-power is checked now, it will never regain its strength. If it is not checked, civil war is inevitable; and, with all my horror of bloodshed, I could be better resigned to that great calamity than to endure the tyranny that has so long trampled us...."

Maria Child had imagined that at Wayland she and her husband had at last finished "building castles in the air." But news of John Brown's raid on Harper's Ferry in October 1859, prompted the now 57-year-old woman to write a friend: "Recent events have renewed my youth and strength, and filled me with electricity, and one word of apology for slavery makes the sparks fly." She thought the raid an act of "sublime" madness; but she honored that "brave old man," and wrote him in prison, offering to serve as his nurse. The offer, politely declined, won her the scorn of Governor Henry Wise of Virginia as well as a scathing reprimand from Mrs. Margaretta Mason, wife of the Virginia Senator. In reply, Maria Child proclaimed that Negro bondage must once and for all be done with. "The fact is," she concluded, "the whole civilized world proclaims slavery an outlaw, and the best intellect of the age is active in hunting it down."

Maria Child's reply, printed in a pamphlet which sold over 300,000 copies, was appropriate. She was, after all, the daughter of a man who had boasted that his first vote had gone to General George Washington and his last to Colonel John C. Frémont. As long as Francis blood ran in her veins, she could not be silent while slavery existed. "I never was one who knew how to serve the Lord," she had written in 1856, "by standing and waiting." And during the war she worked tirelessly making flannel underwear for Union soldiers and writing letters and articles in behalf of black freedom.

Until her death, Maria Child did all she could to further the cause of human freedom. The best any of us can do, she declared, "is to follow, fearlessly and faithfully, the light within our own souls. In no other way can the individual so help the race." She had been enlightened by the men in her family concerning the importance of human liberty; but she extended it to include the equality of women as well. "I have walked in fetters all my pilgrimage," she wrote in her old age, "and now I have but little farther to go. But I see so clearly that domestic and public life would be so much ennobled by the perfect equality and companionship of men and women in all the departments of life, that I long to see it accomplished, for the order and well being of the world."

The Civil War, of course, revolutionized relationships between former masters and slaves. And to a degree it affected the relationships of men and women as well, especially in the Southland. "Women, wives and mothers," wrote Mary Chesnut in wartime, "are the same everywhere." She had grown up in the moonlight and magnolia South, in a land of plenty where the gentry lived off slave labor. There were "dinners the finest in the world, deer-hunting, and fox-hunting, dancing, and pretty girls, in fact everything that the heart could wish." Until Fort Sumter, she knew no other way of life except what she had seen at those favorite vacation places for Southerners at Newport, Rhode Island, and Saratoga Springs, New York, and during a brief visit to London in 1845. But war shocked her into new insights. "Our silver and gold," she found herself asking, "what are they? when we give up to war our beloved?"

It was her husband who had rowed out to Fort Sumter to demand its surrender. When his mission failed and she heard the consequent boom of cannon, she fell on her knees and prayed as never before. With her husband's first leave-taking, she wept in anguish. And with her first sight of mutilated bodies, she felt sickened. But, like Margaret Fuller and Maria Child, Mary Chesnut played her part. She wrote letters requesting money, clothes, and nurses; she too served, only in her case for the soldiers of the Confederacy; she took carriage loads of peaches and grapes to the hospitals and carried away the haunting remembrance of "eyes sunk in cavernous depths and following me from bed to bed."

In time she grew accustomed to the sight of "stumps of limbs not half cured, exhibited to all"—what was left of men who had once been the elite of "a polished and refined people." She watched stoically as "our world, the only world we cared for," was "literally kicked to pieces." "We are two lone women, stranded here," a friend of Mary Chesnut's bitterly lamented between tears. These were women whose marriages were intended to keep Southern bloodlines strong; now many of them were without husbands or sons; that is, without men to carry on the tradition of a patriarchal system. Mary's father-in-law had warned, "With this war we may die out. Your husband is the last—of my family." James Chesnut, Jr., was his only living son and he and Mary were childless. Was anything worth it, "this fearful sacrifice, this awful penalty we pay for war?" She answered her own question by invoking her father-in-law's image: "Partly patriarch, partly grand seigneur, this old man is of a species that we shall see no more—the last of a race of lordly planters who ruled this Southern world, but now a splendid wreck. His manners are unequaled still, but underneath this smooth exterior lies the grip of a tyrant whose will has never been crossed."

Colonel Chesnut was not unrepresentative of 19th-century American men. Few of them were ready to share in an equal human exchange desired by well-educated and talented women of the period like Margaret Fuller, Maria Child and, to a somewhat lesser extent, Mary Chesnut. These women could see in chattel slavery a parallel to their own unhappy condition. Moreover they exhibited excesses of energy in their interaction with men that less enlightened women rarely dared display. Indeed, they thought the day was not far off when women would come into their own on the basis of equality with men. The quality of United States in the future, according to Maria Child, might yet be measured "by the character of its women."

The Civil War was the trauma of 19th-century America. Southerners had a vision of their own independence, and the North one of liberation for enslaved blacks. But neither side thought in terms of woman's liberation. Margaret Fuller, Maria Child, and Mary Chesnut fought a quiet battle and yet remained in loving and mutual relationships with men. And each made their own relationship work. Though overshadowed by his dynamic wife, the shy and uneducated Ossoli had fought for Italian freedom. Maria Child's improvident David failed at raising beets and depended on her for financial and moral support, even as he fought courageously against slavery and other forms of injustice. And a politically prominent James Chesnut fought in a losing cause while Mary Chesnut witnessed first-hand the crumbling of the Southern system.

Margaret Fuller, Maria Child, and Mary Chesnut were indeed women for all seasons. Not surprisingly women liberationists of today see in their efforts to achieve self-realization a foreshadowing of their own struggle for complete equality between the sexes.

10

Modernization and Traditionalism in Jacksonian Social Reform

HORACE MANN
DOROTHEA L. DIX
ORESTES A. BROWNSON

by Gerald N. Grob
Rutgers University

Between 1820 and 1860 American society appeared moving toward fulfillment of the ideals of its Revolutionary founders. The movement to rid the nation of its archaic and immoral system of slave labor was accompanied by a variety of attempts to eliminate the social injustices that stained the nation's fabric. During these decades the foundations were laid for a universal and free public school system. Institutions were also established for the care of the distressed—orphans, the mentally ill and retarded, and sick and old persons unable to survive without some form of assistance. Correspondingly, demands for equal rights for all persons grew in intensity. Most reformers were firmly convinced that man had the power and ability to create a new environment, one that ultimately would help to shape free and moral human beings capable of realizing their broadest potentialities unrestrained by outmoded and repressive inherited traditions.

In one sense this traditional portrait of nearly four decades of American history as an "era of reform" is accurate. But it also leaves many questions unanswered. What made many Americans receptive to social reform between 1820 and 1860? Where did activists come from and what were their goals? How can the dissatisfaction with existing institutions at this time be explained? What was responsible for the apparent failure to create a more perfect social order? And why did those individuals who were neutral or opposed to rapid institutional change fail to retard or reverse it?

Given these problems, how then can we view 19th-century reform? The answer lies not only in understanding individual social activists and their opponents, but—more importantly—in comprehending the context in which they functioned. For however one interprets the evolution of American society in the 19th century, the nation obviously was undergoing a profound transformation in its institutions and social structure as well as in its economy.

Modernization, of course, is a complex and varied process. It involves a massive increase and widespread diffusion of human knowledge about the physical world as well as a conviction that such knowledge provides man with the means by which to control his environment. Demographically, modernization is characterized by new social patterns, an increase in life expectancy, higher levels of health, greater social and geographical mobility, and a sharp rise in the rate of urbanization. Economically, there is a greater specialization of labor, a shift from subsistence to commercial agriculture, and the dominance of a high level of industrial and technological development. Inherent in modernization is the creation of an urban-industrial society where functions are increasingly performed by formal institutions rather than by such primary groups as the family or small village community. Accordingly, newly established specialized structures perform a variety of functions considered vital to the health and well-being of the citizenry.

Neither Horace Mann nor Dorothea L. Dix—two of the most eminent mid-19th-century activists—would have accepted the characterization of themselves as modernizers. Nor would Orestes A. Brownson—one of the most significant traditionalists of this era—have conceived of himself as an opponent of economic and technological change. More significantly, all three saw themselves simply as devout Christians seeking to implement their faith. In some cases this faith led to social activism; in others it became the reaffirmation of a traditional and hierarchical social order. The modernization of American society, therefore, was accompanied by ideological and philosophical diversity that often mirrored fierce social and intellectual conflict.

After first gaining fame as a psychiatric reformer, Horace Mann eventually emerged as the single most influential figure in American education. As Secretary of the Massachusetts State Board of Education, he helped to found a universal, free, compulsory school system held together by an elaborate bureaucratic structure. Dorothea Dix achieved an international reputation for her crusading efforts to set up institutions for the care and treatment of the mentally ill. She was also active in prison reform and played an important role in organizing nursing care during the Civil War. Both, therefore, contributed to the creation of what subsequently evolved into elaborate organizational structures that assumed responsibilities for functions previously reserved for the family, church, or local community. To put it another way, they were among the indispensable agents of modernization. In a certain sense their careers are best understood in terms of a paradox; though creating the new institutional forms that symbolized the dominance of the modern state, they conceived of their work as furthering a religious imperative and perfecting a traditional, and in most respects a premodern, society. The deeper implications of their achievements would only become apparent after their deaths.

Orestes Brownson, on the other hand, was the most famous convert to Catholicism in mid-19th-century America. Thereafter he spent his career as a critic seeking to return to an authoritarian and hierarchical society governed by eternal religious and moral truths. Rejecting much of the prevailing faith in democracy, he became a powerful foe of the emerging secular order, although in the end he himself was overwhelmed by the massive economic and technological transformations in American society.

By the 1850s Mann, Dix, and Brownson were well known in the United States and abroad. Yet little in their childhood and youth presaged their subsequent eminence. All were children of families of modest means; their roots went far back into the colonial period. Mann was born in 1796, Dix in 1802, and Brownson in 1803, the first two in Massachusetts and the last in Vermont. At that time agriculture and shipping were the dominant economic activities in New England. Boston, the largest town of that region, contained only about 25,000 people in 1800. All three, consequently, grew up in a homogeneous and predominantly rural society that stressed traditional values. The transformation of their world lay in the future, for factories, cities, and a large immigrant population—all of which was part of the modernization process—were not to become characteristic until they reached adulthood.

*   *   *

Horace Mann came from a relatively poor family that lacked formal education and insisted upon the inculcation of habits of industry and moral virtue. His childhood was not especially happy, for his health was frail and the extreme Calvinistic teachings of the Reverend Nathaniel Emmons, the local minister, caused him considerable mental agony. When he was but 12 years old, he repudiated the Calvinistic doctrine, which held that man was incapable of saving himself, a break that was both traumatic and irreversible. "From that day," he later recalled, "I began to construct the theory of Christian ethics and doctrine respecting virtue and vice, rewards and penalties, time and eternity, God and his providence, which, with such modifications as advancing age and a wider vision must impart, I still retain, and out of which my life has flowed." In his later career Mann demonstrated repeatedly that his personal religious belief in individual responsibility was a primary force in his numerous undertakings.

Although Mann possessed considerable intellectual ability, he did not attend school regularly. In 1814, however, he decided to prepare for college. Under the direction of a brilliant though eccentric tutor, he completed a course of study that enabled him to enter the sophomore class at Brown University. Brown was a Baptist institution, but it was preferred by many orthodox Calvinists who disliked Harvard's Unitarian atmosphere. Although some of Brown's undergraduates were religious conservatives, they nevertheless espoused democratic political theories that supported the idea of social change. Mann had a brilliant academic record, graduating with highest honors in 1819. By this time he had already demonstrated his belief in the infinite perfectibility of the human race. The subject of his valedictory graduation oration, "The Gradual Advancement of the Human Species in Dignity and Happiness," was a theme that he would reiterate throughout his career.

Brown regarded Mann so highly that soon after graduation it appointed him a tutor in Latin and Greek. Two years later he left to study law at Judge James Gould's well-known law school in Litchfield, Connecticut. He was admitted to the bar in 1823 and practiced law, first in Dedham and then in Boston, for the next 14 years. Driven by a desire to excel, Mann soon established a lucrative law practice that brought him a growing reputation and financial success. Like other young men with ability and ambition, he turned to politics and in 1827 was elected to the Massachusetts General Court. He gave strong support as a freshman legislator to government promotion of railroads; even then Mann identified technological and industrial progress with human happiness.

*   *   *

Career choices facing young men like Mann were varied, and they could easily occupy different roles as they matured. For Dorothea L. Dix, on the other hand, the world was more confined; society's expectations for young women were considerably more restricted. The overwhelming majority of women were taught to look froward to marriage and motherhood. Such roles were by no means inferior or unimportant, for the family prior to industrialization and modernization had functions that only later would be transferred to other institutions. Yet while marriage and motherhood were the accepted norms, there was always the possibility of breaking with them. Such an act required courage, will, and determination. Indeed, what is surprising about mid-19th-century American women was not that so few exhibited these characteristics, but that so many deliberately sought different horizons.

Dorothea Dix's early years and career offered little evidence that she would ultimately become one of the most influential women of her age. Born in a rural community, she had an unhappy childhood. Her mother seemed incapable of offering affection and her father was often intemperate. Her desire to leave home was so great that at age 12 she travelled alone to Boston to live with her well-to-do grandmother (whether she received permission is not known). The move did not bring contentment; she felt keenly the absence of affection and was unable to develop close relationships with others until relatively late in life.

Having made rapid progress in her own schooling, Dorothea Dix, then only 14 years old, decided to open a school for small children in Worcester, where she was temporarily residing with another relative. By the time she returned to her grandmother's home in 1819, her character had matured. She had become an ambitious young woman of singular forcefulness and determination. Against her grandmother's advice and while continuing to manage the household affairs, she opened another school in Boston. She also came under the influence of William Ellery Channing, the renowned Unitarian minister, and her religious commitment deepened in intensity. During the 1820s she briefly embarked on a literary career, publishing several children's books as well as a volume that embodied the ideals of duty, perfection, and Christian piety. In the succeeding decade she continued a teaching career. But in 1836 Dix suffered a nervous and physical collapse that compelled her to abandon her school. She then went abroad, remaining in England for a year and a half. Fortunately, she was financially independent—a bequest from her grandmother providing an annual income of approximately $3,000, a substantial sum by the standards of that day. In 1837 she returned home, still seeking a career that would permit her to serve society and at the same time fulfill her own ambitions.

*   *   *

Like Dorothea Dix, Orestes A. Brownson had an unsettled childhood. His father died shortly after his birth, and his mother, who struggled for six years to keep the family intact, was finally forced to place him in the home of an older couple. There the young boy became engrossed in theology, a concern that would later dominate his never-ending search for meaning and lead him briefly into the ministry. At the age of 14 Brownson was reunited with his family in upper New York where he briefly studied at a local academy. Forced by circumstances to seek employment, he never again attended a school or college; his education would come from internal ambition and avaricious reading. Meanwhile, his interest in theology grew in intensity. Searching for ultimate truths, he moved from one sect to another. For a time he flirted with Calvinism, but found its pessimism too stark and its notions of justice unacceptable. After briefly teaching in the Midwest, he became a Universalist minister. But Universalism proved no more satisfactory than Calvinism, for it seemed to reject the authority of the Scriptures without providing a definitive substitute. "I am amiable and honest, I have intelligence and even some learning; I have wronged no one, and have helped the needed," he confided to himself. "Yet nobody heeds me, nobody loves me, nobody cares for me." Brownson, at age 26, had still to find contentment or meaning.

* * *

Had American society remained relatively stable and traditional, Mann, Dix, and Brownson might never have had the opportunity to transcend their respectable but hardly distinguished careers. Mann might have remained a successful lawyer and political figure, Dix a teacher, and Brownson a spiritual wanderer. But within a short period of time all three were presented with opportunities that grew out of those forces contributing to the modernization of American society. Each would respond in a manner that would have significance not only for contemporaries but for generations yet unborn.

By the 1840s the United States was beginning to experience the rapid industrialization that within half a century would give it a place among the leading world powers. Accompanying it were dramatic demographic changes. One involved the increase not only in the number but the size of urban areas. In 1790 only six cities had more than 8,000 residents; these contained 3.35 percent of the total population. By 1850, 85 such urban areas contained nearly 12.5 percent of the total population. In 1790 not a single city had a population in excess of 50,000, and only two had more than 25,000. By 1850 New York, the largest American city, had considerably in excess of half a million people, while five others had between 100,000 and 250,000 and 20 more ranged in size from 25,000 to 100,000.

Another major demographic shift arose out of the immigration to the United States of large numbers of impoverished Europeans. Between 1830 and 1850, over two and a third million immigrants, of whom nearly a million were from Ireland, landed upon American shores. Although such groups added substantially to the labor force, their arrival presented American society with a series of unresolved dilemmas. Often possessing a different culture, outlook, and religion, they were also poor and tended to concentrate in the burgeoning urban centers, which then had to deal with the social problems arising out of illness, dependency, and acculturation.

The economic, industrial, technological, and demographic changes modernizing mid-19th-century American society posed new challenges. Before 1800 reliance on familial and community traditions and practices made it unnecessary to consider alternative approaches to social and economic problems. The family, local community, and church were regarded as the basic institutions of society. Thus the family was charged with educating and socializing children; schools were simply auxiliary aids designed to support but not replace the family. In cases involving distress and dependency, the local community attempted to maintain the integrity of the family by providing needed assistance. Consequently, the modern concept of social policy—which involves replacing traditional institutions with new public structures or procedures on a regional or national basis—was largely absent for most of the 17th and 18th centuries.

By the 1830s and 1840s Americans were encountering the residual problems that followed in the wake of social and economic change. Periodic unemployment, growing class cleavages, and tensions that accompanied the effort to create a modern labor force, all combined to undermine traditional society. Older modes of alleviating individual and familial distress appeared obsolete. The spontaneous and informal manner in which rural communities handled problems of sickness and dependency, for example, did not operate as efficiently in urban areas, where an extraordinarily high rate of geographical mobility tended to limit informal and traditional means of dealing with distress. Such considerations militated against established approaches and favored more systematic and institutionalized patterns.

The problems arising out of dependency and disease were by no means unique. Familial responsibility for education now seemed inefficient, and fear was widespread that immigrant and working-class families would not be assimilated within the new industrial order. The thrust toward modernization, then, created conditions conducive to the establishment of a universal, free, and compulsory system of education. In building schools, colleges, hospitals, prisons, houses of refuge, asylums —to mention only a few examples—Americans manifested an awareness that existing practices and structures were no longer appropriate to their society. A changing world provided such reformers as Mann, Dix, and Brownson with challenges and opportunities even if they themselves were not completely conscious of the underlying forces that made their own creativity possible.

First indications that Horace Mann's destiny transcended the practice of law came shortly after his election to the Massachusetts legislature. By 1829 he had come to believe that intemperance was the prime cause of crime and poverty. Hostile toward either prohibition or total abstinence, he supported instead a moderate system of licensing to bring drunkenness under some form of social control. Uncommitted to any rigid ideology, he saw nothing wrong in using the power of the state to deal with a problem beyond the control of the individual or the local community. The cause of intemperance did not bring Mann reputation or fame. But his leadership in helping to found a state insane hospital thrust him into a limelight that he would occupy until his death in 1859.

After 1800 a steady movement developed in the United States away from local toward institutional care of the mentally ill. Combining to give rise to the establishment of both general and mental hospitals were demographic changes, a growing sensitivity to social and medical problems, a surge in philanthropy, and an acquaintance with new medical and psychiatric advances in France and England. The first hospitals were products of private philanthropy, although they received public subsidies as well. Almost from the start, they had limited admissions to relatively well-to-do groups capable of paying the high costs of protracted care. Responsibility for dealing with the problems associated with mental disease consequently shifted slowly to public hospitals under state authority. These were supported by funding from both state and local governments.

By the mid-1820s concern over mental illness was on the rise. Investigations by the Boston Prison Discipline Society revealed that mentally ill persons were commonly confined in welfare and penal institutions. Efforts to provide other alternatives were made in the legislature in 1827 and 1828, but not until Mann assumed leadership in 1829, did these succeed. Speaking several times before the legislature, he spelled out the case for public facilities for care and treatment. Justice and mercy required public intervention, he argued. In addition, to provide therapeutic hospitals to cure the insane was more economical than to maintain them in custodial institutions. Above all, the state could no longer evade its moral responsibility for the welfare of these unfortunate persons.

As a result of Mann's efforts, the legislature in 1830 authorized construction of a state lunatic hospital. Located in Worcester, the new hospital opened in 1833. Under the leadership of Dr. Samuel B. Woodward (the first superintendent) and Mann (the leading figure on the board of trustees), the Worcester hospital quickly gained a national reputation and inspired other states to found their own public mental hospitals. By 1860 virtually every state had at least one, and some had more. For better or worse, care of the insane became a public responsibility.

Just as Mann was achieving widespread recognition, personal tragedy altered his career. He married Charlotte Messer, daughter of the President of Brown University, in 1830. Less than two years later she died. For Mann her death resulted in a spiritual crisis that lasted for more than a decade. "Oh, Dearest! Dearest!," wrote Mann in his private journal five years after her death. "How far removed from everything upon earth, how unutterably alone, I dwell in this world. Its beauty is perished. Its music is discord. Its pleasures have become pain, but none of its pains have become pleasures. And will this always be . . . yes. I had rather it would, than that I should ever forget thee, my beloved wife'" The grieving young lawyer began a process of self-reflection. Had he been guilty of excessive ambition? Had the quest for material rewards and fame corrupted his very being? Even his religious faith was called into doubt. Out of this profound personal crisis Mann emerged chastened and more mature. Henceforth he would seek a career that might serve mankind.

In 1837 an opportunity presented itself that would radically alter Mann's career and ultimately make him one of the most influential figures in the history of American education. In that year the Massachusetts legislature debated the disposition of the common school fund (which was used to supplement monies raised by towns for support of public education). Heretofore Mann had not been active in strictly educational causes. Nevertheless, his association with several advocates of public education, coupled with his own inclination to meet social responsibilities, served to involve him. Yet in reality his interest in education did not represent a radical departure from his earlier concern with the mentally ill. If the "calamities and sufferings of men" arose out of either ignorance or disbelief of the laws "impressed upon our being by our Creator," he pondered, might not *the* most fundamental change involve the proper education of human beings in their formative years. Would they not thereby know and follow the natural laws governing mankind? And would they not thus avoid incurring the penalties of misbehavior?

But the legislature, Mann believed, seemed to be composed of men of limited vision, and it rejected appropriation bills for school support. But the session was not a total loss, for Mann and his followers managed to secure enactment of a law establishing a State Board of Education. The new agency would collect and distribute information—the first step toward creating an orderly system for the proper education of children. Composed of non-salaried members, the Board was authorized to employ a paid secretary, a position that Mann agreed to take despite a heavy personal financial sacrifice. For the first time he possessed an institutional base that allowed him to affect the way in which American society socialized and educated its children. Indeed Mann's work as secretary of the Board from 1837 to 1848 would help lay the foundation, for a universal, free, and compulsory system of schools joined together by an elaborate bureaucratic and hierarchical structure.

Embarked upon a new career, Mann proceeded to push for a fundamental restructuring of both the form and substance of education. A changing world, he believed, demanded innovation. The new industrialism and the increasing heterogeneity of the population had fragmented a traditional, stable, and deferential society. Consensus on basic moral values had bound society together in an earlier age. The family provided much of the cohesive force. Parents were responsible for socializing and educating their children as well as inculcating virtue and morality. But Mann thought the family's role and authority had so diminished that it was incapable of performing its indispensable functions. Likewise social and class conflict was apparently undermining the social order, while immigration was bringing to American shores people whose customs, beliefs, and culture were not always consistent with accepted behavioral norms. How, then, could the nation avoid being torn apart by these forces? Could a republican society continue to exist if its citizens lacked both knowledge and virtue? Mann had an answer to these troubling questions. *"The Common School,"* he proclaimed, *"is the greatest discovery ever made by man."* Other institutions had to deal with the consequences of human weakness and imperfectibility. Prisons had to reform the character of criminals; mental hospitals had to cure individuals whose behavior was abnormal. But schools were unique; they would receive children whose characters, minds, and bodies were not yet corrupted by an immoral society. Properly conceived and structured, they could serve as both preventive and antidote; ultimately they would eliminate institutional coercion, since they would develop the moral faculties and inculcate internal restraint. The school would thereby replace family, church and village in molding the character of the child. On the school rested the future well-being of American society, if not of mankind. "In a Republic," Mann proclaimed, "ignorance is a crime."

When Mann began his career, formal education in Massachusetts was decentralized and lacking in clear purpose. Although tax-supported and non-sectarian schools existed in many areas, there was no agreement on matters relating to discipline, curriculum, teacher preparation, attendance, structure, or the basic objectives of schooling. Mann's role was essentially catalytic; he helped to define both the goals of schooling and the structure appropriate to them. For over a decade he was the foremost spokesman for educational innovation, carrying his message not only to his Massachusetts constituency but also to the American people everywhere.

The goal of schooling, Mann argued, was to indoctrinate children in the basic precepts of American morality, religion, and culture. In an age of dynamic technological and economic change, schools would constitute a stabilizing force. They would overcome class barriers, prevent strife, and ensure the dissemination of skills necessary to an increasingly industrialized nation. Mann had no doubts about what constituted morality. In a virtuous society men were frugal, honest, industrious, public spirited, philanthropic, temperate, and hard working. Schools for their part would shore up and maintain the characteristics of an earlier and more homogeneous society. In short, they would reunify a divided nation and provide the basis for widespread material prosperity.

To define the proper goals of education was only half of the job. The other half was to provide a structure capable of realizing these goals in practice. Again Mann turned to institutional solutions. Past difficulties, he argued, had arisen because of the absence of an effective *system*. Required now was the formulation of a plan to systematize and to rationalize schools, thereby guaranteeing the performance of those functions for which they had been established. Political and sectarian considerations, he insisted, should not be permitted to intrude. Isolated from base partisanship and narrow self-interest, schools would be free to instruct the community in its responsibilities.

Tax-supported schools, according to Mann, must be integrated within a cohesive structure. Grading of classes was a first step; examinations given at regular intervals would determine whether students had met basic curriculum requirements. Reading and other text materials would reflect the graded nature of the curriculum as well as embody moral values. All children within stipulated age ranges would be required to attend schools for certain periods. State and local school administrations would be created in order to insure educational uniformity and to make certain that both pupils and teachers were following their prescribed roles. Teachers would be trained as professionals, and school committees would no longer be permitted to employ those lacking proper credentials. Establishment and licensing of normal schools (later teachers colleges) would ensure the continued growth of education as a profession. Above all, public education would be removed from the hands of well-meaning but misinformed amateurs and become the institutional means by which professionals would fulfill their unique and important mission.

The more Mann threw himself into educational reform, the more he grew intolerant of those who had the audacity to disagree with him. To Mann, the battle over education became a struggle between morality and immorality, between narrow-minded and selfish individuals and those who eschewed self-interest. "You and I and others," he wrote to Henry Barnard, his counterpart in Connecticut, "have to work on it, with embarrassment and obstruction, but when I look afar into the future and see the beautiful and glorious development it shall have in other hands, I find not satisfaction in my toils, merely, but I feel a pride in being stationed at this more honorable post of labour. Let us go on and buffet these waves of opposition with a stout arm and a confiding heart."

Dissenters from Mann's educational philosophy included religious groups which rejected his reduction of religion in the public schools to a common set of largely Protestant beliefs and values. Opposition also came from educators who resisted efforts to standardize their schools, often because it meant their displacement from positions of authority. Working-class groups and ethnic minorities sometimes expressed implicit displeasure with schooling by poor attendance, high dropout rates, and opposition to school expenditures. Nevertheless, Mann's vision proved all but irresistible, and by the late 19th century centralized and bureaucratic school systems characterized American public education.

In 1848 Mann temporarily abandoned the field of education; in that year he was elected to the House of Representatives as an antislavery member of the Whig Party. In Washington he demonstrated the same passion that marked his career as an educational innovator. "My zeal grows and glows to continue the contest of evil," he wrote to a friend in 1856. "I love the good causes more than ever; more than ever I want to fight for them; and the most painful idea connected with death is that I must be at most a looker on and not a participant." Eventually Mann received the Free Soil nomination for the governorship of Massachusetts. His defeat in the 1852 elections occurred at the very moment he was being offered the presidency of the newly-established Antioch College in Ohio, a position he accepted and retained until his death in 1859. But the last decade of his life was anticlimactic; his most enduring contributions had occurred during his tenure as secretary of the Massachusetts State Board of Education.

No doubt Mann would have been surprised at the fruits of his labor. His faith in education reflected an underlying religious commitment; virtue and stability were the end products of a proper education. Although he often spoke about the relation of education to industry, he saw the former as a predominantly religious and moral venture. Nevertheless, he did not minimize the economic rewards of schooling or the potential benefits to industry in the form of a literate work force. Even his support of an educational bureaucracy was designed to implement his basic goals. Yet in the succeeding century the school system he helped to design became one of the enduring symbols of an industrialized and modernized America. Seeking virtue and morality, Mann helped pave the way for the advent of a new and different world.

*   *   *

As with Mann, an unforseen event embarked Dorothea L. Dix on a new career. Following her return from England in 1837, she seemed to drift aimlessly. Boston's small but influential intellectual community did not attract her. More doer than thinker, a quiet life of contemplation seemed peculiarly inappropriate. But how could a lonely spinster find personal fulfillment and still serve humanity? "Life is not to be expended in vain regrets," she wrote to her closest friend in 1838. "No day, no hour comes but brings in its train work to be performed for some useful end, the suffering to be comforted, the wandering led home, the sinner reclaimed. Oh, how can any fold the hands to rest and say to the spirit, 'Take thine ease for all is well'?" Thus when John T. G. Nichols, a young Harvard Divinity School student, asked her if she knew someone who could teach a Sunday school class to female convicts in the East Cambridge jail in 1841, she herself volunteered. At the jail she was horrified to discover a group of insane persons confined with hardened criminals. Moreover, they had suffered from years of neglect. Deeply touched by what she saw, she was determined to improve and expand institutional facilities for the mentally ill.

Recognizing that an unknown and unmarried woman could accomplish little, Dix turned then to Samuel Gridley Howe and Charles Sumner for advice. Both men agreed that the public conscience needed to be shocked. They recommended a comprehensive personal examination of prison conditions, a task that would take many months of arduous work. Howe also reminded Dix that her health was delicate, but the newly-discovered cause superceded personal considerations. Shortly thereafter she began her first investigation, which took nearly a year and a half. While she was visiting every jail and welfare institution in the state, Howe helped out by preparing several exposés for the press.

In January 1843, Dix finally completed her investigations and presented the findings in her famous "Memorial to the Legislature of Massachusetts," the first of many similar documents. Combining moral outrage and knowledge, it gave a highly detailed picture of conditions at virtually every jail, house of correction, and almshouse in the state. "I come to present the strong claims of suffering humanity," she told the legislators. "I come to place before the Legislature of Massachusetts the condition of the miserable, the desolate, the outcast. I come as the advocate of helpless, forgotten, insane, idiotic men and women; of beings sunk to a condition from which the most unconcerned would start with real horror; of beings wretched in our prisons, and more wretched in our almshouses. And I cannot suppose it needful to employ earnest persuasion, or stubborn argument, in order to arrest and fix attention upon a subject only the more strongly pressing in its claims because it is revolting and disgusting in its details." Insisting that the Commonwealth had a moral, humanitarian, and legal obligation toward the mentally ill, she called on the legislature to fulfill its duty and provide for additional facilities at Worcester's overcrowded state hospital. Persuaded further by Mann, Howe, and others, the lawmakers appropriated the necessary funds.

For the next three decades, Dix tirelessly followed a similar course of action in other states. After arriving in a state, she spent considerable time in surveying actual conditions. Then she presented her findings to the legislature, usually in the form of a lengthy and impassioned memorial. Unconcerned with arousing public opinion, she then turned with unerring political instinct to those leaders with the power to innovate. Indeed, her singular devotion to the cause often resulted in consternation among her friends, some of whom felt that she took unnecessary liberties with the truth. As one hospital superintendent wrote to another: "I see Miss Dix has been over your state & *Memorialized* your legislature. I hope good will result from it—& trust that her experience in this state [New York] may make her more courteous in observing and publishing. In this state I am afraid she did hurt by *coloring* & by not accurately observing. She was often mistaken & this has thrown a doubt over all her statements with many." In this respect Dorothea Dix's personality was similar to that of Horace Mann. Like other innovators, both tended to classify humans and institutions as either good or evil. Those who opposed their efforts did so for selfish and partisan reasons.

Dix's unflagging devotion to the mentally ill gave her a key position in the history of American psychiatry and mental hospitals from the 1840s to the 1870s. Many hospital superintendents owed their positions to her influence, and it became a common practice for younger men to consult with her about their future plans and aspirations. Nor was her position as an arbiter and leader merely titular, for often she was called on to adjudicate or to pass judgment upon internal institutional conflicts. Few of those concerned with the problems of the mentally ill—whatever their views—could afford the luxury of ignoring this remarkable and determined woman.

By the close of her career Dorothea Dix was responsible for founding or enlarging over 30 mental hospitals in the United States and abroad. Although the groundwork had often been prepared by others, her role was to act as a catalyst and to bring the specific project to fruition. In many ways her most important contribution was to stimulate the thrust toward broadening the role of government in providing institutional care and treatment of the mentally ill. Her influence was national and international in scope precisely because she insisted on excluding virtually all extraneous issues (prison reform being one of the few exceptions). She was one of the few New England social reformers who received a warm welcome in the South because she never coupled antislavery with psychiatric innovation.

Dix's work, of course, would have been all but futile without some base of support. Such backing existed, for most states already possessed groups of people committed to the amelioration of distress and to social improvement through the expansion of governmental activities. However one may view 19th-century American society, it is clear that the creation and strengthening of formal institutions represented a dominant trend. Dix's insistence upon institutional care for those mentally ill consequently struck a responsive chord among those who were dedicated to the creation of a new and better society.

Shortly after embarking on her new career, Dix came to the conclusion that a virtual revolution was required in the manner in which resources were allocated for the care and treatment of the insane. At that time public mental hospitals were expected to be self-supporting in their operating expenditures. Income was derived from three sources: families who paid for private patients; local communities, which were responsible for poorer and indigent residents; and states, which paid for foreign-born and indigent patients or else provided a lump sum subsidy (all capital expenditures came from the states). In 1848 Dix next presented a lengthy memorial to Congress requesting legislation that would provide for the distribution of 5,000,000 acres of federal land to the states, the proceeds of which would be used for the support of the indigent insane. For six years she labored arduously to convince Congress that the project was both desirable and important. Success finally seemed to come in 1854 with the passage of legislation setting aside not 5,000,000 but 10,000,000 acres of federal land. The moment was one of triumph and satisfaction. "And as I rejoice quietly and silently," she wrote her closest friend, "I feel it is *The Lord who has made my mountain to stand strong.* . . . As for myself longing now and then for rest and truely, it is pleasant to think of the time when labor will not be associated with pain and weariness." Her victory proved illusory, however, for the act met with a veto from President Franklin Pierce, and Congress was unable to muster sufficient support to override it. For the remainder of the 19th and the early part of the 20th century responsibility for the mentally ill continued to be borne by state and local authorities.

During the Civil War years Dix would abandon for the only time in her career her struggle on behalf of the insane. Immediately upon the outbreak of hostilities she went to Washington and offered her services for the care of sick and wounded soldiers. In April 1861, she was commissioned as the first "Superintendent of United States Army Nurses." Her passion for efficiency and humanity seemed peculiarly suited to the task at hand. Although the Civil War was one of the first of the modern wars in terms of strategy and weapons, its medical care unfortunately was traditional. The result was a staggering number of casualties and fatalities, mostly from wounds and disease (aseptic procedures were still nonexistent). The Medical Bureau of the army was largely a paper organization.

Dix's experience in Washington, however, proved an unhappy one. The struggle between the Medical Bureau and volunteers like her and others associated with the Sanitary Commission inhibited her effectiveness. By October 1863 the conflict was so acute that a reorganization was instituted; it stripped Miss Dix of virtually all her authority over the nurses. Although she remained in Washington until the fall of 1865, her power was all but gone.

Too strong-willed to be discouraged by her wartime experiences, Dix in 1867 resumed her earlier career as the leading protagonist for the mentally ill. Slowly, however, the ravages of age began to take their toll, and in 1881 she finally retired to the state hospital at Trenton, New Jersey, where the trustees had provided her with quarters in appreciation of her services. She remained there until her death in 1887.

* * *

Horace Mann and Dorothea Dix were practical activists who promoted institutional solutions for contemporary social problems. Orestes Brownson, on the other hand, was more the thinker. Meaning and significance were of greater importance to him than action; consequently, he was less concerned with institution building than with identifying the ideal foundation upon which any moral and just society must rest. A pilgrim in search of ultimate truths, Brownson moved with startling rapidity from one ideology to another. Beginning his career as a social and economic radical, he ended up as a convert to Catholicism and a critic of modern society.

During the late 1820s and the 1830s, Brownson made his way through a bewildering variety of religious and secular reform movements. The socialist ventures of Robert Owen and Fanny Wright with which he was briefly connected gave him no fulfillment. He was attracted to, and involved with, the workingmen's political parties that grew out of the depression of 1828–29, but concluded that labor was no match for capital. Convinced that society must rest on a bedrock of eternal religious truth, he became a Unitarian minister in 1832 and subsequently occupied pulpits in Walpole, New Hampshire, and Canton, Massachusetts. Slowly but surely he acquired a reputation as one of New England's most outspoken intellectuals and authors.

By this time Brownson had come to the conclusion that life could not be understood solely in terms of logic or rationality; some truths were beyond the reach of the intellect. What humanity required was a new church that embodied eternal religious truths. The Reformation had demonstrated the failure of Catholicism, but Protestantism was less a church than a collection of sects. Although lacking precision, Brownson was seeking a synthesis that would unite his religious overview with worldly concerns and thereby offer a guide to human action based on transcendent principles.

Brownson's concern for philosophical issues did not lead him to ignore contemporary problems, as was shown by his participation in labor politics. The fact that his ministry was located in a Massachusetts community with a working-class population forced him to confront practical concerns rather than intellectual abstractions. Yet Brownson did not respond by seeking an environmental transformation. Instead, he concluded that moral reform must precede social reform. "To effect any real reform," he wrote in 1834, "the individual man must be improved. . . . The reformer's concern is with the individual. That which gives the individual a free mind, a pure heart, and full scope for just and beneficent action, is that which will reform the many. When the majority of any community are fitted for better institutions, for a more advanced state of society, that state will be introduced, and those institutions will be secured." But how could people become wise and virtuous? The answer lay in the abolition of the social inequalities that hampered people, especially working men and women, from receiving the kind of education that would cleanse and purify their souls. But Brownson failed to demonstrate how virtue would follow education should the latter be under the aegis of a still corruptly governed nation.

In 1836 Orestes Brownson moved from Canton to Boston, where he was immediately absorbed into the vibrant life of the nation's foremost intellectual community. Members of Boston's tightly-knit intelligentsia usually maintained cordial personal relationships, if only because they were seeking a common consensus. But Brownson did not fit the typical mold. Strong-willed and determined, he did not hesitate to expose, usually in a blunt and undiplomatic manner, the inadequacies of arguments with which he disagreed. With an occasional exception, he lacked close friends. Acquaintances found him rigid and dogmatic even though respecting and sometimes fearing his intellectual capabilities. "Brownson," noted Ralph Waldo Emerson, "never will stop and listen, neither in conversation, but what is more, not in solitude." Moreover, he manifested these very same qualities in his relations with his wife and children, demanding obedience rather than affection. Rarely did he permit family responsibilities to intrude upon his work.

Although Brownson's reputation among Bostonians was that of a contentious social reformer, he also evinced a strong interest in religion and to this end promoted a vague ecumenical movement intended to create an ideal church. The rationality of Unitarianism, he noted in *New Views of Christianity* (1836), did not take into account the affective side of human nature. His vision of a new church rested on the proposition that man was made in God's image and possessed the power and ability to remake society into the Kingdom of God. Religion and social reform were therefore inseparable; the former was a prerequisite for achievement of the latter.

Brownson's thinking in the mid-1830s was still largely abstract. Although he clearly sympathized with the working class, he had not moved beyond his conviction that inner reform must take precedence. The depression ushered in by the panic of 1837 provided a new perspective, however, and he slowly modified his position. Inner reform was all very well, but how could it aid unemployed and starving people? Using the *Boston Quarterly Review* (which he began in 1838) and later *Brownson's Quarterly Review,* he lashed out against the enemies of the people.

Employing a class analysis, he urged that the alliance between government and business be destroyed and that the former be restored to popular control. States' rights, he added, were the guardian of liberty whereas centralization of authority promoted the power of small propertied groups.

Logic impelled Brownson to move into politics in the late 1830s, and his journal became a staunch supporter of the Democratic Party. In the midst of the presidential election of 1840, he published his widely read essay on "The Laboring Classes." Capitalism, he proclaimed, must be destroyed so that true equality could prevail. "Wages is a cunning device of the devil, for the benefit of tender consciences, who would retain all the advantages of the slave system, without the expense, trouble, and odium of being slave-holders." Explicitly repudiating the necessity of inner or moral reform, Brownson railed against "priests" and the clergy in general. They were "miserable panderers to the prejudices of the age, [and] loud in condemning sins nobody is guilty of, but silent as the grave when it concerns the crying sin of the times.... As a body they never preach a truth till there is none but whom it will indict." Destruction of the priesthood and revival of a purified Christianity were but two of the elements in his program. His more practical proposals included a sharp limitation of monopoly and privilege and the abolition of the inheritance of property. These propositions rested on the belief that the personal economic relationships of a bygone era could be restored; he never envisaged a modernized and industrialized America.

But Brownson's program was too radical for the Democratic Party, and it disavowed him. The Whigs attempted to exploit the situation by insisting on identifying him with their opponents. Their presidential candidate, Benjamin Henry Harrison, easily defeated the incumbent Democrat, Martin Van Buren, in the election of 1840. The outcome was altogether disheartening to Brownson. His faith in the people had been ill-founded. So too was his belief in democracy as a political system. Government, he decided, had to rest on an entirely different foundation.

Moving toward a strict constitutionalist position, Brownson urged initially that sharp limitations be placed on government power. Moreover, he became friendly with John C. Calhoun, who had reached a similar conclusion much earlier. While Brownson disliked slavery, he did not boggle at the thought of an anti-business alliance of Southern slaveowners and Northern workers. In a public address he attacked the Northern critique of slavery.

> You of the South consist of freemen and slaves, of gentle and simple and so do we of the North. In both sections we find at bottom the same distinction of classes, though while you have the manliness to avow it, we have the art to disguise it from the careless observer, under the drapery of fine names. You call your slaves by their proper name, and while you impose upon them the duties of slaves, you relieve them from

the cares and burdens of freemen; we call our slaves freemen, and impose upon them the labors and burdens of slavery, while we secure to them none of the advantages of freedom. The only advantage we can claim over you is, that our slaves being of the same race and color with our freemen, are individually less hopelessly slaves than yours. The class is as permanent with us as with you; but individuals of the class may more easily escape from it. . . . But on the other hand, if our slaves are under certain aspects less slaves than yours, our freemen are less free than yours.

But increasingly Brownson turned toward strictly religious questions. The election of 1840 had demonstrated that the people were neither wise nor virtuous; perhaps his faith in them was wrong. His hope of realizing the Kingdom of God on Earth rapidly receded and was replaced by a singular concern with the salvation of men's souls. Disillusioned with the rationality of Unitarianism, he undertook once again a search for metaphysical meaning and truth. Yet, he was unable to abandon completely his class analysis, for he still believed that the "growing industrial feudalism" continued to be the single greatest threat to modern society. But how could this threat be thwarted? Brownson's dilemma was compounded by his new assumption that human nature was utterly corrupt. "With ignorant, depraved men," he wrote in 1844, "can you have a rightly organized society?" Slowly but inexorably he found an answer in the Christian epic of sin and redemption as manifested in the traditions and theology of the Catholic Church. Human reason and rationality were too fallible; they required the aid of divine revelation and the "tradition of the race."

Brownson faced the most important decision of his career. If the Catholic Church was the repository of the one true faith, how could he remain outside its fold? But to most Americans, Catholicism was synonymous with superstition and with a power-hungry and depraved hierarchy. Its strength in the United States lay with the Irish, an ethnic group generally considered to be mired in alcoholism, ignorance, stupidity, and crime. Nevertheless, by mid-1844 Brownson had concluded that there was no alternative between Catholicism and other religions. Since truth lay with Catholicism, his only choice was conversion. In October 1844 he took the final step and joined the Catholic Church. So intense were his feelings that he forced his family to follow him.

Brownson's conversion destroyed whatever credibility he possessed among the Protestant intelligentsia. James Freeman Clarke, the famous Unitarian minister, portrayed him as one who was forever changing his views:

> He has made the most elaborate and plausible plea for eclecticism, and the most elaborate and plausible plea against it. He has said the best things in favor of transcendentalism, and the best things against it. He

has shown that no man can possibly be a Christian, except he is a transcendentalist; and he has also proved that every transcendentalist, whether he knows it or not, is necessarily an infidel. He has satisfactorily shown the truth of socialism, and its necessity in order to bring about a golden age, and he has, by the most convincing arguments, demonstrated that the whole system of socialism is from the pit, and can lead to nothing but anarchy and ruin. . . . He labors now with great ingenuity and extraordinary subtlety to show that there must be an infallible church with its infallible ministry, and that out of this church there can be no salvation. But formerly he labored with equal earnestness to show that there could be no such thing as a church at all, no outward priesthood or ministry.

Given Brownson's personality and temperament, his commitment to Catholicism was total. Three years after his conversion he noted that every Catholic "from the fact that he is a Catholic, has the world and the devil for his enemies." Not surprisingly he turned his immense energies to elevating the spiritual and intellectual standards of his fellow Catholics as well as to proselytizing Protestant America with the true faith. His earlier radicalism was muted; reality simply reflected the wishes of God. The world was but a temporary abode for humanity, for "what matters the inconvenience which we may be required to put up with?" Humanity need not concern itself with political, social, or economic problems; its only concern was salvation.

Between 1844 and 1876 Brownson elaborated his new faith in the light of contemporary problems. He condemned the revolutions of 1848 in Europe and insisted that liberalism was destructive of religion, law, and order. Social questions could be adjudicated only in terms of eternal moral principles. Since obedience to the state meant obedience to God, it followed that the Church had to guide and give sanction to the state. Religion and politics were inseparable, since only the former could legitimatize the latter. Still, Brownson's earlier radicalism was not entirely eradicated. When the balance between liberty and authority was threatened, the Church, he held, should place its moral authority on the side of liberty. Just as he opposed the revolutions of 1848, so did he oppose the rising tide of reaction. The Church, he maintained, had to adjust to the problems of a changing world. This attitude did not enhance Brownson's popularity among his co-religionists, many of whom feared and distrusted him.

During the 1840s and 1850s Brownson occupied a position midway between his youthful radicalism and his later conservatism. The debate over slavery, for example, intensified his concern for law and order. In 1847 he defended slavery by insisting that it did not include dominion over the soul. "[It is] our duty," he remarked on one occasion, "to accept the distinction of classes as a social fact, permanent and indestructible in civilized society." But as the Civil War approached, Brownson grew more resentful of the planters' attempt to rule the nation through their domination of the Democratic Party. When armed conflict erupted in 1861, he rushed to the support of the Union. If the destruction of Southern power required the abolition of slavery, then Lincoln's policy of opposing secession by force was justified. His endorsement of the war regained the friendships of many who had been alienated by his conversion to Catholicism. Conversely, it offended some Catholics who were mostly staunch Democrats and fearful that the war might conclude in emancipation. Brownson became further estranged from many of his co-religionists because of his conciliatory attitude toward Protestantism and his rejection of the temporal authority of the Church.

At the war's end Brownson was growing old and physically infirm. The loss of two of his sons during the conflict contributed to his malaise. The Papacy's turn to the right under Pius IX and its rejection of compromise with modernism left Brownson peculiarly vulnerable. Making his peace with Rome during the final decade of his life, he became a spokesman for orthodoxy and conservatism. He insisted that property was a sacred right, that governments lacked authority to change the established order, that justice and right lay with the aristocracy, and that egalitarianism and disrespect for constituted authority threatened the fabric of society. In an essay on democratic principles written in 1873, he explicitly rejected the doctrine that "the people . . . are the origin and source of all authority and all law, that they are absolutely supreme, and bound by no law or authority that does not emanate from themselves." Politics could not possibly be separated from the moral order, which he defined as "justice, eternal and immutable right" constituted by divine sanction and placed under the authority of the Pope, Christ's vicar on Earth.

By the time of his death in 1876 Brownson had come full circle. Beginning his career as a seeker who espoused liberal if not radical causes, he ultimately despaired of man's ability to change the world according to predetermined goals. By aligning himself with the established order, he explicitly rejected both modernism and contemporary industrial society. Whereas Mann and Dix consciously promoted change by human intervention, Brownson resolutely set himself in opposition by supporting an organic social order with a hierarchy of authority that reached through the Church and ultimately to God. The secular thrust that accompanied modernization, however, proved too strong and Brownson's hopes were overwhelmed by the pace of industrial, technological, and social change.

A supreme individualist, Brownson had few friends and many enemies. His fellow Catholics were often angered by his pronouncements and by his refusal to conform completely and they never overcame their suspicions of him. Nor were Protestants more tolerant of his idiosyncrasies.

Independent to an extreme, Brownson mirrored the transformation of his world. No doubt his irrepressible independence and his isolation from organized and institutional protest contributed to his inability to influence his countrymen. Whatever the reasons, his was a voice in the wilderness, little heeded and soon forgotten by friend and foe alike.

Horace Mann, Dorothea Dix and Orestes Brownson provide a fascinating contrast. The former two were firmly convinced that their institutional solutions to problems could only benefit their countrymen. Their goal was a nation in which virtue and prosperity would be distributed among all citizens, thereby facilitating self-government. They had little doubt about the precise definition of virtue and goodness, which they equated with the behavioral norms of their own social class. They believed that organization was an appropriate means of overcoming the disintegrative forces that threatened the foundations of order and stability. The institutions for which they fought—schools, hospitals, asylums, jails—were the means by which society would progress and confer benefits upon its people. In part their favorable view of formal institutional structures was a reflection of the growing importance of organization in a society that glorified the individual but which was inescapably crossing the threshold into modernization and industrialization. Yet their personal vision of America remained essentially traditional; they saw structural innovation as a means of restoring a premodern social order.

Brownson, pondering the relationship of religion to society, ultimately rejected the belief that human nature was essentially good or that mankind could solve its pressing problems. His concern with abstract analysis—a quality that was even present during the radical phase of his career—removed him from actual involvement, and he remained an intellectual apart from the society in which he lived. When his advice went unheeded, he decided that a corrupt humanity could only act affirmatively with divine guidance. He thoroughly distrusted those secular institution builders like Horace Mann and Dorothea Dix who claimed divine sanction for their activities. Ultimately Brownson found his answer in the Catholic Church, which in his age was identified with the defense of the existing order and opposed to liberalism and modernism.

Curiously enough, neither the fears of Brownson nor the hopes of Mann and Dix were ever fully realized. American society never became fully egalitarian, nor did its political system become a vehicle for social and economic change. If Brownson's fears did not materialize, neither did his dream of a hierarchical social order built on eternal religious truths and divine revelation ever approach reality. Future conservatives might adopt him as one of their patron saints, but to the overwhelming majority of his countrymen he remained an enigma with few redeeming personal qualities.

The results of the efforts of Brownson's counterparts also proved to be quite different from their original objectives. The schools for which Mann fought were intended to turn out virtuous, intelligent, and industrious children; the structures he proposed were designed to facilitate this end. But in practice the American school evolved along very different lines. Future generations would be confronted with a new set of problems: a school system that often appeared rigid and unyielding; a system that was marked by an unresolved tension between professional demands for autonomy and community insistence upon control; a system that educated children with very unequal results.

Much the same was true for mental hospitals. Dix, of course, had conceived of these institutions in therapeutic and remedial terms; from the very beginning they were forced to accept increasing numbers of chronic cases which came to constitute a significant proportion of their resident population, thereby undermining their intended curative functions. Hospitals were supposed to remain small to promote the types of relationships deemed conducive to recovery; instead they grew in size, thereby hastening the transition from a charismatic-type institution to one dominated by administrative concerns. In theory all patients received the same type of care; in practice class, ethnicity, and color played a significant role in determining the nature of care and treatment. Interpreting their role in medical and ameliorative terms, superintendents of institutions were rapidly transformed into administrators who became more and more involved with largely managerial problems. Considerations of order and efficiency overshadowed therapeutic efforts.

*   *   *

The careers of Horace Mann, Dorothea Dix, and Orestes Brownson, then, can be understood in terms of a paradox—one endemic to the human condition. In a rapidly changing world each sought the union of stability and morality. Despite some fundamental differences, their goal was to ensure that traditional values and ideals would continue to dominate the lives of their countrymen. Brownson ended up as a conservative who appeared obsolete in a modernized America. The institutions bequeathed by Mann as well as Dix proved an equally perplexing legacy, for they were rapidly absorbed into a secular and urban-industrial society with an entirely new set of values as well as problems. Beneficent innovations in an earlier day, the schools, hospitals, prisons, and welfare institutions would seem to some 20th-century Americans to require radical surgery if they were not to subvert man's humanity. The legacy of Mann, Dix, and Brownson—like the legacy of all human beings—proved ambiguous and troublesome to future generations.

11

The Abolitionist Controversy:
Men of Blood, Men of God

JAMES GORDON BENNETT
WILLIAM LLOYD GARRISON
JOHN BROWN

by Bertram Wyatt-Brown
Case Western Reserve University

In 1860 Daniel R. Hundley devoted a chapter of his *Social Relations in Our Southern States* to the "swearing, tobacco-chewing, brandy drinking [Southern] Bully" who was "cocked and primed to flog the entire" Yankee breed of "crazy old milk sops!" Southern "short-boys" and tipplers of "bust-head, red-eye, and blue-ruin," the author observed, had Northern counterparts, no less willing to put abolitionists "through a course of sprouts in short order." Hundley was poking fun at an authentic, serious theme in the racial and sectional controversy. Grog-shop ruffians were not the only ones to swagger with "vaporing bravado." William Lloyd Garrison, veteran pacifist and abolitionist, also spoke in similar but more eloquent terms. Caught up in the excitement following John Brown's abortive raid at Harpers Ferry, Garrison rallied a Boston audience: "Give me, as a non-resistant, Bunker Hill, and Lexington, and Concord, rather than the cowardice and servility of a southern plantation." Definitions of manhood involved more than the mere possession of the necessary generative fixtures.

The antebellum cult of virility, a romantic concept in a time of romanticism, had universal appeal. Yet only a handful could ever have met the full ideals of manliness extolled in these years. Quite likely, then, the "Vaporing bravado" and "murderous blamnations" that Hundley satirized

215

may have masked inner doubts. "Cowards prove their courage by their ferocity," John Brown acidly observed, referring to his Southern captors. There is considerable accuracy to his observation. Passionate chest-thumping was highly self-conscious in these decades. Perhaps an inner voice had to be stilled. In 1844, for instance, Sydney Howard Gay, a young abolitionist, surrendered his most intimate self-examinations to his fiancee. "The least reflection," he confessed, "on my manliness or truthfulness makes me shrink and wince like a very chicken." Actually, he was no less stalwart than most contemporaries, though more candid; but the age required assertions of warrior-spirit and "forthright" denunciations of an adversary's "cowardice and servility" from its young men. It is always hard to be reasonable and conciliatory when claims and counter-claims of masculinity and degeneracy become common in public exchange. In times of rapid social, industrial, and political expansion, men sometimes find it necessary to portray themselves in such elemental terms. In their upbringing, ideological commitments, and male identifications, James Gordon Bennett, editor of the New York *Herald*, William Lloyd Garrison, and John Brown exemplified different expressions of a common theme—the meaning of 19th-century American manhood.

*   *   *

Of these three remarkable publicists, James Gordon Bennett was by far the most contradictory in character, combining traditional and innovative styles. Born in Scotland in 1795, Bennett fathered modern journalism. He introduced the financial, sports, theater, and society columns, the Washington bureau, and the foreign-correspondent byline. He also helped establish the Associated Press and wire service. Unlike his old-fashioned rivals in the newspaper industry, Bennett profited from high circulation and cheap newsstand prices. His search for a mass market and his experimental operations for his paper paralleled similar trends in the way Northerners conducted all their affairs. The *Herald* did not exist just to make money; its intent was also to promote "the intellectual happiness of the age." Only "through the medium of a daily newspaper," he claimed, "Conducted on cash principles—(Christ also did business on the cash system)"—could age-old "superstition ... be crumbled to the Earth," he claimed. No less secular was his defense of urban existence while others gushed about the joys of country living. New York, he boasted, would soon become "the big throbbing heart of the nations," the "New Jerusalem," reigning a thousand years. These convictions and accomplishments implicitly sharpened the distinction between the energetic Yankee and unprogressive Southerner. Such convictions made painful listening to Southerners; yet Bennett was their most influential ally in the alien world of Northern business and bustle.

The paradox is not mysterious. Bennett possessed that ardor for Americanism that so many immigrants have displayed for their adopted land. Perhaps a simple desire for public acceptance prompted, in part, an apology for the South. Sectional parity and racist custom were the twin pillars of the Old Republic; the antislavery cause threatened both. Then, too, it was a matter of proximity. Abolitionists were spreading their "disorganizing" gospel close at hand. Slaveholding "Fire-Eaters," though equally menacing, rumbled in the distance.

Self-interest, identification with proslavery constitutionalism, and a journalist's near-sighted eye for news on the doorstep helped to explain Bennett's rebukes of "amalgamationists," "disunionists," "socialists," and "nigger-worshippers"—the gaggle of epithets that he generally invoked as occasion suggested. But the explanation for such epithets had biographical sources as well. Bennett grew up near the village of Keith, in remote Banffshire, far from the intellectual and economic hubs of Glasgow and Edinburgh. For all his boasting of city life, Bennett retained the prejudices of his youth. Like American Southerners, Scotsmen resented their colonial dependency upon an industrial, urban, and imperious neighbor. Aware that English churchmen had induced Parliament to end West Indian slavery in 1833, Bennett would warn New Yorkers in 1838, 'The abolitionists of England are operating here. We know the fact" that "a conspiracy" is underway that "will astonish the whole Union." Such hysteria was partly a result of Scottish enmity toward the ancient foe as well as typical American anglophobia.

Bennett felt such provincial irritations the more keenly because Catholic parents belonged to a persecuted minority. Despised by Englishmen and Scots Presbyterians alike, the anti-Reformation Catholics had fought at Culloden (1746) for the clans, the True Faith, and Bonnie Prince Charlie, last of the Jacobite Pretenders. Stripped of ancient holdings, dirks, claymores, even war-apparel—the kilt and tartan—the Highland clans disintegrated. "A warrior cannot battle in trousers," young James Bennett heard the oldtimers say. In 1780, the right to wear the male gear was restored. By then some Scotsmen had been domesticated in school, factory, and countinghouse. But the back country nourished the old hostilities. Tales of lost glories and British barbarities still burned deep enough in the rural Scottish mind to help form Bennett's animosities.

The Bennetts themselves lived by a peasant code of hard work and simplicity, one also familiar to Southern farming folk. That free-booters and brigands appeared on the family tree supported special claims to masculinity, Bennett thought. Likewise, he admired Southern whites for being untamed and eager to establish agrarian dynasties. In his opinion, they robustly preserved the old ways—personal and family honor, "the good old orthodox religion," and racial and feminine subservience. Planters, he exclaimed, were the last rampart against anarchistic equalities, "filthy mixings," "the poison of rationalism and German mysticism, spiritualism and all the noxious delusions of the age." Bennett always loved the poetry of Robert Burns and the novels of Sir Walter Scott, both celebrants of the grim folkways and warlike nobility of the Scottish Border. Such romantic fare could also be found on library shelves of a plantation mansion.

Life on the Bennett freehold—even the rituals of the kitchen table— also bore a relation to Southern custom. Only his hard-fisted, formidable father was allowed the right to wash up before dining. A chalk line, drawn on the rough table top, separated the hired hands from the inner family circle. Age, gender, relation to the patriarch and, for the "hinds," occupation and seniority in service, determined the seating arrangements. A Southerner would have recognized such distinctions between those who *belonged* and those who were always on the periphery. In fact, Bennett's early milieu was hardly less agrarian, primitive, and socially rigid than the world of the Southern whites. Orderliness and stability, it was thought, required deferences to a hierarchy designed by God; only zealous "levelers" and abolitionists would dare challenge it.

Bennett had no desire, however, to establish a Southern plantation dynasty, with slaves replacing the "hinds." Indeed, after nine boring months on the staff of a South Carolina paper in 1826, he had fled with relief back to New York City. His rationalizations for the Southern way were mostly nostalgic, sometimes even equivocal; but the vehemence of his attacks on blacks and reformers paradoxically derived from rebellion against the Scottish past as well as allegiance to it.

As a schoolboy in Keith, Bennett had to rely on his wits, not his pinched looks and scrawny, thin-rumped frame. His father, impressed by his 14-year-old son, who excelled at Latin and Greek, sent him to Aberdeen to study for holy orders. Since eldest sons ordinarily inherited family lands, the paternal choice suggested special reasons. The Bennetts were a minority within a minority, being among the handful of Catholic Scots who did not have to slave for English overlords at bare wages. The measure of relative prosperity also shielded them a little from the insults of the hated, dominant Scots Presbyterians. In gratitude, the family felt obliged to surrender its eldest, gifted son to the Holy Church.

Several years' study did not bear the expected fruit. James Bennett could not summon the courage to tell his father, but news of his defection from a godly career and even from Catholic persuasion eventually reached the cottage at Keith. Out of fear and rebellion, Bennett abandoned Scotland forever at age 24, putting an ocean between himself and rejected familial duty. Bennett's life thereafter was a perpetual justification of his claim to independence. Moreover, he had absorbed the heretical opinions of Tom Paine and Lord Byron, both heroes to students during the Napoleonic age, and would argue as much to himself as to the readers of the *Herald*, "Have I not a right to create a belief and a church of my own?" His chief purpose became the fashioning of an alternate credo, one in which abolitionism, a religious dogma, he thought, had no place at all.

Journalism, not religion, served Bennett's need for self-expression. With the zeal of a man running away from himself, he worked an 18-hour day and fashioned a rowdy, secular style of reportage that rivals called "polluted vulgarity"; or, as a later age would term it, "yellow journalism." Crude though it was, such a style reflected a compulsive reaction to the earlier religious authoritarianism in which he had been reared—an anti-religious gospel, as it were. After several years' struggle, Bennett founded the *Herald* in May 1835. An early office, which was on Nassau Street, was a dank basement, an appropriate site, some said, for the "hellish" editor. Above it were the headquarters of the leading religious and benevolent societies of the times. It amused Bennett to have close at hand solemn, stiff-collared pietists, so like the arrogant Presbyterian "blue-noses" familiar to his youth in Keith.

Within a few months Bennett became spokesman for those common-school educated masses that shared his aggrieved iconoclasm, gut patriotism, male imperiousness, and racial insensitivity. Pursuing the widest possible readership, Bennett rejected political affiliations and patronage ties. He wanted to be free to criticize the mighty at will. "An editor," he preached, "must always be with the people, think with them, feel with them, and he need fear nothing. He will be always right, always popular, always free." Bennett's trinity was free expression, popular advocacy, and defiance of moral coerciveness. His political preferences, it followed, were not surprising.

Andrew Jackson, victorious hero of New Orleans, was reincarnated as "the old fighting Borderer of prior centuries, cracking crowns with the fiercest, repaying injury with compound interest; a right sufficient captain of men." Scots-Irish himself, Old Hickory was a duelist, slaveowner, Indian-fighter, horse-race gambler, enemy of effete federal bankers, foe of eastern drawing-room snobs and of abolitionist "incendiaries." Democrats —even Tammany Hall—often enjoyed the *Herald*'s irreverent support. So did anyone who gave expression to virile Americanism, which was Bennett's most obsessive theme. If Charles Darwin had not translated the existing doctrine of survival of the fittest into scientific terms, Bennett would still have kept the harsh spirit of a natural order alive.

In line with the theme, the *Herald* defied popular convention by lurid celebrations of sexual and other equally titillating events. Two hundred and fifty "beautiful and apparently accomplished young women," Bennett announced, were busy nightly in the city, while uptown "husbands are leaving their wives—clergymen kissing widows—widows enticing clergymen." In 1836, he shrewdly reported the hatchet-murder of Ellen Jewett, lovely resident of Rosina Townshend's bawdy house. He used personal interviews, verbatim conversations with the accused (a dashing apprentice), the police, and the madam herself. Rivals disdainfully accused him of contaminating public sensibility and exploiting his own sins, like "a vampire returning to a newly found grave yard." Bennett retorted that he was a respectable bachelor, too shy for such goings-on. (In his mid-40s, he married a Brooklyn piano teacher, but the *Herald* remained his sole obsession.) As a young gallant, the editor confessed, he had once visited a Nova Scotia brothel. But the girls told his companion, "Never bring that homely scoundrel to our house"; he "gives us the ague." Such self-deprecation went far to increase the loyalty of his subscribers.

The desperate search for fame and personal justification resulted in nine separate scuffles with those scandalized by his columns. James Watson Webb, hot-tempered editor of the *Morning Courier and Enquirer*, assaulted Bennett on Wall Street for accusing him of criminal stock fraud. He "cut a slash in my head one and a half inches in length," Bennett gleefully reported. "The fellow, no doubt, wanted to let out the never-failing supply of good humor and wit ... and appropriate the contents to supply the emptiness of his own thick skull." Circulation rose dramatically. The stooped Scotsman thrived on making himself the news of the hour and boasted that "neither Webb nor any other man can intimidate me. I will never succumb." One is reminded of Garrison's belligerence; "I am in earnest—I will not equivocate—I will not excuse—I will not retreat a single inch—AND I WILL BE HEARD."

Bennett's editorial position on abolitionism was certainly predictable, one that brought together menacing ideas—clerical manipulation, feminine encroachments upon male prerogatives, and threats of black insurgency, in the form of sexual lust for white women and of slaughter of white males. Bennett did not invent such slanders, but he expanded their scope, relating prejudices to the valid complaints of ordinary Americans beset by a changing and unfamiliar world. Proslavery and racist attitudes were part of the noisy rhythm of Northern life. The *Herald* columns included attacks upon politicians who used racist "sentimentalities" for their own greedy purposes, bankers who knew "the art of rifling the poor" and cheating "the mechanics," fee-grabbing lawyers, do-gooders "who look after everybody's business but their own," and Wall Street brokers, artists of "fraud and deception." Then, too, there were the professors at New York's "colleges, all poor and proud, except Columbia which is rich and lazy, educating only 100 students, yet complaining of hard work." Equally appealing to *Herald* readers were diatribes against the "rogues" in, but mostly out of, state prison. Fearful of rising taxes, New Yorkers chaffed at the "chiselers" on state bounty—the "paupers in the poor house," exclaimed Bennett, and the rest who were "heading there as fast as intemperance and indolence can carry them." Like the workers in New York's dockyards and factories, Bennett fumed about wealthy misers who cut workers' pay so that their sons, the city's "500 dandies," could strut about until they closed "their career with a pistol or a glass of laudanum," the popular drug addiction of the age.

Bennett was more or less singular in his attacks upon "wheedling judges" and other figures in New York's refined and established circles. His imagery fed the appetite of the city-dweller who thought himself a victim of pound-of-flesh bosses, swell-heads, banks, business houses, tax collectors, and parasitic politicians. Then there were the dreamy radicals, "white-coated philosophers," revival deacons with their array of Sunday schools and tract dispensing volunteers—and they, too, preyed upon the ordinary urbanite, and they, too, were targets of Bennett's shafts.

Bennett also portrayed himself as a victim, but one willing to give as much as he got. His readers, as letters to the editor testified, were convinced that he was generous to his friends and to workers, gallant toward women (the deserving ones), godly as only a man free of formal church ties could be, forthright toward his adversaries, moral and respectable, and sound on national and local issues. In a way Bennett was, though he was also misanthropic (refusing even a social glass of wine), virtually friendless, with a bad stomach and a glum, rather cross-eyed expression. The fact that respectable citizens thought him "too pitchy to touch," as a friend of Abraham Lincoln's once exclaimed, only enhanced his reputation among ordinary readers. Many Southerners and Westerners also admired him. To the public at least, he was the kind of fellow a bricklayer thought he would want for a friend.

Antebellum Americans, like many today, clothed themselves and their fears with easily grasped stereotypes that make sense of the incomprehensible and ease their feelings of doubt and insecurity. The result was not consciously nasty, though it could be, particularly during the numerous anti-abolitionist riots of the 1830s in New York City and elsewhere. Bennett served a popular function. He articulated the disenchantments and bawdy preoccupations of the voiceless. At the same time, Bennett himself felt compelled to cry out against self-guilt. There remained a personal connection between his attacks upon abolitionism and the world he had left behind in Scotland.

Three years after the *Herald*'s birth, James Bennett returned to Banffshire for a visit to his widowed mother's home. On the afternoon of his reunion at Keith, Bennett read the last letters from Cosmo, his younger brother, dead from causes Bennett attributed to the austerities of seminary living. He burst out in tears of anger and grief, raging about the house in what his relatives thought was a near-demented state. Bennett said nothing about Cosmo's futile clerical sacrifice upon the family altar, the role that he himself had so long ago escaped. But he swore an oath: "For the negligence that led to his death, my holy mother, the Church, must suffer some, and by my hands! See if she don't!" After a 23 year absence he abruptly left the old homestead the very next morning.

New York's Catholic bishops were not the only emissaries of God to feel Bennett's wrath. He arraigned those clergymen who made special appeal to the Almighty and the public in an evangelistic or dogmatic way. "A more corrupt, infidel, foolish, ignorant, witless, lazy, degenerate and rotten race of clergy," he said, "has not existed since the time of Caiaphus and Ananias, the high priests and high scoundrels of Judea." Bennett returned to the Old Testament prophets for the origins of the unmanly spirit of the clergy. "I don't think much of Moses," Bennett declared. "A man who would take 40 years to get a party of young women through the desert is only a loafer... Moses himself... was the first white man who married a Negro woman, and thus gave a sanction to amalgamation and abolition."

Bennett was aware that most Northern clergymen feared abolitionism as much as he deplored it. He applauded whenever the churches and benevolent societies prevented the passage of antislavery resolutions, but, like the equally vehement Garrisonians, he believed clerical motives were not holy or forthright. In 1860 the *Herald* editorialized, "The abolitionists may demand that the Gospels shall be altered so as to make out our Saviour a Garrisonian," yet "only one thing prevents the societies from splitting with the Almighty Nigger, and that is the Almighty Dollar."

Like many of the *Herald*'s subscribers, Bennett feared that middle-class pieties would feminize the nation. They would snatch the convivial tankard from the honest toiler, close down dance halls and theaters, shut up the Post Offices and railroad depots on Sundays, encourage blacks "to seek white mates," and bring on a return to the theocratic tyrannies of puritan New England. Ancient social and gender rankings would disappear along with "the purity of anglo-saxon blood." All these policies threatened the traditional image of the male as master of his own destiny, arbiter of his own morals and sexual habits, protector of his own dependents, whether within the family or outside it on the plantation. Bennett dwelt almost obsessively upon the modern breed "of unsexed females," abolitionist products of "finishing" schools, where indeed they "are 'finished,' as we once heard John Randolph say in the House of Representatives, 'finished, Mr. Speaker, yes, sir, finished for all useful purposes.'" But if antislavery women wore breeches, as he claimed, they consorted with men in "petticoats—vent your mawkishness on that!" In Bennett's opinion, Wendell Phillips and Garrison, like their clerical cousins in "white cravats," fought from behind the whalebone and cotton padding of their female allies, even though their doctrines were "boldly outrageous" and "madly fanatical." This double accusation of cowardice and satanism explained in part the passions that prompted a near-riot at the Broadway Tabernacle in 1850, the symbolism that surrounded

John Brown, and the outbreak of war itself in 1861. But first the Garrisonian counter-style requires explanation.

*   *   *

In many respects, William Lloyd Garrison represented the very antithesis of those values that Bennett and the anti-abolitionists espoused. Where the *Herald* editor glorified the male characteristics that he claimed to embody, Garrison rejoiced in following the standard of the Golden Rule. "If pride, ambition, and every sinful propensity, have been slain within me," Garrison modestly confided, "if love, joy, peace, long-suffering, gentleness, goodness, faith, meekness, temperance, 'the fruit of the Spirit,' dwell in me, it is solely 'by the grace of God.' " Garrison admitted that if he had not already "nailed natural vanity and love and human praise to the cross of Christ, such things would be likely to puff" him "up." Both Garrison and Bennett were egocentrics par excellence. Each thought himself and his mission extraordinary, almost superhuman.

Bennett drew his definition of manliness partially out of his Scottish heritage; Garrison's source was the hardy puritanism of old and New England. One of his heroes was "the martyred patriot of England—the great Algernon Sydney," a Puritan nobleman executed in the 1683 uprising against Charles II. There was always a trace of Cromwellian iron in Garrison's exhortations, and his speeches echoed the Biblical phrases of New England's ministers. Though we must bear "the vicious slanders of worldly men," Garrison intoned, "Deliver us from a boastful, vainglorious, self-confident spirit: but oh! what strength in Christian faith! what triumph in Christian endurance! Let us use, then, the dialect of Christian conquerors!" The Prince of Peace apparently carried a sword, though Garrison insisted that it was always sheathed.

"Muscular Christianity" of this kind was highly popular in the 19th century, culminating in the kind of male body building that Teddy Roosevelt celebrated. Despite his unique religious and reform beliefs, the role of strenuous Christian Achiever did not originate with Garrison; he merely applied the idea to anti-slavery and other issues. Consistent with this role, Garrison identified bluntness with manly duty. "In all my writings I have used strong, indignant, vehement language, direct, pointed scorching reproof," he wrote in 1830, shortly after release from a Baltimore jail for libeling a slave-trading New Englander. "Many have censured me for my severity—but thank God! none have stigmatized me with lukewarmness. 'Passion is reason—transport, temper—here.' " Typical of the polarized view of sexual roles in this day, Garrison struck out in a manner reminiscent of Bennett himself: "Men of natural softness and timidity, of a sincere and effeminate virtue, will be apt to look on these bolder, hardier spirits" of the antislavery crusade "as violent, perturbed and uncharitable." But the cause of "God's oppressed," he continued, required the services of those brave souls eager *"to move and shake nations,"* even at their own peril.

Defining the male role in terms of Christian sacrifice, selflessness, and boisterous exposure of wrongdoing, Garrison found the Southern system as demonic as Bennett pronounced it wholesome. Slavery, he insisted, made men—both master and slave—into beasts because unbounded, absolute power recognized no moral or even institutional check. Slavery, in Garrisonian opinion, encouraged the animal appetites and weakened capacities to control temptation. The Victorian moralist, however, thought that the Christian ideal of life demanded self-discipline in mind, body, and action. The age, then, stressed bodily restraints of a very inhibiting sort; but, oddly enough, permitted the most self-worshipping boastings. Teetotalism, sexual abstemiousness, cold-water bathing, rejection of "stimulants" like tea, coffee, sometimes meat, all were considered to be a means to physical purity. Garrison, like most other root-and-branch moralists, opposed "the dreadful vice of masturbation," a pleasure that supposedly led thousands of young people to insanity, physical decay, and moral ruin. On this issue, he was quite unlike Bennett, whose cure would have been a visit to Rosina Townshend's. Abolitionists like Garrison, however, thundered against such "sinks of pollution." However much "licentiousness pervades the whole land," Garrison claimed, "the 16 slave states constitute one vast brothel." Therefore, abolitionism was an effort "to save a million of the gentler sex from pollution, field labor, and the lash. *It is to put an end to an impure and disgraceful amalgamation."* The sexual imagery used in the Garrisonian attack was almost as graphic as Bennett's smirky apologies, but Garrison was deeply serious and theoretically if not actually correct about the Freudian implications of Southern racial attitudes.

Although early background never explains the whole man, Garrison's determination to be the purest foot-soldier in Christ's faithful army may have been in part a reaction to his father. Born in 1805, ten years after Bennett, he barely knew Abijah Garrison before being separated from him. A genial ne'er-do-well who drifted aimlessly about New England's grog-shops with fellow sailors, Abijah left household duties entirely in the hands of his ill-matched and pious wife. When Garrison was six, Abijah abandoned the family in Newburyport, Massachusetts, and settled in Maine with another woman. Humiliated, forced to take menial jobs, "Fanny" Garrison raised her children as best she could. The eldest boy, James, took to the sea and to the bottle in unhappy imitation of the departed Abijah. James died of chronic alcoholism in 1842. Imbued with a sense of special destiny that his worrisome mother imparted, William Lloyd apprenticed as a printer. Unlike Bennett, however, he realized that this occupation was a conventional vehicle from which to preach Federalist orthodoxy and, later, racial salvation. Bennett had deliberately rejected the priestly function. Garrison embraced it gladly.

Yet the youthful editor, like Bennett, used journalism to express rebellious feelings. The antislavery cause was, of course, a worthy and inspiring enterprise; and Garrison's contribution to it was both imaginative and effective. Nevertheless, he too wished to create a church and a set of beliefs of his own. Such a goal was common enough in the Jacksonian era. Individual approaches to personal and common problems multiplied, reflecting the social tensions and romantic feelings that accompanied commercial and political change. Perhaps Garrison found the answer in perfectionism—loyalty to the only legitimate government— the government of Christ; conceivably it was a means to fame in contrast to his father's obscurity and fall from respectability. In any case, he defied social norms and institutions by advocating radical policies that only a handful of followers could admire. Churches, he thought, chained the conscience to outworn Sabbatarian regulations and sectional timidities. Government masked an underlying military coercion that only total separation of North and South could begin to alter. Political parties corrupted even the antislavery officeholder. The pure of heart, Garrison asserted, ought not to vote simply because to do so was the expedient thing; expediency was a pernicious tactic. Claiming allegiance to the moral government of Christ, Garrison insisted that racial brotherhood would arrive with the millennial coming. Meanwhile, he arraigned the slightest deviation from righteousness. His policy, which included feminine liberation, made the purity of abolitionism obnoxious to the average citizen. To be sure, it also advertised both Garrison and his cause.

In some respects, few journalists were more traditional than the *Liberator*'s editor. No memorable innovations arose from its dreary columns. Not without reason, Bennett disliked the "one-idea" papers of which Garrison's was merely another struggling sheet. These efforts, he said, became "after a time, terrible bores, even to the people whose convictions they express." But Garrison was a modern agitator, perhaps the first and the best—not a truly professional journalist like Bennett. In that respect, he displayed an ingenious parasitism. With only occasional flashes of wit and stunning phrase, the *Liberator* thrived on the publicity that Bennett and other opponents provided—with their ridicule of Garrisonian "moonshine." Garrison did not initiate the violence that gave meaning and public influence to the cause of racial freedom. Consequently, there was always a latent provocation in his non-resistant rhetoric. But in emotional intensity, the moral antislavery rebukes of William Lloyd Garrison and the hot-tempered bellicosity of James Gordon Bennett were quite alike.

The annual convention of the Garrisonian American Anti-Slavery Society in May 1850, at New York's Broadway Tabernacle, juxtaposed all the themes of racism and equality, fear and hope, manliness and cowardice. The sessions coincided with an intense Congressional dispute over slavery, and a civil conflict over the territorial spoils of the Mexican War seemed likely. Only later in the fall, after President Zachary Taylor's timely death, did sectional negotiation postpone the conflict. But the scenes in the cavernous, overcrowded revivalist tabernacle prefigured events of a decade later.

For some days prior to the antislavery assembly, Bennett urged *Herald* readers to demonstrate the city's loyalty to the "Glorious Union" between North and South. These "besotted zealots," he cried, are "very much excited about the wrongs of their colored brethren and sisters. They mix with them, fraternizing, slobbering over each other, speaking, praying, singing, blaspheming, and cursing the Constitution." Aware of earlier mob reactions to the Garrisonians, Bennett specifically cautioned that passions be restrained. Otherwise, the abolitionists could claim to be "martyrs to their false patriotism, false pride, and sincere folly." Warming to the task, Bennett continued, "Never in the time of the French Revolution was there more malevolence and unblushing wickedness avowed than by this same Garrison."

Among the 6,000 attending the sessions were Captain Isaiah Rynders and a large contingent of Tammany "b'hoys" who represented Bennett's views from their gallery seats. Recently ousted by the Whigs from his post of U.S. Customs weigher, Rynders held power through his Democratic ward gangs of "Calithumpians" and "Rip Raps" as well as his ownership of the Empire Club gambling casino. Individuals actually may conform to the most exaggerated caricature. So it was with Rynders, a florid-faced, beefy, half-German, half-Irish ex-boatmen—the perfect symbol of the hard-headed anti-abolitionist. Garrison was the first speaker. Answering Bennett's editorial charge of fomenting "blasphemous atheism," he attacked the iniquities of the American church system. "The slaves believe in a Jesus that strikes off chains," he exclaimed. But for whites "Jesus has become obsolete." In fact, "Jesus is the most respectable person in the United States. . . . Jesus sits in the President's chair." Uncomprehending the gang in the balcony rumbled ominously. "Zachary Taylor," Garrison drove on, "sits there which is the same thing, for he believes in Jesus. He believes in war, and the Jesus that gave the Mexicans hell."

At that point, Rynders shook a fist and shouted: "I will not allow you to assail the President of the United States. You shan't do it!" Rynders then swung down to the stage on a gaslight standard and headed for the podium. "Have some respect for the ladies," cried an abolitionist from the floor. Rynders parried, "I have always respected the ladies, but I doubt very much whether white women who cohabit with the woolly-headed negro, are entitled to any respect from a white man." Somehow, Garrison restored order and scored the "cowards" who hid "behind the safe and popular side of slavery" and had "no fight in them" for anything but "political preferments." When he had finished, Rynders demanded that his side be given the floor.

"Professor" Robert Grant, with a dirty bandage wrapped around one hand, then stepped up at Rynders' command. His lecture, like his clothing, was a shabby affair that "scientifically" linked Negroes with the primates of the jungle. Horace Greeley's *Tribune*, Bennett's reform-minded competitor, wryly observed that "if anybody present was proved the nephew of a rather dull ourang outang, it was Professor Robert Grant; if anybody the first cousin of a very vicious monkey, it was Capt. Isaiah Rynders."

The abolitionists could not have found a more emphatic refutation than in the argument of their next speaker—Frederick Douglass, the brilliant and light-skinned former slave. He replied, "I cannot follow his argument. I will assist him, however. I offer myself for your examination. Am I a man?" Thunderous applause gave the instant response. But Captain Rynders countered: "You are only half a nigger." In mock deference, Douglass cuttingly replied, "Then I am half-brother to Captain Rynders!" Even Bennett's *Herald* conceded that Douglass' subsequent address was the best of the day. Douglass and another equally impressive black orator, had insured that the rowdies could not halt the momentum of the meeting.

That evening the two forces again confronted each other in a smaller hall, this time with greater expectation of a bloody outcome. Stephen S. Foster, a fiery Garrisonian, almost immediately accused the Rynders "working men" of being mere tools in a plot hatched by Bennett and fearful city merchants. But Foster was wrong. The ward-heelers and butcher-boys were not pawns of upper-class interests: they vented their genuine frustrations against a middle-class group of moralists with cultural and religious assumptions that they themselves could never easily accept. To them abolitionists were a sinister and alien force ready to impose religious and racial tyrannies.

The next reform speaker served as an easy target for the hooters in the gallery. Charles Calistus Burleigh, another reform editor, wore his fiery red hair in long ringlets to the shoulders; he also had a beard to match. Even Garrison was unhappily aware that, for all his gifts, Burleigh subjected himself "to the unjust suspicion that he was a weak and eccentric individual." As Burleigh strode toward the platform, someone shouted to Garrison: "Say, Judge, tell us whether that is a man or a woman"; and another: "Why don't Douglass shave that tall Christ and make a wig for him?" The guffaws grew so loud that Burleigh could not be heard.

Meanwhile, Rynders commissioned another Tammany hack to replace the ineffectual "Professor." Thomas Moore, a policeman recently discharged for being drunk in a "house of ill fame," took command. His resolution accurately reflected working-class feelings: "Resolved, That this meeting will not countenance fanatical agitation whose aims are the overthrow of the churches, a reign of anarchy, a division of interests, the supremacy of a hypocritical atheism, a general amalgamation, and a dissolution of the Union." What these "humanity-mongers" ought to do, Moore continued, was to investigate "the progress of degradation among negroes of the North, and the increasing inequality and poverty of the free whites and blacks of New York." One might argue that the authors, James Bennett among them, included the blacks in this protest against grinding urban conditions as an indication of raceless proletarian solidarity. But their actual object was to contrast the allegedly dreamy abstractions of reform idealism with a more visceral spirit—that paradoxical, mindless notion that there are some good "niggers," so long as they kept their place.

Crowd feelings were growing dangerously overheated. What almost triggered a general melee, however, was not slavery and antislavery as such, but rather the issue of virility. Burleigh tried to regain the attention of this restless crowd and finally cried out in desperation, "You are a God-abandoned people! O, misguided men! You know not what you do!" "Boo, hoo, oo-oo!" yelled the "b'hoys" in high falsetto, waving their handkerchiefs and flapping their wrists. At once, Garrison, outraged, moved Burleigh aside: "There is not a man among you. If you are men of intellect, come up here on this platform. Pick out your man, if you have a man among you who dares to say 'boo to a goose,' which I very much doubt. You have not the manliness to say you are friends of slavery." At least Southerners, Garrison shouted, "have the courage for that." Wendell Phillips then denounced the "cringing wretches" of the North who were doing the South's bidding like slaves themselves. No set of "sacrilegious scoundrels," no "hireling band of Southern aristocracy," no "purlieus of Park Row," Phillips cried, "shall drive us hence. We are able to protect ourselves, and we shall do so." In fact, where better to die "than here—here on this platform—martyrs alike to Freedom and Liberty?" Scuffling broke out on the floor. The ladies present headed for the aisles. Anticipating the worst, Garrison hastily called for adjournment. The Rynders gang replied, "Oh, oh! come, Judge, no more gassing; let up on us, we have given you a good show." Three cheers went up for the *Herald* and its editor.

Just then Sheriff Carnley and a band of police arrived to protect the Library Society's hall and disperse the crowd. Meanwhile, the Hutchinson Family Singers in the gallery struck up an antislavery tune to soothe the throng. Captain Rynders shouted up to the songsters, "You long-haired abolitionists, if you don't stop singing, I'll come up there and bring you down." Pushed along by Carnley's men, the wool-hat boys left with the others. The hymn-singing, the police, and the rough good-humor of the workingmen had averted a general riot. One of the last to leave the scene, Rynders was overheard to complain that contrary to the libels of the *Tribune*, he did *not* count apes among his forebears.

Garrison had no doubt that Bennett was the real instigator of the most heated antislavery convention in a number of years: "For all that transpired, that was brutal, profane, indecent, outrageous ... the miscreant editor of that polluted journal is to be held directly responsible." Although Bennett exhibited a murderous spirit "unsurpassed in the annals of assassination," Garrison claimed, "we freely forgive this abandoned man for all the evil he has sought to inflict upon us; for we cherish no other feelings toward him than those of the deepest compassion." Considering Garrison's version of forgiveness, revenge itself might have been a milder balm. Bennett pointed out that, despite Garrison's disavowal of human government, the Boston editor was demanding that New York officials indict him for inciting a riot. For his part, Garrison saw no contradiction. After all, he maintained, Bennett was "the employer, the principal—Rynders and his gang were only his tools, and are scarcely to be held accountable for their insane behavior." Summing up abolitionist philosophy, Garrison argued that the Society would continue to "procure the abolition of slavery by peaceful agencies, in a voluntary manner, through conviction and repentance on the part of all who are guilty of upholding it, whether in the North or at the South." Carnal weapons were not a solution, he said. Antislavery stalwarts used only spiritual ones for "the pulling down of the strongholds of American slavery."

From 1831 to 1859, the abolitionist crusade, splintered and faction-ridden though it was, remained more or less faithful to the non-violent posture that Garrison insistently preached. The policy was based on a fallacy traditional to American reform; namely, the idea that with proper guidance from enlightened (middle-class) leadership the masses would respond to rational argument. Even slaveholders were expected to rally, as Garrison phrased it from the Bible, to "the foolishness of preaching." To the abolitionist, slavery was a *problem*, like drinking, dueling, cruelty to small animals, and prostitution. For these sins there was the simple remedy of personal repentance, backed by appropriate laws that reflected thousands of individual acts of contrition.

Anti-abolitionists like Bennett and most Southern whites considered slavery a *condition*, not a problem. Race subordination was like poverty, war, government, bloodlines, and hierarchies of individual talent—that is, it was part of the natural order of things. Such matters could be adjusted for better or worse, but the condition itself was immutable and divinely sanctioned. Neither party was totally accurate. Abolitionists were deluded in thinking that the elimination of the problem, "the peculiar institution," would bring on a racial millennium. Bennett's error had a sounder historical foundation, but he romantically overestimated the durability of slavery and ignored the drift toward free-labor capitalism.

Curiously, however, the misperceptions of both parties hastened a revolutionary transformation that could scarcely satisfy either group. Garrisonians had to believe in the efficacy of individual conversion, since the mass of the citizenry—where power resided—was normally phlegmatic and self-concerned. Yet the tactics of "moral suasion," which aimed at antislavery recruitment, had struck another target—confrontation. Abolitionists stirred the blood, not the heart. Garrisonian pacifism, like the offer of forgiveness, provoked indignation. However, without the fulminations of Bennett and others like him, Garrison, Phillips, and Douglass could never have staged so effective a drama that contrasted manly righteousness against ignorance and venality. Each protagonist fed the bellicosity of the other. Gradually, the indifferent and casual observer was being forced to take a stand. But the task of escalating these issues of race and masculinity to the threshold of war itself fell to a former shepherd and insurrectionist.

*   *   *

Shortly after news arrived that John Brown, two of his sons, and most of the fellow conspirators had been captured or killed at Harpers Ferry, Bennett sent a special reporter to Charlestown, Virginia. The *Herald's* coverage was by far the most vivid, detailed, and stirring of any newspaper reporting up to that time. Through it Bennett inadvertently contributed enormously to the polarization of sectional feelings and actually to the dignity of the anti-slavery cause. For the *Herald* as well as other papers in competitive imitation projected the image of Brown as a divine, consecrated man of God *and* blood. "I hold that the golden rule, 'Do unto others as you would that others should do unto you,' applies to all who would help others to gain their liberty," Brown informed the *Herald's* readers. Unlettered though he was, Brown—no less than Bennett and Garrison—showed a masterly grasp of publicity. As Henry Thoreau, one of his most ardent admirers exclaimed, "No theatrical manager could have arranged things so wisely to give effect to his behavior and words."

John Brown's rise to his remarkable prominence involved a strange personal history, which included a growing self-awareness of godly manhood. In a letter of 1857, Brown related a moving account of his inner feelings as child and adult. Written in the third person, as if composed by someone seeking a special detachment, it described how his father, a stern, old-fashioned Edwardsean Calvinist moved the family from rural Connecticut to the Indian-infested Ohio frontier. Born in 1800, Brown was then five years of age, just old enough to feel the tensions of resettlement. When he was eight, Brown lost his mother, and his father promptly married a teenage girl, 20 years his junior. John Brown recalled that he "never adopted" his step-mother "in feeling," but continued to pine after his own mother for years. As the letter revealed, the boy channelled his nervous affections into the possession of pets and toys, particularly "a Yellow marble . . . but at last he lost it beyound [sic] recovery. It took years to heal the wound; & I think at times he cried about it." Finding little love at home, he was compelled to place faith in things that, like his real mother, slipped away too quickly. Since abandoned children often blame themselves for their misfortunes, Brown himself may have thought that God (as well as his grim father) had punished him for misdeeds by depriving him of his mother.

At school, Brown recorded, he was so unhappy and distracted that he "learned nothing of Grammer [sic]" and little arithmetic. Schoolmates thought him a bully "excessively fond of the hardest & roughest plays." Dreaming of eventual successes that would silence those whom he could not impress, Brown spent lonely hours at home where he was captive to such self-isolating fantasies. Moreover, he tended to lie compulsively, a habit, he confessed, that was "very bad & foolish" and practiced "to screen himself from blame," since he could not suffer to be reproached. Authority generally provoked Brown's anger unless paternally identified—whether on Earth or in heaven—and praise from older residents, he admitted, filled him with "self-conceit." Outwardly, however, he came to manhood singularly devoted to the visible and publicly approved virtues of hard work, neatness, and practical realities.

Later events did not alter Brown's private convictions of future omnipotence and present distress. Two marriages, the steady accumulation of children (20 by these wives), and many jobs brought more sorrow than pleasure. One baby, for instance, died when two older children plunged the infant in a bath of scalding water. Or witness Brown's business affairs, mostly sheep-raising and tanning, in which he demonstrated a romantic impulsiveness that led inevitably to debts and disputes. Brown took solace by worshipping not a forgiving God, but rather the crucified, atoning victim of human depravity.

When John Brown's eldest son had engaged in some naughty escapades, the father listed them—a "fearful toting up of debits," John Brown, Jr., recalled—in a moral ledgerbook. And then, rather than continue punishment, John Brown stripped off his own shirt and ordered his son to lay on with the remaining two-thirds of the "account." Throughout the ordeal, he cried out, strike "harder, harder, harder!" until the horrified boy could see the blood oozing down his back. The lesson presumably was modelled after the atonement of Christ on the Cross and would be later repeated by Brown himself on the Charlestown gallows. Religion, punishment, countinghouse bankruptcy, paternal anguish, a masochistic pleasure in the pain of receiving the blows for whatever sins he himself felt guilty—all combine to shape the life of John Brown, a charismatic leader beset by feelings he could not otherwise express. But like most religious zealots—and Brown was essentially that—he somehow managed to utilize even his inmost fears and hopes creatively, and by a peculiar alchemy transforming them into a conquering spiritual power.

Brown, it should be noted, was also the model of the dedicated puritan, replete with rather conventional sentiments: "Diligence is the mother of good luck," "God helps those who help themselves," were among his favorite aphorisms. One of the sources of his loathing for the South, not surprisingly, derived from this Puritanism. Vices of idleness, self-indulgent drunkenness, profanity, wild disorder, sexual profligacy, mean-spirited mastery over the souls of others—these crimes against God and morality were identified with "the *foul and loathsome* embrace of the *old rotten whore,* slavery." Temperamental difficulties could hardly explain Brown's genuine sympathies for the blacks.

Brown had little reason to be proud of his accomplishments until going to Kansas in the mid-1850s. There, with his sons, he discovered a godly, revolutionary calling—the struggle for freedom on the borders of slavery. "Transfixed . . . in a kind of trance," Brown watched his guerilla band hack at the fallen bodies of allegedly proslavery farmers near Pottawatomie Creek.

There may have been a psychological basis for the Kansas violence and for Brown's extravagant scheme of arming slaves with the arsenal guns at Harpers Ferry. For him, the enterprise represented atonement for past disappointment and self-thwarted ambitions, as well as an investment in immortality. Writing to his wife after the effort had failed, he declared, "I have been whiped [sic] as the saying is but I am sure that I can recover all the *lost capital* occasioned by that disaster; by only hanging a few moments by the neck, & I feel quite determined to make the utmost possible out of a defeat." (Italics the author's.) At last, the mission for which he confidently believed God had summoned him was fulfilled.

The bloody border chieftain of the Kansas plains and the benign, radiantly calm Christian martyr of the Charlestown prison combined the tense duality of Brown's character. From capture to the scaffold steps, Brown looked forward with "all joy," as he said, to the moment when hated authority meted out punishment and opened the avenue to personal vindication and black liberation. Almost to the end of the raid, Brown could have escaped to Virginia's hill country. His intention, though not wholly conscious, was instead the performance of a religious, testamentary act of sacrifice. It ended all past confusions and made him feel whole and purposeful in a way denied to most men.

Brown's appeal to many of his contemporaries in the North is not terribly perplexing. He evoked adulation because his actions seemingly cut through the Gordian knot of moral vexations. Yearning for saintly heroes in an age of vulgar preoccupations, money-exchange ethics, and moral complacencies, New England luminaries like Theodore Parker, Thomas Wentworth Higginson, Ralph Waldo Emerson, and Henry Thoreau perceived Brown as the ultimate expression of romantic Christianity and 19th-century manliness. Brown's deeds gave the lie to those who thought Yankee abolitionists generally soulless, calculating and money-conscious. Garrison's hot words, after all, were only words. Brown translated them into bold action. "Walter Scott would have delighted" to depict John Brown, Emerson proclaimed. "All gentlemen, of course, are on his side," though not "people of scented hair and perfumed handkerchiefs, but men of gentle blood and generosity. For what is the oath of gentle blood and knighthood? What but to protect the weak and lowly against the strong oppressor?" As Francis Lieber, a prominent Columbia professor, scornfully observed, "Brown died like a man," while "Virginia fretted like a woman."

Even James Gordon Bennett came to recognize that abolitionists possessed the courage that he admired, though not in a cause that ever gained his approval. Remarking upon the contrasting timidity of some Republican leaders after the Harpers Ferry raid, Bennett mused, "Truly there is as much difference between the manly heart and the politician's gizzard, as physically between the massive form of the Abolitionist and the insignificant figure" of a political time-server. "Would not a Southern gentleman respect the former far more than the latter?" Bennett cared nothing for racial freedom—no more so than did hundreds of thousands of other Northern citizens. Nevertheless, he recognized manly acts, even in a "crazy scoundrel" like John Brown. He also acknowledged loyalty to the Northern clan. Complaining bitterly about abolition "mischief" and canting "Black Republicanism," Bennett nonetheless would remain loyal to the Union in 1861. It was a fitting conclusion since Bennett had done so much to test antislavery mettle and publicize the crusade.

The American ideal of manhood was only a myth. Yet it gave meaning to life itself and helped to mobilize armies on both sides of the Potomac. In an effort to deny cowardice, thousands went to their death. Furthermore, this cult of manliness demonstrated that events of history are sometimes determined less by actual circumstances than by the perceptions of them. In these ante-bellum years, tragedy and inspiration, prejudice and progress, delusion and reason, fear of emasculation and hope of glory conspired together, producing results for which later generations could be soberly grateful.

12

The Peculiar Institution: Defended, Accommodated, and Attacked

JOHN C. CALHOUN
HENRY CLAY
ANGELINA GRIMKÉ

by Charles M. Wiltse
Dartmouth College

After the Missouri Compromise of 1820, the elimination of slavery, the South's "peculiar institution," became the major goal of American reform, while its defense formed the hard core of the nation's conservatism. The northern challenge to Missouri's admission as a slave state forced the South to come to grips with both its conscience and its future. Many of the framers of the Constitution, including slaveholders like James Madison, had assumed that the institution, without renewal, would be progressively diffused and would eventually disappear. The Constitution's provision prohibiting the Congress from halting the foreign slave trade prior to 1808 was only a gesture, for it had already been stopped by the states. In 1790 there were some 750,000 slaves out of a population of approximately four million. Over the next three decades, the proportion of slaves to total population remained relatively unchanged —a little more than 18 percent. However the production of cotton, which came to absorb the bulk of slave labor, increased from 3,000 bales in 1790 to 335,000 bales in 1820.

By the latter date cotton planters, to a man, had convinced themselves that their staple could not be grown and prepared for market without slave labor. If Congress could abolish slavery in Missouri, it could end it anywhere, given the requisite majorities in both houses. Missouri was admitted with slavery but only by a compromise that brought Maine simultaneously into the Union as a free state. The Senate thus remained evenly divided, but to the South, already numerically weaker than the North, equality in the upper house at best afforded shaky ground on which to rest the future of its way of life. Thereafter, the specter of slavery was present in every debate that implied to any degree the supremacy of the federal government over the states. Slaveholders came to oppose all legislation pertaining to internal improvements, the tariff, and a national bank, lest such measures unintentionally concede an excess of power to the federal government.

In the North the great religious revival of the 1830s both fed upon and nourished a growing antislavery mood. Though the defense of slavery was also grounded in Scripture, its immediacy derived from the tariff and the falling price of cotton. Southern planters were absolutely convinced that the one was the cause of the other. With equal obstinacy they believed that the power to override the states by imposing a distasteful tariff might one day be invoked to alter their slave labor system. This possibility, which achieved nightmarish proportions after the slave revolt of 1822, gave a do-or-die impetus to the fight against the tariff as well as to the developing intellectual defense of slavery.

The South's most refined constitutional and intellectual argument came from its most able political theoretician, John C. Calhoun. The South Carolinian's tightly reasoned arguments were countered by a well-organized and vocal abolitionist movement that preferred to rest its case on morality rather than legal hair-splitting. Angelina Grimké has been chosen here as the representative of the antislavery crusade not only because of the importance of her role but because, like Calhoun, she was a South Carolinian. Somewhere between these two extremes were great numbers of Americans, Northerners and Southerners alike, who were prepared to accept whatever the national verdict might be so long as it was indeed national. Henry Clay, whose name is associated with three great North-South compromises, fell into this intermediate group.

* * *

No figure in American history has been more controversial than John Caldwell Calhoun, the gaunt, emaciated Senator from South Carolina, the very personification of the antebellum South. He has been variously called a pure-hearted patriot and a traitor to his country, a man of "enlarged and liberal views" and the "philosopher of reaction." By accident of birth and residence, the acknowledged spokesman for a minority interest that came under intensified attack during his lifetime, he spoke for this interest in a period of growing sectional hostility. From an ingenious interpreter of the economy of cotton, he became the "Sentinel of the South" and finally the section's foremost apologist for slavery. Calhoun did not devise the concept of slavery as a "positive good," but he gave it a currency no other man of his time could have done. He himself was a man of strong moral convictions. While he could not defend, nor even accept, an immoral institution, he could and did so rationalize Negro slavery that it became in his hands not evil but good, a blessing to bondsman and master alike!

The Calhouns were only 50 years from Ulster when John Caldwell was born in 1782 in Abbeville District, South Carolina, high in the Appalachian foothills. His family had migrated there in stages from Lancaster, Pennsylvania, by way of the Valley of Virginia. John's early education was meager, but his capacity to learn seemed without limit. He studied a few scattered months at a fly-by-night field school taught by an itinerant teacher and for two years at the academy run by his brother-in-law, Moses Waddel, near Appling, Georgia. Then in 1802 at the age of 20, he enrolled with the junior class at Yale College where his primary interest almost inevitably was history and politics. In New Haven he witnessed at first hand the full bitterness of the Federalist opposition that culminated in the separatist threats of the Essex Junto. He had time to ponder New England's reaction to the Louisiana purchase, which seemed to open the way for more slave states. And he saw political rivalry in neighboring New York State end in the fatal duel between Aaron Burr and Alexander Hamilton. For a few months after his graduation from Yale in 1804, he read law in Charleston; then in the summer of 1805 he entered Judge Tapping Reeve's famous law school at Litchfield, Connecticut.

In the summer of 1807 young Calhoun was back in South Carolina completing his legal training in his native Abbeville. It was there he heard the electrifying news that the American frigate *Chesapeake* had been fired upon by a British warship outside Hampton Roads and forced to strike her colors. Ever since the Revolution Great Britain, in fact, had been interfering with American commerce and kidnapping American sailors for her own navy, but protest hitherto had not survived diplomacy. This time it was different. For a brief time a sense of outrage united the country as it had never been before. Had President Jefferson called for war at that moment the American people would have followed; but his answer was to impose an embargo, and the wound festered. Especially indignant apparently were those who had been born since the Declaration of Independence. One of these birthright Americans, Calhoun prepared resolutions and made his first political speech. In the fall of 1808, he was elected to the South Carolina legislature and two years later to Congress. His personal future was secured at about the same time by his marriage to a cousin, Floride Bonneau Calhoun, who brought him not only a modest fortune but also entree into the tidewater aristocracy.

Thereafter Calhoun's rise was mercurial. In November 1811 he took his seat in the House of Representatives where he quickly identified himself with the War Hawks, mostly new and youthful Congressmen who were hot for war with Britain since the *Chesapeake* affair. Although Kentucky's Henry Clay was making his first appearance in the House, he was the acknowledged leader of this group, which succeeded in electing him Speaker. In turn, Clay took care of them through his committee appointments. Calhoun served on the Foreign Relations Committee; he became its chairman in time to draft the report calling for war with Great Britain. Working with and through Secretary of State James Monroe, the War Hawks, in effect, forced hostilities on a reluctant President Madison.

Calhoun's vigorous nationalism in support of the War of 1812 and of the measures for economic renovation that followed, won him the post of Secretary of War in the cabinet of Madison's successor, James Monroe. There he quickly demonstrated great administrative skill and a capacity for leadership of the first order. By the end of 1821, Calhoun's announcement that he was a candidate for President surprised no one, and except for his youth it seemed not unreasonable. Who then could have foreseen that in ten years time this same ardent and popular nationalist from South Carolina would be asking the cotton growing states to ignore an act of Congress and defy the authority of the national government?

Calhoun's bid for the presidency in 1824 soon proved to be bad politics, for it brought him into immediate conflict with rivals whose claims were based on longer if not more distinguished public service. Moreover, the United States was in the midst of the Era of Good Feelings, the second and last time in American history when there were no political parties—only factions among Jefferson's Republicans. Secretary of State John Quincy Adams felt that his office made him the natural heir; Secretary of the Treasury William H. Crawford was the inheritor of the old but still active Virginia–New York political alliance; Henry Clay certainly had a claim based on distinguished service as Speaker and as one of the peace commissioners who negotiated the Treaty of Ghent ending the War of 1812. He would be an ideal man to break the "Cabinet Succession" and to give the growing West a President. But Andrew Jackson, the popular hero who had won the only decisive victory of the war, was soon to be the front runner. Against any of these Calhoun had little chance, and he soon withdrew, to become the successful candidate for the vice presidency. When the 1824 presidential election was thrown into the House of Representatives because no candidate had a majority in the electoral college, he bent over backward to avoid indicating a preference. As the fourth man, Clay had been eliminated, and ill-feeling developed between Calhoun and Crawford. But both Adams and Jackson had backed Calhoun for Vice President, and he had won with a clear majority. He could not now take sides, or so he believed.

Ultimately the House chose Adams, but within a year Calhoun joined the opposition that was rallying around Jackson and calling itself the Democracy. Calhoun's new political stance was directly related to the tariff issue. As a member of Congress, he had voted for the tariff of 1816, which was designed to protect war-born American industry from ruinous foreign competition. The tariff of 1824, which doubled the 1816 duties, was another matter. The predominantly agricultural southern states exchanged their staples, especially cotton, for manufactured goods. England was both their market and their supplier. Southern planters reasoned, not illogically, that the value of cotton sold must be equivalent to the value of manufactures bought. It followed that every tariff-fostered increase in the price of manufactured goods, to the extent that it reduced imports, would be accompanied by a decline in the price of cotton. The 1824 tariff passed by a narrow margin with southern members united in opposition. As they foresaw, the price of cotton dropped sharply.

Cause and effect or not, no cotton planter would believe otherwise. Henry Clay, the foremost advocate of the tariff, was the presumed successor to Adams, whereas Jackson was himself a cotton planter whose interest would be served by keeping the duties down. More important, the administration did not question the federal government's power to impose a tariff; but to a mind like that of Calhoun, preternaturally acute through generations of living with bondsmen, the same power in the hands of a northern majority might one day be used to emancipate the slaves. Calhoun remembered all too well the Missouri Compromise debates, which had forced the South to affirm for the first time that slavery was a permanent institution. Many Southerners, and particularly South Carolinians, believed the antislavery argument publicly advanced in these debates had inspired the Denmark Vesey rebellion of 1822. Though quickly crushed, it had frightened the South into tightening slave codes and moving toward greater repression. By 1825 Southerners were convinced that tariffs, internal improvements, and anything that tended to increase the power of the federal government were a threat to slavery.

Cotton prices continued to fall, and from the cotton states came rumblings, first of discontent, then of rebellion. Those from Calhoun's own South Carolina resounded the loudest of all. When Congress passed the tariff of 1828—called the "Tariff of Abominations" by its opponents—Calhoun assumed the role of polemicist, preparing the case not only against the tariff itself but also against a system that permitted tariffs to be enacted. In his *South Carolina Exposition and Protest*, published by the state legislature in December 1828, he outlined a defense against the uncontrolled power of the numerical majority. In a brilliant analysis anticipating that of Karl Marx in the *Communist Manifesto* 20 years later, Calhoun demonstrated how capitalism would sharply divide society into owners and operatives. Wealth, he reasoned, would concentrate in the hands of the former, while labor eventually would be reduced to a subsistence level. This condition could be avoided by giving each major interest group a veto upon the will of the numerical majority. Since each of the states was dominated by a major interest, they would perform this role. As matters stood, the manufacturing interest controlled the numerical majority, but by acting through the states, the agricultural interest might interpose to arrest legislation to its detriment. Details of the exposition would be refined later, but here in embryo was the doctrine of nullification. According to Calhoun, the tariff was unconstitutional because its action did not apply equally to all of the states. Consequently any state adversely affected could declare the tariff null and void within its own borders. Calhoun, it should be emphasized, premised this elaborate political procedure on the United States Constitution, which he interpreted as a compact among sovereign states. While delegating certain specified functions to a general government, he had the states retain their individual sovereignties, which they could exert as they saw fit.

Calhoun did not actually invoke the nullification doctrine. He let it dangle for all to see. In particular, it was a warning to Andrew Jackson, who had just won the presidency from Adams. Calhoun had been re-elected vice president, but he wanted Jackson to understand that the South had supported both of them in expectation of tariff reform.

Jackson's first year in office passed with no move in that direction. Nor was there any in his second year. Cotton prices continued to fall, and Calhoun's restless young followers threatened to invoke his doctrine with or without his leadership. He held them off for the time being, but events conspired to force his hand. David Walker's militant *Appeal to the Coloured Citizens of the World,* appearing in the fall of 1829 and calling on slaves to strike for their freedom, violently if necessary, had brought near panic to the South. Once again slave codes were tightened and vigilance intensified. Nor was Southern equilibrium fully restored when the long simmering anti-slavery opposition burst into flaming rhetoric with the appearance of William Lloyd Garrison's *Liberator* in January 1831. And then in the following August came Nat Turner's rebellion, which frightened slaveholders into a common fellowship of fear. In January 1832 the Virginia Legislature debated emancipation, and by the razor-thin margin of a single vote defeated Jefferson's old plan for gradual emancipation. The tariff of 1832, which the South considered no better than its predecessor, was enacted in mid-summer, and in November Jackson was triumphantly re-elected, this time with Martin Van Buren of New York as his running mate.

No longer able to restrain the South Carolina dissidents, Calhoun placed himself at their head and implemented the theoretical remedy of the exposition. Late in November 1832 a special state convention chosen on the issue of nullification declared unconstitutional the tariffs of 1828 and 1832 and enjoined their enforcement within South Carolina.

Senator Robert Y. Hayne was then chosen Governor and Calhoun elected to his vacant Senate seat. He resigned the vice presidency and proceeded to Washington where for 15 stormy years he represented the Palmetto State in particular and the South in general as the great champion of states rights and as the most vocal apologist for slavery. The tariff issue was compromised and the Ordinance of Nullification consequently was withdrawn. But at the same time Jackson had also shown that given sufficient provocation, the federal government could and would use force to uphold the law.

And the law just might be the abolition of slavery! So Calhoun set himself to guard against that frightening contingency under whatever guise it might appear. Thereafter he fought every act that might extend the power of the federal government, either directly or by implication. Because the South was already a hopeless minority, Calhoun sought to curb majority power by identifying a political balance that would parallel the existing balance of interests. If each major interest group might veto legislation it considered harmful, the South could not only block tariff measures but also defeat any future move to emancipate the slaves. By a skillful exercise of dialectic, Calhoun would have shorn the federal government of its sovereignty, supplanting it by a consensus of pressure blocs.

Though Calhoun's course over the next decade remained single minded and undeviating, his response to the panic of 1837 struck a popular note. He was instrumental in establishing the treasury as a substitute for the now defunct Bank of the United States. After the comic opera presidential election of 1840, his hopes rose once more and he began to see himself as John Tyler's successor. He resigned his Senate seat early in 1843 to avoid taking any positions that would be unpopular nationally. Although his lieutenants did a yeoman job, Calhoun's cause was again hopeless, and he withdrew before the nominating convention began its deliberations. Almost immediately he was recalled to public life, this time as Secretary of State in Tyler's cabinet. The annexation of Texas was his special mission. Always a man to say what he thought, Calhoun literally destroyed his chances for the presidential nomination by making a vigorous pro-slavery argument justifying annexation. He did this in an official despatch to the British minister. In the end Calhoun succeeded in bringing about annexation, but the aftermath was to be a war with Mexico, which he strongly opposed. In still one more of his political maneuvers, Calhoun returned to the Senate in time to denounce the conflict, to help frame the 1846 tariff, which abandoned the principle of protection, and to debate the question of the status of slavery in the territory acquired from Mexico as a result of the conflict.

The territorial issue forced the Compromise of 1850. An all-Southern convention had already been summoned to meet in Nashville in June.

Southerners were all too aware that exclusion of slavery from California and New Mexico would foreshadow massive anti-slavery majorities in both houses of Congress. In that event, few doubted that secession of the Southern states from the union would be proposed at Nashville. But California, her population swollen by gold fever, had opted to exclude slavery and had Senators and Representatives present when Congress met in December 1849. They brought with them a free state constitution for approval. The broad compromise offered by Henry Clay was rejected by Calhoun, who saw no further hope of maintaining parity between North and South, even in the Senate. He had less than a month to live. While Calhoun sat in his seat, too feeble to address his fellow legislators, Senator James Mason of Virginia read his last speech for him on March 4, 1850. Still bent upon the protection of slavery, Calhoun demanded that a sectional veto be added to the Constitution, even if it meant creating a dual presidency.

Who really knows for sure what goes on in the mind of another? Calhoun certainly loved the union and would not willingly have seen it destroyed. Yet he thought it worth preserving only if it dispensed what he considered to be equal justice to all its members. For the South dependence on the ballot alone would never suffice; it could always be outvoted by the free states. Calhoun's most important legacy was his reasoned defense of minority interests, through a species of functional federalism he called the "concurrent majority." The doctrine had worked in the case of the tariff. But as a defense of slavery it did not and could not work, for in the long run morality cannot be compromised. Although the concurrent voice of the slave interest died away with the muffling of the guns at Appomattox, interest groups, in one form or another and for better or for worse, still manage to veto the will of the numerical majority.

*   *   *

Henry Clay and John C. Calhoun were cut out of different kinds of political cloth. Calhoun was the disembodied intellect, driven by some inner compulsion to analyze the political activities that went on around him. From his analysis he produced sweeping theories for universal application. For his part, Clay was never happier than when he was at the very center of the political stage. He was far more concerned with political process than with abstractions or with far-reaching theories about the nature of government. The Kentuckian was the complete politician, not in the machine sense that described Martin Van Buren, but in the more primary role of organizer, doer, and leader. He had magnetism, charm, wit; he had a restraining sense of values; and he had a superb measure of what we today would call "horse sense."

When Henry Clay first erupted upon the national scene, he was already past master of the art of managing men. Though still in his early 30s, there seemed to be no height that was unattainable. Clay himself assessed his prospects with complete confidence. But as the bitter sectional struggle began to draw the lines ever more tightly, Clay found himself caught in the middle. Calhoun was unequivocally the symbol and spokesman of the slaveholding South, as Daniel Webster of Massachusetts was of the industrial and commercial North. Clay, the self-appointed spokesman for the West, was torn both ways. In the border state of Kentucky he lived, and loved, the life of a Southern gentleman. His home, "Ashland," near Lexington, was a plantation of more than 500 acres with some 50 slaves, and there he dispensed lavish hospitality. But the crop that Ashland produced was not the cotton that required free trade for a profit; it was hemp that needed ample protection from foreign competition. Moreover, Clay lived not on the Atlantic slope, where broad and deep rivers carried commerce effortlessly to the sea, but beyond the mountains where nature required the aid of man by way of canals, locks, and highways. Far removed from the East's financial centers, banknotes (which constituted the only currency aside from unmanageable gold and silver) had a way of declining in value as they circulated farther from the issuing institutions. Only the federal government could, in fact, guarantee a stable medium of exchange. Soon Clay's "American System," defined as a central bank, a protective tariff, and government-financed internal improvements, was openly at war with the interest of those whose prosperity was pegged to the economy of cotton. Just as Calhoun's mature life was devoted to the defense of slavery and the South, so time and again did Clay give his energy and political skill to compromising sectional hostilities.

Born near Richmond, Virginia, April 12, 1777, Henry Clay was the seventh of nine children, with seven more to come by his mother's second marriage. His formal schooling was minimal, but the times themselves were an education. Heroes of the Revolution walked the Virginia earth to be seen and heard by an eager and ambitious lad. When Clay's family moved to Kentucky in 1792, the 15-year-old Henry remained in Richmond as a deputy clerk of the High Court of Chancery. Chancellor George Wythe, who soon became Clay's mentor, was the venerable teacher of law to an earlier generation that included Jefferson, Marshall, and Monroe. Late in 1797, young Henry Clay set out to join his family in Kentucky. He carried in his pocket a Virginia license to practice, a smattering of learning in his head, and the deep conviction of a Jeffersonian Republican in his heart.

In the Blue Grass State politics became Clay's life. Though he was a successful lawyer from the start of his career, the law never meant more to him than a way of earning a living and a stepping stone to political advancement. Marriage to Lucretia Hart in 1799 brought him both social prestige and a modest property. Within five years he was in the lower house of the state legislature and later became its Speaker. In 1806, he was chosen to fill out two months of an unexpired term in the United States Senate, although he had still not reached the required age of 30 when the term expired. He was back in the Senate again for a few months in 1810, but preferred election to the House of Representatives, where he sat with Calhoun and other young War Hawks in November 1811. A little older and more experienced in the legislative art than most of the others, Clay was their choice for Speaker and he skillfully used that office to generate war with Great Britain. The story of that bungling conflict need not be recounted here, save to say that when peace talks reached the negotiating stage, Clay was named by President Madison one of the United States Commissioners to meet with British representatives at Ghent in Belgium. There he was teamed with tough-minded, suspicious, puritanical but immensely able John Quincy Adams, then Minister to Russia, and the former Secretary of the Treasury, Albert Gallatin, who had been one of the pillars of the Republican party from its origin. Gallatin's fabled tact was to be sorely tested as peacemaker between Adams and Clay. Two other members of the delegation, Federalist Senator James A. Bayard of Delaware, and Jonathan Russell, Minister to Sweden, played secondary roles in the negotiations.

No two characters could have been more unlike than Adams and Clay. Short and rotund, Adams was the complete scholar. He was up before dawn and already working at his books and papers, when the tall, lanky Clay would be returning from a night of card playing and good fellowship. Even their goals for the negotiations were unlike; Clay was determined that Great Britain be excluded from the Mississippi River, while Adams was equally adamant about preserving American rights in the North Atlantic fisheries. Each, so it sometimes seemed to their fellows, was willing to sacrifice the other's interest to achieve his own. A generally satisfactory treaty nevertheless resulted, and Clay then joined Adams and Gallatin in a separate mission to London to negotiate a commercial treaty.

Broadened by his European experience, Clay was back in the House when Congress met in December 1815. He was again chosen Speaker. Powerfully aided by Calhoun and others of the old War Hawks, he now sought to heal old wounds with a program of national development that would encourage industrial growth, supply internal transportation, and through a national bank provide the uniform and stable currency so necessary for commerce. The system was left incomplete by President Madison's veto of the internal improvement bill on his last day in office, but New York pointed the way for the states to take up the slack by its financing of the Erie Canal without federal assistance. A new age was at hand. Subsequently the United States would direct its energies toward economic self-sufficiency and internalize its political conflicts. The old

Federalist party of Alexander Hamilton and John Adams offered only token opposition to James Monroe in 1816 and did not again contest a national election.

With new goals, new parties, and new men to lead the nation, who deserved better of his countrymen than Henry Clay? Ambition for the presidency was deep-rooted in the popular Kentuckian, and he cared not who knew it. But circumstances, some of them of his own making, were beginning to work against him. Arrogant and proud he was, and sensitive where his "honor" was concerned. He was also quick to see any threat to his ambition. Monroe, for instance, had offered him the secretaryship of the War Department before it went to Calhoun, but Clay thought he deserved to be Secretary of State, a position from which Jefferson, Madison and then Monroe himself had been catapulted into the White House. He turned it down, and then from his vantage point in the House began a desultory war upon Administration measures. When Andrew Jackson, the military hero of the battle of New Orleans, moved into Florida in pursuit of a band of Seminoles and in the process hanged two Englishmen and seized a Spanish fort, it was Clay who invoked the specter of military dictatorship and denounced the general's action. He did this partly to embarrass Monroe's administration, but also because Jackson was beginning to loom as a formidable Western rival.

When Missouri applied for admission to the union with a pro-slavery constitution, Clay upheld its right to do so, and at the same time he supported the compromise that forbade slavery elsewhere north of 36°30'. A second Missouri Compromise, which explained away a clause in the state constitution excluding free blacks, was of Clay's devising. His middle-of-the-road attitude toward slavery was clear both in 1820 and thereafter. He had no strong moral scruples for or against it. In his first years in Kentucky he had advocated gradual emancipation and would return to this position near the end of this career. He was one of the prime movers in establishing the American Colonization Society, which came into being January 1, 1817, and was its first vice president. Conceivably he was willing to accept almost any expedient that aimed at sectional harmony. And there was something to be said for Clay's position, for it made possible the compromises by which alone the nation survived its first three quarters of a century.

Clay withdrew from Congress in 1821 to rebuild his personal fortune; perhaps he also wanted to think about his future. He was back in Washington however, when the 18th Congress convened in December 1823, and was again chosen Speaker. Now an avowed candidate for the presidency, he was pitted against Jackson who had recently eliminated Calhoun, against John Quincy Adams, and against William H. Crawford, who would receive the endorsement of a thinly attended party caucus. Clay's platform was unchanged from the early post-war years. He championed and forced through the House the protective tariff of 1824; he continued to uphold the hard-pressed Bank of the United States, which had been badly mismanaged; and he voted at every opportunity for the internal improvements that Madison had pronounced unconstitutional. Despite his personal popularity, his qualifications, and his charisma, Clay was badly beaten. Since no candidate had a majority of the electoral vote, the House of Representatives had to choose from among the three highest candidates. Clay was the fourth man and therefore was eliminated. When the balloting came, Clay's followers voted for Adams, who won out over Jackson despite the General's greater popular support. When the Kentuckian accepted the position of Secretary of State in Adams' cabinet, the Jackson managers understandably cried out "Corrupt Bargain."

Over the next four years Clay worked to forge a party from the ill-assorted groups that for one reason or another backed the administration or opposed the Jacksonians: Old Federalists, pro-tariff Republicans from the West, free soil men, and slavery advocates who wanted land reforms or feared Andrew Jackson. Unwisely, Clay chose to make an issue out of United States attendance at a Panama conference of Latin American states. True, he had supported Latin American independence before Adams and Monroe were ready to recognize it, but joining in this nascent pan-Americanism was something altogether different. As a slaveholder, Clay should have foreseen the reaction of the South when it was publicized that Haiti, product of a successful slave rebellion, would be represented at the conference. After a bitter fight, a byproduct of which was a bloodless duel between Clay and John Randolph of Roanoke, the Senate confirmed the delegates. But thereafter the administration did not win another contest with Congress. Adams was easily beaten for reelection in 1828 and the Age of Jackson began.

For the next two years Clay was out of public life, although his presence was very much felt behind the scenes. With a view to his own election in 1832, he continued to rebuild the National Republican party, soon to be called the Whigs. Jackson's veto of the Maysville Road bill gave him a peg on which to hang his opposition. The 65-mile strip of narrow, steep, and often muddy road connecting Maysville, Kentucky, on the Ohio River with Lexington was a link in the network that by 1830 not only joined the eastern seaboard with the western outposts (Ft. Smith, Arkansas, Ft. Leavenworth, Kansas, and Ft. Snelling, Minnesota) but also the Great Lakes cities with the Gulf. When Jackson denied federal funds to improve the Maysville Road, Clay saw an opportunity to uphold internal improvements, always popular in the West, against an administration that appeared to oppose all of those great elements of national progress including the tariff and the Bank of the United States.

Clay returned to public life late in 1831 when he took his seat in the United States Senate; his friend John J. Crittenden had withdrawn in his favor. A few days later a National Republican party convention nominated him by acclamation. At this juncture Clay persuaded Nicholas Biddle, president of the Bank, to apply at once for recharter. This action was highly premature since the institution had still four years to go on its existing charter. Clay reasoned that Jackson would alienate a portion of his following if he signed such a bill and another portion if he vetoed it. Clay was also instrumental in the passage of a new tariff law that the South found no less objectionable than the existing one. Here he ignored Calhoun's warning and the rebellious mood of the cotton states.

Neither Clay's protectionist bid to the manufacturing states nor Jackson's ringing veto of the Bank recharter bill helped the National Republican candidate. Clay suffered a worse defeat than had Adams four years earlier. But it was only South Carolina's nullification of the 1828 and 1832 tariffs that finally convinced him that the cotton states would not accept protection—or the extension of the federal government's authority. When Congress reconvened, Clay quietly worked out the details of the 1833 compromise tariff bill that would abandon the principle of protection and reduce duties to the revenue level of 1816 over a ten-year period. With the support of Calhoun, John Tyler, and other nullifiers the measure was passed; but so was the Force Bill, authorizing the President to collect the tariff by force if need be.

Clay had once more made peace, and for another half dozen years he and Calhoun worked in harmony. And when Jackson removed the public deposits from the Bank of the United States, the Whig party was born in opposition. Clay's Whigs and Calhoun's Nullifiers combined to censure the President, but they failed to defeat his handpicked successor, Martin Van Buren, in the election of 1836. The strategy was wrong. Clay, who surely deserved something from his party, was passed over as the Whigs put up multiple candidates in hopes of throwing the election into the House of Representatives where they held a majority. But with the Jackson machine behind him, Van Buren beat them all—Daniel Webster, Hugh Lawson White of Tennessee, and William Henry Harrison of Ohio, one of the few American generals who had won a battle in the war of 1812. Harrison's showing was unexpectedly strong, so the Whig convention in 1840 again passed over Clay and named the old general as its candidate for the Presidency and John Tyler of Virginia, a Calhoun Nullifier, for vice president. The Whigs offered no program— had there been one Tyler could not have been on the ticket—but none was needed. The unlucky Van Buren had been engulfed by the Panic of 1837 and simply to defeat him was program enough.

Harrison won easily, and then to the surprise of Whig stalwarts, he named not Clay but Webster as his Secretary of State. As a result Clay sought to control the administration from his dominant position in the Senate. When Harrison died after one month in office, Clay began to put pressure on his successor, John Tyler. In the end he succeeded, for though the unsympathetic Tyler vetoed one Whig measure after another, no Clay man would serve in his Cabinet. Even Webster found it expedient to withdraw midway in the term.

Slavery was now back in the forefront of public consciousness. In an ill-conceived effort to suppress abolition literature, the post office denied the mails to "incendiary publications," while the House of Representatives passed a "gag rule," tabling all anti-slavery petitions without reading or reference to committee. Feeling over both of these actions was still running high in the free states when Tyler undertook to annex Texas, which permitted slavery. It was then that Webster withdrew, to be succeeded after an interval by Calhoun. Clay, meanwhile, was nominated by the Whigs as their candidate in the 1844 presidential election. But before Texas was finally annexed, he was defeated by another slaveholder, James K. Polk of Tennessee. New York state accounted for Polk's victory. There the antislavery Liberty Party, contesting its second election, had taken away a sufficient number of Whig votes from Clay to swing the state to Polk.

The nation's antislavery forces were now entering on to the political scene. They had been given great impetus by the annexation of Texas and the war with Mexico that was the inevitable aftermath. The prospect of extending slavery into the new lands acquired from Mexico triggered unprecedented nation-wide protest. It prompted a new Free Soil party, which for the first time gave a solid political base for the anti-slavery movement. And it boded ill for the waning political fortunes of Henry Clay whom the Whigs once more passed by in choosing their candidate in 1848. Ironically, the Whig candidate, the "war hero" General Zachary Taylor, a Louisiana slaveholder, won the election. Henry Clay's chances of being elected to the presidency were now gone.

After 1848, the extension or restriction of slavery in the territories overshadowed all other political issues. The discovery of gold in California swelled the population of that territory and made some action by Congress imperative. But feeling between slave and free states ran so high that no action seemed possible. In this crisis—and crisis it truly was —the Kentucky legislature once more sent Henry Clay, aging but still magnetic, back to the Senate; he had plans for a compromise already in his mind. These included California's admission to the Union as a free state and the establishment of territorial governments without mention of slavery for the rest of the Mexican cession. Texas was to surrender all claims to parts of New Mexico, and in return the Federal government would assume the state's public debt. The hated slave trade was to be ended in the District of Columbia, but slavery itself was not to be abolished there without the consent of Maryland and Virginia. There would be a new and more drastic fugitive slave law, and Congress was to renounce any power to regulate the interstate slave trade. Calhoun and Taylor were dead, Millard Fillmore was president, and Webster was back as Secretary of State before Clay's Compromise proposals finally passed in August.

But pass they did, with only trivial modifications. It was Clay's last great effort to make peace between North and South, whose diverging needs and aspirations he understood so well. And for a decade more it worked, although the Fugitive Slave Law proved exceedingly ill advised. Henry Clay of Kentucky, the great pacificator, died in the summer of 1852 with the Union he loved still intact. The nation had always withheld from him its highest honor, but it was he who largely gave it the reprieve that ultimately allowed it to survive.

*   *   *

The Grimkés were a South Carolina Huguenot family, like the Bonneaus to which Calhoun's wife belonged; and like the Bonneaus they were fully integrated into the slaveholding culture of the state. John Faucheraud Grimké was educated to the law in England, but returned to his native Charleston in time to fight in the American Revolution. He served as a delegate at the Constitutional Convention in Philadelphia and approved its results. Already a judge at that time, he would be the state's Chief Justice in the last 20 years of his life. The family lived in Charleston but like so many others whose occupation condemned them to the swampy low country, they had a plantation retreat in the highlands reserved for those times when Charleston became unhealthy. Judge Grimké was wealthy, conservative, aristocratic, Episcopalian, a considerable slaveholder, and allied by blood, marriage, or interest with most of the other conservative slaveholding families. His wife was an aunt of Robert Barnwell Rhett, a staunch Calhoun supporter and one of the earliest of the Southern "fireaters."

A more unlikely family to produce two militant abolitionists can hardly be imagined. Worse still, the pair were women who had to prove their right to speak before they would be heard! Driven by a fanatical loathing of slavery, which they themselves had seen in all its horrors, the Grimké sisters, Angelina and Sarah, became the first female agents of the American Anti-Slavery Society as well as pioneer propagandists for women's rights. Angelina was the younger and more gifted of the two though hardly more courageous than her sister. Their impact upon the major reform movements of their time was immense. They could talk to and about the South, because they were not only Southerners, but "ladies." In the North their abilities, their breeding, and their dedication opened doors for them almost at will. Neither Sarah or Angelina was by any stretch of the imagination physically attractive, judging from their photographs; they ill fit the stereotype of the delicate Dixie belle. Their faces had character, to be sure, but certainly not beauty. It took an abolitionist zealot to make a bride of Angelina, while Sarah was never to wed.

Angelina Grimké was born in Charleston in 1805, the last of 14 children. Her sister Sarah, 13 years old and already a lonely, questing child, by her own request stood godmother to her new sister to whom she remained deeply devoted in an almost parental relationship through life. Sarah was early aware of the moral problem posed by slavery. The subject was not discussed and literature on it was not available in the South but this sensitive girl, upon entering womanhood, found ample cause for dissatisfaction in her own observations of the system. How could men and women of the highest social standing beat helpless slaves for trivial reasons and then conduct family prayers and appear as pillars of the church? Still unprepared to speak, she saw her own question answered when Angelina fainted one day in school at the sight of the whip's bloody marks on the legs of a black child.

The turning point came in 1819 when Sarah was a 27-year-old spinster. Frustrated in an attempt to study law, she was increasingly critical of the society in which she lived. Judge Grimké, seriously ill, decided to visit the celebrated Dr. Physick in Philadelphia and chose Sarah to be his only companion. His case was already hopeless. Within a few weeks the judge died quietly in the comparative exile of the unfamiliar New Jersey coast. Her filial duties performed, Sarah stayed on for two months with a Quaker family whom she had met in Philadelphia. She returned to Charleston with more critical eyes to see the brutal side of slavery as she never had before. For a time she attended a Quaker meeting in Charleston, something not easy for a Grimké to do, but she was dissatisfied with the equivocation of the Southern Friends on slavery. Needing a more positive condemnation, she left early in 1821 for Philadelphia, never again to return to the South except for brief visits.

Angelina, meanwhile, was substantially retracing the ground her sister had already traveled, but with a more decisive personality and a nature that was activist to the core. Disillusioned with the Episcopal Church because its members would not acknowledge the existence of sin in slavery, she left it to join the Presbyterians, who had a new and promising minister. Soon she was teaching a Sunday school class and conducting a monthly interfaith prayer meeting. She beseeched the minister to explain why professing Christians apparently saw no wrong in enslaving other Christians. While conceding the moral wrong of slavery, he had no answers save prayer and patience, and these were not enough for the likes of Angelina Grimké. After a visit from Sarah, whose new simplicity she greatly admired, she too tried the Charleston Quaker meeting, now reduced to two old men who disliked each other. She rebuked them and for her trouble was told to mind her own business.

Angelina spent the next summer with her sister in Philadelphia, where she saw and heard nothing to change her feelings. At 23, however, she was not yet ready for exile, preferring instead to reform the Charleston Quakers and her own family. Both efforts met with stout resistance, and she acknowledged her failure. The final indignity came when she was formally expelled from the Presbyterian Church, which she had already left. Her avenues at home were closing fast. Late in 1829 she joined Sarah in Philadelphia, this time for good. Angelina's dilemma was based entirely on her abhorrence of slavery. Of South Carolina's opposition to the tariff, of the doctrine of nullification fresh from Calhoun's hands, of the crisis in cotton, she was uncaring. And certainly she must have been aware of political issues, for the best of the anti-nullification pamphlets was written by her brother Thomas. Her world had narrowed, but it was of an intensity that even Philadelphia could not long endure.

The Grimké sisters found the City of Brotherly Love almost as repressive as Charleston. The Quakers formed a tight organization of their own, and one could join only after months or years of probation. The liberal Quakers, the Hicksites, outnumbered the orthodox, but were given no doctrinal concessions on that account. Women were to be quiet and demure, which did not include speaking out in meetings, nor challenging the authority of the elders on the question of slavery. Sarah talked until bluntly told to hold her tongue. Angelina sought, but was denied, permission to attend Catherine Beecher's school in Hartford.

The momentous political events of 1831, 1832, and 1833 seemingly passed the sisters by. They were aware of the appearance of the *Liberator*, with its unrestrained attacks on the hated institution, but they were still too close to their own genteel upbringing to approve Garrison's tactics. They read, of course, about Nat Turner's rebellion in Virginia. And they were surely aware of the organization of the American Anti-Slavery Society late in 1833, since it took place in Philadelphia. The new society turned the anti-slavery cause from colonization to immediate emancipation; it insisted on education for the blacks and an end to race prejudice.

The sisters would not have been welcome in the AASS had they been ready to go so far, for they were mere women and this was man's work. But they were moving closer. And 1834 was a critical year. Race riots erupted in New York and Philadelphia. John Greenleaf Whittier and Samuel May were stoned in Ralph Waldo Emerson's home town, Concord, Massachusetts. Prudence Crandall's valiant but losing battle to maintain a school for Negro girls in Connecticut was widely publicized. And most importantly for the Grimké sisters, although they were not yet aware of it, Theodore Weld, by his eloquence, leadership, and dedication, converted the students of Lane Theological Seminary in Cincinnati from colonization and gradualism to immediate abolition of slavery. Lane's president, Lyman Beecher, did not agree and the rebels moved to Oberlin. Theodore Weld emerged from these developments as the acknowledged leader of the Western antislavery forces.

Events were now moving with great rapidity for the sisters. The year 1835 saw more race and anti-abolition riots, including one in Charleston where a mob broke into the post office and publicly burned large quantities of abolitionist literature. Angelina took the plunge, joining a Female Abolitionist Society. About the same time William Lloyd Garrison, in the *Liberator*, denounced the widespread disorders and appealed to his fellow Bostonians to give a fair hearing to a visiting English abolitionist, George Thompson. Though Angelina had never met Garrison, she wrote him a personal letter of commendation; for the first time she took a stand in favor of immediate emancipation. Without asking permission, Garrison published the letter, with suitable introductory remarks. Her Quaker friends condemned her action and Sarah was horrified, but Angelina Grimké had crossed her personal Rubicon.

Now identified irrevocably with the radical abolitionism, Angelina moved surely and decisively toward full participation in the movement. It came in 1836 with the publication of her *Appeal to the Christian Women of the South*. The concept was brilliant and the execution flawless. "It is because I feel a deep and tender interest in your present and eternal welfare that I am willing thus publicly to address you," she began. "Some of you have known me as a relative, and some have felt bound to me in Christian sympathy . . . It is because you have known me that I write thus unto you." She then went back to the book of Genesis and proceeded through the Bible to show that the Hebrew slavery, so often cited by Southern polemicists as sanction for their own peculiar institution, was in fact not slavery at all but a form of compensated servitude. She quoted the Southern slave codes most effectively to emphasize the difference. In her hands the Bible became one long antislavery tract. "Can we love a man as we love *ourselves if we do and continue to do* unto him, what we would not wish anyone to do to us?" The very language of the pamphlet, rich in analogy and illustration, was itself almost Biblical and gave the tract a form of sanctity for those to whom it was addressed.

After establishing the case against slavery in many and varied ways, Angelina addressed herself directly to the timidity, the hesitancy, the long repression she knew to be in the character of her female readers. What can you, as a woman, do?, she asked. Read; pray; speak; and finally act. And for sanction she again turned to the pages of Scripture, where time and again, from Miriam to Pilate's wife, she found women leading and speaking out for justice.

The *Appeal* quickly proved to be one of the most influential pieces of abolition writing. Shortly after its appearance the Grimké sisters left Philadelphia to settle in New York. There in November 1836 they attended an "Agents' Convention" of the American Anti-Slavery Society. It was not a convention in any legitimate sense, but a training school for those who were to go out as antislavery missionaries. The Grimkés were the only women in a consecrated group that included Garrison, Arthur and Lewis Tappan, and Theodore Dwight Weld who directed the training program. Weld quickly recognized Angelina's special talents and gave her personal training as a speaker. He recognized other qualities as well, for the two were married a little over a year later.

Angelina first began speaking against slavery under the auspices of the New York Female Anti-Slavery Society, but she was not content to lecture only to women. So great had her reputation become that the problem almost solved itself, for wherever she spoke men came to hear her. In May 1837 she followed her successful *Appeal* to the Southern ladies with another address to "The Women of the Nominally Free States." In June the sisters, escorted by Garrison, visited John Quincy Adams at his home in Quincy. The ex-President, now a congressman, was in the thick of his fight against the House of Representatives "gag rule." Wise in the ways of politics, Adams knew that he could win his case only by tying it to the constitutional right of petition. The sisters, however, thought he was temporizing on the great moral issue.

Meanwhile, Catherine Beecher, the formidable eldest daughter of Reverend Lyman Beecher, had published an answer to Angelina's *Appeal.* Entitled "An Essay on Slavery and Abolition with Reference to the Duty of American Females," it took a harshly antifeminist view. The Beecher pamphlet played into the hands of those who resented participation of the Grimké sisters in the antislavery movement simply because they were women. Angelina answered in a series of "Letters to Catherine Beecher," while Sarah wrote "Letters on the Equality of the Sexes" for the New England *Spectator.* Next followed a "Pastoral Letter of the General Association of Massachusetts to the Congregational Churches under their care" and another from the Andover Theological Seminary, both denouncing Garrison's tactics as well as the appearance of women on the lecture platform.

By this time the Grimké sisters were among America's most famous women—or most notorious, according to the point of view. In February 1838 they spoke by invitation before the Massachusetts Legislature and were an unqualified success. In six months time 40,000 people heard them in New England, where the antislavery message found an increasing number of sympathizers.

After Angelina's marriage to Theodore Weld in May 1838, the period of feverish activity came to an end. There were many reasons. The day after the wedding, for instance, the Welds took part in the dedication of "Pennsylvania Hall" in Philadelphia. The Hall had been built by reformers to provide an auditorium and headquarters for several antislavery organizations. The following day as the newlyweds were attending sessions of the Anti-Slavery Convention of American Women, a mob had gathered outside the hall. Twice they broke in, but were ejected. Rocks were crashing through the windows when Angelina spoke, unperturbed, eloquent, incisive. "What is a mob?" she asked, as glass fell on the floor at her feet. "What would the breaking of every window be? Any evidence that we are wrong, or that slavery is a good and wholesome institution? What if that mob should now burst in upon us, break up our meeting and commit violence on our persons—would this be anything compared with what the slaves endure?" Before the night was done Pennsylvania Hall was burned to the ground along with all of the precious records and documents it housed. The incident occurred with the apparent sanction of the city's mayor, the police, and the fire department.

It was Angelina's last major speech for many years. The duties of homemaker were new and arduous to her; they absorbed all of her energy despite the much needed assistance she would receive from Sarah, who lived with the Welds. Her health suffered from experimental dieting, and there were three children to raise. Despite their household activities, the sisters collaborated with Weld on a lengthy pamphlet called *American Slavery as It Is* (1839). Consisting of hundreds of personal statements by eyewitnesses to the cruelties of slavery—the sisters, needless to say, contributed their own recollections—the book was by far the most powerful and most effective piece of antislavery literature before *Uncle Tom's Cabin*. "No one, who has not been an *integral part* of a slaveholding community," declared Sarah's narrative, "can have any idea of its abominations." 100,000 copies of the pamphlet were sold in the first year. Thereafter the sisters helped Weld with his own publications, but they themselves kept out of the limelight.

The times indeed were changing and so was the focus of the antislavery cause. In 1840 the movement entered its political phase with the organization of the Liberty Party. Though the party candidate James G. Birney, a converted Alabama planter, polled less than one percent of the popular vote, the start had been made. Eight years later the Liberty Party merged with the Free Soil Party, and in 1856 their political heirs, the Republicans, carried the anti-slavery fight to the seats of power.

* * *

From the Missouri Compromise to the Civil War itself the controversy over slavery was never far from the mainstream of American history. Whatever the immediate issue might be—tariff, public lands, transportation, banking, manufacturing, territorial expansion—the "slave question" quickly became an abrasive factor in the discussion. By the middle 1830s the South, guided, led, and ultimately propelled by Calhoun, took the position that her peculiar institution was beyond criticism or even comment, lest the slaves overhear and become restive. The prospect of slave rebellion was a constant nightmare that invoked ever more repressive measures. Southern fears were fanned by the endless torrent of antislavery literature produced by dedicated reformers like the Grimké sisters, but all attempts to suppress it had an opposite effect, arousing not abolitionists alone, but those who came to the defense of the constitutional right of free speech. Between the extremes of pro- and anti-slavery advocates was the great body of Americans who wanted only to go about the business of living. To them, any reasonable middle ground, any workable compromise such as Clay proposed, would have been acceptable. Indeed, the Compromise of 1850 was favorably received by a popular majority, but it gave to neither extreme all that it desired and consequently renewed the sectional conflict. *Uncle Tom's Cabin* in 1852 went far to solidify Northern sentiment against slavery, while the Kansas-Nebraska Act and the Dred Scott decision removed the last national barriers to the extension of the hated institution. The three approaches to slavery—protection, compromise, and abolition—met head-on in the election of 1860, where the nation made its choice.

13

Different Drums:
The Civil War Era

JEFFERSON DAVIS
ABRAHAM LINCOLN
HORACE GREELEY

by Emory M. Thomas
University of Georgia

"If a man does not keep pace with his companions, perhaps it is because he hears a different drummer. Let him step to the music which he hears, however measured or far away."

When Henry David Thoreau wrote these lines, he expressed more than an ethical ideal; he also described an American reality. Americans during the first half of the 19th century marched to a variety of "different drummers," and indeed they often seemed to try to keep pace with several beats at the same time. By mid-century, however, American drumbeats were fewer in number and harsher in tone. Finally the words "drum" and "marching" lost their metaphorical quality and became litteral realities amid the cataclysm of Civil War.

Reduced to the simplest of terms, the American Civil War was about "different drums"—the noisy extensions of conflicting life styles in the United States. For some time in the North and South, ways of living and looking at the world differed. As Americans, both Northerners and Southerners could and did compromise about specific, real issues before 1860; for two generations these Americans had compromised on slavery, tariffs, foreign policy, and more. Yet divergent life styles became incompatible, and then mutually exclusive. They became so because

255

Northerners and Southerners sanctified their respective ways of life and raised their interests and institutions to the level of ideologies. Divergent lifestyles, interests, and institutions may have been subject to compromise and coexistence; ideologies were not. These ideologies were not material, but moral expressions, and righteousness was not likely to compromise with evil.

The "drum" metaphor is significant here. Just as a drumbeat is more than the sum of its component physical parts—wood, hide, and steel— so also were the sectional ideologies of the antebellum North and South more than the sum of their component interests and circumstances. Just as rhythm and cadence have a transcendent quality distinct from drum and drummer, so did the world views, belief systems, or any other synonyms for ideology have real, separate identity beyond the lives and life styles from which they sprang. So it was that in 1861 the United States was really two nations. Then for four bloody years Americans were in fact two nationalities. In 1865 the United States united once more by force of arms at the cost of 600,000 lives; the "American way" prevailed by right of conquest. Such was the reality and power of "different drums."

Obviously metaphors and generalities can only go so far in explaining the experience of the American Civil War. To amplify these general statements and to understand this very human experience, we must look more closely at some of the humans involved in it. To understand the "drums," we need to become acquainted with some of the "drummers."

Abraham Lincoln, Jefferson Davis, and Horace Greeley were not exactly "average" Americans of the mid-19th century. Lincoln and Davis led their respective nations in wartime, and Greeley was perhaps the most influential newspaper editor in American history. Nor were these men always the most rabid proponents of their respective ideologies. Lincoln, Davis, and Greeley did, however, interact with their times and circumstances in such a way as both to reflect and shape their age. And all three faced, in one way or another, the fundamental issues involved in the Civil War experience.

Lincoln, Davis, and Greeley were part of the ideological conflict that conditioned the era. In time each had to deal responsibly with the question of secession. Davis had to choose his national identity—Southern or American; Lincoln and Greeley had to elect between peaceful secession or union by force. Once the fighting began the three men faced the tasks of defining their respective war aims and in so doing they refined and redefined their ideological positions. Finally each of the three had to set a price for peace, to decide whether any or all of their war aims were worth continuing the bloodshed to total victory or defeat. Because they were strong men in high places, each one dealt with these common questions independently and individually. For this very reason the responses of Lincoln, Davis, and Greeley to the issues raised by ideology, secession, war aims, and peace hopes were crucial, and are significant. And because their responses were identifiably human, these men were and are fascinating.

*   *   *

By the time he was 16 years old, Jefferson Davis already disliked "Yankees." Born into modest circumstances in Kentucky in 1808, Davis spent most of his youth in Mississippi. His father who fought in the Revolution never quite made the transition from "farmer" to "planter"; however Davis' older brother Joseph made a great deal of money very quickly and assumed a place in Mississippi's planter aristocracy. Joseph took charge of his younger brother's schooling and support after their father died in 1824. Jefferson Davis returned to his native Kentucky to attend Transylvania University in Lexington and then with Joseph's aid secured an appointment to West Point. There, for the first time, Davis encountered "Yankees" in any significant numbers. After his first few months at West Point he wrote brother Joseph that his Northern contemporaries were "not such as I formed an acquaintance with on my arrival ... nor are they such associates as I would at present select." Then Davis informed his brother and patron, ". . . As you have never been connected with them, you cannot know how pittiful they generally are."

Chief among the shortcomings of his Northern brethren, to Davis' way of thinking, was their ability to subsist on the meagre allowance paid them as cadets. Davis indeed took a certain backhanded pride in asking his brother for "Cash" (with a capital "C") to sustain him in the style of a Southern gentleman. Already in the young cadet's mind, to be a "Yankee" was to be narrowly frugal and shrewdly Puritanical. In contrast Davis perceived himself and his Southern kinsmen to be genial, openhanded men of the world, practitioners of the good life. As it happened, much of Davis' experience in later life reinforced his youthful perceptions.

Davis received his lieutenant's commission from West Point in 1828, and although he fought in the Black Hawk War (1830–31), he found little more than boredom in the garrison duty that characterized a peacetime army. Accordingly in 1835 he resigned from the army and embarked upon a career as a Mississippi planter. That same year Davis married Sarah Knox Taylor, daughter of Zachery Taylor, much against her father's will. The couple had hardly settled on their new plantation, carved out of Joseph Davis' lands just below Vicksburg, when Sarah Davis died. The young widower chose to express his grief by losing himself in work and study, and spent the next several years in what might appear to have been limbo. Actually he worked long and hard on his plantation "Brierfield," and cultivated his Democratic neighbors. Thus in 1845, when Davis married again and went to Congress, he had labored ten years to become an "overnight" success.

His second wife was Varina Howell whose family had a well-respected Natchez name and not much else. Varina herself was a strong-willed woman who made fast friends and firm enemies with equal facility. Both Davises enjoyed Washington and its Southern Democrats during their initial stay in the capital. When the Mexican War broke out, Congressman Davis resigned his seat and accepted command of the "Mississippi Rifles." Colonel Davis served briefly but gloriously in the war under his ex-father-in-law General Zachery Taylor. They had already reconciled the difficulties that had caused Taylor's disapproval of his late daughter's marriage, and the battle of Buena Vista brought generous praise from Taylor and a disabling wound in Davis' foot.

Davis returned to Mississippi in 1847 a wounded hero, and promptly won election to the United States Senate. After fighting the good Southern fight during the debates over the Compromise of 1850, Senator Davis again resigned from a national office and sought the Mississippi governorship in 1851. At this point and throughout the turbulent 1850s, he played the role of a militant Southern moderate. He took his intellectual cue from John C. Calhoun and pursued sectional interests within a national orientation. Like Calhoun, he threatened secession as a last resort and constantly demanded that the Northern majority prove its good faith toward the South by making appropriate concessions concerning slavery, expansion, tariffs, and such. Davis, however, was not among the ranks of the Southerners "fire-eaters" who despaired of union with anyone and crusaded for a Southern republic.

Ex-Senator Davis lost the Mississippi gubernatorial race to Henry S. Foote in 1851 but soon found political place as Franklin Pierce's Secretary of War. He was an extremely capable Secretary, perhaps the most efficient since Calhoun over three decades before. Although from New Hampshire, Pierce listened closely to his Southern advisors, and in the front ranks of these was Jefferson Davis.

In 1856 Davis ran once more for the Senate and served there until his state seceded in January 1861. Again he championed Southern interests in the Senate; for example in 1859 he led the movement to reopen the international slave trade. Yet Davis left the Union reluctantly. At the conclusion of his farewell speech to the Senate, he reportedly broke down and wept. Still, he concluded, he was more Southern than American and followed Mississippi into disunion. His decision was, at the same time, momentous, dramatic, and natural.

By 1861 Davis had done most, if not all, of those things to which Southerners aspired. He had lived well, served conspicuously, and his contacts with people and place had been primal and meaningful. He had grown up "Southern"; that is, he read the same books literate Southerners read and he thought the same thoughts. By his own achievement and with generous aid from his brother he became a planter aristocrat. As a member of the master class, he could afford to be patronizing toward his slaves and his less successful neighbors. But he felt no guilt over holding slaves; he accepted the South's "peculiar institution" and strove to be a humane master. Indeed, one of Davis' closest lifelong friends was James Pemberton, his body servant since youth and plantation manager in later years.

Davis and his milieu aspired to be comfortable, simple, and open. At base were relationships among familiar people and between men and nature, the high degree of personalism which one scholar termed the persistance of a "folk culture." Whatever nagging contradictions lingered in the reality of the Southern world, Davis and his fellow Southerners believed they had in fact lived out their aspirations. In this Southern version of the "best of all possible worlds," planter aristocrats worked hard, played hard, and served their social inferiors, black and white, faithfully. Black people, Davis and most Southerners believed, were racially inferior and so were best off as slaves. Moreover, Southern non-planter whites deferred to their social and economic superiors out of habit, short range self-interest, and simple neighborliness. These things and more Davis believed. In some cases he believed half-truths, in others lies; but his convictions were supported by his experience. And by the time of the secession crisis these convictions had become articles of faith.

Davis left the Union because he was certain that his world was in peril. Other men had actually initiated the break; Davis took no active part in the secession movement until after South Carolina had acted. Nevertheless he was convinced that the South had the right as well as provocation enough to separate. The Yankee was the villain; and Davis described his activity in 1850 as "the steady advance of a self-sustaining power to the goal of unlimited supremacy." The South, as he saw it, was in the position of the American colonies in 1776, and he was responding to tyranny in much the same way his father had done in joining the Continental Army. Two clauses in Davis' first major address to the Confederate Congress on April 29, 1861, summarized his feelings about the secession crisis. "We feel," he said, "that our cause is just and holy"; and a bit later he added, "All we ask is to be let alone." The Southern lifestyle had become a "cause," a "just and holy" one, and for its sake Davis and his fellow Southerners had chosen to separate.

Jefferson Davis was at home, in "Brierfield," pruning his roses and hoping for a military command, when the messenger arrived to tell him he had been unanimously elected Provisional President of the Confederacy. Varina his wife remembered the scene—Davis' face fell; she despaired that a member of the family had died. Yet he could not refuse the honor. Being President of a rebel nation at war was no easy task. The experience ultimately tested him and his ideological preconceptions much more than anyone could imagine in 1861.

Davis seemed a quite logical choice for President when the Montgomery convention of delegates from seceded states gathered. The Mississipian had worn Calhoun's mantle as Southern rights champion in the Senate; he had military experience at both the executive and field levels; he was no radical, and for a people in search of national respectability at home and abroad, moderation was mandatory. Also Davis *looked* like a president, and Americans have selected chief executives for less cause than that before and since.

His ability and credentials notwithstanding, Davis was a flawed President. Limited as a political personality, he loved and hated too well, and too often chose righteousness at the expense of success. The Confederate President clung to friends when they were clearly political liabilities; he nourished quarrels with political leaders and generals and fed needless dissension by so doing. Davis had difficulty in delegating authority and thus worked so hard at inconsequential matters that his health faltered. Understandably a sick President was hardly capable of that political congeniality a healthy one sorely lacked. When the administration clashed with state governors such as Joseph E. Brown of Georgia and Zebulon Vance of North Carolina, Davis was perhaps right; but he needed cooperation more than the contrition he seemed to demand. In sum Davis was severely lacking in the skills of political and personal give and take. Still, he gave his all for his section and its cause. Although many of those who shouted assent to his election as President later had second thoughts, Davis served them faithfully and perhaps more wisely than they ever knew.

The Confederacy's war challenged Southerners. They expected physical sacrifice; they did not expect to have to sacrifice the fundamental tenets of their lifestyle to the vain hope of victory. Perhaps Davis' greatest achievement as President was his rare insight into the nature of the war and his willingness to calculate its cost. The one, great, overriding Confederate war aim was independence—"all we ask is to be let alone." Most Confederates recognized this, but most Confederates also clung to the vain hope that independence could be bought cheap. Davis was never so sanguine. He foresaw a long, costly struggle. He perceived the necessity of the undermanned, outgunned Confederacy to fight a defensive war. And he realized that a Southern victory might come only at the expense of some Southern "sacred cows." The situation was paradoxical. Confederates sought independence to preserve their cherished way of life; but to have independence they had to win; and to win the South had to surrender some portion of its way of life.

When Davis and other Southern leaders thought realistically about war, they had to confront some very unpleasant facts. Euphoria might sustain the Confederacy's war effort for the short run; but if the Union persevered as Davis believed it would, a state rights confederation would be ill-equipped to respond to the need for centralized direction of a national effort. The South was overwhelmingly rural and agricultural, and however much Southerners disdained "Yankees" with their manufacturing, the South entered an industrial war with little or no industry. The irony was cruel. Confederates struck for independence to sustain a states rights polity and an agrarian economy, yet to achieve it they had to pursue the politics of nationalism and place economic emphasis upon industrialization.

These realities Davis, perhaps more than any other Confederate, understood. Consequently, his administration did several highly "unsouthern" things. Less than a year after the War Office was turning away volunteers because their numbers were greater than the government's capacity to arm and equip them, the Confederate Congress enacted the first draft law ever imposed in North America. Already the President had acted subtly and skillfully to transform the Confederate army from the traditional American amalgram of state militia units into a national force. With the blessing of his Congress, Davis suspended the writ of habeas corpus and invoked martial law in some areas of the Confederacy. Under the sanction of law military commanders could and did impress private property for the use of the army. The Confederacy also levied an income tax and tax-in-kind (ten percent of the gross) on agricultural commodities. It took over all blockade running in 1864 and thus managed the South's foreign trade. Its War Department took an active part in the economy by controlling draft exemptions for laborers, transportation priorities, and raw materials allocations. The draft, impressment, martial law, stern taxation, and economic regulation were novel measures in the South. To Davis' credit he recognized their necessity; unfortunately he was ill-equipped in temperament and political skill to make these actions palatable to Southerners.

The Confederacy had an equally profound impact upon Southern economy. Under Davis' leadership it developed sufficient industry to conduct its industrial war. Such a "crash" program did not of course turn the South into an industrial giant overnight. Still, the Confederacy was essentially self-sufficient in terms of war industry by 1863.

Ultimately the needs of war demanded that the Confederacy sacrifice still more of that way of life it was supposedly defending. War challenged and eventually altered Southern mores to a large degree. For example, when Varina Davis played the role of "first lady" and gave gay luncheons instead of visiting hospitals, she reaped bitter criticism for doing the very things Southern "belles" were supposed to do in antebellum times.

Finally in the fall of 1864 Davis confronted what many Confederates believed was the extreme challenge; he embarked upon a scheme to emancipate Southern slaves and employ them as soldiers. Here the Confederate President employed rare tact and political skill. He began by asking for an appropriation from Congress to purchase 40,000 black men for noncombatant use by the army. Such requests were normal; the details of the bill, though, were indeed unusual. Davis proposed a "radical alteration in Southern law and custom" by suggesting that the laborers be freed in exchange for their loyal service. Congress gave him the appropriation, but denied any hint of emancipation. As things happened the 40,000 laborers bill was Davis' "trial balloon"; next the administration proposed to arm and free the slaves. Congress and the Confederate people debated the measure during the winter of 1864–65 while the nation's military fortunes went from hopeless to non-existent. The issue was all too plain. Arming the slaves was the last, best hope of Southern victory; but arming the slaves also meant the end of the antebellum way of life. Finally Congress passed the administration measure in March 1865. The lawmakers shrank from emancipation, but Davis virtually wrote black freedom into the regulations implementing the act. And even earlier, in December 1864, the President had sent an emissary to Britain and France to offer emancipation in exchange for recognition. The mission was desperate and fruitless, but it served as an index of how far he would go for the sake of independence.

Davis' emancipation and arm-the-slaves proposals came too little, too late. The Confederacy was beyond military redemption by March 1865. Still Davis showed himself willing to make the sacrifice. He had abandoned slavery along with many another tenet of the Southern creed for the sake of independence. As most of his countrymen came to terms with their fate and prepared to live with defeat and reunion, Davis renewed his devotion to the "cause." He spoke of a "new phase" of the war—guerrilla warfare—and assured Confederates that independence was theirs so long as they willed it and resisted conquest.

At this juncture Davis the creative realist lost touch with reality. Southerners may have been willing to give up the major tenets of their way of life for the sake of independence. But finally they had to ask "independence for what?" When they answered, they were manifestly unwilling to commit themselves to guerrilla warfare. Partisans may have kept the "cause" alive a while longer, but they would have had to surrender their ties to people and place. As guerrilla nomads they might indeed have had to conduct reprisals against their own people. The fundamental attachment to people and place, "folk culture," was the one feature of Southernism they proved unwilling to abandon. Davis, however, did not understand. As he fled in the wake of multiple military disasters during the spring of 1865, he tried to exhort his people to renewed resistance. He failed. In the end Davis was captured wearing his wife's shawl and was sent to prison.

When at length the Confederate President left his prison cell, he never quite understood what had gone wrong. Davis had the bad fortune to live long after his "cause" collapsed. During these years he sought justification; he renewed old quarrels with some of his generals, and he spun the old theories about state rights that Robert Lee's surrender had rendered moot. When Davis defended his world view as war leader of a rebel nation, he proved a flawed politician but a creative statesman. When the ex-President tried to justify a cause already lost, he was in many eyes truly as "pitiful" as those Yankee cadets he had despised so many years before.

*   *   *

President-elect Abraham Lincoln made the long journey in 1861 from Springfield, Illinois, to Washington, D.C., in triumph and trepidation. At every stop along the route people wanted to see Lincoln, most to cheer him, a few perhaps to kill him. Everyone wanted to know Lincoln's opinion of the secession crisis and his prediction about the possibility of civil war. On one occasion in New York City he responded to the inevitable questions by telling a story.

As a young lawyer, Lincoln recalled, he used to ride the judicial circuit in southern Illinois. Once during a rainy spell he and some companions found most of the streams along their way swollen far beyond their normal size. As they crossed these streams with mounting difficulty, the party became concerned about the Fox River, which lay ahead and promised to be even more turbulent than the creeks behind them. Night came on, and the men stopped at a tavern. There by chance was the local Methodist presiding elder who traveled about the region extensively. Lincoln and his colleagues were eager to learn from this man about their prospects of fording the Fox. To their questions the elder replied "O yes, I know all about the Fox River. I have crossed it often and understand it well; but I have one fixed rule with regard to the Fox River, I never cross it till I reach it."

Lincoln enjoyed telling stories. Many were ribald; most were humorous; and some were profound. Often, as in the case of the Fox River story, Lincoln told stories as parables to illustrate, or perhaps obscure, his point of view. Sometimes, though, Lincoln's tales told more about Lincoln himself than they did about their supposed topic or lesson.

Like the elder in his story, Lincoln was a profound pragmatist. He crossed rivers when he had to, in what seemed to him the most effective manner available. In fact it may be that this very quality, this down-to-earth, human approach to the crises that beset him, has been the thing that has most endeared Lincoln to generations of his countrymen. Americans can identify with the image of a practical man wrestling one-at-a time with great problems even more than with the genius of his solutions to those problems.

There is high irony, then, in the fact that Lincoln, the model of pragmatic statesmen, did more to express and refine the ideology of the North than did any of his doctrinaire contemporaries. From the time of its founding in 1854 the Republican Party was the practical political expression of the Northern world view. And from the time of his nomination to the presidency in 1860, Lincoln was the ultimate expression of the Republican Party. Upon Lincoln fell the burden of translating principles into action. His measure of greatness among American presidents rests not so much upon the validity of the principles, but upon his translation of them.

As every schoolchild knows, Abraham Lincoln was born in a log cabin in Kentucky. In fact Lincoln and Jefferson Davis were born within 100 miles and about eight months of each other. There the parallels end of course. The Davis family moved south from Kentucky; the Lincolns north into Indiana and then Illinois.

Little distinguished the young Lincoln from other sons of the midwestern frontier. He read more than his fellows and took more interest in the rude and intermittent schooling available to him. He was very tall (6'4"), and quite strong. He enjoyed the tales and rough humor of men. Perhaps Lincoln's best youthful prank involved an attempt to mix the mates of a double wedding when the couples retired for their first night of marriage. Lincoln did most of the same sorts of things as his contemporaries; and some he did a little better than others.

Like Davis, Lincoln in his young manhood served in the Black Hawk War. He saw no action and returned to New Salem, Illinois. For three years he kept store, served as postmaster, dabbled at surveying and "read law." Then in 1836 he hung out his law shingle in Springfield. Lincoln was a rapid success at law and local Whig politics. He worked very hard at both; if it were possible to apply the "work ethic" to politics, Lincoln did so. He was ambitious, true, but more important he believed that he owed himself his best efforts. If these were not sufficient, so be it.

Lincoln enjoyed an easy comradery with men, which made him a Northern counterpart of a "good old boy" and helped him through the rough and tumble of frontier politics. Women, though, were another matter. In 1840 Lincoln became engaged to Mary Todd, a strong-willed, well-born young lady whose social standing intimidated him. He began having second thoughts; he wondered if he truly loved her. He also suffered from attacks of very deep depression, and probably had one of his severe "down" periods at this time. At any rate he broke the engagement. In November 1842, nearly two years after the marriage was originally scheduled, Lincoln finally married Mary Todd.

At the conclusion of ten years of work and maneuver, Lincoln won his party's blessing to run for his district's relatively "safe" Whig seat in Congress. He served as representative from 1846 through 1847 and then returned to Springfield. Although enjoying Washington and national politics, he did little to distinguish himself during his term in the House and resigned to allow another faithful Whig from his district have his "turn." Perhaps, had the sectional issue not assumed crisis proportions that upset the normal order of many things, Lincoln might have ended his political career a one-term Congressman, genial lawyer, and member of the local Whig establishment.

Events, however, moved more swiftly than institutions could adapt during the late 1840s and 1850s. And Lincoln, the moderate Whig, followed the tide. In the wake of Stephen A. Douglas' Kansas-Nebraska Act in 1854, a group composed mainly of Free Soilers and dissident Whigs founded the Republican Party. Although its founders were considered radicals by moderates such as Lincoln, the Party broadened its base to include many segments of the Northern political mind. The Republicans soon swallowed up many Northern Whigs whose old party no longer had a national existence. In 1856 Lincoln took the plunge and joined the Republican campaign to make John C. Frémont president of the United States.

The Republican slogan, "Free soil, free labor, free men," well expressed Lincoln's hopes and his vision. He opposed the expansion of slavery because he considered slavery an evil that might be endured for a time, but could not be permitted to grow. On the contrary, free labor capitalism had to expand; the achievement, work-oriented "American dream" was real and right for Lincoln. He had lived it. Thus, although he was too profound a pragmatist to stand in the front ranks of the idealists and visionary reformers at his Party, he did stand behind them and their motives, if not their methods.

Frémont ran well in 1856 and the Republicans served notice that they were the second instead of the third party. In 1858 Lincoln carried the party banner against Stephen A. Douglas for the Senate. The campaign attracted national attention, at first because Douglas was a national figure and later because of Lincoln's skill and logic during the series of debates in which the candidates engaged. Lincoln lost the election, but won a reputation in the process. By the time Republicans met in Chicago in 1860 to nominate their presidential candidate he was a genuine contender. His managers worked tirelessly and promised much. Lincoln was enough of an unknown political quantity to draw votes away from men such as William H. Seward, Simon Cameron and Salmon P. Chase who had more formidable reputations but also more formidable political enemies. On the third ballot Lincoln caught the front-runner Seward and took the nomination.

In November the Republicans won the election. Their platform attracted support throughout the Northern tier of states. It called for an end to the expansion of slavery, for a protective tariff appealing to business interests, for a homestead law offering free land to western settlers, and for subsidized internal improvements (river dredging, railroad building, and the like). In 1860 the Republican struck the precise balance between ideals and interests to win. In the wake of Lincoln's victory, however, first South Carolina and then six other states of the deep South seceded from the Union. The President-elect faced the most severe crisis in his nation's young life before he even took the oath of office.

Lincoln assumed the "wait and see" posture of his Fox River parable for two reasons. First, he could not act on secession until he was the President, and even then rash action might make the situation worse by driving the border South into the rebel camp. Second, he simply did not believe that the South was serious about disunion; perhaps the planters were committed to a rump confederacy, but not the great mass of common men. When the confrontation came, as eventually it must, Lincoln believed the vast majority in the South would refuse to follow the planter lead. So President-elect Lincoln was silent while Davis and the Southerners formed their Confederacy, and he was cautious following his inauguration on March 4.

For more than a month Lincoln remained cautious. He talked to politicians from the border South. He worked unceasingly to mold his new administration and to satisfy voracious appetites for political place among Republicans. Yet for all his talking and political maneuvering, Lincoln actually did little, and his administration appeared to be in limbo. Republican regulars had believed all along that the neophyte from Illinois would be their "front" man; Lincoln could win the election, then they would run the country. Accordingly on April 1, Secretary of State Seward said plainly that the government had no policy, and it was high time to adopt one. He then proposed to heal the nation's internal wounds by provoking a foreign war. Finally Seward offered himself as the logical man to carry out the bold stroke he had outlined. Lincoln had reached his "Fox River"; he could temporize no longer.

Contrary to appearances the new President did have firm policies in mind upon coming to Washington. In fact, he had three of them. He planned to be his own president; he did not intend to compromise with the Southerners in such a way as to permit the expansion of slavery; and he was determined to preserve the Union no matter what the cost. So he responded tactfully to Seward's tactless memorandum. Gently but firmly he reminded the Secretary of State that he, not Seward, was president. Lincoln then faced the confrontation with the South. He faced it at Fort Sumter, because there the issue was most clear. If Davis chose to make a stand, he would have to do so by firing the first shot. The Confederates, of course, did fire on Sumter, and Lincoln called for volunteers to "put down combinations in rebellion."

From hindsight it seemed inevitable that Lincoln should respond to the shelling of Fort Sumter by mobilizing for war. But hindsight too often leaves important questions unasked. Why did Lincoln decide to go to war to keep Southerners in the Union against their will? And why did the American people follow his lead and risk their lives for an apparent political abstraction? The answer to these questions is that the Union was not an abstraction in 1861; no more than was the "Southern way of life." The Union was real. It was the essential vehicle through which Americans could achieve their destiny. It was an arena for reform; it was a source of economic strength; it was the world's laboratory for democratic idealism. The Union was prerequisite for the growth of free labor capitalism and the *sine qua non* of American nationalism. Lincoln could never quite believe that the majority of Southerners did not share these beliefs, and so he fought a war of liberation to free these Southerners from their planter oppressors. Others in the North shared Lincoln's motivation, but the Union fought more than a war of liberation. It also fought a war of conquest—to humble the idle aristocrats in the South and to impose the "American way" of righteousness upon a "degenerate" people. Consequently even in the grim aftermath of the Union debacle at Bull Run, the war's first real battle, Lincoln and his countrymen persevered. In the process of persevering for the sake of union, however, Northerners found it necessary to say with greater precision what the Union meant. Lincoln's war aim was union—that never changed—but the war forced the President to refine and expand the definition of union.

During the first year of conflict, union sufficed as a rationale for bloodshed. Furthermore, wars tend to contain a dynamic of their own, which demands that they go to completion. Once blood is spilled, victory becomes an end in itself. By the summer of 1862, however, Northerners needed more than the words "victory" and "union" to justify the effort. Victory seemed possible, but far in the future, and union demanded definition. At this juncture, for these and other reasons, Lincoln determined to add emancipation to his stated definition of union.

Lincoln opposed slavery even though some of his best friends were slaveholders. His solution to the "problem" had been compensated emancipation for whites and colonization (deportation) for blacks. Yet the conduct of the war brought tremendous pressure to bear on the President. Strong-minded men like Charles Summer in Congress and Salmon Chase in the Cabinet argued in favor of immediate emancipation. Generals asked what to do with the human "contraband" captured from the Rebels. And the war was going badly in the summer of 1862—stalemate in the West, defeat in Virginia. Thus Lincoln decided to move on the subject of emancipation. Characteristically he proceeded deliberately and tactfully. He waited for a military victory and on September 22, 1862, announced his intention to free the slaves in rebel-controlled areas. It was, at the same time, a stroke of humanitarianism and political genius. The Emancipation Proclamation did not free a single slave on the day it went into effect, since Confederate Southerners did not recognize the validity of proclamations by "foreign" presidents and loyal unionist slave-holders were excluded from its terms. Still, Lincoln put himself and his government on record for emancipation, and in essence doomed slavery in the United States. He did so without driving border slave states such as Missouri, Kentucky, and Maryland out of the Union. And he did so without destroying the Republican majority in Congress as some of his advisors feared might happen in the 1862 "off-year" elections. Most important, though, Lincoln gave greater meaning to the war for union. Anti-slavery had been a part of that war all along, part of Lincoln's definition of union; but now the President had articulated the fact. He allowed the "war for union" to become a "crusade against slavery" as well.

Naturally the President and his party expended most of their time and energies presiding over the war effort. Yet the administration also took long strides toward making a reality out of its ideological vision for the nation. The clear Republican majority in Congress and the absence from Washington of otherwise-minded Southerners made the task easier. The non-military legislative record of Lincoln's presidency was impressive. Indeed one historian has termed this legislation the "blueprint for modern American."

Beginning in 1861 a series of tariffs were passed that progressively raised duties and set the tone for more political accommodation to industrial capitalism. In 1862 the Republicans fulfilled another campaign pledge by approving the Homestead Act. The law promised free land for those who would settle on it, but also offered public land for sale at $1.25 per acre. This latter provision opened the door to speculators who "settled" on the best plots and resold them at $15 an acre. The National Banking Act of 1863 outlawed state bank script and effectively standardized union currency. In 1864 Congress passed the Contract Labor Law, which permitted employers to bring in draft-exempt workers from abroad. Such legislation, together with lucrative war contracts, aided the American business community substantially. Taken as a whole the actions of Lincoln's administration well served the American transition from a preindustrial to an industrial state. The President himself was probably no "tool" of moneyed interests; his legislative record was the natural, sophisticated extension of his personal commitment to hard work, thrift, and such capitalist virtues. But "tool" or not, the results were the same. The business of the country was very much in the process of becoming business.

When asked, Lincoln ever maintained that his sole war aim was preservation of the Union. At the height of the agitation over emancipation, during the summer of 1862, the President went so far as to write an open letter to Horace Greeley in which he said, "my paramount object in this struggle *is* to save the Union, and is *not* either to save or to destroy slavery. If I could save the Union without freeing *any* slaves I would do it, and if I could save it by freeing *all* the slaves I would do it; and if I could save it by freeing some and leaving others alone I would also do that." Lincoln meant these words and to the disgust of many of his contemporaries was no doctrinaire reformer. But as the war dragged on he expanded his definition of union until it became synonymous with the interests and ideals of the Northern world view. The President thus became the pragmatic agent of American ideology. The Union that Lincoln insisted his enemies rejoin would not be the same Union they had left.

However much Lincoln eschewed reforming zeal, the thrust of his war aims and peace hopes was to remold the South. He still believed that the mass of Southern men were good, hard-working, frontier democrats like himself. He felt that peace and reunion would bring these people to the fore. The process of war, he hoped, would destroy the planter class, and a generous peace would insure the repudiation of planter leadership in the South by the common-man majority. Consequently the president resisted the heavy-handed peace tactics proposed by the radicals in his party. He "pocket-vetoed" the Wade-Davis Bill, which passed Congress in the summer of 1864; it projected a stern reconstruction for the South to be superintended by Congress. Always he insisted upon reunion and assumed that the union he proposed would itself reconstruct the South. At the abortive Hampton Roads peace conference in December 1864, the President insisted upon union, even to the point of holding out some hope of compensation to the Southerners for their emancipated slaves. And once he had the Union all but restored in April 1865, he counselled the commander of his military garrison in Richmond, "If I were in your place, I'd let them up easy—let them up easy."

A few days after his visit to the fallen Confederate capital of Richmond, Lincoln became one of the war's last casualties. His death was not a little ironic, because his countrymen lauded him in death as they never had in life. It spared him from seeing the South frustrate his hopes for reunion and reject the Union he had fashioned. Perhaps though, had the pragmatic idealist Lincoln ever reached the "Fox River" of Reconstruction, he would have made the crossing.

* * *

Late in the year 1861, some members of the Lincoln administration made informal overtures to Horace Greeley, editor of the New York

Tribune. If the *Tribune* should consent to become an unofficial "organ" of the government, the newspaper would receive in exchange advance notice of events and decisions occurring in high places. Greeley consented and the President was delighted. Lincoln said of Greeley, "Having him firmly behind me will be as helpful to me as an army of one hundred thousand men." As it happened Greeley did not long remain "firmly behind" Lincoln; nevertheless the President gave ample witness to the influence of this strange little man.

Born in Amherst, New Hampshire, in 1811, Greeley was "Hod" to the friends and neighbors of his youth. The robust sounding nickname was more appropriate to Greeley's parents, however, than to himself. His father and mother were sturdy farming people who enjoyed drink, tobacco, dance, and song. "Hod" Greeley was a shy, priggish prodigy who in time crusaded against most of the things that gave his parents pleasure. Perhaps Greeley associated creature comforts with poverty and hard times because his parents were never prosperous and often poor. The Greeleys lost their farm in the panic of 1819 and moved once to recoup their savings, then again to western Pennsylvania, to begin farming once more. During his family's difficulties Greeley himself retreated to books and shut himself off whenever there were no family chores to perform.

Greeley's most revealing practice during his early teens was that of lecturing girls against wearing corsets. He even devised a test to determine for sure whether his female companion was bound together with stays and strings. He dropped a handkerchief and challenged the young lady to pick it up. Whenever she did so, Greeley changed the subject. His interest in corsets seems purely that, a puritanical fetish; he seemed to care not at all about the contents of these worldly devices.

Greeley did not accompany his family on the move to western Pennsylvania. He had taken a job as an apprentice printer in East Poultney, Vermont, and remained there to learn his trade and earn his keep. While working on the East Poultney *Spectator,* Greeley reinforced his intellectual talents and bent his emotions toward religious pietism, temperance crusades, anti-slavery sentiment, and the Federalist Party. In journalism he had found his element, a vehicle with which to exercise his gifts and vent his moral fervor.

The *Spectator* folded in 1830, and Greeley rejoined his family in Pennsylvania. He did not stay long. A brief stay on his parents' lean, backwoods farm convinced him to leave his kin to their toilsome fate and strike out for New York. He began his journey to the nation's mecca with $25 in his pocket.

After a short term with a job-printing firm, Greeley founded his own family weekly, *The New Yorker.* The periodical enjoyed modest success in spite of its editor's periodic attempts at belle lettres. Greeley realized his limitations, however, and let others contribute stories and poems so that he could devote most of his attention to criticism and comment. The long-time Federalist evidenced his distaste of Jacksonian democracy. He distrusted mobs, labor unions, women's rightists, and abolitionist agitation; predictably he supported the National Bank against the assaults of "King Andrew."

In 1836 Greeley married a young schoolteacher and set up housekeeping in a modest neighborhood. The couple were never very "close" because Greeley could not allow domestic concerns to interfere with his journalistic pursuits and also because the Panic of 1837 so damaged *The New Yorker* that Greeley had to work all the harder to support his family. In 1838 Greeley began "commuting" to Albany where he edited the *Jeffersonian,* a Whig organ of Thurlow Weed, which sought to make William H. Seward Governor of New York. The venture succeeded, and in 1840 Greeley edited another Weed paper, *The Log Cabin,* as an organ of the Whig campaign to elect William Henry Harrison president. Finally in 1841 Greeley began publishing his own paper the New York *Tribune.*

Greeley's mind and heart shone clearly in the pages of the *Tribune.* A man of great enthusiasms; he flirted in turn with utopian socialism, transcendentalism, abolitionism, women's rights, and the temperance movement among others. He changed his mind often (notably on abolitionists and women) and in fact might have justifiably been charged a dilettante and hypocrite. However Greeley did display a fundamental consistency. He was a romantic reformer by nature; never mind if he altered his opinion of specific reforms. During the panic of 1837 he acquired new respect for the plight of the poor and thereafter believed that government ought to do positive good for society's downtrodden instead of merely preventing evil. He was an elitist, armed with moral rectitude, and eager to impose righteousness upon his fellow man. Greeley, in short, was an extreme expression of the idealistic, reforming bent in the Northern mind. And he attracted readers and converts, not only because of the substance of his ideals, but also because of the passionate, vigorous prose with which he expressed them.

Greeley remained a staunch Whig until 1854, when he accepted the Republican alternative to the nationally defunct Whig Party. In the process he split with Weed and Seward, a division that festered ultimately into open political warfare. At the Republican Convention in 1860 Greeley dedicated himself to preventing Seward's nomination and hoped to get the latter's Senate seat for himself. As it happened, Greeley "backed the wrong horse"; he worked for Edward Bates, a conservative, 65-year-old Whig from Missouri. The *Tribune* supported Lincoln once he won the nomination, but Greeley still believed Bates would have been a more prudent choice. He never quite appreciated Lincoln. In truth, he always seemed out of his element in the rough and tumble of practical politics; and Lincoln, to the bookish idealist, seemed the epitome of politics in the raw. Seward's defeat at the Republican Convention and Lincoln's victory in November were cause for rejoicing; but Greeley then fretted more over Weed's and Seward's successes at patronage in the new administration than about Southern secession. Once again he miscalculated; he did not believe the Southerners were serious.

When Greeley did confront the prospect of secession, his response was quite curious, on the surface at least. In the columns of the *Tribune* he bade the South to "go in peace." "Whenever a considerable section of our union shall deliberately resolve to go out, we shall resist all coercive measures designed to keep it in." This editorial, published in November 9, 1860, attracted much attention throughout the country because of its sentiment and its source. In reality, though, Greeley did not mean what he said. He admonished the South to secede, believing she would not do so. In Greeley's mind the Union was "a reality, an entity, a vital force, and not a mere aggregation." Thus secession was not only unconstitutional, but also unthinkable. All that was necessary was to call the South's bluff. Then the "reality" of the Union, which Greeley believed was a universally held concept, would silence the few hot-heads who preached secession. If, however, the South should persist in its folly, Greeley opposed compromise, which "only panders the South's insanity." He was opposed to war, but "we do not capitulate to traitors."

Greeley's stance on secession was characteristic of the man. At first he refused to believe that any sane person would deny the virtue of Union. When the Southerners proved him wrong, he reacted with the fury of a woman scorned, and after the Sumter crisis the *Tribune* was constant in its demand for blood.

Greeley gravitated wildly when defining the ultimate purpose of the war. In 1861 he was belligerent and convinced that the war was about his beloved Union. For a time, then, the *Tribune* served as an administration paper. But by 1862, Greeley could not understand why virtue was not everywhere triumphant, and he despaired of the North's military leadership. "Buell ought to be shot, and Grant ought to be hung," he privately confided; and, in the *Tribune,* he attacked McClellan's "tinsel imitation" of war. Greeley then concluded that the war must be about slavery as well as union. God was on the side of union but wanted it cleansed of the stain of slavery. He began working with Radicals in Congress toward emancipation and on August 20, 1862 published his "Prayer of Twenty Millions" editorial, which demanded that Lincoln "fight slavery with liberty." Although Greeley could not know it, the President had already decided to issue the Emancipation Proclamation and only required a military victory to emancipate from a position of strength instead of weakness. The *Tribune* applauded the Proclamation when it came, but expressed some concern over those slaves in loyal areas who were excluded from its provisions. Still, in Greeley's mind, the union had struck a blow against slavery; victory must be at hand. When victory did not immediately follow emancipation, Greeley once more despaired. He began talking about the "best available peace" and considered restoration of the old union without emancipation. Consequently he alternated between the Rebels and the war itself as the proper object of distaste. For example, after the Confederate victory at Chancellorsville, he lamented, "My God! it is horrible—horrible; and think of it, 130,000 magnificent soldiers so cut to pieces by less than 60,000 half-starved ragamuffins!" But in the wake of the New York draft riots in July 1863, he had second thoughts about the war. The mob remembered his support of the draft, attacked the *Tribune* office twice, and sang songs about hanging "Horace Greeley to a sour apple tree." Mrs. Greeley spent the week of the riots with a keg of gunpowder in the basement of their home. If the mob came she planned to flee into the woods, then ignite the trail of powder leading to the keg, and blow up some of the rioters along with her house.

Greeley's reenlistment in the war effort and rapprochement with the Lincoln administration was short-lived. By 1864 he was again hoping for peace negotiations and opposing the President's renomination. In the summer of 1864 he actually made contact with semi-official Rebel agents in Canada and offered himself as a free-lance peace negotiator. Lincoln wrote that Greeley might pursue peace as long as union and emancipation were understood as absolute conditions. But Greeley went to Niagara to meet the Rebels without mentioning conditions, and the venture was a fiasco. Despite some harsh words about the President's conduct of the "Niagara Conference," Greeley supported Lincoln's re-election. And despite the embarrassment caused him by Greeley's well-meant duplicity, Lincoln welcomed the *Tribune*'s help.

In the end victory produced the peace and restored the union for which Greeley crusaded. The editor shared Lincoln's hopes for a generous, speedy restoration. But whatever else Reconstruction was, it was neither generous nor speedy. Greeley clung to his ideals during the postwar years, and they led him down strange paths. He turned on the Republican Radicals and then on the Republicans altogether. Greeley ran for President in 1872 as a Democrat. He *was* true to his ideals. He simply never reconciled his zeal for perfection with the realities of politics and personal interests. Having scoffed at Lincoln's temporizing and pragmatic leadership, Greeley apparently realized Lincoln's greatness only after the assassination and called the martyred President, "the one providential leader, the one indispensable hero" of the war of union. He even had second thoughts about the Rebels. In the name of his own notion of justice, he journeyed to Richmond on May 13, 1867, and signed his name to Jefferson Davis' bail bond. "Hod" Greeley was not a "man of the world" as his youthful nickname tended to imply. Still his ideals and reform enthusiasm stamped him as very much a man of his world. That he was increasingly out of step with the real world as he grew older revealed more about the world than about the indomitable Greeley.

The "real world" eventually overcame each of the "drummers" we have heard. Davis finally lost touch with the reality of the Southern world and ended his life beating a broken drum. Lincoln was a victim of an ideological intensity he scarcely shared but which he molded and effectively led to victory. Having directed the "drummers" he never completed his march. And Greeley just beat essentially the same drum during his whole life—long after his beat was obsolete. Nevertheless in their prime each of these men—Davis, Lincoln, and Greeley—played upon the essential themes of their era. They not only reflected their respective world views; they strove to act them out.

14

Cavalier, Yankee, and the Malleable Man in the Reconstruction Process

WADE HAMPTON

CHARLES SUMNER

ROBERT BROWN ELLIOTT

by Joel Williamson
University of North Carolina

In a sense, the Civil War came because Southern whites by 1861 had generated a relatively clear-cut concept of their own identity, one that in large measure rested on chattel slavery and the black presence. Psychologically, they made a virtue out of a vice, an asset out of what the remainder of the Western world considered a liability. Likening their society to the democracy of ancient Greece, Southern whites saw themselves as the spiritual heirs of the once great Athenians.

On the other hand, Northern whites, with an increasingly polyglot population, had quite deliberately opted not to face the identity crisis. Instead they delayed it, generally stressing what America was *not*, rather than what it was. The United States, for instance, would *not* be monarchial, aristocratic, or church-ridden, and of that there was no question. Neither would it be slave-ridden although, abolitionists aside, there was a general disposition to allow it to remain where it was south of the Mason-Dixon line. But beyond extolling the virtues of American freedom, republicanism, and equality, the Yankee North, in fact, moved quite gingerly toward the realization of a thorough-going democratic society.

In only one area, perhaps, did virtually all Northerners (and many Southerners too) have a universally affirmative philosophy: they shared an idealized and romantic nationalism, an image of one nation indivisible in the common cause. Hundreds of thousands of young Americans were about to die for that cause. Their bodies strewn grotesque in death upon the fields of Gettysburg were offered as tokens "that government of the people, by the people, for the people, shall not perish from the earth."

On the eve of the Civil War white Southerners of every social class were united in support of a culture erected on what John C. Calhoun called the "mudsill" of slavery. Almost defiantly they acclaimed slavery to be ordained by God, something that they themselves were unique in recognizing. Since the 1830s slavery, they believed, was producing in the South a highly superior civilization dominated by a proudly aristocratic elite, a civilization still in the process of improvement and refinement and yet to reach its apex. Southerners, like Northerners, worshipped at the 19th-century shrines of duty, honor, loyalty, patriotism, Christianity, and womanhood. But in the South, those ideals were held to have solid content. Internalized individually and externalized socially, they were firmly grounded in knightly rituals not unlike those found in Sir Walter Scott's Waverly novels, especially *Ivanhoe.* For example, a whole code of feminine behavior developed, and an answering code existed for gentlemen. These codes stressed honor and dictated behavior, including prescriptions for courage and grace. Finally patrician character embodied a sense of *noblesse oblige:* from the gifted for the less gifted came a sense of responsibility, a protectiveness, and a paternalism.

Thus Southern culture was both like and unlike that of the North, but somewhere the American organism had split and become two. One emerging nation had divided to become two peoples, two souls, two regional cultures of differing characters, the one cavalier and the other Yankee. And when conflict came, it was a struggle as uncivil as only a fratricidal war can be. It was an American Revolution fully as much as the Revolution that their ancestors had fought four generations before. Essentially, one side had determined what it would become, and the other what it would not.

That Southerners identified themselves with such clarity helped them to seize the initiative and to act assertively in secession and war and, ultimately, to win after Reconstruction. From the first, the lack of a clear sense of self hobbled the Northern effort and established a pattern whereby the South acted—and the North reacted. It began in the harbor of Charleston where Southerners boldly attacked Fort Sumter. The North then reacted. In the war itself, three daring and sharply pointed Southern invasions of the North were massively met and quickly crushed; yet for four years powerful Northern armies literally wallowed on Southern soil before their offensive was perfected. It was almost as if the Union armies had flowed into victory instead of having won it. Ultimately, blue coated Yankee soldiers flooded the South in such numbers that the rebellion of the Confederate states was crushed under their avalanche.

The pattern of action and reaction continued during Reconstruction. For some weeks after Appomattox, Southerners waited for the prescription of the bitter medicines that would purge them of treason. When the prescription came from President Andrew Johnson, however, it was surprisingly mild. Quite understandably, Southern aristocrats began to revert to their traditional ways, and their restored governments moved to reinstate a form of quasi-slavery through the Black Codes. Moreover, in several localities the white populace subdued the more aggressive freedmen in bloody riots. Again, Northerners could not act in regard to the South, but they could react. Increasingly frustrated, they supported the Radical policy of reconstruction; and they grew in numbers and so too did their spokesmen in Congress. Gradually, a new and narrowly focused reconstruction program emerged centering on the ex-slaves. But significantly it came at the instigation of the South, not the North.

Whereas in 1865 the North had supported only a second-class, natural rights citizenship for blacks in the form of protections for life, liberty, and property, it now moved on to insure those rights by opening the courts, the ballot boxes, and political offices to black people. Northern interest in the South was intense by 1867, when the military was bluntly used to create Republican governments in the Southern states. But Northern interest cooled noticeably when those governments were assumed to be underway late in 1868. Two years later, with the passage of the Fifteenth Amendment—which assured that no one would be denied the suffrage because of race, creed, or color—the cooling turned to frosty indifference.

Ku Kluxers in the early 1870s had momentarily revived interest. But this revival was fainthearted and expertly parried by Southerners, and state after state was redeemed by the Old South leadership and its heirs. The South was successful in its efforts at redemption because it was now careful never to act in a way to evoke a Northern reaction. Nowhere was the North openly attacked; nowhere was the government directly defied. Wherever they went in the South, Union soldiers were perfectly safe. White Republicans in the South, however, were in danger and blacks in mortal peril.

The North had prevented disunion; but it could not prescribe what the restored union would be. It *could* not reconstruct the South because it *would* not construct itself. Indeed, Reconstruction was not a failure of force on the part of the North, nor one of goal or will; it was a failure of the North to define itself. The North chose not to choose, not to face the identity crisis in its adolescence, and therein it set the Southern white free and deserted the Southern black.

The process by which all of this had taken place was personified in the lives of three men, two from South Carolina—one white and one black—and the other a descendant of 17th-century New England Puritans. Wade

Hampton, a Civil War hero and later governor of South Carolina, led conservative whites in regaining political control of their State during the Reconstruction period. He represented that Southern culture that had been vindicated and perfected by the Civil War and Reconstruction. Charles Sumner, the senior Senator from Massachusetts, would define the North's ideals, particularly as they related to the black man, and seek to implement them primarily in a section of the country other than his own. Robert B. Elliott was in a position to advance the interests of his fellow blacks, but he was unable to resist the values and temptations of white America.

*   *   *

That Wade Hampton III was 47 years old when Reconstruction began has great significance. He was not only a son of the Old South, he *was* the Old South. So much marked by tradition, so deeply grooved, he could be no other than what he was. Probably more than anyone else after the war, Hampton spoke for the enduring South.

In the role of Southern spokesman, Wade Hampton had high visibility. Even before the war, he had some national reputation as a moderate, as an opponent of slavery in principle and of immediate secession. During the conflict, he became one of Robert E. Lee's favorite aides. After Jeb Stuart's death, Hampton was the most eminent cavalry leader in the eastern theater of war. Unlike Lee, Jefferson Davis, and other prominent leaders of the Confederacy, Hampton did not withdraw from active political life after Appomattox. Further, whereas other Southern leaders had statewide prominence, Hampton had a sectional reputation. In the fall of 1865, a correspondent of the *Nation* travelling in the South recognized Hampton's political power when he wrote that "the Southern people can be reached quickest through the medium of such men as R. E. Lee and Wade Hampton." Hampton's appeal derived from his personification of the best values of the Old South: he had courage, he had grace, and he was ruled by a high sense of personal honor and loyalty. Before hostilities he had known considerable wealth and prosperity, and he had been reared with a deep and comfortable sense of self. Those gifts had carried him and his people through the war. With Lee's surrender, he suffered both the South's crushing defeat and its great poverty. But he never deserted the faith. Remaining true to himself and to others, he ultimately redeemed himself and that older South.

The Hampton name was first brought to the new world by William Hampton who landed at Jamestown in 1620. Hardworking farmers and pioneers, the Hamptons were to move on to South Carolina. There they were Indian fighters on the raw Carolina frontier and subsequently distinguished themselves as soldiers in the American Revolution and the

War of 1812. The same aggressiveness and opportunism that characterized the Hamptons in battle served them as well in time of peace. They became highly successful and wealthy plantation owners. Their main property consisted of Millwood, a huge holding along the Congaree River in the South Carolina upcountry not far from the newly established state capital at Columbia. The Hamptons innovated in the cultivation of short-staple cotton and acquired a sizable number of slaves. True to their earlier pioneering and acquisitive spirit, the Hamptons also carved new cotton and sugar plantations out of the Louisiana and Mississippi wilderness.

Wade Hampton III, with whom we are concerned here, was born on March 28, 1818. He grew up at Millwood, where his surroundings included a great white-columned mansion, amid five acres of gardens, kitchens, storehouses, barns, carriage houses, stables, and slave quarters. "Mauma Nelly" cared for Wade in his early childhood, but his still vigorous grandfather tutored him almost from infancy in riding, shooting, and the manly arts. At the Rice Creek Academy and at the South Carolina College, where his father and grandfather served as trustees, young Wade received a formal education. But most of all, like his father before him he was trained primarily to take over the eventual management of Millwood, which together with the Louisiana and Mississippi properties were becoming a giant business enterprise for that day. But business was mixed with pleasure, and every summer the Hampton family journeyed to White Sulphur Springs in the mountains of western Virginia. There at palatial resort hotels, they mixed with the other great planting families of the South. Through it all there was business, pleasure, and politics, and the clear beginnings of a unique sectional culture.

Two years after graduating from college in 1838, Wade Hampton married his half cousin, Margaret Preston of Arlington, Virginia. The marriage was not unappropriate as a symbol of the closed nature of Southern high society. Shortly thereafter the young planter and his bride were established upon their own estate, Sand Hills, near Columbia, and in 1840 their first child was born. During the next few years, Wade Hampton spent much of his time attending to business, commuting between the eastern and western family holdings. He interrupted these labors in 1846, to accompany his brother-in-law on a European trip that included a visit to England where he dined with the Duke of Wellington and met several members of the country's nobility.

Returning home, Hampton assumed increasing responsibility in the family business. At Christmas time in 1850, he was with his father at Houmas, the Louisiana plantation, distributing clothes to almost 1,000 slaves. As Wade reported to Mary, his youngest sister, each slave was given according to sex "a blanket, pair of stockings, hat, handkerchief, a calico dress, check apron, fine bleached shirt, and fancy pants." Five years later, Hampton suffered a devastating personal blow, the death of his wife, but he bore this tragedy courageously, for he was always aware of those who were dependent upon his steady attention to duty and of the many blessings still left to him. During the next few years, he continued to steep himself in the family business, buying, selling, managing. When his father died in 1858, he inherited the mantle of family leadership. About 3,000 slaves, some the property of his three unmarried sisters, were under his care. In 1858 he married Mary McDuffie, daughter of the late George McDuffie a fire-eating South Carolina Congressman. He had probably known Mary for most of her 28 years, but they became very close only in the mid 1850s, when he was advising her on the management of her inherited plantation. In 1860 Mary Hampton bore her husband a son and life again seemed full.

Wade Hampton III was one of the South's richest men, but his life was not all business. In the early 50s he had entered the South Carolina legislature as a representative and in the middle 50s moved up to the state Senate. Known as a moderate he was conspicuously against the proposal to re-open the African slave trade. He was also a leading moderate in a state rife with pro-secession sentiment. Secession, he stated calmly and deliberately, was "inexpedient and without sufficient provocation." His objective was "the union of the South for the preservation of the South."

Hardly a typical South Carolina planter, Hampton was nonetheless typically Southern. When war came, he accepted a colonel's commission and immediately began to raise Hampton's Legion, a body of six companies of infantry, four of cavalry, and a battery of artillery. With his own money he imported two Blakely cannon and 400 stand of Enfield rifles from England. As Wade Hampton II had brought military experience to the plantation, now his grandson brought vast plantation experience to the military. Having once supervised slaves, he now supervised the military drills of a thousand of Carolina's most favored sons. When his Legion went onto the field at Manassas, it was prepared to do its duty. Six hundred of Hampton's men arrived sleepless and unfed just in time to be thrown against a Union flanking movement. All but engulfed by the blue-coated tide, the South Carolinians nonetheless delayed the advance. Finally retiring to a line with Stonewall Jackson's troops, the Legion joined in a counterattack, which won the field. Hampton's horse was shot from under him and a bullet had opened his scalp, knocking him to the ground during a charge against an artillery battery. But bandaged and bloody, he resumed command.

There could be no question of Wade Hampton's courage; he was truly a great soldier. Calculatingly aggressive, he took awesome risks. In the battle before Richmond in the spring of 1862, he was shot in the foot. Still mounted, he had the regimental surgeon probe and remove the bullet and galloped away to rejoin the battle. Afterwards, Hampton became a brigadier in Jeb Stuart's cavalry and there were still more of hard riding, shooting, and sabre slashing.

At dawn on July 2, 1863, Hampton arrived at Gettysburg with Jeb Stuart's cavalry. While the men were resting after an exhausting ride, he scouted ahead and was caught unaware by a lieutenant of the Sixth Michigan Cavalry. With a heavy downstroke of his sabre, the Yankee officer slashed through Hampton's hat cutting a four inch gash in his scalp. Whirling about on his horse; Hampton stuck his revolver in the lieutenant's ribs and pulled the trigger. A hollow click—misfire. The lieutenant raced away with Hampton close behind and snapping the pistol at him. Fortunately for the Union officer, there was a break in a fence and he galloped through it, finally joining up with his regiment. "It was a half-mile race for life," the lieutenant later recalled. "I heard his pistol snap three time at my back, and also his parting curse. . . ."

The next day Hampton, head bandaged, participated in a charge against the Union cavalry. Immediately he attracted the enemy and bluecoats swarmed about him. His head again was cut open and blood poured down his face almost blinding him. He drove off some of the attackers with pistol and sabre, but more Yankees rushed in for the kill. Badly wounded, Hampton spurred his horse over a fence, but, in midflight, caught a piece of shrapnel in his side. Gushing blood from his head and side, his skull fractured, he was taken from the field.

In May of 1864, Jeb Stuart was killed and Hampton, now fully recovered from his wounds, succeeded to the command of Lee's cavalry. Outnumbered, outgunned, and outhorsed, he did his best to shield Southern troops from the ever-pressing Ulysses S. Grant. By the fall, the Confederates were barely holding Richmond and Petersburg. On October 27 Hampton received the most grievous wound of all. In a melee with Union cavalry his son Preston was struck in the groin by a bullet and fell to the ground badly wounded. His brother Wade rushed up and was himself struck in the back by another bullet. Their father galloped over, swung down, held the half-conscious boy in his arms and cried, "My son, my son." The boy could not speak. Wade junior was helped to his saddle and led off, while Preston was carried away in a wagon with other wounded. When General Mat Butler rode up to his commander, there were tears on Hampton's face and a cold rain was falling on the field. "Poor Preston has been mortally wounded," said Hampton. He remounted and rode beside the wagon, where a physician was cradling Preston's head. Hampton looked at his son. "Too late, doctor," he said quietly, wheeled about, and rode back to the fight. Preston died, the second Hampton to perish in the war.

Hampton fought out the war like a mechanical man, facing Sheridan's cavalry in the North, and then turning to face Sherman's army in the

South. When the end finally came, he did not want to yield, and tried to persuade Jefferson Davis to take what cavalry as would join them and push across the Mississippi, there to fight with their backs to the Rio Grande and Mexico until they either won or were punched out of the land. Finally, and only when his wife persuaded him to his responsibility to those who remained alive did Hampton capitulate to duty and not to the Yankees.

Hampton had great physical courage, but he also had moral courage, which Reconstruction gave him ample opportunity to demonstrate. After the war, he turned back to business. The home plantations had been utterly demolished. Moving his family into an overseer's house that somehow had escaped destruction, Hampton managed to take care of immediate needs on the Congaree lands in the summer of 1865. In the fall he put the family's western North Carolina estate in order, and by Christmas time, 1865, he was out on the broad acres of Mississippi. Impoverished and deeply in debt, he had taken out loans before the war against lands that were devalued much below the amount of the debts. Consistently honorable, Hampton did not renege; he commenced the struggle to pay his creditors.

Neither did Wade Hampton renege upon his duties as a Southern leader. Other eminent Confederates retired from political activity. Jefferson Davis, surrogate for Confederacy, carried it into retirement at "Beauvoir," his Mississippi plantation. Lee did the same in becoming president of Washington College. But Hampton brought the values of the Old South into Reconstruction. Asked to head a group of slaveholders who would migrate to Brazil, he declined, urging his countrymen to remain and "to devote their energies to the restoration of law and order, the re-establishment of agriculture and commerce, the promotion of education, and the rebuilding of our cities and dwellings which have been laid in ashes." Though he himself was still proscribed from politics, Hampton advised all those who could legally do so to participate in the re-establishment of civil government. In spite of his disabilities, he came within a few votes of being elected governor of South Carolina in the fall of 1865.

Throughout the Reconstruction years, Hampton maintained that the South had surrendered with honor, was meeting its obligations in good faith, and was expecting the North to do the same. Even as Radicalism gained in the North and military rule was reimposed upon the South in 1867, Hampton hewed to that line. Opposing appeasement and expediency, he urged Southerners to register and vote against the Radical program. Expediency, he declared, was "that fatal fallacy which has lured us so far on the road to destruction, that Trojan horse which has brought with it an Iliad of woes." Far from being fearful of Negroes, he proposed that some be enfranchised under precisely the same tests applied to white men. But the battle was quickly lost: the military registered all blacks, and South Carolina proceeded to elect a totally Republican government.

Turning to his private affairs, specifically to his debts, Hampton was engaged in another losing battle. His land daily declined in value. Characteristically, he was both stubborn and stoical. "I am only solicitous to serve the interests of my creditors and to protect my name from any stain," he told a friend. "If these objects can be accomplished I will give up all I possess with far greater pleasure than I ever experienced in its acquisition." On Christmas Eve of 1868, he went into bankruptcy in Jackson, Mississippi, with debts of more than a million dollars.

Still Hampton had other interests. Peace seemed sweet indeed after the horrors of war and the deaths of his son and brother. He hunted, fished, and enjoyed family and friends. He also engaged in business ventures. With two other former generals, he formed the Southern Life Insurance Company, and for a time he served as the president of a Maryland firm, the Baltimore Fire Extinguisher Works. While in Baltimore, he was also highly active in the organization of Confederate veterans. Once again in 1872, Hampton participated in the national political battles but once again was the loser. All this would change in 1876.

On June 28, 1876, Wade Hampton as grand marshal led a parade through Charleston's streets, celebrating the 100th anniversary of the Revolutionary War victory at Fort Moultrie. The column, including militia from Massachusetts as well as South Carolina, moved through the town to a public park where various orators mounted a platform to speak. The speeches were organized around a theme of reconciliation—conservative South Carolinians would support a reform regime led by Daniel H. Chamberlain, the incumbent carpetbag governor from Massachusetts. On a westbound train the next day several former general officers of the Army of Virginia, including Hampton, sat talking. Martin Witherspoon Gary, one of Hampton's young generals and a firebrand, chaffed at the idea of fusion with the conservative Republicans. He was convinced the Democrats could win on a "straightout" Democratic ticket. But more importantly he discovered that Hampton was of similar mind. From that moment, the "Straightout" campaign began. Gary urged Hampton to run for the governorship. Hampton pled poverty: his furniture had just been sold at public auction at the courthouse door in Columbia for less than $120. Gary persisted, however, and Hampton gave in.

At their convention the next month, the state's Democrats rejected fusion with the Republicans and nominated Hampton by acclamation. A curious campaign followed. Running on a platform of "reconciliation, retrenchment, and reform," Hampton spoke in moderate terms for law and order, and for fair treatment for the blacks. But numerous white paramilitary groups made a show of force. After several outright riots, Governor Chamberlain asked President Grant for aid. Some federal troops arrived and more were offered; however, the local general did not request them, probably because he was sympathetic with the local whites. Grant ordered the military clubs to disperse. Hampton himself had never licensed such violence nor even recognized the existence of these clubs. "We cannot disperse," he responded "because we are not gathered together." All during the summer and fall, federal troops marched up and down South Carolina's dusty roads, repeatedly arriving at the scene of violence just in time to count the still warm and bleeding bodies. Organized violence was rampant in the state, but no one could convincingly name its perpetrators. On election day, local militia commanders stationed their men a discreet distance from the polls, thereby enabling the white population to exploit the situation to the fullest. Whites went early to the polls, voted, and then did not leave, crowding around the officials and the ballot boxes so tightly that no one else could approach. At other locations they rode their horses all day at breakneck speeds around the polling places so as to run down any who dared attempt to cross. Sometimes, when a black man approached the polls, two Democrats would stage a fight, draw pistols, and fire at one another with menacing inaccuracy.

When the election was over, no one could say for certain who won or who might have won in a fair election. Probably about 9,000 black men would have had to vote for Hampton for him to win. It is very unlikely that they did so. Both sides claimed victory and shortly thereafter, two governments, each claiming to be legal, were operating in Columbia. Again Chamberlain called on Grant for aid. Again the President responded with the military, which proceeded to give physical control of the state's properties to the Republicans. Angry whites gathered on the broad grounds around the capitol and violence seemed imminent. But a tall, portly man, the graying Hampton emerged from the state house door. Speaking carefully and calmly, he urged the crowd to avoid violence and disperse quietly. "I have been elected your governor, and, so help me God, I will take my seat," he concluded. Within minutes the crowd had dissolved.

Hampton steadily held his people in check. Taxpayers paid ten percent of their year's taxes to the Hampton government and none to Chamberlain's. Hampton issued a pardon to a woman in the state penitentiary and significantly the Republican-dominated State supreme court upheld him. Support for the Chamberlain government slowly eroded. The Hampton presence was responsible. When South Carolina's rifle clubs scheduled parades in Columbia and Charleston on Washington's birthday in 1877, Grant forbade them. Hampton bowed, but in so doing pointed to his own people as exemplifying law and order and willing to obey constituted authority. He had at last outgeneraled Grant, and Rutherford B. Hayes, coming into the White House on March 4, recognized the North's defeat. By invitation, Hampton arrived in Washington on March 28, which happened to be his 59th birthday. On the following day, he met the new President. On April 2, the administration decided to remove the troops that had been occupying the Palmetto State. On the tenth, the last 30 soldiers marched smartly out of the State house. The next morning, Hampton entered the building as governor. South Carolina had been redeemed.

As Governor, Wade Hampton perfected the redemption. But he did not proscribe the vanquished. For Hampton had grace in victory as well as in defeat. During the war, he repeatedly exhibited a chivalric consideration for his enemies, a tolerance that bordered upon indulgence. Hampton now demonstrated the same magnaminity toward the best of the "scalawags" as well as to the blacks, an attitude that disturbed the firebrands among his followers. One scalawag headed the committee investigating the frauds of the Republican administration, and the secretary of the senate for the old regime was allowed to remain in office for a time under the Democrats. Most of all, Hampton showed no disposition to eliminate Negroes from the political process. Possibly he believed that the great mass of blacks were for him and had so voted in the 1876 election. In any case, his regime was marked by a paternalism in which few Negroes were elevated, but none proscribed because they were black. Like the planters of old, Hampton took care of all his people, black and white, large and small, male and female.

In 1879, Hampton went to Washington as United States Senator. And in the nation's capitol, it could be truly said, he resided as a Bourbon. He had learned nothing and he had forgotten nothing. No legislation bore his name, and none even reflected his special influence. He was content to let well enough alone. In the late 1880s, an agricultural depression gripped South Carolina, producing a rebel political movement led by some of Hampton's old supporters. They seized control of the Democratic party in 1890 and elected Ben Tillman governor. Next, they proceeded to depose the general. Now hissed, booed, and shouted down, Hampton refused to assail former political allies. Instead, he quietly retired.

When Cleveland became President in 1893, Hampton was appointed a railroad commissioner, thereby easing his personal financial problems in his last years. He had a comfortable home on Senate Street in Columbia, where he frequently sat on the veranda, received relatives and friends, and played with grandchildren. The McKinley administration took away his office, but he accepted no other. Increasingly, he turned his attention to veterans' organizations and to nostalgic reminiscing about the war.

In April 1902, Wade Hampton became seriously ill. From time to time he drifted off, had vague reveries about the war and the death of his son Preston. Just before he himself died, the 84-year-old Hampton momentarily regained consciousness. "God bless all my people," he said, "black and white."

*   *   *

The Sumners came to Massachusetts from Kent, England, in 1635, only scant years after the Hamptons came to Virginia. On January 6, 1811, following a long line of Puritans, Charles Sumner was born in Boston. He progressed through the Boston Latin School to Harvard and on through Harvard Law School. In Cambridge he became the protege of Justice Joseph Story of the Harvard law faculty and later of the United States Supreme Court. Briefly Sumner was reporter for the circuit court of appeals, and between 1835 and 1837 he lectured at Harvard. For three years thereafter, he lived in Europe and Great Britain, enjoying the company and friendship of many eminent persons. Back in Boston, Sumner began to practice law and early established a reputation as a brilliant attorney. His circle of friends included many of New England's most distinguished intellectuals. He was a lifelong intimate of the poet Henry Wadsworth Longfellow and close to such reformers as William Ellery Channing, Samuel Gridley Howe, and Horace Mann. Inspired by them, he embraced one cause after another, beginning with penal and educational reform, the peace movement of the 1840s and, finally, the anti-slavery crusade.

Charles Sumner was an endlessly complex man. He had an almost inexplicable personality. Indeed one of the strangest things about it was that he really had none, at least until middle age. As the perceptive Julia Ward Howe observed of him in his early 30s, he had "no heart," by which she meant no feelings of his own. Lacking a distinctive personality, Charles early fell into the habit of appropriating the personalities of others. Initially he aped his father, the sheriff of Suffolk County, a notably cool man who was himself marked by having been born out of wedlock. Charles Sumner tried desperately to please him—and everyone else—but his father was never able to give the approval he needed. At Harvard, young Sumner exchanged his father for Joseph Story—emulating him so thoroughly, he almost became more like Story than Story himself.

When Charles Sumner went abroad in 1837, President Josiah Quincy of Harvard predicted that he would return with a cane. And he did, because that was the fashion. In Europe and in England, he saw everything and liked everything he saw. He was in a "constant state of astonishment and delight" with Thomas Carlyle, who for his part thought Charles Sumner "the most completely nothin' of a man that ever crossed my threshold." He was also taken by John Bright and indeed with everybody and anybody he chose to notice. He admired the French system of law and thought of revamping the American legal system in a sort of Code Sumner like the Code Napoleon—until he encountered the superior English system. On the Continent he charmed Prince Metternich in Vienna and fell in with the American artists in Italy. In Florence he affected the artistic pose so completely as to feel free to offer pointers to the sculptor Horatio Greenough on how to improve the latter's shockingly nude statute of George Washington. And with no difficulty, he identified with the romantic poets of his day.

Back home in Boston in 1840 and practicing law, Charles Sumner's penchant for imitation continued. When his friend Samuel Gridley Howe, who pioneered in working with the deaf and the blind, fell in love with Julia, one of the beautiful and charming Ward sisters of New York, Charles also showed signs of falling in love, taking up the fruitless pursuit of Julia's younger sister. And there were other instances of Sumner's identifying himself with the personal affairs of his friends. When Henry Wadsworth Longfellow married Fanny Appleton, Charles Sumner went along on the honeymoon, reading funeral orations to the newlyweds while on the train taking them to the Catskills.

After the marriage of his two closest male friends in 1844 and at the age of 33, Charles Sumner felt deserted, embattled, persecuted, and desperately sick. So convincing was he in illness, whether real or feigned, that even physicians pronounced his case fatal and his many friends came around to his mother's house to pay their last respects. Then, rather suddenly he decided to recover and to emulate William Ellery Channing, the great Unitarian minister who had breathed new life into the tired body of New England Puritanism. Channing had been a revolutionary when Charles Sumner first came to sit at his feet. His concerns—for the penal system, education, peace, and slavery—became Sumner's. Writing with admiration, if not reverence of the old man, who died in 1842, Charles Sumner declared: "What seemed to me a sight almost sublime was this weak old man, almost fading out of life, with a voice affected by the debility of his frame, uttering words that pass mountains and seas, overcoming the impediments of distance and boundaries, and ... pleading trumpet-tongued for humanity, for right, for truth."

When Charles Sumner returned to the world it was as invalid *cum* reformer. From Channing he had learned that man was perfectable through the management of the environment and that progress toward an "age of Humanity" was ordained by God. With Samuel Gridley Howe, he campaigned for penal reform and joined Howe and Horace Mann in the movement to improve teaching methods in the common schools. And then, in 1845, he gained his first taste of national fame when he gave the Fourth of July Address, "The True Grandeur of Nations," and he loved it. Before a Boston audience studded with admirals and generals, he proceeded to denounce all wars and to remand military leadership to the level of mass murder. With that speech Charles Sumner had indeed become a new man.

In the beginning his ideas were those freely and easily available—indeed unavoidable—in New England. With Channing, he learned to think out the causes more precisely and to construct programs toward ideal ends. When his friends seemingly deserted him, he espoused these programs even more vigorously and publicly. If the world caught up with him, he would again move out ahead. And when the world did not applaud, he denounced his critics, saw conspiracies everywhere, carried his doctrines to the extreme, and would fight for them to the death. Though made for martyrdom, he was not one who would go willingly to the cross.

Sumner's opposition to militarism soon placed him in the vanguard of those who were against the Mexican War (1846–48), and from it he moved into the anti-slavery crusade. By a fluke of politics he was elected to the United States Senate in 1851, and he used that forum to press constantly for the rights of man, especially black men.

In 1856, Sumner delivered a celebrated speech against the crime that the slaveholders were perpetrating against the Kansas territory. As a part of this speech, he deliberately made a personal attack upon South Carolina Senator Andrew Butler, a warm and generous man as well as a slaveholder. Two days later, the Senator's nephew, Preston Brooks, following the South's code of honor, which held that one chastised an unequal with a horsewhip or a cane, came into the Senate and approached Sumner at his desk. "Mr. Sumner," he said. As Sumner seemed about to rise, Brooks struck him over the head with a heavy cane. Then he struck him again and again. Desperately, Sumner struggled up, wrenching his desk, bolts and all, from the floor. Still Brooks rained blows upon him. Finally, Sumner fell to the floor, senseless and bleeding. For more than three years, Sumner's seat in the Senate remained empty. When he returned to it in 1859, he knew himself to be the living embodiment of the great cause of the rights of man.

In 1860 Sumner's Republican party was victorious, and he himself gained great power as the Chairman of the Senate Foreign Relations Committee. He used that power to gain administration support for programs designed to improve the condition of black people in America. Repeatedly, he would push out into the advance, the South would act, and Northern opinion would react to his lead. During the war years, the Massachusetts senator was a prime mover in the abolition of slavery in the District of Columbia and in emancipating slaves for the purpose of enlisting them in the Union Army.

When Lincoln died, Sumner had already gone on record as opposed to presidential Reconstruction, which was then moving rapidly ahead in Louisiana. He rejected Lincoln's plan because it excluded Negro suffrage. Within a week of an all night vigil by the bedside of the dying President, the Senator had a long discussion with the new chief executive, Andrew Johnson. He came away certain that Johnson would enfranchise both black men and all loyal Southerners. But back in Massachusetts, it soon became evident to Sumner that something had gone awry. Southern state governments were being organized one after another on the basis of white supremacy. Immediately, in the summer of 1865, Sumner took the field in behalf of equal rights for the blacks. He found a surprising lack of sympathy for this cause in the North generally, in New England in particular, and even more particularly in his beloved Massachusetts. Furthermore, he discovered a great willingness to abide by Johnson's program. The North easily made a distinction between the abolition of slavery and equal rights for blacks. While some veteran abolitionists like Wendell Phillips would continue the good fight, others like William Lloyd Garrison, simply considered that their job had been done. Among New England's intellectuals, Henry Wadsworth Longfellow was one of the few apparently to agree with Sumner and the poet was famously non-political. Most of all, the younger generation of New Englanders clearly indicated that it did not want to get involved. Politicians taking the popular pulse, found that it beat not at all for equal rights for blacks.

Yet events would soon give practical substance to Sumner's ideals. Driving for a moderate party, Andrew Johnson gave increasing leeway to the South, which had taken the president's program as an invitation to establish distinctly antebellum type governments. Disregarding how the North might greet such measures, these new governments passed Black Codes, all allegedly designed to protect Negroes from their own supposed inadequacies. But they all remanded blacks to a quasi-slavery. Most Northerners were outraged, and in December Congress was emboldened to turn away those Southerners who came to its doors with certificates of election. Johnson added fuel to the flames by criticizing congressional Radicals, especially in an intemperate 1866 address on Washington's birthday in which he mentioned the extremists by name, including Sumner. Then, in the spring, the President vetoed the Civil Rights Bill, designed as an answer to the Black Codes. In the wake of the veto Sumner worked like a fury, flying about the capital, buttonholing Congressmen. On April 6, the Senate overrode the veto.

During the following summer, when riots broke out in the South, it came clear enough that Southern whites were not prepared to recognize black equality, civilly or otherwise. The Northern reaction showed in the fall elections; a flood of Radical representatives came into the Congress. Sumner, the prophet vindicated, had not changed on the issue of equality for all. But the nation had changed. The South had shown its colors and the North had responded. Suddenly finding himself in step, the senior senator from Massachusetts felt gloriously.

Part of his euphoria came from marriage. A confirmed bachelor with a heart condition (which had resulted, he believed, from the fearful beating administered him by Preston Brooks), Sumner had taken a youthful bride. Or possibly she had taken him. Alice Mason Hooper was a rich widow of the Massachusetts gentry. After her husband had died in the war, she had frequently come to Washington to serve as nurse in the military hospitals. Rich, elegant, thinly beautiful, she did not lack for suitors. But she was taken by Sumner. In October they married, and briefly, in that winter in Washington, he was supremely happy.

And Sumner's fondest wish, black suffrage, became a reality. Once again the South did its part. One Southern state after another rejected the Fourteenth Amendment, which had been proposed by Congress. The Amendment established federal and hence Negro citizenship. After its rejection, Southerners had calculated there would come a bargaining in which they would give up some things in return for others. To their surprise, what they got instead was the re-establishment of military government. By order of Congress, the military then proceeded to register all legitimate voters in the South, and these included practically every adult black male. Northern Republicans though politically embarrassed by requiring the South to do what they refused to do at home, not only secured the acceptance of the Fourteenth Amendment in the former Confederate states, but also moved to enfranchise blacks in the District of Columbia and in the territories of the United States. They also insisted on universal male suffrage before they would admit the states of Nebraska and Colorado to the union. Charles Sumner now found himself in perfect accord with his heretofore often most unharmonious universe.

Sumner's marital and moral happiness, however, was soon to end. Pressing work in the Senate and the demands of a highly social young wife proved to be incompatible. Alice Sumner suffered only briefly. She continued to make the rounds of Washington society. Her frequent appearances in the company of a young Prussian diplomat, brought reproaches from Sumner and they quarreled bitterly. Shortly afterwards she left for Europe and eventual divorce.

At the same time, Sumner, moving out ahead of his Republican colleagues, had concluded that both the Fourteenth Amendment and the Military Reconstruction Act were insufficient. On March 6 he introduced his own bill, which would bar from political participation not only the political and military leaders of the Old South, but also those authors, publishers, editors, speakers, preachers and anyone else who had urged secession and supported the rebellion. Further, the new state governments would be required to recognize that a republican form included systems of "public schools open to all." Finally, he urged that every rebel landowner convey to his former slaves "a certain portion of the land on which they have worked." Reconstruction could never be completed, he thought, "unless in some way we secured to freedmen a piece of land." Before the month was over, most of his colleagues were highly disturbed upon learning that Sumner meant his principles of equal citizenship should apply to Northern as well as the Southern Negroes. Consequently Sumner's ideals were not implemented, but his very reassertion of them isolated him from the mass of his party and people.

When the Fifteenth Amendment was hammered out in Congress, Sumner took no active role. He had long felt that a simple congressional act was sufficient to insure black suffrage and he scoffed at constitutional quibbling about human rights. The following winter, during the session of 1869–70, Sumner came into his own again as the Senate leader in matters also pertaining to Reconstruction. Most Southern states had proceeded to organize rapidly under the military, and their representatives were admitted to Congress. Georgia, Virginia, and Mississippi, however, proved recalcitrant. The predominantly white Georgia legislature peremptorily expelled 28 black representatives from its midst on the ground that conferring the vote upon Negroes did not automatically mean that they had the right to hold office. Led by Sumner, the Senate refused to seat Georgia's representatives. In Virginia, conservative native whites had gained control. After a more difficult fight, Sumner secured Senate agreement that Virginia would not be readmitted until it met the old requirements, and also ratified the Fifteenth Amendment, insured blacks the right to hold office, and established a uniform system of public schools. When Mississippi still later offered itself for readmission, Sumner was largely instrumental in persuading the Senate to join the House in imposing the provisions pertaining to Virginia upon that mostly black state. Mississippi accepted the terms, and sent Hiram Revels to Washington as the nation's first black Senator. "Liberty and Equality are the two express promises of our fathers," Sumner exclaimed. "Both are now assured."

Sumner was perfectly aware that he was working for a new nationalism in which state rights would largely disappear. As the guarantor of equality, the federal government would look for guidance beyond the Constitution to the Declaration of Independence as well as to the transcendant ideals of human rights. Nor did Sumner's new nationalism stop with the United States. He would expand the American system throughout the Western Hemisphere. Endorsing the acquisition of Alaska, he also looked forward to replacing the British in Canada. In the Caribbean his imperialism was made hesitant only by his conviction that the United States ought not to buy at high prices what must inevitably fall to her anyway.

But, again, Sumner's effectiveness was ephemeral. In April the troublesome Georgia question reappeared, this time centering on whether state elections would be held in 1870. Sumner and the Georgia Radicals opposed elections because Conservatives were almost certain to win. In a series of close votes, he and his followers were defeated, marking a significant new turning away by the North from Radical Reconstruction. Southern action, however, was still producing Northern reaction. In May, the same Senate passed the First Enforcement Act against the rising Ku Klux Klan and other such Southern organizations. Once again Sumner, moved out ahead with his own solution for the continuing disorders in the South—increased racial integration. He introduced a measure outlawing discrimination by common carriers, hotels, churches, cemetery associations, and schools. Although the bill was rejected in committee, it would be revived and become the last of Sumner's efforts in the cause of racial reconstruction.

By 1872 Sumner had fallen out with the Grant administration over the annexation of Santo Domingo and was at odds with many of his old allies who were now in the Liberal Republican movement. The latter desired amnesty for those few thousand Southerners still proscribed under the Fourteenth Amendment. But Sumner's readings pointed to an unrepentent South; indeed to one that was intent on reducing the former bondsmen to a new servitude. He moved an amendment to the Liberal Republican amnesty bill calling for an end to discrimination in all public places—the ultimate in his proposals for equal rights. He could not imagine any further legislation on the matter. This Civil Rights measure, he was sure, would "be the capstone of the reconstructed Republic."

The capstone, however, was not laid. The Senate allowed the civil rights amendment to be attached to the amnesty bill and then voted down the entire measure. Yet within the month, Sumner again introduced the bill. With true prescience, he pronounced the segregated school a nursery of injustice. "How can you expect the colored child or the white child to grow up to those relations which they are to have together at the ballot box," he asked, "if you begin by degrading the colored child at the school and by exhalting the white child at the school?" Discussion of this second bill clearly revealed that the Liberal Republican Party cared little about the civil rights of blacks and that Grant's supporters were willing only to play politics with the issue.

Plagued by failing health and failing politics, Sumner went abroad at the end of the 1872 session. He returned to Washington somewhat restored in both respects. But during the next year, he was largely ineffectual. The Civil Rights bill was re-introduced, and it was his prime concern. Early in 1874, his health gave way and he was obliged to take to his bed. His friends, including two eminent Washington black men— Wormley the hotel owner and Downing the caterer—took care of him. In agonizing pain, half conscious, indeed dying, he still was concerned with his "bill." When Senator George F. Hoar, his fellow Senator from Massachusetts, came to him, he said, "You must take care of the civil rights bill—my bill, the civil rights bill, don't let it fail." An hour later, Frederick Douglass entered the room and Sumner implored, "Don't let the bill fail." About 2:30 on the afternoon of March 11, Sumner died.

Ralph Waldo Emerson, after the Brooks episode, had spoken of Sumner's "white" soul. In spite of all his foibles, Sumner ultimately was that pure soul Emerson saw; he personified the soul of America as it travelled down that tortuous road toward a national identity. His guide was the Declaration of Independence, with its ringing pronouncement that all men are endowed with certain natural rights. He hewed unswervingly to it. But Americans wavered and yielded to a confusion of identity. Sumner had outlived his time. Indeed, he was outside of his time. He would have been more at home in the world of Thomas Jefferson than he was in that of Ulysses S. Grant. Sumner was a revolutionary in a time when the revolution had, in fact, gone backward. His greatness was not so much on failing magnificently—nor even in trying so assiduously—but in holding up the light to illuminate what might have been and was not.

*   *   *

The most famous speech in advocacy of the Civil Rights bill was not made in the Senate by Charles Sumner but in the House of Representatives by a 31-year-old black man, Robert Brown Elliott, of South Carolina. Even so, Elliott spoke with the words and in the spirit of the dying senator.

There was a curious scene on the floor of the House on January 5, 1874. Alexander Stephens, recently the vice president of the Confederacy and now a representative from Georgia, led off with an address against the Civil Rights bill. Insisting that he had not the slightest prejudice against anyone on account of race, Stephens, an acknowledged expert on Constitutional law, argued that the powers that would be given to the federal government under the bill properly belonged to the police powers, reserved to the states. Elliott, the champion of the bill, rose like a David to contest Stephens, the august Goliath of legal learning. He was indeed a proper David. A very dark man of medium height, he wore his hair short and sported a neat and closely cropped mustache. A woman journalist observed that his teeth were "perfect and white in strong contrast with surrounding color," and admired a physique that was "deep in chest, broad in shoulders, shapely in limb." Other reporters commented upon his obvious intelligence and education and his great gift of oratory. The *New York Times* remarked that "the African love of melody was noticeable in the harmony of his delivery."

No doubt a part of the fame of Elliott's speech came from the fact that he was black. To racist America, an intelligent black man was indeed a curiosity. As word went out that Elliott was to answer Stephens, both the House floor and the gallery quickly filled.

Elliott began by meeting head-on the argument to the effect that Supreme Court decisions in the recent Slaughter House cases gave the powers to regulate schools and other such local institutions to the state alone and that the Thirteenth and Fourteenth Amendments had not delegated such powers to the federal government. Every judicial decision, Elliott said, should be interpreted in the light of the question brought before the Court. Reviewing the Slaughter House cases in detail, he pointed out that the Supreme Court had refused to accept the argument of the plaintiffs, a group of New Orlean butchers, that the amendments protected them from being forced to use certain slaughter houses licensed by Louisiana. Those amendments, the Court had said, were specifically designed for the protection of the freedmen and could not be applied in such a way as to prevent a state from the ordinary exercise of its police powers. The rule in the Slaughter House cases, Elliott indicated, was "what you give to one class, you must give to all; what you deny to one class, you shall deny to all, unless in the exercise of the common and universal police power of the State, you find it needful to confer exclusive privilege on certain citizens, to be held and exercised still for the common good of all." Would one argue, asked Elliott, who had just been denied service in the dining room of a railway station on his way to Washington, that such exclusions were for the good of all? "Is it pretended anywhere," he continued, "that the evils of which we complain, our exclusion from the public inn, from the saloon and the table of the steamboat, from the sleeping-coach on the railway, from the right of sepulchre in the public burial ground, are an exercise of the police power of the state? Is such oppression and injustice nothing but the exercise by the state of the right to make regulations for the health, comfort and security of all her citizens." Bitterly, he persisted, "Are the colored people to be assimilated to an unwholesome trade or to combustible materials, to be interdicted, to be shut up within prescribed limits?" How could one see justice for either black or white? Would one say, he asked "that my good is promoted when I am excluded from the public inn? Is the health or safety of the community promoted?"

When Elliott finished, his audience broke into loud and long applause, and his colleagues gathered to congratulate him. Further praise came in Boston three months later. On March 11, Sumner died and Boston's blacks designated April 14 as a memorial day for him. High point of the occasion would be a meeting in Faneuil Hall where Sumner had made his first major anti-slavery speech almost 30 years before. Before that gathering of whites and blacks, Elliott acquitted himself superbly, tracing out the march toward liberty represented by Sumner's life. Again, as with his speech on the Civil Rights bill, it was almost if Sumner himself had given it.

Who was this black man who had answered the arguments of the best legal minds of the white South and who had come to Boston to eulogize Sumner on his home ground and in his own terms?

"Elliott, Robert Brown," runs the entry in the official publication bearing the biographies of members of Congress (biographies based primarily upon information supplied by members themselves) "a Representative from South Carolina; born in Boston, Mass., August 11, 1842; was of the Negro race; attended High Hollow Academy, London, England, in 1853, and was graduated from Eton College, England, in 1859; studied law; was admitted to the bar and practiced in Columbia, S.C.; member of the State constitutional convention in 1868; member of the State house of representatives from July 6, 1868, to October 23, 1870; assistant adjutant general South Carolina 1869–1871; elected as a Republican to the Forty-second and Forty-third Congresses. . . ."

Robert Brown Elliott "was born and educated in Liverpool, England, where he also learned the printers trade," wrote his biographer Peggy Lamson after some very impressive historical detective work. Liverpool had been the center of the British slave trade and included in its population a considerable number of blacks. Early in his life, Elliott was a sailor in the Royal Navy. He travelled widely and improved his education. In addition to being a superb speaker and writer in English, he knew Latin, French, and Spanish. Obviously, he was well acquainted with classical literature. He came to Boston after the war, perhaps in 1866 or 1867. There he worked as a typesetter, lived in the black community in Boston's West End, was prominent in a literary society, and married an intelligent and handsome mulatto girl. In March 1867, precisely as Radical Reconstruction began in the South, he became the associate editor of *The Leader* in Charleston.

Before his appearance in Charleston, Elliott was, as Mrs. Lamson says, "a man of mystery." Her own sketch of his early life is hypothetical. What she does establish beyond a reasonable doubt is that much of the personal background which Elliott claimed was untrue. There is no record or remembrance of Elliott's birth in Boston. There was no High Hollow Academy that can be found. It is patently impossible that Elliott graduated or even attended Eton College. Elliott asserted that he studied law in England under Sergeant FitzHerbert, "Sergeant" being a rare and senior title among English barristers. Mrs. Lamson looked at the list of sergeants for likely years and found no FitzHerbert among them. Further, Elliott sometimes suggested that he had been in the Union army during the war. But again official or unofficial records and lists provide no evidence. Mrs. Lamson concludes that Elliott was suddenly catapulted into politics by the momentum of the times, that he had not time to become a naturalized citizen and hence created an American identity for himself. According to his nature, the one he created was highly complimentary; it explained his qualities so well that no one thought to look closely at his story.

Not having an American past that he cared to avow and continue, Elliott was uniquely free to become what he would. In this way he was completely representative of his people. They, too, had a past—a slave past—upon which they did not wish to dwell. Their eyes were lifted to the Sumnerian ideals of the future. Elliott and his people both lent themselves to America to be shaped in its image.

When Elliott came to South Carolina, he brought with him the best ideals of Charles Sumner's Massachusetts. In March 1867, at the age of 24, he became the associate editor of the state's black newspaper, *The South Carolina Leader*. Previously, it had been run by a black minister who was, perhaps, responsible for the Paulistic slogan on the masthead: "First the blade, then the ear, after that the full corn in the ear." With Elliott, all of that changed to "Equality and Union." Charles Sumner himself could not have said it so simply. Almost symbolically, Congress passed the first of the Reconstruction acts in the very month of Elliott's arrival, and the vigorous young man threw himself into the politics of his people.

Robert Elliott and Reconstruction unfolded together. He helped in the giant task of organizing black Carolinians for the Republican party. When a convention met in Charleston in January 1868, to draft a new state constitution, he represented Edgefield County in the deliberations. Again he had changed his scenes, from Charleston to the middle of the state; he represented an overwhelmingly rural constituency and one lately out of slavery. These were people very unlike any that he had ever lived among before. Yet he represented them well. In the convention Elliott opposed, as Sumner would have done, a bill that would legitimatize those debts contracted for the purchase of slaves. "The importance of this subject overcomes my reluctance to obtrude my feeble opinion," he began, as he always did, with a show of modesty. Then he launched into an assault upon the recent peculiar institution. He further distinguished himself in that assembly as the defender of universal manhood suffrage by opposing poll taxes and literacy requirements for voting.

Soon Elliott went into the state legislature again as the representative of Edgefield. In the very first session of this Republican-dominated assembly, he ran for speaker, but was defeated by the scalawag, Franklin J. Moses, Jr. A graduate of the South Carolina College and son of a State supreme court justice, Moses would become the "Robber Governor" of his native state in 1872. In September, 1868, while serving in the legislature, Elliott was one of the first black men admitted to the South Carolina bar.

In the following spring, Elliott became, as 26, the state's assistant adjutant general, charged with the organization of the militia. Subsequently he became Colonel, then General Elliott. The militia, nominally headed by Speaker Moses, soon became the instrument by which the incumbent governor, Robert Scott, organized his faction within the Republican Party. Scott freely used the officers and monies of the state's military arm for his own political purposes. For instance, he turned the census takers of 1870 into enlistment officers for the militia. Elliott participated in that corruption. Not only did he use his office to strengthen the Scott machine and to promote his own election to Congress in 1870, but he also bought property and spent money far beyond what must have been his legitimate income. Although joining in the general corruption, Elliott did his job well. He had no difficulty in assuming an imperious military manner. As he wrote to a local militia commander, "Sir, you will please send to the Department immediately the remaining rolls of militia for your county or compulsory steps will be taken to make you do so." His political faction was totally successful in the 1870 elections; Scott was re-elected governor, and Elliott himself was sent to Congress.

As a congressman, Elliott was vaulted into national politics. In 1872 he was the orator of the day at the tenth anniversary celebration of the abolition of slavery in the District of Columbia. In the same year he also led the South Carolina delegation to the national Republican convention in Philadelphia. Only 30, Elliott was among the first blacks to address that body, and was loudly applauded by the delegates after pledging 900,000 black votes to the Grand Old Party. Although on this occasion Charles Sumner had deserted President Grant, Elliott remained firm for his nomination. With Grant's victory, the Congressman's star continued to rise. In December 1872, he sought election to the United States Senate but was badly defeated even though his fellow blacks held 106 out of 156 seats in the South Carolina legislature. The victor was John Patterson, a Pennsylvania railroad man, who spent $40,000 bribing legislators to gain senatorial honors. He was called "Honest John" Patterson because, it was said, if he promised a bribe, he would surely pay it.

Elliott reflected almost perfectly the low moral climate that prevailed in politics of South Carolina as well as in the nation during Reconstruction. Defeated by bribery, he in turn took money rather carelessly both for his political operations and for his personal use. Nor is there any indication that he felt any guilt about these peculations or that he made any pretensions to fiscal honesty. Clearly, he did not demand honesty of his friends. During the whole of his political career, for example, he was strangely sympathetic with the elegant and notoriously corrupt Franklin Moses, Jr.

Elliott's contradictions in behavior are striking, inexplicable, and almost schizoid. Affecting all manner of idealistic principles, he was simultaneously a patron of blatant scoundrels. As a case in point, he announced himself sternly against amnesty for Southern leaders. Yet in 1872 he introduced a private bill in the House to relieve James D. Tadewell, prewar mayor of Columbia, a Confederate officer, and a lawyer, of his disabilities under the Fourteenth Amendment. In January of 1873 the two became law partners! This quixotic pattern, as his biographer described it, of "shifting from loyalty to antagonism and back and sometimes back once again," continued during the closing years of Reconstruction.

In the spring of 1874, Elliott returned in triumph to South Carolina where he was repeatedly honored for his civil rights speech. Suddenly raising the standard of reform, he told audiences that great political and moral changes were occurring in the North and that South Carolina was being severely criticized for its corruption. That corruption, he added was properly blamed on the black electorate, which was in the majority. Blacks, he warned, must reform the State, "and that speedily." If they did not, the national Republican Party "would be compelled to cut off the rotten branch." Elliott then proceeded to promote reform, paradoxically, by successfully defending his old friend, Frank Moses, now Governor, from being convicted of stealing $6,000 in state funds. Not only did Elliott excuse Moses, but he himself promptly took $500 from a fraudulent fund to finance his own campaign for election to the general assembly in the fall of 1874. And then, in the following spring, when the new reform governor, Daniel H. Chamberlain, vetoed a blatantly corrupt money bill, Elliott, as Speaker of the House, seized upon a technicality to rule the veto invalid, thereby licensing the continuation of corruption.

When the legislature convened in the fall of 1875, Elliott was a key leader in another move that not only betrayed reform but also was the single most important action that eventually led to the overthrow of Republicanism in South Carolina. Duplicity marked his behavior in that 1875 session. Eight circuit judges were to be elected to serve the state. Led by Elliott, the Republicans stalwarts in the legislature made a show of fiscal restraint and seemed to endorse reform, thereby lulling the opposition into a false sense of security. When it appeared that Governor Chamberlain would be absent from the capital on the day that the judges were to be chosen, he requested Elliott, as a personal favor, to postpone the vote until his return. Elliott readily agreed, and seemingly made such arrangements. But hardly had the governor's train departed, before the wheels of state reversed. On "Black Thursday," as conservatives called it, the two houses came quickly together and proceeded to the vote.

Elliott came down from the speaker's chair to declare menacingly that the Republicanism of every member would be measured by his vote. The first choice of the lawmakers was William J. Whipper, a black man and Elliott's good friend. Then Elliott himself nominated for the second district the very capable incumbent, a white *Democrat!* Not only had he deceived Chamberlain, he also had flagrantly betrayed his own black Republican colleagues. Then for judge of the third district Elliott returned to party loyalty, but only to desert reform by supporting none other than Frank Moses, who was elected.

The sequel was depressing. All of the talent, all of the energy, all of the courage Elliott might muster could not save him or his people. In 1876 he ran for Attorney General and claimed victory in the election. But in the spring of 1877, the office was taken from him by Wade Hampton's Redeemers. For a time, Elliott attempted to practice law in Orangeburg, the center of state-supported education for blacks. But he discovered that the courts were no longer very accepting of black lawyers. In 1879 he was appointed a special inspector of customs in the Treasury Department. For two years he travelled from port to port in the South. He relished the police aspects of his new job, fairly bristling with ideas to catch smugglers and crooks. Once again he had adjusted to a new environment. In late 1879 he returned to politics, supporting his boss, John Sherman, the Secretary of the Treasury who was then in pursuit of the Republican presidential nomination. That campaign found a new use for black politicians. Southern black voters might be useless in the general elections, but their leaders could be a powerful factor at Republican nominating conventions. For decades afterward, no Republican candidate was selected without strong support from Southern black politicians. In the 1880 Republican convention Elliott managed Sherman's effort among black delegates. When his candidate lost, he swung behind James A. Garfield. In 1881 he was transferred to the New Orleans customs office. His finances were precarious at this time, his wife was in ill health, and he himself suffered from malaria. In his new position, he found endless fault with his superiors and with the local Republicans. Some months later, he was dismissed from the customs service. During the next two years Elliott eked out a declining existence as a lawyer in the New Orleans police courts. Meanwhile, he suffered recurrent bouts with malaria, which finally took his life on August 9, 1884. He was then 42, but his true death had occurred some years before.

Elliott, the malleable man, reflected the condition of his people during Reconstruction. They did not succumb to the political corruption that prevailed in that era. Instead they acted according to the examples of courage, grace, and honor as offered by the Hamptons, and by the idealism of the Sumners. They used to the fullest the temporary license granted by Northern intercession in the South and successfully constructed viable communities and ways of life for themselves. They established family farms, black schools and churches, and a black culture that was unique and valuable. In this most essential sense, then, Reconstruction was not a failure for black people.

But Reconstruction was a failure for America at large. At the least, it failed to realize the promise of American life. Perhaps, after all, Robert Brown Elliott fits best into white America. He failed both as a leader of his people and as a person became, in effect, he became too white. His friends and fellow politicians were corrupt and he fell in step with them too easily. Inevitably he would not survive an era of reform. He learned much from Sumner and the reformers, but he cut learning short. Had he been a more perceptive student, he would have known that the true reformer must himself be reformed. But, after all, Elliott lacked roots, and it is perhaps unfair to ask too much of him. Ultimately, Elliott was a surface man, but the people he represented went deeper.